Negotiating Trade

Negotiations between governments shape the world political economy and in turn the lives of people everywhere. Developing countries have become far more influential in talks in the World Trade Organization, including infamous stalemates in Seattle in 1999 and Cancún in 2003, as well as bilateral and regional talks like those that created NAFTA. Yet social science does not understand well enough the process of negotiation, and least of all the roles of developing countries, in these situations. This innovative book sheds fresh light on three aspects of this otherwise opaque process – which strategies developing countries use, coalition formation, and how they learn and influence their counterparts' beliefs. This book will be valuable for many readers interested in negotiation, international political economy, trade, development, global governance, or international law. Developing country negotiators and those who train them will find practical insights on how to avoid pitfalls and negotiate more effectively.

JOHN S. ODELL is Professor of International Relations at the University of Southern California. He was editor of *International Organization*, 1992–1996.

Negotiating Trade

Developing Countries in the WTO and NAFTA

Edited by

John S. Odell

CAMBRIDGE
UNIVERSITY PRESS

CAMBRIDGE UNIVERSITY PRESS
Cambridge, New York, Melbourne, Madrid, Cape Town, Singapore, São Paulo

Cambridge University Press
The Edinburgh Building, Cambridge CB2 2RU, UK

Published in the United States of America by Cambridge University Press, New York

www.cambridge.org
Information on this title: www.cambridge.org/9780521679787

© Cambridge University Press 2006

First published 2006

Printed in the United Kingdom at the University Press, Cambridge

A catalogue record for this publication is available from the British Library

ISBN-13 978-0-521-86178-6 hardback
ISBN-10 0-521-86178-0 hardback

ISBN-13 978-0-521-67978-7 paperback
ISBN-10 0-521-67978-8 paperback

Contents

Part III   WTO Dispute Settlement Negotiations

Figures

Tables

Contributors

COSIMO BEVERELLI, Graduate Institute for International Studies, Geneva

CHRISTINA L. DAVIS, Princeton University

CÉDRIC DUPONT, Graduate Institute of International Studies, Geneva

AMRITA NARLIKAR, University of Cambridge

JOHN S. ODELL, University of Southern California

ANTONIO ORTIZ MENA L. N., Centro de Investigación y Docencia Económicas (CIDE), Mexico City

STÉPHANIE PÉZARD, Graduate Institute for International Studies, Geneva

SUSAN K. SELL, George Washington University

J. P. SINGH, Georgetown University

JAMES MCCALL SMITH, George Washington University

Acknowledgments

The authors and I are most grateful for generous assistance that helped make this book possible. The University of Southern California's Center for International Studies hosted a workshop at which the team planned the research, and the Center financed field research. The authors then presented preliminary findings at a conference at the Palais des Nations in Geneva on November 6 and 7, 2003. Associate Professor Cédric Dupont of the Graduate Institute of International Studies, Geneva (GIIS), volunteered to help organize and host the conference and played a central leadership role, and the Graduate Institute provided administrative support. The Geneva International Academic Network kindly financed the conference and the drafting of an interim report. Director Patrick Low and Counselor Jean-Daniel Rey (WTO), Director Manuela Tórtora (UNCTAD), and Minister Didier Chambovey (Switzerland) gave invaluable advice and support. UNCTAD provided a conference room and the Swiss Mission to the WTO welcomed participants with a reception.

At the conference veteran negotiators and academics contributed thoughts and suggestions for improving the papers. We are indebted to UNCTAD's Secretary General Rubens Ricupero of Brazil, and the WTO's Director General, Supachai Panitchpakdi of Thailand, who generously shared ideas about effective negotiation practice from long high-level experience. Excellent prepared comments on individual papers were presented by Ambassador K. M. Chandrasekhar (India), Counselor Kyonglim Choi (Korea), Director Esperanza Durán (AITIC), Minister Magdi Farahat (Egypt), Expert Marisa Henderson (UNCTAD Secretariat), Counselor Cristina Hernández (CASIN), Ambassador Alejandro Jara (Chile), Director Patrick Low (WTO Secretariat), Counselor and Professor Gabrielle Marceau (WTO Secretariat and GIIS, Geneva), Ambassador Carlos Pérez del Castillo (Uruguay), Ambassador Eduardo Pérez Motta (Mexico), and Ambassador Luiz Felipe de Seixas Corrêa (Brazil). We are equally thankful, for their wise advice, to Professors Pierre Allan (University of Geneva), Thomas Cottier (University of Bern), John Cuddy (GIIS), Heinz Hauser (University of St. Gallen),

Urs Luterbacher (GIIS), Jongryn Mo (Yonsei University), David Sylvan (GIIS), and Gilbert Winham (Dalhousie University). We owe special thanks to Professors Jongryn Mo and Gilbert Winham for help to our team in 2003.

We are grateful to an anonymous referee for detailed comments on an earlier draft of the book, and to Cambridge University Press editor John Haslam and the Press staff for their support and assistance. None of these friends should be held responsible for opinions or any errors in this study.

1 Introduction

John S. Odell

Negotiating international trade agreements has become a full-time job for developing countries. They negotiate often in pairs, in regional groups, and as members of the World Trade Organization (WTO), where they make up the majority of members. The WTO in particular is one of the premier sites where globalization will be either managed or mismanaged. Some official talks aim for deals that shape international rules and state policies. Other talks seek settlements for legal disputes arising in the shadow of those rules. Ultimately all this bargaining helps determine who receives the gains and bears the burdens of trade, with powerful consequences for local communities across the globe.

Less developed countries have become dramatically more active in trade negotiations in recent years, as their policies and societies have become more dependent on trade. Even the smallest traders are better organized and prepared than in the past. They were prominent players in WTO ministerial conferences in Seattle in 1999, Doha in 2001, and Cancún in 2003. The results – for the entire world – depend more than ever on how developing countries negotiate.

Yet social science still does not understand the process of trade negotiation – as distinct from the institutions, laws, and economics of the issues – well enough. In particular, negotiation process research has underrepresented the experience and needs of developing countries, where the large majority of the world's people live. Empirically grounded research on their negotiations is still in its infancy. What happens inside these frequent talks between delegations? What negotiation strategies have developing country delegations attempted and have they made any difference, considering the power disparities they face? How do they process information and influence their counterparts' beliefs during the talks? Why do some bargaining coalitions hold together while others fragment? Most centrally, what accounts for the varying outcomes we see? Is it possible to generalize about this complex process? Can one find any valuable lessons for practitioners who will face future negotiations?

The theme of this book is that the content of developing countries' international trade agreements varies with the process of negotiation that produces them, and in turn that process depends partly on the institutions in which the process unfolds. The trade superpowers – especially the United States and the European Union – dominate this process, of course. For smaller and poorer players, achieving their objectives is a daunting challenge. But this book's main message is that even so, their decisions about how to negotiate make a material difference to the results, for them and for the world.

This chapter summarizes the innovative ways in which we develop this theme. By *the international negotiation process* we mean a sequence of actions in which two or more governments address demands and proposals to each other for the ostensible purpose of reaching an agreement and changing the behavior of at least one party.[1] The central elements are the actions of official negotiators, but this complex international process often involves others. Government officials also interact with constituents, international officials and non-state actors.

Our specific conclusions concentrate on three variable aspects of the negotiation process that are likely to affect the outcome: coalition design, strategies used by states and coalitions, and dynamic subjective interactions. We also flesh out the general idea that variable properties of the institutional setting of a trade negotiation will shape the process and in turn its outcome.

Things besides this process also matter, of course. Trade negotiators must take various conditions as given and are not able to exert much influence over them, except perhaps indirectly over the long term. Exogenous elements of the negotiator's context – such as the cultures of the countries participating, the interstate distribution of power, existing international institutions, existing domestic institutions, technological change, and other market trends – are conceptually "outside" the negotiation process and almost certainly have important effects on official negotiated outcomes too, at least indirectly. But our premise is that such conditions in the negotiators' environment do not predetermine any official outcome completely. We assume they leave significant space in which decisions by governments and delegations, including those from developing countries, tip their collective outcomes toward impasse or agreement and shape the distribution of costs and benefits. We attempt to offer something distinctive by exploring this space, rather than abstracting from negotiator

---

[1] The terms "negotiation" and "bargaining" are used interchangeably here, as in much of the literature. Some scholars draw a distinction between the two, but this practice can divide research in one tradition from related insights developed in the other. I believe integration is what this literature needs.

decisions and behavior as much political economy research has done. Some might consider this behavior a rather special element in the grand sweep of history. But many governments repeatedly invest great effort and expense to conduct these negotiations, and companies, other non-governmental organizations, and the media spend yet more resources trying to monitor and influence them. We assume something significant is going on.

We analyze two types of trade negotiation. In complex episodes like the Uruguay Round and the Doha Round, dozens of governments seek to reach multilateral agreements to regulate access to markets and write rules for the world trading system. Chapters 2 through 5 investigate WTO deal-making and chapter 6 investigates a regional deal. In the second type represented by chapters 7 and 8, two or a few more governments attempt to negotiate settlements to disputes taking place in the shadow of these rules. When WTO members file legal complaints attempting to achieve fuller compliance, they often engage simultaneously in settlement bargaining with the defending states. In fact most disputes brought to the General Agreement on Tariffs and Trade (GATT) and WTO have been settled by negotiation or dropped before the adjudication process has run its course.[2]

A broader aim of this book is to flesh out an under-exploited overlap of two lively multi-disciplinary bodies of scholarship: international political economy and negotiation analysis. Scholars working in each of these communities are accomplishing a great deal but are not always able to keep up with advances in the other, and we see opportunities for deepening knowledge over the long term by exploring their possible intersection. We draw on and combine elements from both.

This is also scholarship designed to be relevant. The main questions about which we seek to generalize spotlight possible courses of action and factors that will determine the results. A central goal is to add to the body of empirically grounded scholarship on the economic negotiation process that is available to support participants in these negotiations and their constituents.

Section 1 of this chapter sets the scene by highlighting major changes in the participation of developing countries in trade negotiations in recent years and by situating our contributions in published literatures. The following section introduces key assumptions and analytical terms that will appear in other chapters without further definition. A third section summarizes our specific contributions, and a fourth points toward implications for future research and future negotiations.

---

[2] Busch and Reinhardt 2003; Davey 2005.

4   *John S. Odell*

1   **Participation explodes, negotiation process
       scholarship lags**

After 1990 developing country participation in dispute settlement talks
increased, and their participation in multilateral trade negotiations
exploded. During and after the GATT's Uruguay Round (1986–1994)
more developing countries shifted their policies toward reliance on international markets for development. After creation of the WTO in 1995,
more countries reinforced or established their missions in Geneva. Most
notably, in 1999 during preparations for the WTO's ministerial conference in Seattle, developing countries voiced concerns and injected dozens
of formal proposals into the negotiation process. This participation explosion drew in many smaller trading countries that had been passive or
not signatories at all prior to 1994. Many states increased their investment in training their officials for international commercial negotiations,
with the help of UNCTAD, the WTO, and regional organizations. Many
delegations formed or joined bargaining coalitions to defend common
negotiating positions through direct coordination. Almost every member
state sent its minister to Seattle and again to Doha in 2001 and Cancún
in 2003. These events and developing countries' role in them became
front-page news worldwide.

Newer organizations are now part of the negotiator's context as well.
The South Centre and the Agency for International Trade Information
and Cooperation are intergovernmental organizations created to support developing countries in trade negotiations and headquartered in
Geneva. Non-governmental organizations have become quite active not
only in public protests but also behind the scenes in some cases, supplying applied analysis and proposals to developing country delegations.
Chapter 3 in this book documents such a case.

Meanwhile, developing countries have been targeted as defendants in
far more legal disputes under the WTO than under the GATT. From
1995 through 2000, they were defendants in 81 cases – amounting to
37 percent of all disputes – which was dramatically higher than the 8
percent of disputes that had targeted developing countries during the
GATT period. This is partly because there are far more developing country members, they have far more legal obligations under the new treaty,
and their trade has expanded. Each of these cases, along with 64 others during 1995–2000 in which a developing country initiated a complaint,[3] created an occasion for a possible settlement negotiation. From
2000 through mid-2004, developing countries, especially some in Latin

[3] Busch and Reinhardt 2002.

America, sharply increased their use of the system as complainants, filing against other developing countries as well as developed countries. Some complaints, such as those by Brazil and India against certain US and EC policies, seemed aimed in part at influencing the Doha multilateral negotiations.[4]

Simultaneously many developing country governments were also busy negotiating over trade inside their regions. The Caribbean Community and Common Market (CARICOM) has existed since 1973. The Association of Southeast Asian States (ASEAN) and the South American countries of the Mercado Común del Sur (MERCOSUR) launched free trade areas in the early 1990s. The Andean Pact and the Central American Common Market were reactivated during that time. Western hemisphere states began to negotiate a Free Trade Area of the Americas in 1994. In 1997 the South Asian Association for Regional Cooperation agreed to make itself into a free trade area. The African, Caribbean, and Pacific Countries engaged in continuing talks with the European Union. African states have negotiated a variety of sub-regional and region-wide trade and monetary pacts since the 1960s. They launched the African Economic Community in 1991 and the African Union in 2002.[5]

Empirical negotiation process research has not kept up with this participation explosion, however. We do have voluminous literatures from economics and law on the effects of past agreements, problems, proposals for future agreements, and developing country stakes in these deals.[6] But scholarship concentrating on what developing country delegations and others do during negotiations and why is only beginning to accumulate. Histories and memoirs of GATT rounds sometimes touch in passing on roles played by developing countries.[7] A few studies describe and analyze particular negotiations from earlier years – for example when newly independent African states first bargained with the European Community,[8] textile exporters faced demands for restrictions in the 1960s and 1970s,[9] Latin American governments and South Korea faced the United States during that period,[10] and a bloc of developing countries campaigned in the United Nations for a new international economic order.[11]

---

[4] Davey 2005; Petersmann 2005.   [5] World Bank 2001.
[6] A sampling of recent works could begin with a special issue of *The World Economy* 2000, UNCTAD 2000, and articles and books by the prolific World Bank trade research group, such as Michalopoulos 2001, Panagariya 2002, Hoekman, Mattoo, and English 2002, later working papers at www.worldbank.org/research/trade, and their references. This would only scratch the surface.
[7] Preeg 1970; Evans 1971; Winham 1986; Oxley 1990; Hampson and Hart 1994; Paemen and Bensch 1995; Croome 1999.
[8] Zartman 1971.   [9] Destler, Fukui, and Sato 1979; Aggarwal 1985.
[10] Odell 1980, Yoffie 1983, Odell 1985, Bayard and Elliott 1994.
[11] Rothstein 1979; Zartman 1987. Also see Hoda 1987.

6   *John S. Odell*

During the Uruguay round as some poorer countries developed further and their governments became more active in Geneva, several more publications discussed their bargaining options and experience.[12] After 1999 the increasing contention in trade negotiations, as developing country governments and non-governmental organizations became much more active in and around the WTO, attracted the attention of a few more authors.[13] A handful of statistical studies has traced effects of political institutions on regional trade agreements without observing the negotiation processes involved in reaching those agreements.[14]

Excellent statistical studies of GATT and WTO dispute settlement have illuminated which countries have filed the most complaints, which have gained the greatest policy change at which stages of the proceedings, and reasons for the observed differences.[15] Yet these studies are by nature limited to information that is publicly available for hundreds of cases and to what can be measured. The method is not able to analyze much of what happens inside any settlement negotiation. Few empirical studies describe how dispute negotiators behave in these talks and ask how their process might affect the outcome.

Reasons for the relative shortage of empirically grounded analyses of the process itself – even studies of richer countries' experience – are not difficult to find. Insiders seldom have the inclination, liberty, and time to publish what they have learned about negotiation strategy and tactics, especially not in societies where such talents are extremely scarce and absorbed for other purposes. Outsiders find it virtually impossible to observe intergovernmental negotiations directly, and alternative methods must be devised. The best methods for indirectly discovering what occurs – reading archives and interviewing participants scattered over several continents – involve costs high enough to deter many scholars. Others shy away from empirical study of this process because they prefer to limit themselves to claims that can be supported with quantitative data, and no such data exist on negotiating strategies and other key process elements.

Two established multi-disciplinary bodies of literature are, however, very much part of our conceptual context. The literature of international

[12] E.g., Hamilton and Whalley 1989; Nau 1989; Whalley 1989; Winham 1989; Tussie and Glover 1993; Arriola 1994; Shukla 1994; Stephenson 1994; Sell 1995; Raffaelli and Jenkins 1996; Winham 1998; Watal 2001; Steinberg 2002. Higgott and Cooper 1990 first described and analyzed the Cairns group. Additional studies are cited in later chapters.
[13] Singh 2000; Duran 2001; Ramamurti 2001; Das 2002; Crystal 2003; Drahos 2003; Ives 2003; Jawara and Kwa 2003; Narlikar 2003; Page 2003; Sally 2003; Narlikar and Tussie 2004; Bernal et al. 2004.
[14] Mansfield, Milner, and Rosendorff 2002; Mansfield and Reinhardt 2003.
[15] Hudec 1993; Busch and Reinhardt 2002; Busch and Reinhardt 2003.

political economy is a mix of economics and political science and has devoted extensive attention to trade policies, especially in the United States and to a lesser extent in other industrial countries.[16] The second literature of negotiation analysis has been fed by streams from business, law, political science, psychology, and sociology, and not so much by economic theory since early game theory.[17] Negotiation analysts have suggested concepts for understanding the negotiation process at many levels, from the local community to world politics, though again without great attention to developing countries in trade negotiations. In the former genre, game theoretical methods are prominent and the latter is mostly not mathematical. Several recent review articles discuss the seminal works, accumulating findings, and remaining challenges of each tradition. This is not the place for additional comprehensive reviews.

For now, suffice it to say that the two traditions have tended to specialize in somewhat different ways and have not fully developed the potential bridges between them. To simplify greatly, political economy research on trade policies has often abstracted from the behavior of international negotiators, concentrating more on the sectoral market conditions, exchange rates, institutions, and politics surrounding them to explain trade policies. Few political economists have conducted empirical research designed to generalize about the negotiating behavior of developing countries and their partners. Skeptics sometimes complain that the assumptions on which political economy models depend are too strong to provide accurate explanations. Meanwhile, it is fair to say that many international negotiation studies have not yet exploited insights from economics or political-economic institutionalism very fully. Skeptics here sometimes complain that they cannot find many clear causal hypotheses in negotiation studies. Nor have negotiation analysts often applied their process ideas in the empirical domain of developing countries' trade negotiations. There are exceptions in both cases and some are mentioned here. Our purpose is not to disparage either tradition; it will be apparent that we incorporate elements of each. The point is that we see our work as an attempt at cross-fertilization that will contribute to each. The third section will be more specific. One study also suggests a different possible bridge to constructivism, which is not a substantive

---

[16] For reviews see Nelson 1988, Marks and McArthur 1990, Odell 1990, Milner 1999, Hoekman and Kostecki 2001, and Frieden and Martin 2003. These reviews show that most political economy research concerning trade policies has concentrated on aspects other than negotiator decisions and behavior, and that developing country negotiations have been especially neglected. Rodrik 1995 emphasizes other gaps.

[17] For reviews see Jönsson 2002 and Sebenius 1991. The sub-school represented by Sebenius, following Raiffa 1982, begins the work of bridge-building that we continue.

theory but a set of basic premises under which to investigate inter-subjective phenomena in world and domestic politics.[18]

2   Main question and assumptions

We concentrate in this book on one main analytical question or dependent variable: what determines the outcome of a trade negotiation involving developing countries? Any negotiation outcome has two dimensions – whether the process ends in impasse or agreement,[19] and which parties receive which gains and losses. The value of an outcome to a government varies by degrees rather than simply between success and failure. Gains and losses are almost impossible to measure precisely, however, even on economic issues. Some trade negotiations end with agreement on an agenda for another negotiation, so that the ultimate value of a gain in agenda formation – keeping an item out or getting one in – depends on later events. Some outcomes take the form of changes in international rules, and efforts to forecast rules' effects face great inherent uncertainty. Some final gains and losses are intangible. Here we attempt to classify and compare outcomes qualitatively.

Any notion of gain or loss implies some reference point. In this book the primary reference point is the status quo before negotiations. Was the country or coalition better off or worse off than before, and how much so? In several chapters, two outcomes will be compared with one another. What counts as a gain for a country will be defined in light of the objectives of the country's government rather than the authors' personal values. The negotiation outcome for present purposes also refers to the terms of official agreements themselves and not the behavior of markets later. Exports expand and diminish for reasons other than negotiated government agreements; the analysis of trade itself is also a substantial enterprise, and many others supply it.

Our primary method is the single case study or the focused comparison of two or three cases of negotiation. Most authors choose these established methods because one primary research goal is to add accurate observations and descriptions of the negotiation process to the literature. Without careful case studies it is difficult for an outsider even to know what happens in confidential government negotiations, and accurate description is a prerequisite for valid explanations and generalizations about the process. Through process tracing, these studies provide more

---

[18] Finnemore and Sikkink 2001.
[19] A third possible category is a signed agreement that fails of ratification, like the 1948 charter for the International Trade Organization. This book does not explore any such cases.

accurate and meaningful description of those cases than would be possible by measuring only a few variables in each case along with many other cases in a statistical study. But we seek more than descriptions of a few episodes. We use them inductively to generate some modest middle-range hypotheses that may prove promising for investigation and use in other cases. In some cases we apply a published hypothesis to interpret a new case. Note that we do not claim to test any hypothesis here or to reject alternative approaches in general. Our goals are different. We do claim that ignoring the negotiation process would miss key reasons for the outcomes we study. But these cases have not been selected randomly and larger numbers of cases selected neutrally would be needed for true tests. Developing data quantitatively measuring negotiation strategies or other elements of this process in actual international negotiations would be a large-scale undertaking, and case studies should be valuable prerequisites for efforts to create valid measures and models.[20] We do speculate about the likely limits of each hypothesis. Chapter 5, rather than using a case study of actual negotiations, experiments with the innovative technique of observing how developing country delegates behave in WTO training simulations, and does generate some data from this setting.

Two premises

To frame answers to the main question, we begin with two assumptions. First, the actors in trade negotiations make decisions using bounded rationality. The assumptions of classic unbounded rationality have proven highly fruitful and surely will continue to be so. Much other social science research, including the negotiation analysis tradition, has shown that a different set of assumptions has also been highly fruitful, and the premise of this project is that it will continue to be so. Here agents are rational in the sense that they aim to achieve objectives as effectively as they are able, but their rationality is bounded in two senses, in keeping with Simon's definition.[21] Agents lack not only complete information but also the ability to perform the computations needed to optimize. (Much political economy work has recognized certain limits on information while continuing to assume that players optimize.) Negotiators lack full information, for instance, about other countries' reservation values, true priorities across issues, and domestic politics. The others have well-known incentives to

---

[20] In 2002 *International Negotiation* published a special issue (volume 7, number 1) exploring the difficulties and possible remedies.

[21] Simon 1997, 291, emphasized both these dimensions. Much evidence for their relevance has accumulated in economics and political science as well as psychology. See Conlisk 1996 and Odell 2002 for comprehensive reviews.

misrepresent some information. Before the beginning of a multilateral trade negotiation, delegates cannot know exactly which issues will be on the agenda and exactly how they will be defined. These features will be determined by negotiation.

Thus in practice a boundedly rational player cannot deduce a single optimal strategy simply and directly from material interests. Even if she could specify every possible course of action available to her country, she is unable to forecast exactly what would happen with each alternative. The outcome in multilateral talks will depend on how parties B and C respond to each alternative, not to mention how markets would respond. How B responds often depends on how C responds. How government C responds will in turn depend on how its citizens value the alternative outcomes. Constituents and bureaucracies often disagree on such matters, and so how C responds will also depend partly on domestic politics inside C's country.

To take another example, identifying a government's reservation value empirically is also too complex and uncertain an operation to permit exact computation. The parties' reservation values – the worst deals they would prefer to accept – collectively determine whether they have a positive zone of agreement or contract zone. Given that negotiator B can be expected to misrepresent her own state's bottom line, identifying the true value would require putting some exact value on the best course of action party B could take if this negotiation ended in deadlock. Choosing one outside alternative as best (abbreviated as the *batna* – best alternative to negotiated agreement) implies knowing what other governments and markets would do in each scenario. If the outside alternative is a conflict, how likely is it and what would be the costs and any benefits? Judging which deal is the minimum also implies estimating which deals could be sold in B's domestic politics. That will depend on how many political resources its leaders spend to secure ratification, which will depend in turn on the other demands upon those resources at the time. The number of combinations to evaluate escalates quickly beyond the computation capacity of even the most developed government. One veteran GATT and WTO negotiator declares flatly: "Most delegations don't know their own bottom lines,"[22] not to mention those of other states.

In this world, the only way to make timely decisions is to use mental short cuts – to consider only a few alternative strategies, overlook many complexities, and make rough subjective judgments about risks, others' resistance points, and odds of success. Since such judgments and strategy choices are unavoidably subjective, they are open to biases, framing

---

[22] Interview, Florence, Italy, July 3, 2004.

tactics, and persuasion – the negotiation process. Persuasive and coercive tactics frame the choices in particular ways and influence a negotiator's judgment about what would happen to her country if she refused the deal on the table. Thus in the boundedly rational world, the reservation value is not fixed and exogenous; it is subjective and partly endogenous to the negotiation process. Actual signaling is complicated by a haze of biases on the receiving side. Biased judgments (in developed as much as in developing states), reinforced by pressures from special interests, can drive players into deadlocks when theorists would say their countries enjoy a positive zone of agreement.[23]

Assuming bounded rationality is not, however, equivalent to assuming that errors or personal idiosyncracies are all that determine behavior. In this book it does not mean abandoning efforts to generalize about negotiation. Bounded rationality is a premise, an increasingly popular platform for research designed to improve our generalizations about aspects of the process, including the subjective level, that are otherwise difficult to study. It encourages us to improve our knowledge by, among other things, factoring in some fascinating insights being developed in psychology.[24]

A second primary assumption is that international institutions like the GATT and WTO are products of negotiation in the first place and also may influence later negotiations. In the jargon, institutions are endogenous to the negotiation process and subsequent negotiations are endogenous to the institutions under which they occur. As long as the discussion remains at such a high level of abstraction, however, it is next to impossible to document more specific causal relations. Many political economists have chosen to abstract from what delegations and mediators do, pretending temporarily that this process does not matter, in order to study how background conditions and fixed institutional properties may affect outcomes. This book uses the same partial method but from the opposite direction, as is common in negotiation analysis. Most of the time we abstract from the institutional context, setting aside variations of that type temporarily in order to study the intervening process and its effects. This is not true of every chapter, however. At some points we also introduce institutional variation to see what difference it might make.

We refer to negotiators as individuals since inevitably individuals are the primary actors and hence the natural focus for a negotiation analysis.

[23] Arrow et al. 1995.
[24] Growing numbers of economists, political scientists, and psychologists are taking up the challenge of building on Simon's foundation. For other interesting initiatives, see Todd and Gigerenzer 2003 and McDermott 2004 from the psychological side. See Alexander 2003 and Kydd 1999 for a sense of how evolutionary game theorists have been responding to limitations of traditional game theory.

The role of international negotiator is played by officials at various levels, from the middle up to the ambassador, the cabinet minister, and occasionally the head of state at summit meetings. This simplification is not meant to imply that agents are completely autonomous from their principals and their bureaucracies, or that personal idiosyncrasies and relationships will necessarily determine policies. These too are matters for empirical investigation and they undoubtedly vary. Trade negotiators are embedded in agencies and governments, and some of their perceptions are shared by fellow citizens rather than purely idiosyncratic. At least some trade negotiators are instructed and the instructions are often products of domestic bargaining.

3   Contributions

Our specific conclusions concentrate on three variable aspects of the negotiation process that are likely to affect developing countries' outcomes – coalition design, strategies used by states and coalitions, and dynamic subjective interactions. Furthermore we flesh out the general idea that variable properties of the international institutional context will shape this process and in turn its outcome. Individual chapters offer additional specific insights as well. This section will group and summarize these four sets of conclusions one at a time, ceteris paribus, for clarity of understanding. In practice the variables are related. They may be intertwined more or less simultaneously throughout an actual negotiation.

Coalition design

Most theorizing about international negotiation – both formal[25] and non-formal[26] – has concentrated on bilateral interactions. The challenge of simplifying and generalizing about the far more complex multilateral variety has been daunting and we have a long way to go. One of the defining distinctions of a multilateral negotiation is that parties can and tend to

---

[25] Powell 2002.

[26] Jönsson 2002. Young 1994, chap. 4, and Zartman 1994 review alternative perspectives on multilateral negotiation and Hampson and Hart 1994 develops an application to trade. In the last few years a number of studies of particular multilateral episodes have also appeared. Elsewhere a large political science sub-literature investigates the formation of coalition governments at the national level. But most of this research assumes a body that makes decisions by majority vote. In the WTO, which makes multilateral decisions under the consensus rule, the only winning coalition must consist of all members. There too, however, coalitions can influence the process leading up to the decision, as this book will show. In the European setting these have been labeled "process coalitions" (Elgstrom et al. 2001).

form coalitions as one way of cutting down the complexity, promoting their preferences, and learning. For us, a *coalition* is a set of governments that defend a common position in a negotiation by explicit coordination. We do not include in this category a set of states that happen to act in parallel without explicit coordination, or a set of delegations that exchange information and meet to seek compromises but do not defend a common position. A trade coalition may be defined according to a common product interest or a common ideology. Some trade coalitions are relatively informal and short-lived while others last longer with a title and a regular meeting schedule. A coalition operating at a given stage is a product of the negotiation process at an earlier stage rather than a structure exogenous to this process. For a given state, then, a sophisticated negotiation strategy will often include tactics for building coalitions, for splitting rival coalitions, and for defending against efforts by outsiders to break one's own.[27]

Regarding developing countries in multilateral trade negotiations, a few works published late in the Uruguay Round describe coalitions operating at that time.[28] Recently more studies have touched on specific coalitions – observed[29] and potential[30] – and Amrita Narlikar (2003) has offered a comprehensive analysis of developing country trade coalitions.

This book provides new evidence that the design and membership of developing country coalitions affect the subsequent process and outcome. Three aspects of coalition design are highlighted. First, a comparison of negotiations on services and intellectual property rights during the Uruguay Round (chapter 2 by J. P. Singh) asks why developing countries gained more and lost less in 1994 on services than on intellectual property rights issues, the opposite of what might have been predicted in 1986. This study suggests, for one thing, that coalitions defined in terms of specific issues or sub-issues are likely to do better than ones encompassing several issue-areas, other things being equal.[31]

Chapter 2 also suggests a second testable hypothesis that coalitions that include important players, such as major developing or developed countries, are likely to gain more for developing countries than those that do not. Chapter 7 by Christina Davis on negotiating in WTO legal disputes

[27] See Sebenius 1995 and Sebenius 1996 for interesting theoretical ideas about this part of the process.
[28] Hamilton and Whalley 1989; Kahler and Odell 1989; Higgott and Cooper 1990; Kumar 1993; Tussie 1993; Dupont 1994.
[29] Luke 2000; Duran 2001; Page 2003; Bernal et al. 2004; Narlikar and Tussie 2004.
[30] Wang and Winters 1997; Bjornskov and Lind 2002; Drahos 2003.
[31] But note Narlikar's (2003) skepticism about this hypothesis. She argues that many issue-based coalitions are short-lived, new ones must be created repeatedly, and the negotiating transaction costs are too high for many poor countries to make this practical.

proposes the analogous proposition that developing countries that file a complaint with the support of interested developed country members will negotiate better outcomes than those that act alone. Chapter 7 illustrates with a dispute coalition combining Chile, Peru and Canada, which negotiated gains from the European Union in a dispute over its barriers to their fish exports.

Third, case studies of two coalitions operating in multilateral talks in 2001 prior to and in Doha suggest that the larger the coalition, the less it will lose and the more it will gain, provided that it manages the fragmentation problem discussed below. The logic is that the credibility of the coalition's threat to block the entire WTO will be lower if the group is smaller, and will rise with the number of states that would have to be coerced or persuaded to abandon their group. In 2001 the larger of the two coalitions sought a new declaration concerning the application of the WTO agreement on intellectual property rights to matters of public health (chapter 3 by John Odell and Susan Sell). The smaller coalition that gained less and lost more, the Like Minded Group, also illustrates how initial coalition design can constrain a group's choice of strategy and tactics during the subsequent process (chapter 4 by Amrita Narlikar and John Odell). The LMG was defined as countries committed to the principle that the Uruguay Round package had been unbalanced, rather than uniting countries that shared the same preference on a specific issue, and it encompassed several issue-areas. This credibility logic might operate differently in the realm of dispute bargaining. There, if a small set of countries seeks to convince panelists that an offending practice should be judged inconsistent with the rules, and if the coalition has rules, facts and legal reasoning on its side, adding members may make little difference in convincing the panel. But a larger coalition operating jointly might still influence the defending state's decisions in settlement negotiations. This issue could be investigated empirically.

Strategies

A second set of conclusions concentrates on the negotiating strategies negotiators use and the effects of their strategies. The meaning of *strategy* often shifts according to the goal sought. We read that one country in international relations followed a "containment strategy," another a "liberalizing strategy," and so forth. Without some fixed standard meaning, it is difficult to compare attempts to use the same strategy, to ascertain conditions when it is more or less successful, in short to use the concept in generalizations. For developing generalizations about the negotiation process and interpreting particular cases it will be helpful to have a typology for uniformly classifying general courses of action available to negotiators, regardless of the issue. Here *strategy* means a set of behaviors or tactics that are observable in principle and associated with a plan to achieve some objective through negotiation. This behavioral meaning differs from the meaning in earlier international cooperation research and in game theory.[32]

Suppose the behavioral options vary along a conceptual continuum between two polar ideal types: distributive behavior and integrative behavior.[33] On one end of the spectrum, a *purely distributive strategy* is a set of tactics that are functional only for claiming value from others and defending against such claiming, when one party's goals are partly in conflict with those of the other. Specifically these tactics include opening with high demands, refusing all concessions, exaggerating one's minimum needs and true priorities, manipulating information to others' disadvantage, taking others' issues hostage, worsening their alternative to agreement, making threats, and actually imposing penalties. When a state joins the WTO it gains access to a major new distributive tactic for worsening another state's alternative to negotiating a satisfactory dispute settlement: filing a legal complaint under WTO rules. A defensive distributive strategy consists of analogous behaviors to offset other parties' distributive tactics and protect as much as possible against losing value. This strategy is not restricted by definition to the most powerful. When a weaker state asks others for benefits and refuses to grant any negotiating gain to others, it is attempting a strict distributive strategy. Distributive tactics such as delay and refusal to make concessions are common among all states. This strategy can also include the tactical retreat – agreeing to accept less than demanded earlier or give up more than conceded earlier. A purely distributive strategy runs the risks of discouraging the discovery of opportunities for mutual gains and provoking deadlocks and conflict.[34]

A *purely integrative strategy* would be a set of tactics instrumental to the attainment of goals that are not in fundamental conflict and hence can be integrated for mutual gain to some degree. One subset of these tactics

---

[32] Strategies here are not limited to two binary choices. Most behavioral strategies do not specify every possible response to every conceivable contingency.

[33] The terms are due to Walton and McKersie 1965, though this pioneering work of negotiation analysis thought of distributive bargaining as a two-sided interaction rather than a strategy for one side to consider, and likewise for integrative bargaining.

[34] The negotiation analysis tradition has developed a long list of possible distributive tactics. Political economists and others have carried out several partial investigations of conditions when threats and other distributive tactics are likely to gain more and less in trade and other spheres. E.g., Hufbauer, Schott, and Elliott 1990; Schoppa 1993; Bayard and Elliott 1994; Noland 1997; Schoppa 1999; Drezner 2003.

involves sharing information relatively openly to explore common problems or threats in a search for mutual gain solutions. Another well-known
integrative move is proposing an exchange of concessions or fallbacks that
might benefit more than one party (as opposed to demanding a concession without compensation). Legislative logrolling is a well-known example. In GATT talks, proposing a formula for cutting all tariffs, including
those of the speaker's state, embodies such an exchange of concessions. A
third subset of integrative tactics involves reframing the issue space itself
in a way that eases impasses.[35] These are behaviors for gaining (through
cooperation with others), not ways of giving up value. Simply yielding
concessions under pressure without any compensation is part of a process of shifting value from one to another rather than creating joint gain.
But integrative tactics, used exclusively, will expose the player to at least
some risk of exploitation by others.

Experienced negotiators often attempt to overcome the risks of each
pure type by blending tactics into a mix. Tactical elements from the two
ends of the continuum may be mixed either simultaneously or sequentially.[36] Thus the conceptual spectrum runs from purely distributive, to
mixed-distributive (including a minority of integrative elements), to balanced, to mixed-integrative. Purely integrative strategy is difficult to find
in international negotiations. An appendix to this chapter provides operational definitions for classifying behavior along this spectrum.

This typology carries several caveats. It refers to only one party's
behavior; it does not assume other parties will necessarily match its strategy. To describe a party's strategy is also not to make a claim about
whether it has succeeded; it describes an attempt. Nor does it amount
to a judgment whether the strategy was good or bad. The typology aims
only to describe the observed negotiating behavior. Making evaluative
judgments is more complex; it requires specifying the standard by which
to judge and considering alternative courses of action. The same general
strategy could be judged preferable in some circumstances and inferior
in others. The proposed typology is not the only conceivable typology,
but it does have the advantages that the options are defined in terms of
observable behavior and are not restricted to particular goals.

In practice a negotiator or delegation may not choose a strategy all at
one time and in a self-conscious way. Some may make decisions one step

---

[35] Integrative tactics are elaborated further in Odell 2000, chapter 7. In the negotiation analysis tradition Zartman's conception of the "deductive" process for overcoming impasses
has been influential (Zartman and Berman 1982). Recent empirical studies by Elms
2003, Farrell 2003 and Ives 2003 shed new light on effects of integrative tactics in
trade.
[36] This meaning of mixed strategy is not the same as in game theory.

at a time and accumulate a set of actions without considering them as a set. Some conceivably may even act without thinking carefully about their objectives at all. Be that as it may, our premise is that it will be fruitful, for purposes of research and generalization about negotiation, to classify observed behavior using these concepts.

Four of our chapters focus on strategies used by developing countries. Their evidence supports the conclusion that a developing country or a coalition will gain more in most conditions if it employs what we call a mixed-distributive strategy than if it follows a purely distributive one, other things equal.[37] The mixed strategy allows other delegations to claim some gains to show their constituents, moving the deal above the others' reservation values, and hence is less likely to produce a breakdown. Evidence from the Dillon and Kennedy Rounds indicates that developing countries that offered concessions on their imports gained far more for their exports than passive countries.[38] Both Mexico in NAFTA in the early 1990s (see chapter 6) and the 2001 WTO coalition for TRIPS and public health (see chapter 3) used sequential rather than simultaneous mixing. They opened with distributive tactics and later mixed in some integrative moves. The Mexico case suggests that simultaneous mixing would have opened Mexico to greater risk of exploitation by its powerful neighbor to the north.

The Like Minded Group of developing countries in the WTO in the period 1998–2001 illustrates what we call the strict distributive strategy throughout, and it gained less than the TRIPS/health coalition. This case suggests the additional generalization that for a developing country coalition, gains from this strategy will diminish to the extent that the group fragments and loses its credibility. This strategy encourages outsiders to attempt to divide and rule, and once defections begin they tend to stimulate more. A mixed strategy is unlikely to create as intense an incentive for outsiders to attempt to split them. The Like Minded Group demanded that Northern countries concede changes in the existing rules in favor of the South before launching a new round, threatened to block consensus otherwise, and refused overtures toward integrative bargaining, as a group. The European Union and the United States used mixed strategies and separate deals to split the coalition, which lost its credibility, collapsed into acquiescence in Doha, and came away with relatively small gains and a major loss. Both these coalitions were operating in the same international institution, the WTO, during the same time, but the institution left space for different strategies to contribute to different outcomes. There

---

[37] Here we apply a hypothesis from Walton et al. 1994 and Odell 2000, chapter 7.
[38] Finger 1974 and Finger 1976.

are conditions in which a strict distributive strategy will gain more, but they are not easy for poorer countries to arrange.

Thus another variable in the process is what coalition members do, if anything, to maintain unity in the face of splitters' efforts. Many developing country coalitions probably do nothing in response to these attempts. But if coalition members attempt to persuade other members to spurn such attempts, the credibility of the coalition's threat to block a deal will remain higher and will induce outsiders to think more about concessions, again other things being equal. The 2001 coalition on TRIPS and public health illustrates one effective response to attempted splitting. This coalition was large and hence vulnerable to the free-riding problem, and the United States did attempt to break its unity with lesser offers to a subset of members. Some leading members responded vigorously and convinced others they could gain more if they rejected the lesser offers. The outcome was a significant gain for the developing country coalition as a whole relative to the status quo ante, at the expense of the United States, Switzerland, and global pharmaceutical firms.

One important phase for applying a strategy is during agenda setting, which can shape the ultimate distribution of gains as well as the potential to expand the pie. Comparing Uruguay Round negotiations over services and (initially) counterfeit goods, chapter 2 concludes that failing to monitor and participate carefully in agenda setting (as the property rights agenda expanded) increased developing countries' losses. Later ministerial conferences in Seattle, Doha and Cancún were concerned centrally with setting the agenda for the Doha round, and experience there suggests many more governments learned this general lesson well. Nevertheless, many of them still lack the resources to gather information about domestic developments in other countries in the detail needed to have early warning of specific campaigns to change the agenda.

Strategy choices made during dispute settlement bargaining may also affect developing country outcomes in that setting. Ecuador, the world's largest exporter of bananas, faced discrimination against its chief export to the European Union during the late 1990s. Ecuador's strategy in the famous banana dispute was innovative, sophisticated, and tenacious, and it surely increased Ecuador's negotiated gains beyond what it would have received otherwise (see chapter 8).

Dynamic interactions on the subjective level

A third set of ideas in this book concentrates on the subjective elements of the international negotiation process, which can themselves tip its direction and the outcome, despite institutions and domestic veto groups attempting to impose constraints. Bounded rationality implies that part of the negotiation process occurs at the subjective level. Given uncertainties and biases on all sides, delegations go to negotiations partly to gather information and to influence one another's thinking, including that of constituents. Thus when deciding what to do, negotiators want to understand how various possible moves will affect other parties' beliefs and feelings as well as their markets. A voluminous literature has documented effects of policy makers' beliefs on foreign policy decision making,[39] as well as effects of heuristics and biases on negotiator behavior.[40]

Specifically, a key part of normal processes of policy making and negotiation is a contest among partisans each attempting to establish the dominant subjective frame of reference. Cognitive psychologists assume that all human beings are subject to *framing*. Tversky and Kahneman theorize that when a person makes a choice, his or her mind goes through two phases. In the first, a preliminary analysis of the decision problem "frames the effective acts, contingencies and outcomes. . . . Framing is controlled by the manner in which the choice problem is presented as well as by norms, habits, and expectancies of the decision maker."[41] Only then does the person evaluate the framed prospects and choose one.

That is, preferences themselves sometimes vary with the way an issue is framed. Not all preferences are exogenous and stable, even on economic issues clearly affecting the individual's material welfare. For example, economist Richard Thaler finds that

The number of options on a 401(k) menu can affect the employees' selections. Those with a choice of a stock fund and a bond fund tend to invest half in each. Those with a choice of three stock funds and one bond fund are likely to sprinkle an equal amount of their savings in each, and thus put 75 percent of the total in stocks.[42]

Companies and politicians pay the advertising and public relations industries billions each year for attempts to create or modify consumers', voters' and legislators' preferences, by placing their products or proposals in the most favorable possible frame and omitting discordant information. The possibility that preferences vary with framing seems even greater when we move from individuals' choices to governments' choices over economic

[39] Young and Schafer 1998 is a recent review. Janis 1972 and Jervis 1976 are influential exemplars.
[40] Odell 2000, chapter 5 and works cited there. More of this literature is cited in chapter 5 of the present book.
[41] Tversky and Kahneman 1986, 73.
[42] Lowenstein 2001, 70. Also see Kahneman, Knetch, and Thaler 1990, Rabin 1998, and earlier works cited there.

policy and negotiating positions, where complex but intangible ideas of national interest including political values also enter in.[43]

Framing is common in negotiations. Experimental studies find that when there is considerable uncertainty about interests, opening bids tend to frame the counterpart's belief about the likely outcome. The worse the opening bid by A, the worse the deal B believes is likely.[44] One of the most investigated instances of framing concerns loss aversion. Many experiments have found that negotiators framed with the goal of avoiding losses make fewer concessions and reach fewer agreements than negotiators framed to achieve gains, even when the monetary consequences of the agreements are identical.[45] People are willing to take a greater risk of no deal to avoid a loss than they will take to make a gain of the same magnitude, all other things equal.

Several chapters make new contributions on the subjective level. During the NAFTA talks Mexican negotiators supported their defensive demand to exclude concessions on oil by framing it as analogous to demands by Washington and Ottawa to exclude issues of their own like migration, rather than allowing Mexico's defensive demand to be framed as requiring Mexico to sacrifice one of its offensive demands.

Chapter 3 supports the proposition that a developing country coalition seeking to claim value from dominant states will increase its gains if it persuades the mass media to reframe the issue using a reference point more favorable to the coalition's position, other things equal. In 2001 governmental and non-governmental advocates of a WTO ministerial declaration on TRIPS and public health attempted repeatedly to reframe subjective understandings of TRIPS via the mass media. The agreement's original advocates had framed it as an alternative to allowing piracy of private property. Opponents beginning in 1999 attempted to reframe TRIPS using a different reference point – as a barrier to treating AIDS and other dire threats to public health. The case study illustrates how the attempt was executed, how the global pharmaceutical firms responded, and how this campaign encouraged pressure on US and other Northern official negotiators from within their own politics toward compromise in the WTO talks.[46] (Thus this example also illustrates again how international negotiations are often two-level games.)

---

[43] Odell 2002.   [44] Lax and Sebenius 1986, 135.
[45] Bazerman and Neale 1992, 39. See Levy 1997 for a review of applications of prospect theory to international relations.
[46] Reframing can also be part of a more integrative strategy. Negotiators, mediators and consensus builders like WTO council chairs sometimes attempt to reframe a contentious set of issues, carving up the issue space itself along different dimensions, in an attempt to break an impasse and broker a mutual-gains deal.

Other reframing attempts have not had as great an effect, and the chapter speculates about conditions that will be more and less favorable for future attempts.

Chapter 3 also suggests parallels between these insights based on psychology and insights about the subjective level developed by political science constructivism, most of which takes off from sociology. Recent empirical studies in this constructivist tradition have attempted to account for the outcomes of international negotiations – mostly on military and human rights rather than trade issues – by reference to NGOs' and governments' attempts at argumentation and persuasion.[47] These scholars, like many lawyers, stress the power of a good argument to change minds as distinct from the power that comes from coercive threats. Other contributions suggest that international norms help define and change states' interests.[48]

This book also provides new evidence for the proposition that developing country gains will rise with their delegates' efforts to compensate for their own judgment biases.[49] The NAFTA study finds that such compensatory efforts helped Mexico reach a favorable agreement without conceding on oil. By hiring US lobbyists and other steps, the team improved its estimate of the true US reservation value, offsetting a tendency to overconfidence that has been documented in negotiation research.

Gains are also likely to rise with tactics to increase the subjective credibility of commitments.[50] Mexico's NAFTA team took several specific steps to increase the credibility in Washington of their commitment to their reservation value on oil. Ecuador's strategy in the bananas dispute (in chapter 8) illustrates other steps. Likewise, a threat to block a consensus in the WTO or walk away from regional talks unless one is satisfied must be believed to have an effect. Thus negotiators sometimes take steps to influence those beliefs, and the effects of those steps tip the process in a particular direction in some cases. Forming a coalition and holding it together are means of increasing credibility, and splitting a rival coalition will undermine its credibility. Credibility tactics by coalitions and their results are illustrated by the WTO's Like Minded Group and the TRIPS/health coalition in 2001.

---

[47] See review essays by Finnemore and Sikkink 2001, Goldgeier and Tetlock 2001, and Checkel 2004. Chapter 3 gives other citations. Exceptions that explore trade issues include Schoppa 1999, Tsygankov 2001, Eising 2002, and Farrell 2003.

[48] Klotz 1995; Finnemore 1996.   [49] Odell 2000, chap. 5.

[50] Many political economists followed Schelling 1960 in thinking about this slice of the international negotiation process, though not often by gathering evidence on tactics actual negotiators use to increase or defend credibility. Sample Martin 1992; Cowhey 1993; Moravcsik 1998; Martin 2000.

More generally, negotiation on the subjective level involves a process of complex learning. As parties make demands and proposals and react to others, each receives new information and factors it into subsequent decisions. Each case study in this book documents simple learning by negotiators followed by behavioral consequences. During the Uruguay Round developing country officials learned that the United States and others meant to enlarge the agenda of intellectual property rights far beyond what had been discussed in 1986, and their attention and resistance intensified, belatedly. During the NAFTA talks Mexican delegates learned new information about the US reservation value. After Seattle the Like Minded Group learned that demands for one-way concessions on its signature issue of implementation were not generating many meaningful concessions, despite their threats to block the launch of the Doha Round, and eventually members began to defect. During dispute bargaining with Peru over food labeling, the European Union learned that a WTO panel was going to rule against the EU regulation, which led to a change in Brussels' bargaining behavior.

But we know that learning is more complex than simply adding information to a pile of facts or updating probability estimates. The starting point – limited rationality including a thick matrix of predispositions and partisan biases – implies opportunities for signals and other new information to be interpreted in ways different from those intended by their senders.

Chapter 5 by Cédric Dupont, Cosimo Beverelli, and Stéphanie Pézard generates new evidence specifically about information processing and its distortions for the case of developing countries and trade. This study observes the changing beliefs of developing country trade officials while they are participating in a three-day training simulation. Officials are organized into four delegations negotiating over tariffs and subsidies and play roles representing those found in actual WTO talks. This evidence suggests that developing country negotiators revise initial beliefs and converge in the direction of common knowledge in three respects. For instance they learn more about one another's true reservation values and the bounds of a zone of agreement during successive rounds.

At the same time, however, developing country officials playing these roles, like subjects in earlier experiments, also demonstrate uncertainties, biases and heuristics that can channel learning and thus subsequent interactions in particular directions. For example, many delegates enter the negotiation with excessive optimism about their own knowledge. They make tactical choices based on fixed rules of thumb rather than responding to clear new information from others' moves. They discover it is difficult to tell which aspects of others' actions are relevant signals and which extraneous. There is evidence of self-serving bias regarding whose offers are fair and who is responsible for delays. The tactics of individuals playing key roles can strongly tip beliefs of other delegations about how cooperative each country is likely to be. Signaling in this hazy environment is difficult to carry out accurately and convergence is not smooth or complete. This chapter points to evidence of these phenomena in other chapters as well as some practical remedies.

Chapter 5 raises two important challenges to Bayesian models of bargaining and learning. It indicates that the assumption that common knowledge among players will make for effective learning is too strong. These trade officials fell well short of the degree of common knowledge assumed in the models, at least in the brief time available. Second, models that attempt to represent biases in updating assume all players learn and change the same way, but this is not what is observed here. Thus this study suggests avenues for future research by modelers as well as other scholars.

Difference in institutional context changes process and thus outcome

Political economists have contributed a number of theoretical ideas about possible connections between international institutions and the outcomes of bargaining embedded in them.[51] One of the most influential ideas has been that institutions like the GATT and WTO improve the efficiency of negotiations and help members overcome collective action problems. The multilateral forum economizes on the transaction costs of conducting multiple bilateral negotiations. Theorists say institutions add information that would not be available otherwise. Organizations monitor conditions in the issue area and compliance with agreements and thus help expose cheaters, implying that states will be more willing to sign agreements.[52] Others have proposed that international institutions sometimes inject focal points into negotiations that states would otherwise not find.[53] Institutions like the European Union or the WTO encourage linkages between unrelated issues that would not occur in the absence of the international institution.[54] Others have contended that when states negotiate an enforceable international trade agreement, their governments sometimes use the international institution to overcome resistance of

[51] For reviews see Milner 1992, Hasenclever, Mayer, and Rittberger 1997, Martin and Simmons 1998, Frieden and Martin 2003.
[52] Keohane 1984.
[53] Garrett and Weingast 1993, Young 1994. But see the dissent in Moravcsik 1999.
[54] Martin 1992.

domestic opponents.[55] They may "lock in" commitments to liberalism, tying the hands of future governments and creating higher obstacles for social forces that would prefer more interventionist or protective national policies. Still others argue that the GATT/WTO rule permitting state A to retaliate against exports of state B if B's practices in another sector violate the rules means that A's threat to retaliate will stimulate the targeted exporters in B to lobby domestically for concessions in dispute bargaining, to escape the retaliation.[56] On the other hand, it has been argued that the more precise information the institution provides during multilateral negotiations for further liberalization, the more accurately it also informs potential "losers" of what they stand to lose. Stripping away the "veil of ignorance" alerts them to oppose trade-offs and causes greater restraint on liberalization.[57] A recent article finds that developments in the GATT/WTO context have paradoxically given members the incentive to form discriminatory regional groups to enhance their global bargaining leverage.[58]

The question of why states comply with any international obligations has also stimulated much theoretical debate and empirical research by political economists, legal scholars, and constructivists. Much early political economy work abstracted from the negotiation process as an explanation for compliance.[59] Legal scholars and some constructivists contribute a type of process understanding.[60] A few works have concentrated specifically on ways in which negotiation shapes compliance and implementation.[61]

The trade negotiator's institutional context does change on occasion, and two chapters observe such variations to study the effects such differences might have on the dispute negotiation process and outcome. Chapter 7 by Christina Davis reminds us that most fundamentally, creating the GATT and then the WTO in the first place, with their dispute settlement procedures, gave members and only members an additional negotiating tactic for claiming value from others in a dispute. If state A complains to B about its trade practices and neither is a member, B has some alternative to satisfying A with a negotiated agreement, such as unilateral action or doing nothing. But if both are WTO members and A decides to file a legal complaint under WTO rules, doing so is likely to worsen B's perceived alternative to negotiated settlement, whenever

[55] Goldstein 1996.   [56] Frieden and Martin 2003, 122.
[57] Goldstein and Martin 2000.   [58] Mansfield and Reinhardt 2003.
[59] Simmons 1998 reviews some of this literature. Works specifically on GATT and WTO dispute settlement have been cited above.
[60] Raustiala and Slaughter 2002; Checkel 2001; Hurd 1999.
[61] Jönsson and Tallberg 1998; Spector, Zartman, and Sjostedt 2003.

the rules can be interpreted as prohibiting B's practice. Now if B refuses to make a concession after a violation ruling, the costs of impasse may well be greater, including a loss of reputation from violating international trade law. This worsening of the alternative is likely to be even greater when the complaint also raises the odds of the WTO setting a precedent that could jeopardize other trade measures besides the one in litigation.

Chapter 7 compares Vietnam's recent dispute with the United States and Peru's with the European Union, both concerning labeling of fishery exports. Vietnam was not a WTO member. US practices harmed its catfish exports and Hanoi proposed to negotiate, but Washington virtually refused to negotiate in this case. Except for one brief period, the United States resorted to its outside alternative – unilateral actions inconsistent with WTO rules. Not being a WTO member, Vietnam lacked access to this legal-framing tactic to worsen Washington's BATNA.[62] Meanwhile Peru's sardine exports were also damaged by European labeling practices. A member state, Peru chose to file a WTO complaint. While the proceedings were underway, these two sides attempted to negotiate a settlement but could not come to agreement. After the panel and the Appellate Body ruled in Peru's favor, Brussels and Lima settled on an agreement that gave Peru a significant improvement over the status quo ante. Peru clearly gained more than Vietnam. The chapter notes other differences that were also relevant.

One 1994 change in the rules of the global trading system enabled a new distributive tactic, the threat to cross-retaliate. A winning complainant could now be authorized to respond to a failure to comply with one WTO agreement by retaliating under a different agreement. Chapter 8 by James McCall Smith describes the first use of a threat to cross-retaliate, by Ecuador in 1999, to influence the European Union in dispute settlement bargaining over bananas. Not satisfied with the initial European offer, Ecuador threatened to withdraw European intellectual property rights in Ecuador. This move along with several other elements of its aggressive but calibrated distributive strategy, such as taking advantage of the WTO consensus norm, helped Ecuador gain significantly compared with the status quo ante, and gain more than other small exporting countries that did not use the same tactics. Smith's chapter illustrates how earlier institutional design choices may shape subsequent negotiations among members, sometimes in unintended directions. It also shows again that, within a given institution, even a small developing country's

---

[62] For Davis, legal framing is different from framing as defined in cognitive psychology, as her chapter explains.

choices among bargaining strategies and tactics can have their own direct effects on what it gains or loses.

4   Future research, theoretical bridges, and practical implications

The process through which developing countries negotiate their trade agreements, then, exerts a significant influence on the outcomes in both deal-making and dispute settlement, judging from the cases we have studied. Many of these outcomes were counter-intuitive from the perspective of familiar theories and facts known before the process began. Not all choices made along the way were fully predictable from markets, power structures, and institutions. Ignoring process variations would have caused us to miss key elements needed for an accurate understanding. Later chapters present counter-factual examples suggesting how a different process would have led to a different outcome. These cases also suggest possible generalizations about the negotiation process in other cases. Naturally these studies by themselves, like most studies, can supply only partial and provisional support for general conclusions.

But they also point beyond themselves to useful future research projects that would close the gaps further. First and most simply, studies of other cases could check the ideas suggested here and confirm, modify or reject them. It would be especially valuable to better isolate conditions under which each idea holds, if it does. When does a strict distributive strategy or the reframing tactic gain the most and the least? Will a coalition including a member of the Quad states always gain more for developing countries than a coalition restricted to developing countries, and if not, what determines the difference?

Second, future research could do more to explore the relations among these aspects of the negotiation process, in trade and other realms. How do strategies as defined here affect the formation and breakup of coalitions in general? How do coalitions affect information processing? Do cognitive biases limit behavioral strategy choices, say between the strict and the mixed distributive type? Which substantive biases most strongly determine responses to attempts to use integrative tactics in the trade realm and elsewhere?

Third, the scope of this research can be and is being expanded to illuminate other aspects of the international negotiation process, its contexts, other parties' experience, and other types of economic negotiation. This book explores only one slice of the more general phenomenon. As for contexts, we need deeper and more specific knowledge about how changes in objective market conditions affect developing country negotiations with multinational corporations over investments, and with the International Monetary Fund over financial crises. There is opportunity to pin down more exactly the conditions and mechanisms through which changes in international security conditions shape the economic negotiation process. Greater progress could be made in understanding whether and how changing international norms shape the negotiation process on economic issues. Industrialized countries' and transition countries' coalition designs, strategy choices, and signaling problems in trade, monetary, and environmental negotiations also could benefit from more empirically grounded study. Odell 2000, chapter 9, offers a more comprehensive agenda for research on economic negotiation. An Economic Negotiation Network publicizes new projects and publications and links researchers and interested readers. This network is found on the World Wide Web at www.usc.edu/enn, and it includes current contact information for this book's contributors.

Still more broadly, this book and the growing research effort of which it is a part speak to scholars in two schools of thought that have not fully exploited the theoretical intersection of their traditions. We incorporate certain ideas from each and merge them selectively. From the negotiation analysis tradition we incorporate and develop the basic concept of the negotiation process, the BATNA, distributive and integrative strategies, coalitions, cognitive biases, and the tradition's typical qualitative method. From the international political economy tradition we build on basic concepts such as rationality, market competition, gain and loss, the reservation value, the contract zone, commitment credibility, information, incentives created by institutional design, and characteristic methods including variables, exogenous conditions, and causal hypotheses.

If the results of this merger are regarded as productive, the broader implication is that further selective integration of this type could be progressive for each tradition. Future work in the negotiation analysis tradition could, without abandoning its main commitments, experiment more with political economic ideas about institutions, considering the incentives they create and tracing their impact on negotiator decisions and the dynamic process. This tradition could compare institutions with different properties to explore the effects of institutional variation on negotiations. Analysis of negotiations over economic issues could give more attention in its conceptualization to the markets that the governments are trying to regulate, as sources of variations in negotiator behavior, as distinct from the psychological and cultural sources. Researchers working in this tradition could devote much more attention to developing country experience, and work harder to generate testable causal hypotheses from their case studies. One chapter suggests further possible benefits from exploring related insights of constructivism.

International political economists could, without abandoning their main commitments, factor the international process more consistently into explanations of trade policies. This tradition could devote more attention to behavior and interactions of negotiators themselves, in both model building and empirical research. The concept of information could be broadened step by step by considering more of the rich insights available from psychology and sociology. This tradition might explore further the insight that certain common biases documented by negotiation analysis could distort the reception of signals in predictable ways. More generally, political economists might look to this neighboring negotiation literature for additional ideas about the causal mechanisms that operate during bargaining. Those open to suspending a core commitment could also experiment with modeling decision rules other than optimization.[63] Political economists too could devote much more attention to the experience of developing countries.

We hope it is also clear enough that this book generates specific implications for the practice of trade negotiation. These new studies point to ways negotiators may reap gains and limit losses by choosing particular coalition designs, negotiating strategies, and subjective tactics, and avoiding others. These practical lessons for delegations, their constituents, and international organizations are also summarized in Odell and Ortiz 2004. Globalization, as challenging as it is for developing countries, does not eliminate all choices. True, weak economies, structural power inequalities, a shortage of attractive alternatives, and moves by strong states and multinational firms certainly constrain and channel those choices. But trade institutions and the negotiation process embedded in them also leave some real opportunities to influence results. The daily news indicates that developing country governments are discovering some of these possibilities, and it seems certain the trade negotiation process will never be the same.

Appendix

An operational definition for classifying and describing negotiating behavior

A. Distributive or value-claiming strategy. Code a party's strategy as "pure distributive" if any of the following tactics are observed and no

---

[63] One political science example is Bendor 1995.

more than a small minority of the behavior fits the definition of "integrative strategy."

Both defensive and offensive variants. The negotiator:

- criticizes the other country's or countries' actions or arrangements, blames them for the problem under discussion;
- attempts to exclude from the agenda issues on which her own country would probably have to make concessions;
- rejects or ignores demands for concessions or delays their consideration;
- avoids saying her own country is partly responsible for the problem under discussion, avoids expressing concern for the other's objectives or a desire for a mutual-gain outcome, avoids making a proposal characterized as beneficial to other parties or the world as a whole;
- manipulates information for her own advantage: avoids revealing information about own genuine objectives and priorities; makes arguments whose effect is to support her demands or refusal to concede and does not present information or arguments that are inconsistent with that position; e.g., argues that the other's alternative to agreement is worse for them than they realize, that our alternative is better than they realize, or that the other's forecasts showing future improvement for us (in absence of agreement) are not convincing, or that she simply does not have the capacity to deliver what is demanded, or that the other's proposal would harm our side or others;
- establishes a commitment to a particular outcome, by means of some public action tied to that outcome such that accepting less would be costly to the negotiator or her country;
- denies that he or she believes the other's commitments.

Offensive variant: The negotiator also:

- demands concessions for the benefit of his or her own country without offering concessions in exchange;
- takes steps to worsen the other's alternative to agreement and improve her own; e.g., unilateral actions or negotiations with third parties that would help compensate it for a breakdown in relations with the other or provide itself with a superior alternative, or raise the cost of a breakdown for the other; actions could include introducing draft legislation for official consideration at home or "talking the national currency down";
- files a legal complaint against another state under global or regional rules and demands a change in current policy or practice that will benefit the complainant. The complainant typically perceives this move as responding to and righting a wrong done earlier. In any case, relative to the status quo and from a neutral standpoint, the move's effect on the negotiation process would be to help shift value from the respondent to the complainant rather than to make both better off as they see it;

- launches an antidumping or similar complaint through its national institutions, which could be done for external bargaining purposes as well as for the stated purposes;
- threatens to take action harmful to others unless they yield the desired concessions;
- actually imposes such penalties and implements its alternative to agreement.

Defensive variant. The negotiator also:

- brings a counter-complaint under international rules against a state that has filed a complaint against it;
- threatens or imposes counter-sanctions.

B. Integrative or value-creating strategy. Code a party's strategy as "pure integrative" if the following tactics are observed and if no more than a small minority of the behavior fits "distributive." The negotiator:

- states that the parties have an interest in common or expresses concern for an objective held by the other;
- proposes negotiations designed to benefit both or many sides, usually aiming to agree on a joint approach to a common problem or an exchange of concessions;
- praises the other and avoids public statements criticizing the other country or blaming it for the problem or issue under discussion;
- invites the other to state frankly its genuine concerns and objectives and their priority order, as distinguished from its demands and proposals;
- proposes and implements a series of meetings whose only or main purpose is to engage the parties in joint study of problems and objectives they have in common;
- uses and refers to information about the issue or problem without shaping it to her own side's advantage; engages in an "even-handed" discussion of all the facts whether favorable or unfavorable to her side;
- proposes an exchange of concessions for mutual benefit or accepts a mediator's proposal that entails such an exchange;
- argues that a different conception of the other's interests or a redefinition of the issues themselves could lead to an agreement that would benefit both parties;
- proposes a formula or agreement described as helpful to other parties as well;
- agrees to abide by binding arbitration, which can shorten a conflict and reduce its costs for all parties.

C. Mixed or combined strategy. Code a party's behavior in a conflict or negotiation as a "mixed" strategy if distributive and integrative tactics are mixed in some proportion, either simultaneously or in a sequence dominated by claiming in one phase and value-creating in another.

REFERENCES

Aggarwal, Vinod K. 1985. *Liberal Protectionism: The Politics of Organized Textile Trade*. Berkeley: University of California Press

Alexander, J. McKensie. 2003. Evolutionary Game Theory. In *The Stanford Encyclopedia of Philosophy*, ed. Edward N. Zalta. Accessed on June 12, 2005 at http://plato.stanford.edu/archives/sum2003/entries/game-evolutionary/

Arriola, Salvador. 1994. La Ronda Uruguay: una experiencia de consulta y coordinación de American Latina y el Caribe. In *La Ronda Uruguay y el Desarrollo de America Latina*, ed. Patricio Leiva. Santiago: CLEPI/PNUD

Arrow, Kenneth, Robert H. Mnookin, Lee Ross, Amos Tversky, and Robert B. Wilson. 1995. *Barriers to Conflict Resolution*. New York: W. W. Norton

Bayard, Thomas O., and Kimberly Ann Elliott. 1994. *Reciprocity and Retaliation in US Trade Policy*. Washington, DC: Institute for International Economics

Bazerman, Max H., and Margaret A. Neale. 1992. *Negotiating Rationally*. New York: The Free Press

Bendor, Jonathan. 1995. A Model of Muddling Through. *American Political Science Review* 89: 819–40

Bernal, Luisa E., Rashid S. Kaukab, Sisule F. Musungu, and Vicente Paolo B. III Yu. 2004. *South-South Cooperation in the Multilateral Trading System: Cancún and Beyond*. Trade-Related Agenda, Development and Equity Working Papers, 21. Geneva: South Centre

Bjornskov, Christian, and Kim Martin Lind. 2002. Where Do Developing Countries Go After Doha? An anlaysis of WTO positions and potential alliances. *Journal of World Trade*. 36 (3): 543–62

Busch, Marc, and Eric Reinhardt. 2002. Testing International Trade Law: Empirical Studies of GATT/WTO Dispute Settlement. In *The Political Economy of International Trade Law*, eds. Daniel L. M. Kennedy and James D. Southwick, 457–81. Cambridge: Cambridge University Press

2003. Developing Countries and GATT/WTO Dispute Settlement. *Journal of World Trade* 37 (4): 719–35

Checkel, Jeffrey T. 2001. Why Comply? Social Learning and European Identity Change. *International Organization* 55 (3): 553–88

2004. Social constructivisms in global and European politics: a review essay. *Review of International Studies* 30 (2): 229–44

Conlisk, John. 1996. Why Bounded Rationality? *Journal of Economic Literature* 34 (2): 669–700

Cowhey, Peter F. 1993. Domestic institutions and the credibility of international commitments: Japan and the United States. *International Organization* 47 (2): 299–326

Croome, John. 1999. *Reshaping the World Trading System: A History of the Uruguay Round*, 2d and revised edition. Geneva: World Trade Organization

Crystal, J. 2003. Bargaining in the Negotiations over Liberalizing Trade in Services: Power, Reciprocity and Learning. *Review of International Political Economy* 10 (3): 552–78

Das, Bhagirath Lal. 2002. *Strengthening Developing Countries in the WTO*. Trade and Development Series, 8. Third World Network. www.twnside.org.sg/title/td8.htm.

Davey, William J. 2005. The WTO Dispute Settlement System: The First Ten Years. *Journal of International Economic Law* 8 (1): 17–50

Destler, I. M., Haruhiro Fukui, and Hideo Sato. 1979. *The Textile Wrangle: Conflict in Japanese-American Relations, 1969–1971.* Ithaca, NY: Cornell University Press

Drahos, Peter. 2003. When the Weak Bargain with The Strong: Negotiations in the World Trade Organization. *International Negotiation* 8 (1): 79–109

Drezner, Daniel W. 2003. The Hidden Hand of Economic Coercion. *International Organization* 57 (3): 643–59

Dupont, Christophe. 1994. Coalition Theory: Using Power to Build Cooperation. In *International Multilateral Negotiation,* ed. I. William Zartman, 148–77. San Francisco: Jossey-Bass

Duran, Esperanza. 2001. *The Participation of the Latin American and Caribbean Countries in the Multilateral Trading System.* Geneva: Agency for International Trade Information and Cooperation

Eising, Rainer. 2002. Policy Learning in Embedded Negotiations: Explaining EU Electricity Liberalization. *International Organization.* 56 (1): 85–121

Elgstrom, O., B. Bjurulf, J. Johansson, and A. Sannerstedt. 2001. Coalitions in European Union Negotiations. *Scandinavian Political Studies* 24 (2): 111–28

Elms, Deborah Kay. 2003. When the Status Quo is Not Acceptable: Resolving US Bilateral Trade Disputes. Dissertation, University of Washington Department of Political Science

Evans, John. 1971. *The Kennedy Round in American Trade Policy.* Cambridge, Mass: Harvard University Press

Farrell, Henry. 2003. Constructing the International Foundations of E–Commerce – The EU–US Safe Harbor Arrangement. *International Organization* 57 (2): 277–306

Finger, J. Michael. 1974. GATT Tariff Concessions and the Exports of Developing Countries: United States Concessions at the Dillon Round. *Economic Journal* 84 (335): 566–75

1976. Effects of the Kennedy Round Tariff Concessions on the Exports of Developing Countries. *Economic Journal* 86 (341): 87–95

Finnemore, Martha. 1996. *National Interests in International Society.* Ithaca, NY: Cornell University Press

Finnemore, Martha and Kathryn Sikkink. 2001. Taking Stock: The Constructivist Research Program in International Relations and Comparative Politics. *Annual Review of Political Science* 4: 391–416

Frieden, Jeffry, and Lisa L. Martin. 2003. International Political Economy: Global and Domestic Interactions. In *Political Science: The State of the Discipline,* eds. Ira Katznelson and Helen V. Milner, 118–46. New York: W. W. Norton

Garrett, Geoffrey, and Barry R. Weingast. 1993. Ideas, Interests and Institutions: Constructing the EC's Internal Market. In *Ideas and Foreign Policy: Beliefs, Institutions, and Political Change,* eds. Judith Goldstein and Robert O. Keohane, 173–206. Ithaca, NY: Cornell University Press

Goldgeier, James M., and Philip E. Tetlock. 2001. Psychology and International Relations Theory. *Annual Review of Political Science* 4: 67–92

Goldstein, Judith. 1996. International law and domestic institutions: reconciling North American "unfair" trade laws. *International Organization* 50 (4): 541–65

Goldstein, Judith, and Lisa L. Martin. 2000. Legalization, Trade Liberalization, and Domestic Politics: A Cautionary Note. *International Organization*. 54 (3): 603–32

Hamilton, Colleen, and John Whalley. 1989. Coalitions in the Uruguay Round. *Weltwirschaftliches Archiv* 125 (3): 547–62

Hampson, Fen Osler, and Michael Hart. 1994. *Multilateral Negotiations: Lessons from Arms Control, Trade and the Environment.* Baltimore: Johns Hopkins University Press

Hasenclever, Andreas, Peter Mayer, and Volker Rittberger. 1997. *Theories of International Regimes.* Cambridge: Cambridge University Press

Higgott, Richard A., and Andrew Fenton Cooper. 1990. Middle Power Leadership and Coalition Building: Australia, the Cairns Group, and the Uruguay Round of Trade Negotiations. *International Organization* 44 (4): 589–632

Hoda, Anwarul. 1987. *Developing Countries in the International Trading System.* New Delhi: Allied Publishers Private Limited

Hoekman, Bernard, Aaditya Mattoo, and Philip English, eds. 2002. *Development, Trade, and the WTO: A Handbook.* Washington: World Bank

Hoekman, Bernard M., and Michel M. Kostecki. 2001. *The Political Economy of the World Trading System: The WTO and Beyond,* 2d edition. Oxford: Oxford University Press

Hudec, Robert E. 1993. *Enforcing International Trade Law: GATT Dispute Settlement in the 1980s.* Salem, New Hampshire: Butterworth Legal Publishers

Hufbauer, Gary C., Jeffrey J. Schott, and Kimberly Ann Elliott. 1990. *Economic Sanctions Reconsidered: History and Current Policy,*2d edition. Washington: Institute for International Economics

Hurd, Ian. 1999. Legitimacy and Authority in International Politics. *International Organization* 53 (2): 379–408

Ives, Paula Murphy. 2003. Negotiating Global Change: Progressive Multilateralism in Trade in Telecommunication Talks. *International Negotiation* 8: 43–78

Janis, Irving. 1972. *Victims of Groupthink: A Psychological Study of Foreign Policy Decisions and Fiascoes.* Boston: Houghton Mifflin

Jawara, Fatoumata, and Aileen Kwa. 2003. *Behind the Scenes at the WTO: the Real World of International Trade Negotiations.* London: Zed Books

Jervis, Robert. 1976. *Perception and Misperception in International Politics.* Princeton: Princeton University Press

Jönsson, Christer. 2002. Diplomacy, Bargaining, and Negotiation. In *Handbook of International Relations,* eds. Walter Carlsnaes, Thomas Risse, and Beth Simmons, 212–34. Thousand Oaks, California: Sage

Jönsson, Christer, and Jonas Tallberg. 1998. Compliance and Post-Agreement Bargaining. *European Journal of International Relations* 4: 371–408

Kahler, Miles, and John S. Odell. 1989. Developing Country Coalition-Building and International Trade Negotiations. In *Trade Policy and the Developing World,* ed. John Whalley, 146–70. Ann Arbor: University of Michigan Press

34	John S. Odell

Kahneman, Daniel, Jack L. Knetsch, and Richard H. Thaler. 1990. Experimental tests of the endowment effect and the Coase Theorem. *Journal of Political Economy* 98 (6): 1325–48

Keohane, Robert O. 1984. *After Hegemony: Cooperation and Discord in the World Political Economy.* Princeton: Princeton University Press

Klotz, Audie. 1995. *Norms in International Relations: The Struggle against Apartheid.* Ithaca, NY: Cornell University Press

Kumar, Rajiv. 1993. Developing Country Coalitions in International Trade Negotiations. In *The Developing Countries in World Trade: Policies and Bargaining Strategies,* eds. Diana Tussie and David Glover, 205–24. Boulder, Colorado: Lynne Rienner

Kydd, Andrew. 1999. Review of *Individual Strategy and Social Structure: An Evolutionary Theory of Institutions* by H. Peyton Young. *American Political Science Review* 93 (2): 442–43

Lax, David A., and James K. Sebenius. 1986. *The Manager as Negotiator: Bargaining for Cooperation and Competitive Gain.* New York: The Free Press

Levy, Jack S. 1997. Prospect Theory, Rational Choice, and International Relations. *International Studies Quarterly* 41 (1): 87–112

Lowenstein, Roger. 2001. Exuberance is Rational, or at least Human. *New York Times Magazine,* 11 February, 68–71

Luke, David F. 2000. OAU/AEC Member States, the Seattle Preparatory Process and Seattle: A Personal Reflection. *Journal of World Trade* 34 (3): 39–46

Mansfield, Edward D., Helen V. Milner, and B. Peter Rosendorff. 2002. Why Democracies Cooperate More: Electoral Control and International Trade Agreements. *International Organization* 56 (3): 477–513

Mansfield, Edward D., and Eric Reinhardt. 2003. Multilateral Determinants of Regionalism: the Effects of GATT/WTO on the Formation of Preferential Trading Arrangements. *International Organization* 57 (4): 829–62

Marks, Stephen V., and John McArthur. 1990. Empirical Analyses of the Determinants of Protection: A Survey and Some New Results. In *International Trade Policies: Gains from Exchange between Economics and Political Science,* eds. John S. Odell and Thomas D. Willett, 105–40. Ann Arbor: University of Michigan Press

Martin, Lisa L. 1992. *Coercive Cooperation: Explaining Multilateral Economic Sanctions.* Princeton: Princeton University Press

——— 2000. *Democratic Commitments: Legislatures and International Cooperation.* Princeton: Princeton University Press

Martin, Lisa L., and Beth A. Simmons. 1998. Theories and Empirical Studies of International Institutions. *International Organization* 52 (4): 729–58

McDermott, Rose. 2004. The Feeling of Rationality: The Meaning of Neuroscientific Advances for Political Science. *Perspectives on Politics* 2 (4): 691–706

Michalopoulos, Constantine. 2001. *Developing Countries in the WTO.* Bolton, Ontario: Palgrave Macmillan

Milner, Helen V. 1992. International Theories of Cooperation among Nations: Strengths and Weaknesses. *World Politics* 44 (3): 466–96

——— 1999. The Political Economy of International Trade. *Annual Review of Political Science* 2: 91–114

Moravcsik, Andrew. 1998. *The Choice for Europe: Social Purpose & State Power from Messina to Maastricht.* Ithaca, NY: Cornell University Press

1999. A New Statecraft? Supranational Entrepreneurs and International Cooperation. *International Organization* 53 (2): 267–306

Narlikar, Amrita. 2003. *International Trade and Developing Countries: Coalitions in the GATT and WTO.* London: Routledge

Narlikar, Amrita, and Diana Tussie. 2004. The G20 at the Cancún Ministerial: Developing Countries and their Evolving Coalitions in the WTO. *World Economy* 27 (7): 947–66

Nau, Henry R., ed. 1989. *Domestic Trade Politics and the Uruguay Round.* New York: Columbia University Press

Nelson, Douglas. 1988. Endogenous Tariff Theory: A Critical Survey. *American Journal of Political Science* 32 (3): 796–837

Noland, Marcus. 1997. Chasing Phantoms: The Political Economy of USTR. *International Organization* 51 (3): 365–88

Odell, John S. 1980. Latin American Trade Negotiations with the United States. *International Organization* 34 (2): 207–28

1985. The Outcomes of International Trade Conflict: The US and South Korea, 1960–1981. *International Studies Quarterly* 29 (3): 263–86

1990. Understanding International Trade Policies: An Emerging Synthesis. *World Politics* 43 (1): 139–67

2000. *Negotiating the World Economy.* Ithaca, NY: Cornell University Press

2002. Bounded Rationality and the World Political Economy. In *Governing the World's Money,* eds. David Andrews, Randall Henning, and Louis Pauly, 168–93. Ithaca, NY: Cornell University Press

Odell, John, and Antonio Ortiz Mena L. N. 2004. *How to Negotiate Over Trade: A Summary of New Research for Developing Countries.* Available at www.usc.edu/enn/, under members, Odell or Ortiz

Oxley, Alan. 1990. *The Challenge of Free Trade.* New York: St. Martin's Press

Paemen, Hugo, and Alexandra Bensch. 1995. *From the GATT to the WTO: The European Community in the Uruguay Round.* Leuven: Leuven University Press

Page, Sheila. 2003. *Developing Countries, Victims or Participants: Their Changing Role in International Negotiations.* Overseas Development Institute. Available at www.odi.org.uk/iedg/index.html.

Panagariya, Arvind. 2002. Developing Countries at Doha: A Political Economy Analysis. *World Economy* 25 (9): 1205–33

Petersmann, Ernst-Ulrich. 2005. The End of the WTO's "Peace Clause": Strategic Use of WTO Dispute Settlement Proceedings for Advancing WTO Negotiations on Farm Subsidies "in the Shadow of the Law"? In *Reforming the World Trading System: Legitimacy, Efficiency, and Democratic Governance,* ed. Ernst-Ulrich Petersmann. Oxford: Oxford University Press

Powell, Robert. 2002. Bargaining Theory and International Conflict. *Annual Review of Political Science* 5: 1–30

Preeg, Ernest H. 1970. *Traders and Diplomats: An Analysis of the Kennedy Round of Negotiations under the GATT.* Washington: Brookings Institution

Rabin, Matthew. 1998. Psychology and Economics. *Journal of Economic Literature* XXXVI (1): 11–46

Raffaelli, Marcelo, and Tripti Jenkins. 1996. *The Drafting History of the Agreement on Textiles and Clothing*. Geneva: International Textiles and Clothing Bureau

Raiffa, Howard. 1982. *The Art and Science of Negotiation*. Cambridge, Mass: Harvard University Press

Ramamurti, Ravi. 2001. The Obsolescing "Bargaining Model"? MNC-Host Developing Country Relations Revisited. *Journal of International Business Studies* 32 (1): 23–39

Raustiala, Kal, and Ann-Marie Slaughter. 2002. International Law, International Relations, and Compliance. In *Handbook of International Relations*, ed. Walter Carlsnaes, Thomas Risse and Beth Simmons, 538–58. Thousand Oaks, California: Sage

Rodrik, Dani. 1995. Political Economy of Trade Policy. In *Handbook of International Economics*, eds. Gene Grossman and Kenneth Rogoff, 1457–94. Amsterdam: Elsevier

Rothstein, Robert L. 1979. *Global Bargaining: UNCTAD and the Quest for a New International Economic Order*. Princeton: Princeton University Press

Sally, Razeen. 2003. *Whither the WTO? A Progress Report on the Doha Round*. Trade Policy Analyses No. 23. Washington: Cato Institute. Available at www.freetrade.org.

Schelling, Thomas C. 1960. *The Strategy of Conflict*. Cambridge, Mass: Harvard University Press

Schoppa, Leonard J. 1993. Two-level Games and Bargaining Outcomes: Why Gaiatsu Succeeds in Japan in Some Cases but Not Others. *International Organization* 47 (3): 353–86

1999. The Social Context in Coercive International Bargaining. *International Organization* 53 (2): 307–42

Sebenius, James K. 1991. The Negotiation Analytic Approach. *International Negotiation: Problems and New Approaches*. ed. Victor Kremenyuk, 203–15. San Francisco: Jossey-Bass

1995. Dealing with Blocking Coalitions and Related Barriers to Agreement: Lessons from Negotiations on the Oceans, the Ozone, and the Climate. In *Barriers to Conflict Resolution*. eds. Kenneth Arrow and others, 150–82. New York: Norton

1996. Sequencing to Build Coalitions: With Whom Should I Talk First? In *Wise Choices: Decisions, Games, and Negotiations*, eds. Richard J. Zeckhauser, Ralph L. Keeney, and James K. Sebenius, 324–48. Boston, Mass: Harvard Business School Press

Sell, Susan K. 1995. Intellectual property protection and antitrust in the developing world: crisis, coercion, and choice. *International Organization* 49 (2): 315–50

Shukla, S. P. 1994. The Emerging International Trading Order: A Story of the Uruguay Round. In *World Economy in Transition: An Indian Perspective*, eds. G. S. Bhalla and Manmohan Agarwal, 95–120. New Delhi: Har-Anand Publications, for the Indian Institute of Advanced Study at Shimla

Simmons, Beth A. 1998. Compliance with International Agreements. *Annual Review of Political Science*. 1: 75–93

Simon, Herbert A. 1997. *Models of Bounded Rationality.* Volume 3. *Empirically Grounded Economic Reason.* Cambridge, Mass: The MIT Press

Singh, J. P. 2000. Weak Powers and Globalism: The Impact of Plurality on Weak-Strong Negotiations in the International Economy. *International Negotiation* 5: 449–84

Spector, Bertram, I. William Zartman, and Gunnar Sjostedt, eds. 2003. *Getting It Done: Post-Agreement Negotiation and International Regimes.* Washington: US Institute of Peace

Steinberg, Richard H. 2002. In the Shadow of Law or Power? Consensus-based Bargaining and Outcomes in the GATT/WTO. *International Organization.* 56 (2): 339–74

Stephenson, Sherry M. 1994. ASEAN and the Multilateral Trading System. *Law and Policy in International Business* 25 (2): 439–48

Todd, Peter M., and Gerd Gigerenzer. 2003. Bounding Rationality to the World. *Journal of Economic Psychology* 24 (2): 143–65

Tsygankov, Andrei P. 2001. *Pathways after Empire.* New York: Rowman & Littlefield Publishers

Tussie, Diana. 1993. Holding the Balance: The Cairns Group in the Uruguay Round. In *The Developing Countries in World Trade,* eds. Diana Tussie and David Glover, 181–204. Boulder, Colorado: Lynne Rienner Publishers

Tussie, Diana, and David Glover, eds. 1993. *The Developing Countries in World Trade: Policies and Bargaining Strategies.* Boulder: Lynne Rienner Publishers

Tversky, Amos, and Daniel Kahneman. 1986. Rational choice and the framing of decisions. *Journal of Business* 59 (4): Part 2, S251–S278

UNCTAD. 2000. *Positive Agenda and Future Trade Negotiations.* Geneva: UNCTAD

Walton, Richard E., and Robert B. McKersie. 1965. *A Behavioral Theory of Labor Negotiations: An Analysis of a Social Interaction System.* New York: McGraw-Hill

Walton, Richard E., Joel E. Cutcher-Gerchenfeld, and Robert B. McKersie. 1994. *Strategic Negotiations: A Theory of Change in Labor-Management Relations.* Boston: Harvard Business School Press

Wang, Z. K., and L. A. Winters. 1997. *Africa's Role in Multilateral Trade Negotiations.* Policy Research Working Paper, 1846. Washington: World Bank. Also in *Journal of African Economies* 7 (0) (Supplement 1 June 1998): 1–33

Watal, Jayashree. 2001. *Intellectual Property Rights in the WTO and Developing Countries.* London: Kluwer Law International

Whalley, John, ed. 1989. *Developing Countries and the Global Trading System,* 2 vols. London: Macmillan

Winham, Gilbert R. 1986. *International Trade and the Tokyo Round Negotiation.* Princeton: Princeton University Press

1989. The Prenegotiation Phase of the Uruguay Round. In *Getting to the Table.* ed. Janice Gross Stein, 44–67. Baltimore: The Johns Hopkins University Press

1998. Explanations of Developing Country Behaviour in the GATT Uruguay Round Negotiation. *World Competition* 21 (3): 109–34

World Bank. 2001. *Trade Blocs.* Washington: World Bank

Yoffie, David B. 1983. *Power and Protectionism: Strategies of the Newly Industrializing Countries.* New York: Columbia University Press

Young, Michael D., and Mark Schafer. 1998. Is There Method in our Madness? Ways of Assessing Cognition in International Relations. *Mershon International Studies Review* 42 (1): 63–96

Young, Oran R. 1994. *International Governance: Protecting the Environment in a Stateless Society.* Ithaca, NY: Cornell University Press

Zartman, I. William. 1971. *The Politics of Trade Negotiations Between Africa and the European Economic Community: the Weak confront the Strong.* Princeton: Princeton University Press

 ed. 1987. *Positive Sum: Improving North-South Negotiations.* New Brunswick, NJ: Transaction Books

 ed. 1994. *International Multilateral Negotiation: Approaches to the Management of Complexity.* San Francisco: Jossey-Bass

Zartman, I. William, and Maureen R. Berman. 1982. *The Practical Negotiator.* New Haven, Conn: Yale University Press

Part I

Multilateral negotiations

2 The evolution of national interests: new issues and North–South negotiations during the Uruguay Round

J. P. Singh

Are developing countries marginalized in the formation of global rules governing new issues such as services and intellectual property rights?[1] This chapter shows that developing countries gave up fewer concessions in the 1994 services agreement than in the intellectual property agreement, both resulting from the Uruguay Round. The gains developing countries make in 'high-tech' issue-areas have been examined before.[2] Other studies show developing country gains for a host of issue-areas, high-tech and otherwise.[3] These studies stand in contrast to evidence documenting the inability of developing countries to understand or negotiate these new issues,[4] or trading off their acquiescence in these issues in return for concessions in old issues.[5]

A question then arises: Why do developing countries make fewer concessions or gain more in some new issue-areas than in others? This chapter provides a structured focused comparison to explain the difference in outcomes for two Uruguay Round (1986–94) agreements: the General Agreement on Trade in Services (GATS) and the Trade-Related Aspects of Intellectual Property Services (TRIPS). Developing countries made fewer concessions to the North in the former case than in the latter.

Apart from support from this volume's conveners, the Social Science Research Council's Summer Fellowship Program on Information Technology, International Cooperation, and Global Security provided funding for an initial draft of this chapter. I am also grateful to this volume's writers for their comments, especially John Odell and Susan Sell. Ambassador K. M. Chandrashekhar of India to the WTO, Gilbert Winham, Beth Yarborough, and William Zartman also provided valuable feedback.

[1] Intellectual property refers to "creations of the human mind" (Watal 2001: 1) such as pharmaceutical formulas, a trademark, or an industrial design. Services are intangible products or goods such as banking, tourism, telecommunications services, or professional skills.

[2] Grieco 1982; Odell 1993; Singh 2002.

[3] Wriggins 1976; Yoffie 1983; Odell 1985; Zartman 1987; Zartman and Rubin 2000; Singh 2000A.

[4] Braithwaite and Drahos 2000: Jawara and Kwa 2003; Oxfam 2002; Raghavan 2002; Correa 2000.

[5] Croome 1999; Sell 2003.

The outcomes present contrasts with respect to each other as well as to the way the Round started. GATS allowed developing countries to walk with an agreement, allowing specific and tailored commitments across multiple issue-areas, that did not ask them to make concessions too far beyond their domestic liberalization schedules.[6] By accepting TRIPS, developing countries agreed to provide to creators or rights holders limited, or in some cases indefinite, terms for the use of their creations or intellectual property.[7] Developing countries agreed, more or less, to introduce and enforce domestic legislation to conform to TRIPS and also agreed to the multilateral dispute settlement mechanism at the WTO. By doing so, they managed to avoid unilateral sanctions from the United States. They also carved out marginal gains for phase-in periods, compulsory licensing, and parallel imports. For example, article 31 of TRIPS allows the developing world room for compulsory licensing and article 6 allows room for parallel imports from countries that may produce the products cheaper than rights holders.

The differing outcomes are hard to predict from the positions the North and South took before the Uruguay Round started. Intellectual property and services were both new issues and their inclusion on the agenda was opposed by developing countries. However, before the round began, the services issue was heavily contested by the developing world while there seemed to be widespread support for it in the developed world by 1986. Intellectual property issues were not so heavily debated and there was no unified position among the developed countries on this set of issues. Extrapolating from these positions would indicate that the outcomes for GATS and TRIPS for the developing world might be the opposite of what they in fact turned out to be.

This chapter explains the differences in outcomes by looking closely at changing sets of (national) interests regarding services and IP among negotiation parties before and, more importantly, *during* the negotiation process. Interests shape the sets of choices that countries make at the negotiating table. Negotiation outcomes that reflect agreement are obviously the result of convergent choices and, at times, interests as well. Negotiation theory helps to explain how non-convergent interests

[6] Most observers would concur with the following assessment: "Differences in national policy orientation, negotiating strength, and sectoral interests have translated into wide differences in commitments across members, sectors, and modes. Although it might be tempting to use the term 'imbalance' in this context, member governments with low levels of commitments would probably insist that their schedules are a balanced reflection of the Uruguay Round process and of domestic policy constraints that might preclude liberalization of individual areas" (Adlung et al. 2002: 262).
[7] Watal 2003, 361.

are altered to result in agreement outcomes.[8] Four variables, drawn from negotiation theory, here explain interest or choice alteration (See Table 2.1): changing levels of support from domestic constituencies, degree of close attention to agenda-setting by negotiators, degree of effectiveness of unilateral threats made by major powers, and the extent to which developing countries can form various types of coalitions with developed countries on overall or micro agendas.

Negotiations are important in defining global outcomes. Between the power structures – globally or in a particular issue-area – and the formation of global rules is the realm of interest formation and negotiation processes. Variables drawn from the theory of negotiations examined here show how successive interactions among negotiating parties lead to the creation, alteration, or disposal of national interests. Power structures do not predetermine outcomes either; if they did, the North would have gained more in services than in intellectual property. Power structures might predispose negotiations toward a set of outcomes but negotiation interactions themselves shape interests and outcomes, and therefore, the exercise of power.

1 Method and conceptualization

While single case studies point toward developing country success or failure in high-tech and in new issue-areas, a comparison of similar cases or a structured focused comparison is necessary to control for a large number of factors while varying the crucial hypothesized causal factors to specify the underlying conditions for contrasting outcomes.[9] By selecting cases this way, we move toward satisfying the conditions of unit homogeneity and conditional independence necessary for building causal claims.[10]

The two cases selected here from the same multilateral negotiation satisfy several methodological conditions for making causal claims. They

[8] Political economists usually take underlying interests to be constant while examining how choices or preference orderings change. This chapter shows that conceptually and empirically there is no a priori reason to hold interests constant. While choices or preferences can change without altering overall interests, a change in the latter must always change choices as well. Choices, known as alternatives in negotiation theory, when they can be ratified by domestic constituencies are known as win-sets (Putnam 1988).
[9] Odell 2001.
[10] King et al. 1994, 91–95. Given variations of social phenomena, units compared can only be similar, not alike. Unlike elements of a laboratory experiment, negotiation environments are such that we cannot completely divorce independent variables from dependent ones; successive uses of the negotiations tactics examined here thus cannot be presumed to be completely independent of previous outcomes.

Table 2.1 *Differences in negotiation processes and outcomes for GATS and TRIPS from the South's perspective*

	GATS	TRIPS
Status quo at the beginning of the Round	No agreement benefits the developing world's preferences: agenda seen as favoring Northern service industries	Revision of the Paris Convention on patents underway would have benefited the South rather than an agreement via GATT
Differences in domestic preferences	North: in the beginning industry united in support; not so united at the end South: no support in the beginning, strong support at the end	Northern industries close ranks during the round and harden their positions. Southern industries also close ranks in opposing the IP agenda.
Differences in agenda-Setting	South opposes including services on the agenda. Once included, in the two-track format worked out at Punta del Este, it works within the process to influence 'mini-agendas'.	North sneaks in an expansive agenda at the beginning with the South barely noticing that agenda not limited to trade in counterfeit goods. Opposed to this agenda until 1989.
Differences in unilateral threats from major powers	Unilateral threats hardly made: no initial disposition for a particular type of agreement or support from service industries for this.	Unilateral threats effective: North united in the type of agreement it wants from the South and its coalitions strongly argue for this.
Differences in coalition-building	A moderate coalition breaks the deadlock between extreme positions taken by North and South at the beginning of the round. Subsequent coalitions on mini issue-areas include North and South.	Coalitions on IP harden their positions over time. After 1989, South does form a few coalitions with EC on a few mini-issues.
Best alternative for the developing world at the end of the round without an agreement	No agreement might harm service industries in the South, esp. telecom, tourism, construction.	Best alternative is to face unilateral (extra-legal) pressures via US than the somewhat legal order of WTO
Differences in interest formation (reflecting the four differences above)	Interests change for both parties: North's interest for an agreement gets diluted; South starts to support it	US favors an increasingly expansive agenda over the course of the round. South gives in reluctantly.

can be held constant in terms of relevant global power distributions, historical and time context, the international institutional dimension, and international actors involved, thus helping to focus on the dynamics of the negotiation. Developed and developing countries also employ similar overall negotiation strategies, a combination of hawkish and dovish behavior, and tactics (agenda-setting and coalition-building). In both cases, the developing country coalitions are headed by Brazil and India. In addition, GATS and TRIPS are two of the best-known new issue-area negotiations and good representatives of the types of negotiations likely to take place as knowledge-based economies (including intellectual property and services) continue to expand globally. Finally, the two cases examined here include several observations of each negotiation, endorsing the call by King et al. to count the number of observations within a case rather than posit a case as comprising one observation.[11]

Six hypotheses are advanced, which build on the four variables of this chapter – support of domestic constituencies, agenda-setting, unilateral threats, and coalition-building (See Figure 2.1):

1. Unified support on particular positions from domestic constituencies constrains the credible set of agreeable alternatives or win-sets available to negotiators.

2. (Given 1) Attention paid to agenda-setting, coalition-building and unilateral threats, among other negotiation tactics, allows negotiating parties to interact and alter the losses or benefits from a negotiation.

    2A. Close attention to agenda-setting allows negotiators to skew future gains in their favor.

    2B. Coalitions that encompass important players such as major developing or developed country partners are more likely to effect gains for developing countries.

    2C. Coalitions on specific or sub-issues are more likely to effect gains for developing countries than ones encompassing several issue-areas.

    2D. If backed by domestic constituencies, unilateral threats from major players can skew gains in their favor.

Before summarizing the theories explaining the workings of these variables, they must first be made operational. *Unified or divided domestic constituencies* shape the conduct of international negotiators. Unified interests, as they were in the case of service industries in the United States in the early 1980s, limited the number of agreeable alternatives for negotiators. For the United States services became a take-it-or-forget-the-round issue before the Uruguay Round. On the other hand, intellectual property

---

[11] King et al. 1994, 52.

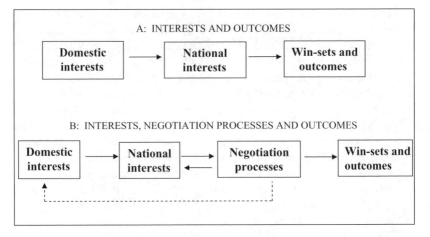

Figure 2.1: Explaining global outcomes with or without negotiations

interests in the North became ever more unified and entrenched as the negotiation process unfolded.

Agenda-setting is a *process* variable leading to inclusion or exclusion of issues being negotiated. In the macro sense, it refers to the big issues included in any trade round: in the micro sense, to issues included or excluded during meetings as the round progresses as negotiating parties work toward formulas and frameworks. Contrary to a common misperception, agenda-setting takes place throughout a negotiation and not just at the beginning. It includes sets of practices used to include, exclude or keep the focus on issues. Three practices in particular – use of popular or attractive frames, degrees of technical and institutional capacity/expertise, frequency of participation in meetings – were important for developing countries to influence agenda-setting during the Uruguay Round. The developed world, on the other hand, slipped in an expansive intellectual property agenda on the developing world which paid close attention to services but much less attention to intellectual property.[12]

Credible unilateral threats refers to the ability of major players to use domestic policy means to constrain the other side's choices during a negotiation. The United States' chief instrument here, especially on

---

[12] Ability to sneak an expansive agenda past negotiators is particularly possible in complicated multilateral negotiations. Both developed and developing countries can be fooled. French officials insist that they hardly noticed in 1989 when audio-visual became one of the sectors to be negotiated as part of the evolving services framework (based on interviews). The French were vehemently opposed to this and finally the EU took an MFN exemption on the issue.

intellectual property, was to flex its muscle through unilateral sanctions-inducing pressures – consistent with section 301 of the Trade Act of 1974 – or refusal to renew privileges such as the Generalized System of Preferences for developing world products. Such unilateral threats must be understood within the context of a negotiation as they are designed to coerce responses from other countries.[13]

Coalition-building refers to strategic alliances with like-minded countries or other coalitions; whether such coalitions are on single or multiple issues, and the extent to which they include developed country partners are posited as crucial variables in the hypotheses above.

An operational definition of the dependent variable, negotiation outcomes, is also necessary. Outcomes are defined as the net gain or loss embodied in an agreement relative to the status quo before the negotiation began. An attempt is also made to posit them against the best alternative developing countries faced at the end of the Round if there had been no agreement on these issues (See Table 2.1).

The hypothesis outlined above on domestic alignments and alternatives comes directly from negotiation theory. The importance of the two levels of international relations, international and domestic, is now increasingly recognized.[14] For international rules to be effective, they must have "domestic resonance."[15] On the flip side, domestic lobbies can tie the hands of negotiators. This chapter shows that these propositions may apply to developing countries – with two twists. First, until recently, most developing countries were excluded from multilateral rounds.[16] Now that they are included, domestic constituencies can build credibility for developing countries' proposals while also serving to limit or expand the alternatives a negotiator might accept. Negotiation alternatives for any country are directly related to the particular alignment of domestic actors and their interests. In Putnam's words: "we may define the 'win-set' for a given Level II constituency as the set of all possible Level I agreements that would 'win' – that is, gain the necessary majority among the constituents – when simply voted up or down."[17] Second, divisions in the ranks of the domestic constituencies of the North can be exploited by developing countries to their benefit or can make effective agenda-setting and coalition-building difficult for the North. Thus, a negotiator involved in market liberalization talks at the international level might find much more room to maneuver if she faces the choice of multiple constituencies at home (those for and against liberalization) than if her country is dominated by a protectionist

---

[13] Odell 2000, Chapter 6.   [14] Rosenau 1997; Keohane and Milner 1996.
[15] Putnam 1988.   [16] Winham 1986.   [17] Putnam 1988, 437.

coalition.[18] Either way, it is negotiation tactics that finally account for the way the interests or choices made by domestic constituencies are shaped and disposed.[19]

Similarly, the presence of multiple issues and actors at the global level offers more alternatives to negotiators than if the talks are bilateral and concentrated around one issue.[20] Several issues in a negotiation allow for more opportunities for coalition-building and agenda-setting while multiple actors allow for more alternatives to arise from the coalitions that might exist. However, if is hard to maintain coalitions that encompass several issue-areas, therefore the caution expressed in hypothesis 2C above.

This study emphasizes micro-level negotiation tactics such as agenda-setting over macro-level strategies such as hawkish versus dovish behavior. Odell's concepts of distributive (hawkish) and integrative (dovish) strategies may in fact be seen as particular tactics deployed by a negotiator.[21] Other scholars also eschew the language of negotiation strategies to detail tactics instead.[22] Thus, it seems that the real substance of any negotiation lies in the particular tactics deployed.

The term agenda-setting as used in this chapter, though an accurate reflection of negotiations, is more expansive than its usual deployment in negotiation literature to only indicate the agenda of a negotiation when it begins. Such a focus on agenda-setting both deepens, as well as departs from, Zartman's three-phase typology of negotiations: (1) the diagnostics phase setting the stage of negotiations, (2) the formula phase defining the zone within which an agreement may be reached, and (3) the details phase in which concessions are traded.[23] Agenda-setting would seem to fall in the first phase, but Zartman acknowledges that diagnostic activities (definitions of issues and positions that may be taken to be the equivalent of agenda-setting) continue into the second formula-setting stage.[24] This was indeed the case with both TRIPS and GATS where even a minimal agreement on the issues to be discussed and the position of the parties did not come about until 1989. Diagnostics are then the macro aspects of agenda-setting. However, agenda-setting also influences the

---

[18] However, having many alternatives may not be a bargaining advantage, per se. With only one coalition back home, the negotiator might argue that her hands are tied and use the situation to extract concessions from the other side.

[19] Domestic alignments, in turn, depend on economic and market conditions, political institutions, number of issues and actors, historical circumstances, and cultural practices among other things. This chapter singles out factors most relevant to its case studies.

[20] Singh 2000A.   [21] Odell 2000 and Appendix of this volume's Chapter 1.

[22] Putnam 1988; Zartman and Berman 1982.   [23] Zartman and Berman 1982.

[24] Zartman and Berman 1982, 87–88.

formula and concession phases by itself, and these are the micro aspects of agenda-setting. Even when a formula is in place and concessions are being traded, each negotiation meeting's agenda may define their shape and scope. For example, even after GATS negotiators agreed by 1989 to incorporate the principle of Most Favored Nation (MFN) into services, the United States sought to change the formula at successive meetings so that it would not be applied unconditionally but be contingent upon other parties making concessions.

The issue of frames is closely tied to agenda-setting and, therefore, included here. Drake and Nicolaides acknowledge that framing helps to define and include issues.[25] Frames are mental shortcuts used by negotiators to simplify and make sense of the issue.[26] Clearly, the issue of framing is neither synonymous with nor a sub-category of agenda-setting. However, framing does help to set agendas, so the two issues overlap. The reason frames are highly politicized media sound bites is to influence negotiators to accede to an agenda. Domestic industries in the United States used the "jobs and growth" frame in services and the "theft and punishment" frame in intellectual property to get their government to put these issues on the Uruguay Round agenda. Framing also helped to mobilize constituencies of support.

In sum, domestic alignments help to specify the zone of agreement, which is dependent on the intersection of win-sets of the negotiating countries. The final agreement depends not just on this win-set but it gets altered via the use of negotiation tactics. As the win-set gets altered the overall interests of negotiators may change as well.[27]

The evolution of national interests[28]

Negotiation tactics such as agenda-setting and coalition-building allow developing countries to effect gains by altering interests and making available agreeable alternatives to negotiators. The previous section described

---

[25] Drake and Nicolaides 1992.   [26] Odell 2002; Tversky and Kahneman 1986.

[27] It is possible that domestic interests are also altered because of changes in the international environment or, in this chapter, negotiations. At a general level this is the third image reversed argument (Gourevitch 1985). For simplicity, this chapter concentrates on negotiator interests. However, examples of domestic interest alteration are not hard to find. Argentina's support for a services agreement, backed by the developing world, changed in favor of an agricultural deal in 1989. As the Uruguay Round proceeded, its agricultural interests realized that they were being left out. Argentina's domestic interests were thus prompted by international factors to realign the national interest in their favor.

[28] This chapter should not be taken as providing state-centric analysis. National interests, as articulated here, are conditioned by the global and local environments in which states operate. The same holds for other actors in global politics.

the way particular negotiation tactics may be practiced. This section describes their role in interest formation and alteration, the strongest theoretical claim made in this chapter.

Negotiations are about human interactions and, thus, the first claim negotiation theory must make for itself is the changing behavior of actors through successive interactions. Take the case of actor interests. The formation of *national interests* as political scientists tend to call them, or *preferences* as economists do, is a contentious topic precisely because they are taken as given – usually derived from global economic or security power structures. At times national interests are taken to be the sum of domestic constituencies' interests.[29] This is myopic. There is no straightforward logic linking power structures or domestic constituencies and interest formation. Social environments, like those offered by international negotiations, create as well as limit the articulation of particular interests.[30] Interest formation is thus a product of both constraints and opportunities. In neo-classical economics, interests or preferences are based on the intrinsic utilities of particular actions for individuals. Kuran notes that such intrinsic utility calculations are the result of cognitive and social processes.[31] He underscores the role of framing devices, mental shortcuts, persuasion, knowledge production, and underlying social beliefs, in calculations of intrinsic utility.

At best, power structures can only constitute the information base from which calculations of intrinsic utility may be derived. However, such calculations are an inherently social act, even when an individual makes them alone, for example with recourse to a framing device. They are also cognitive processes. These social and cognitive processes help an actor make sense of available information. Most theories of interest formation take note of the condition of bounded rationality in which actor interests are shaped with incomplete information. They could also take note of the processes that allow actors to make sense of that information. *Negotiation processes, tactics in the case of this chapter, can thus be seen as the production, dissemination, and disposal of information to actors involved.* That they then result in changing the interests of actors should come as no surprise. As

---

[29] The term *interest* is preferred in this chapter over *preferences*. Economists and political scientists would agree that starting from either helps us specify choices made or the set of agreeable alternatives. However, when economists speak of preference orderings, it is not clear whether they are speaking of interests or choices. Similarly, political scientists start with interests and then speak of preferences, choices, or alternatives that speak to these interests. To avoid confusion, the term preferences is eschewed.

[30] Peterson 2004; Wendt 1999; Katzenstein 1996. Evolutionary economics makes similar claims. See, Nelson and Winter 1982; Murmann 2003.

[31] Kuran 1995, Ch. 10.

in Kuran, this study takes interest formation to be more a social process than an outcome of deductive logic.[32] In taking interests as given, international relations theory therefore partly annuls the very interactions that it tries to explain.[33]

The negotiation of GATS and TRIPS

The difference in outcomes between GATS and TRIPS can be explained through the negotiation histories of these issues that provide interesting similarities and contrasts. Both feature the United States as setting the agenda and building coalitions. Both issues are opposed by the developing world before the Uruguay Round starts though it spends most resources in opposing the services issue. In services, the agenda formation leads to a separate but a parallel track in negotiations; in intellectual property, the South hardly notices the ambiguous language used during the macro agenda-setting that allows the North to sneak in an expansive agenda later. For services, the positions of the North and the South are softened by the development of a mid-level coalition to allow for concessions to both parties. TRIPS features a progressive hardening of the North's position and some cracks (some might say moderation) in the South's stance that eventually lead to an agreement where the South makes most of the concessions.

The negotiation history is divided into four phases here: the pre-Uruguay Round phase up to 1986 ending with these issues on the Round's agenda; the period up to the mid-term review in Montreal that shows the extent of the North-South divisions on these issues in December 1988; the period from Montreal to the Brussels meeting in December 1990 that almost led to agreements; and the final phase when the details of the agreements were worked out.

---

[32] Kuran's main point is more nuanced than the summary presented here. His agents falsify their interests to conform to social pressures and conditions. This point would be consistent with my notion of changing interests but not with those who take interests to be given. We could also conjecture that those exercising the social pressure have less of an incentive to falsify interests, great powers or wealthy developed countries in the case of this chapter. Therefore, the interests articulated by the North in intellectual property and services are taken to be approximations of their true interests here.

[33] A bolder claim about interest formation, beyond the scope of this chapter, would question the assumption of goal directed behavior or maximization of a utility function underlying interest calculation. In as much as these interests arise from interactions, it is unclear how they always lead to goal directed behavior or maximization of utility functions. See Green and Shapiro 1994; Friedman 1996.

Getting to Punta del Este

The September 15–22, 1986 GATT meetings in Punta del Este came at the end of over a decade's diplomacy spearheaded by the United States to make new issues – services, intellectual property and investment – part of the new Round's agenda, especially after the GATT ministerial in 1982. Setting such an agenda would skew future outcomes in its favor. Broadly, the interests of the North regarding services agreement were for an expansive agenda, supported by a broad coalition of industries, while the developing world remained opposed to even its inclusion. The intellectual property agenda was presented in a much narrower sense and, at least, until Punta del Este, did not showcase the kind of concerted and explicit inter-industry support that services did. Until early 1986, the US Trade Representative (USTR) was presenting the IP agenda as aiming for an agreement on counterfeit goods; for its part the developing world missed the cues from the wide-ranging IP industries being mobilized to support this agenda. The developing countries also continued to receive false assurance from the revision of the Paris Convention that had almost gone through and would have weakened the patent regime.

Intellectual property: The moves toward including services and intellectual property in GATT decision-making began with industry groups in the United States as the Tokyo Round of trade talks was progressing (1973–79). At that time, there were existing frameworks governing intellectual property but services were an unexplored territory globally.[34] During the Tokyo Round, famous brand names in the developed countries pushed the European Economic Community and the United States to table a code curtailing trade in counterfeit products. An anti-counterfeiting coalition was announced in 1978 led by Levi Strauss and included brand names such as Samsonite, Izod, Chanel and Gucci. The intellectual property issue was also tied to US negotiations with Hungary over renewal of its MFN and the effort was led by agro-businesses such as Monsanto, FMC, and Stauffer.[35] Monsanto's Jim Enyart was also trying to frame intellectual property as a trade-related issue.[36] The work of big profile firms such as Pfizer and IBM in the US Advisory Committee on Trade Policy and Negotiations (ACTPN) established by the 1974 Trade

---

[34] Important agreements included the Paris Convention for the Protection of Industrial Property of 1883 governing patents, the Berne Convention for the Protection of Literary and Artistic Works of 1886, and the Rome Convention (the International Convention for the Protection of Performers, Producers of Phonograms and Broadcasting Organizations) of 1961. These treaties were administered by the World Intellectual Property Organization, which was formed in 1967 and became part of the United Nations in 1974.

[35] Devereaux 2002, 6.   [36] Sell 1999, 177.

Act in the United States is especially important.[37] This body, chaired by Pfizer's CEO Edmund T. Pratt, took up the cause of making intellectual property rights, hereafter IPRs, a trade-related issue. Strengthening of the Paris Convention was important to Pfizer while IBM sought to extend the Berne Convention to copyright protection of software. (Significantly, the US Trade Act of 1974 introduced section 301, which would be amended in 1984 to declare that IPR infringements were trade barriers.) The ACTPN thus worked not only to effect trade legislation in its favor but it did so by making the otherwise arcane issue of IPRs a trade issue.[38]

ACTPN worked closely with commercial associations in several countries and also with the Pharmaceutical Manufacturers Association and the Chemical Manufacturers Association in the United States to strengthen its ranks. The efforts culminated in the formation of the Intellectual Property Committee (IPC) in March 1986 before the start of the Uruguay Round. IBM Chairman John Opel headed it, with a membership of eleven to fourteen over the Uruguay Round period. The original thirteen members were: Bristol-Myers, Du Pont, FMC Corporation, General Electric, General Motors, Hewlett-Packard, IBM, Johnson & Johnson, Merck, Monsanto, Pfizer, Rockwell International, and Warner Communications.

The patent and copyright interests did not come together automatically in the United States. While IPC mostly represented the patent interest, the copyright interests came together in late-1984 to form the International Intellectual Property Alliance (IIPA), which was the umbrella group for associations representing industries producing and distributing audio and visual content. The copyright interests, representing films, music and books, were initially skeptical about the need for global rules and felt that section 301 was enough.[39]

The developing countries were not organized enough on these issues to anticipate the moves in the United States with any counter-moves. They argued that with existing international treaties, the need for another one, especially via GATT, was minimal. If anything, the developing countries since 1974, with efforts dating as far back as 1967, were trying to push through a revision of the Paris Convention that would have weakened its provisions.[40] Watal notes "that the developing world may have been lulled into a certain complacency" due to the support they received from the developed world for diluting the Convention to allow for compulsory licensing from countries such as Canada, Australia, New Zealand,

---

[37] Ryan 1998, Chapter 4.

[38] In 1988, the loss to US industry annually from IPR infringements was estimated to be $40 billion (US International Trade Commission 1988).

[39] Ryan 1998, 107.   [40] Sell 1999.

Portugal, Spain and Turkey (many of whom had compulsory licensing procedures of their own).[41] The revision almost went through, breaking down in its final stages in 1981 and 1982 at meetings in Nairobi and Geneva, respectively. Countries like India had, in fact, passed laws that made such copying simple and effective.[42] The 1970 Drug Price Control Order set price ceilings on essential drugs and the Indian Patent Act of 1970 disallowed product patents but recognized product processes which, in effect, led to copying of patented drugs from the developed world.

By the time of the 1982 GATT ministerial to discuss the possibility of a multilateral round, there was no consensus that intellectual property was a trade issue, or that it went beyond counterfeiting. Before the ministerial, India's Prime Minister Indira Gandhi gave a major speech to the WHO in May lambasting developed countries for trying to take away compulsory licensing provisions. The delay in accepting the agenda on counterfeit goods at the 1982 ministerial may have allowed for the induction of a much larger agenda on trade in intellectual property later on.[43]

Most moves toward getting intellectual property on the agenda developed after the 1982 ministerial and close on the heels of the Punta del Este meetings. In this regard, strengthening of the intellectual property coalition and use of US trade law and instruments are particularly important. After coming together in late-1984, IIPA lobbied successfully to apply section 301 of Trade Act of 1974 to intellectual property. In 1985, the USTR asked the private sector to forward its concerns on IP issues. The IIPA in a report to the USTR noted that the United States lost $1.3 billion to piracy of copyrighted works in ten countries.[44] A more significant report in 1985 from the economist Jacques Gorlin, commissioned by John Opel, not only synthesized the thinking about intellectual property as a trade issue but also advanced an agenda for multilateral negotiations through OECD and GATT, although it acknowledged that World Intellectual Property Organization (WIPO) would play a consultative role.[45]

By the time of the Gorlin paper, the US government was already pursuing IP issues. Unilateral and determined moves by the United States would later be characterized during the Uruguay Round as offering the developing world a worse outcome than one through TRIPS. Bilateral consultations led to revisions of IP laws in Hungary, Taiwan and Singapore. Unilateral moves were particularly directed against countries that might oppose the United States' IP agenda. President Reagan

[41] Watal 2001, 16.   [42] Gallagher 2000, 282–283.
[43] Croome regards this as a positive development from the point of view of IP interests and international trade. See Croome 1999, 11.
[44] International Intellectual Property Alliance 1985.   [45] Gorlin 1985.

himself cited Brazil and Korea as indulging in unfair trade practices under section 301 in his weekly radio address on September 7, 1985 (coincidentally Brazil's National Day).[46] The agreement with Korea in 1986 was subsequently characterized as a model for TRIPS. The talks with Brazil dragged on for 36 months and although there was no agreement, their role in putting pressure on countries like Brazil to agree to the Uruguay Round IP agenda is undeniable.

In 1985, USTR Clayton Yeutter created the Assistant USTR for International Investment and Intellectual Property. By Spring 1986, Yeutter asked Opel and Pratt to lobby internationally to put IP on the new Round's agenda. The Intellectual Property Committee was formed as a direct result of this request. During the summer of 1986, IPC representatives went to many European capitals and Tokyo to make their case. The IPC travels resulted in a tripartite alliance between IPC, the European Union of Industrial and Employers' Confederation (UNICE), and the powerful Japanese federation of industries, the Keidenran. From summer onwards, the efforts to put intellectual property on the agenda of the new Round were inextricably mixed with the politics of services and the efforts by major developing countries to block their inclusion in the agenda. Interestingly, until April 1986, the goals of the USTR on IP issues remained modest – developing an anti-counterfeiting code and making it subject to the GATT dispute settlement process.[47] In hindsight, the longer it took to shape the IP agenda, the more hardline became the stance of the coalition, and the more expansive its agenda.

Services:[48] The coalition for services in the developed world as well as its agenda showcased an impressive agenda from its inception in the 1970s. The term 'trade in services' owes its origins to the OECD, which conceptualized this agenda before it became a GATT issue. Until the Uruguay Round, there was no umbrella agreement in services although there were a few agreements, mostly of a technical nature, involving particular sectors such as telecommunications, civil aviation, and shipping.[49] These agreements legitimized national monopolies while allowing for 'interconnection' among them and allowed for international rules and decision-making procedures to guard for safety and damage control. Whereas in intellectual property, the existing agreements covered a related set of issues over a number of sectors, in services the agreements governed disparate sets of issues in individual sectors.

The impetus for services trade in the 1970s came from US industries in banking, finance and software and their moves began to coincide

---

[46] Odell 2000, Chapter 6.   [47] Watal 2001, 17–18.
[48] This sub-section builds on Drake and Nicolaides 1992.
[49] Zacher with Sutton 1996.

with the US balance of payments, and later trade, deficits. US multinational corporations (MNCs) began to argue that the country's comparative advantage lay in service industries. Their moves were aided by the OECD whose Trade Committee began to look into the services issue in 1979 (its report came out in 1987). Think-tanks and other institutions (mostly in the United States and United Kingdom) pitched in to show that trade in services was important and growing. The US government reacted by establishing the Interagency Task Force on Services and the Multilateral Trade Negotiations at the White House. The Department of Commerce as well as the USTR also established offices for services. These agencies raised the services issue at the Tokyo Round. What they achieved was a proposal for GATT's Consultative Group of eighteen (G-18) comprising senior trade officials to look into services and other issues.[50] Meanwhile, in 1979, the US Chamber of Commerce was asked by the government to add services barriers to its 1976 list of trade barriers. Foreign governments turned in their own lists after consulting with their firms. Drake and Nicolaides note that these moves were a form of issue-framing shaping the services negotiation agenda in the 1980s. However, until the GATT ministerial in 1982, the United States was more enthusiastic about services than other developed countries.[51]

The hard times of the early 1980s helped to push the services agenda forward. Trade growth was barely one percent, stagflation was high, and with 1982 came the international debt crisis, which plagued the developing world and the world's financial markets. The US Department of Commerce calculated that the services sector accounted for 70 percent of the total employment and 90 percent of growth in employment. Of the total world trade in services of $350 billion, the United States accounted for $35 billion.[52] Service firms such as IBM, American Express, and insurance industries increased their lobbying.

The next step in getting services into GATT was the ministerial in 1982. The Coalition of Service Industries came about in 1982 in the United States and the Liberalization of Trade in Services Committee in the United Kingdom. At a 1982 meeting in Geneva, which included 82 ministers and 800 official delegates, the USTR brought up the new issues and was especially aggressive on the services issue. The Europeans, in the process of establishing an interservices group, advocated a 'go slow' approach. They feared the US advantage in service industries and, except for Margaret Thatcher's United Kingdom, they had no concrete

---

[50] Croome 1999, 2.   [51] Drake and Nicolaides 1992, 51.
[52] Statistics cited in May 1992, 2.

plans for liberalizing service industries, especially the national utility and transportation monopolies.

The reaction from the developing world was predictably negative and, unlike intellectual property, cohesive. The relevant coalition to voice its concerns was the Group of 77 led by Brazil and India at the GATT. Brazil and India argued that services was not a GATT issue and focused on issues of concern to the developing world – protectionism in agriculture and textiles – and asked for the implementation of the standstill and rollback agreements on these areas at the Tokyo Round. With such opposition from G-77 and lack of support from the EC for the US position, the issue of services was put off until the meeting of the Contracting Parties in 1984 where further studies on services would be reviewed.

The next big move, the formation of the 'Jaramillo Group' in 1983 for consulting on services, built on the existing coalitions in services and began to fracture the G-77 coalition. The group resulted from GATT delegates meeting informally to discuss the services issue and got its name from Felipe Jaramillo, Colombia's ambassador to GATT, an authority on international trade policy. Jaramillo convened and chaired the group's sessions, which lasted until 1986. The United States was a central player presenting studies and listing barriers in various countries.[53] In 1984, it submitted a comprehensive report of the state of trade in services globally that detailed statistical tables showing that the United States was not the only beneficiary from services trade.[54] Developed countries and a few ASEAN newly industrialized countries (NICs) began to come around to the US position. In May 1985, the EC declared its support on the services issue with EC's Commissioner for External Affairs Willy de Clerq acknowledging that many EC countries had services surpluses.

In order to break the North-South deadlock, the Swedish trade minister brought together twenty-four trade ministers in Stockholm in May 1984, attended by GATT Director General Dunkel, where the idea of a two-track approach, one for goods and another "separate but parallel" for services, was suggested to jump-start the new round.[55] This meeting seemed to end in consensus but subsequent meetings in Geneva broke down again. In July 1985, India presented a paper to GATT questioning new issues, among other things, and easily got the support of twenty-four developing countries (G-24). Issues of textiles and standstill and rollbacks were brought up again. Thus, by 1985, the battle lines on services

---

[53] May 1992, 4.   [54] US Government 1984.
[55] Croome 1999, 17. What Sweden suggested was already part of the thinking on the subject in international legal journals where the difficulty of applying existing GATT rules to services was acknowledged (Drake and Nicolaides 1992, 63).

particularly, and new issues in general, were between the North and the South. The Jaramillo Group itself was deadlocked by late 1985.

Meanwhile, the United States was working behind the scenes to push for starting the new round – in jeopardy mostly over developing country concerns (and differences in agricultural trade among developed countries) by 1984–85. The G-7 meetings and OECD were important in this regard. As it had done on intellectual property issues with Korea, the United States produced a Free Trade Agreement with Israel in 1985 that its officials began to showcase as a possible services agreement for the future (it also served as a model for the Canada-United States Free Trade Agreement).

In April 1985, the OECD countries became aggressive in trying to start a new round by asking for a preparatory committee (Prepcom) of senior trade officials to start drafting the agenda. As the summer of 1985 ended in bitter North-South disputes, the Prepcom was seen as a way of breaking the deadlock and was established on November 28, 1985.

From Prepcom to Punta del Este: Prepcom meetings took place between January and July 1986 but remained deadlocked and served to illustrate the difficulty of agenda formation. The United States blamed the GATT Secretariat and even flirted with the idea of submitting a draft ministerial declaration to start the new round. As the stalemate at Prepcom ran on, the Swiss Ambassador Pierre-Louis Girard convinced a group of nine (G-9) moderate developed countries (Australia, Austria, Canada, Finland, Iceland, New Zealand, Norway, Sweden, Switzerland) to draft an agenda which G-9 presented as a draft to Prepcom on June 11, 1986.[56]

Brazil and India struck back immediately. On June 23, Brazil's ambassador to GATT Paulo Batista presented an official proposal 'W41' to Prepcom signed by ten hardline developing countries including India. The W41 move backfired; it was seen as extremist and the G-10 support itself, as opposed to the G-24 of 1985, showed a dwindling of developing country ranks. Among other things, it argued for complete standstill and rollback of protectionist measures as a pre-condition for including services and other new issues in the Round. G-10 was concentrating on keeping services out. Watal notes that this was a mistake given the push on intellectual property and the US agreement with Korea.[57]

A direct result of the Brazilian proposal was the explicit defection of twenty moderate developing countries (G-20, including Colombia, Chile,

---

[56] G-9 was a sub-part of the dirty dozen, which also included the United States, Japan, and the EC. Leaving the other three out of agenda-setting would marginalize power politics and put the G-9 in a neutral light.
[57] "The TRIPS proposal of the *demandeur* governments was neither effectively diluted nor countered with other proposals by its opponents." Watal 2001, 20.

Jamaica, Korea) who joined ranks with the G-9. The Korean Ambassador led the G-20 defection.[58] Along with the United States, Japan, and the EC – who played mostly observer roles – the G-9 and G-20 led by Switzerland's Girard and Colombia's Jaramillo began to meet in the EFTA offices at Geneva to prepare what came to be known as the "café au lait proposal", after the Swiss-Colombian leadership. Because of the EFTA meetings, the Prepcom had only four short meetings in late June 1986 to discuss the café au lait proposal, which included services and language on standstill and rollbacks. The language on IP issues in the Swiss–Colombian draft was "ambiguous and general."[59] Other proposals were discussed at Prepcom but the clear winner seemed to be the Swiss-Colombian draft. However, on the last day of Prepcom meetings (July 31), the EC broke ranks and sided with the hardliners (its motives may have been its protectionist agricultural interests pushed by the French). The EC suggested the two-track approach that would allow India and Brazil to save face. Dunkel thus forwarded all proposals to Enrique Iglesias, the Foreign Minister of Uruguay, who would chair the ministerial, with a note indicating that the café au lait proposal was largely favored. This drew sharp critiques in a series of letters from Brazil and India.[60]

The meetings at Punta del Este, September 15–22, started with USTR Yeutter arriving with a US Cabinet decision that forbade him to accept a two-track proposal. Thus, the negotiations on services, moderated by Iglesias, were mainly between the United States, India, and Brazil. They remained deadlocked although the US position had the support of many from the EFTA group. Eventually, Jaramillo proposed a procedural solution, albeit one favoring two tracks: the services talks would be separate as in the EC proposal but conducted by the same officials and the GATT secretariat. In other words, the two tracks, in the language of GATT would be 'a single undertaking' although it did not really apply to services. The United States accepted this proposal and the Uruguay Round was launched and expected to be concluded in four years.

Intellectual property was included under goods negotiations. The subject heading for the three paragraphs dealing with intellectual property at the Punta del Este declaration included wording on trade in counterfeit goods, which might have led major developing countries to believe that

---

[58] Oxley 1990.   [59] Devereaux 2002, 14.

[60] Arthur Dunkel had a hard act to play. Croome (1999) and Devereaux (2002) note that his own interests, especially on public health provision, were sympathetic to the developing world. Even before Punta del Este, he did not want to make pariahs out of the hardline countries (Interview with a participating ambassador, November 28, 2002). However, he drew continual ire from the hardliners and, in India's case, effigies of him were burnt in the streets after the so-called Dunkel Draft on intellectual property was presented in December 1991.

only the latter would be negotiated. In the case of intellectual property, the developed countries had slipped in an agenda without the developing countries taking much notice.

The procedural distinction agreed to at Punta del Este led to the constitution of the Group of Negotiations of Goods (GNG), the Group of Negotiations on Services (GNS), and the round as a whole would be directed by the Trade Negotiations Committee (TNC). Arthur Dunkel and, after July 1993, his successor Peter Sutherland headed the GNG and TNC while Felipe Jaramillo headed the GNS. In keeping with the Punta del Este declaration, fourteen negotiating groups were appointed for goods and one for services in January 1987. Lars Anell, the Swedish Ambassador to GATT, headed the TRIPS group.

Punta del Este to Montreal

A mid-term review was planned for Montreal in December 1988. Developing countries' chief interests were to limit the scope of the services agreement and to try to kill the IP one, even though technically intellectual property was now part of the Round's agenda. As a result, by 1988 considerable conceptual work had been done in shaping the agenda, and formulas thereof, for services liberalization. Building on the precedence of the café au lait proposal, developing countries worked within GNS to effect mini-agendas and build coalitions. A few of them even began to see that a services agreement might benefit them. The intellectual property issues, however, remained deadlocked. If in services, the relatively open process allowed developed and developing countries to arrive at the problem-solving framework; in intellectual property, the framework was presented as a fait accompli by the developed world. The services discussion began to be characterized and framed by the developed world in terms of "jobs and growth"; the latter in terms of "theft and punishment".

Intellectual property: On the part of the developed world the coalition building by IPC strengthened, its representatives' governments began to speak with a common voice in spite of minor differences, and unilateral moves by the United States increased. Developing countries woke up to the expansive way the developed world was defining the Punta del Este agenda and sought to resist it. The first two years of the IP negotiating group were thus spent in trying to define the agenda of the Punta del Este mandate.

The IPC got busy in this period in strengthening its ranks and trying to come up with a monolithic position. In November 1986, IPC representatives met with their counterparts at UNICE and Keidenran to start this process. For the next two years, the IPC arranged meetings with

30 to 40 industry associations every six to nine months to review successive drafts of this framework. The 100-page position paper, called "Basic Framework of GATT Provisions on Intellectual Property" was presented in June 1988. Throughout this process the IPC worked closely with the US government, especially with Mike Hathaway the US TRIPS negotiator and with Mike Kirk of the US patent office. The paper reflected the position of the earlier Gorlin paper on framing a wide-ranging IP treaty via GATT and using its dispute settlement for enforcement. The US pharmaceutical industry did not want to give any ground on the need for compulsory licensing but adjusted its position in order to get the Japanese and Europeans on board. The final TRIPS agreement reflects the Basic Framework to a great extent.

Developed countries were beginning to speak with a common voice and defined an expansive agenda for intellectual property rights (IPRs). By October–November 1987, the United States, Japan, and other developed countries including Switzerland had made it clear that they wanted to use the GATT process to discuss almost all IPRs: copyright, patents, trademarks, designs, geographical indicators, industrial designs, and trade secrets.[61] The EC submission in November, focusing on the enforcement of such rights, was largely in concurrence with the US and IPC positions.[62] Sell notes that the consensus building among developed countries came from following the advice on meetings in enclave committees given in the Gorlin paper. This was the IPC strategy, too.[63] Within GATT, the Quad (United States, Japan, EC, and Canada) and "Friends of Intellectual Property" group were key enclaves.

The hardline developing countries, led by Brazil and India, felt that they had been misled at Punta del Este. They expected the discussions to be limited to counterfeit goods. While they continued to find common cause against IPR protections, they could not find any sympathetic actors in the North to take their side. They critiqued the "Basic Framework" put forth by IPC, UNICE, and Keidanren. The very character of the multilateral negotiations was thus reduced to a two-way game with an asymmetric power distribution favoring the North. In several fora, developing

[61] Watal 2001, 22–23.
[62] The differences among developed countries, apart from the one mentioned on compulsory licensing above, were on the omission of designs from the US list, trade secrets from the Japanese list, and geographical indicators from both of them. The latter was an issue dear to the Europeans and they did not fully come on board on blessing the expansive agenda until this issue was included in mid-1988. Another difference between the United States and the EU was over copyright issues or "neighboring rights" related to performers, producers and broadcasters (this would come up later in audio-visual negotiations as part of the GNS).
[63] Sell 1999, 186–187.

countries sought to exclude patents (especially in pharmaceuticals) from the agenda, but the gambit did not work. The North refused to recognize the compulsory licensing claims in any great measure. Civil society protests in the developing world, that often featured groups from several countries together, served to spotlight developing countries' causes in areas such as seeds procurement and cheap pharmaceuticals, but they were unable to sway the Northern negotiators. They also pointed out that the Punta del Este declaration, specifically sub-sections (iv) and (v) of Section B, did accord them 'Special and Differential Treatment,' in accordance with GATT rules framed in the 1960s. Intellectual property was a make-it-or-break-it issue for India, which faced strong domestic pressure, at times resulting in violent protests, from its farmers and pharmaceutical firms.[64] In October 1988, Brazil submitted its position, which sought to limit the agenda of the negotiating group on intellectual property. However, there were developing countries, Korea and ASEAN among them, who refrained from critiquing the developed country proposals.[65] Many of them were under pressure from the United States on their IP practices.

Concerted pressure on the developing world came from toughening of the US legislation on intellectual property and the pursuit of infringing countries by the USTR. First, the United States began to tie with IP protections the granting of Generalized System of Preferences (GSP), which waived certain tariffs for developing country products. Second, in August 1988, the US Congress added bite to section 301 by passing the Omnibus Trade and Competitiveness Act of 1988 in response to business pressures. The 1988 amendment authorized the USTR to annually list and investigate within thirty days of doing so those countries whose IP practices resulted in unfair access to US firms.[66] USTR began to prepare "priority watchlists" of countries. The inaugural list, coming on heels of pressure from IIPA, included Korea, Brazil, India, Mexico, China, Saudi Arabia, Taiwan, and Thailand.[67] The 301 initiative against Brazil in 1985 was mentioned earlier. The Brazilians amended their copyright law in 1987 and their patent law in 1988. In September 1988, USTR began to investigate Argentina's pharmaceutical patent protections. In 1989, Thailand lost GSP benefits after being named on the 301 IP watchlist.

The net result of all these moves, however, was that there was no consensus on the IP agenda by the time of the mid-term review. Mike Kirk notes that the first two years had been spent talking in generalities that resembled a "Kabuki dance. . . .We would lob principles at the South and

[64] Sharma 1994.   [65] Croome 1999, 114.   [66] Sell 1998, 134.
[67] Ryan 1998, 78. China, Taiwan and Saudi Arabia were not GATT members.

they would either sit there and ignore them or occasionally lob an idea back at us."[68] Before the Montreal meeting, the required text describing the future course of action was difficult to frame. The text prepared by Lars Anell was rejected by the United States for being too weak and by developing countries as being too strong. Thus, this text along with three others (from Brazil, United States and Switzerland) was forwarded to Montreal. The meeting ended in deadlock and adjourned over this issue and, mostly, agricultural issues.

It was, however, in Montreal that Brazil came around, followed by India on the IP issue. India had been the major holdout from the South because of the importance of India's domestic pharmaceuticals industry. Before the Montreal meeting, President Bush called Prime Minister Rajiv Gandhi and pressed upon him the need for India to step out of the way to let the negotiations move forward. If any trade-offs were made at that time, they did not make it to the negotiation floor. Contrary to many published accounts, India's former TRIPS negotiator notes that she did not speak to, nor was instructed to speak to, the textiles or agriculture negotiators to try to get concessions in these issues as a condition for backing down in intellectual property.[69] In April 1989, therefore, the TRIPS deadlock was broken with India now playing a key role in the writing of the text.

Services: Compared to the Kabuki of the negotiating group on intellectual property, the Group of Negotiation on Services (GNS) featured ballroom dances. The developing countries had walked out with their major victory at Punta del Este with the two-track mandate. Now they worked within GNS to try to define principles. While this continued, the interests of a few business groups changed in the United States when they began to fear that they might not gain so much from a far-reaching agreement; on the other hand, the developing countries began to see a few benefits from a services agreement, especially if the agreement could apply to movement of labor supplies from the South to the North.

The GNS decided in January 1987 to take up five tasks, each of which then offered opportunities to shape mini-agendas:
   (i) definitions and statistics of trade in services;
  (ii) inclusion of concepts such as national treatment, MFN, transparency that may be relevant for services as a whole or for particular sectors;

[68] Quoted in Devereaux 2002, 15.
[69] Based on interview with Jayashree Watal at the World Trade Organization, November 5, 2004. She notes that India could have been savvier about backing down on intellectual property but the Indian team was under instructions from the Government of India "to let the text go."

64 J. P. Singh

(iii) lists of the sectors that would be covered;
(iv) inventory of existing international agreements;
(v) listing measures increasing or obstructing trade in services. The "modes of supply" used for delivery came out of examining the first issue.

By 1988, it was agreed that services could be supplied through several modes such as movement of consumers, suppliers, commercial organizations, and cross-border flows. As these required rights of establishment, developing countries capitalized on this to note that service delivery might entail movement of personnel and sought to include this on the agenda (later playing into sensitive immigration issues in developed countries). The issue of sectoral coverage was difficult: many countries had sacred cows – maritime in the United States, audiovisual in the EC, insurance in India.[70] It became clear that rules would have to be designed to include whole or specific features of sectors. It was also not clear if concessions made would apply to all those making any kind of commitments or only to those making reciprocal commitments. A Swiss proposal touted optional MFN applicable only to a few countries.

Given the hostility to services before the round opened, the willingness of developing countries to work within the GNS is significant. Developing countries submitted several papers that helped with technical details on the formulation of principles. Frequent meetings, characterized by collective problem storming, also bred trust: the GNS met twenty-seven times between November 1986 and January 1990 for three to five days each.[71] There were some protests: a few developing countries felt in late 1987 and 1988 that their issues had been ignored, with Brazil taking the lead to add they were being rushed into issues that they barely understood.[72] In 1987, developing countries also turned to the UNCTAD for assistance, which began to coordinate its activities with GNS. The UN Centre on Transnational Enterprises also helped the developing world and helped to articulate their concerns about MNCs and the need for regulation in services.[73]

By the late 1980s, the developing world also began to shift away from its import-substitution policies of the past toward liberalization. Sectors like telecommunications that were also a major part of the GNS exercises were targeted. Developing countries became willing to see that they

---

[70] Croome 1999, 105–106.
[71] Narlikar 2003, 98, notes the origins of this process in the pre-Uruguay Round Jaramillo group: "the information exchange and consultation along the Jaramillo track were critical in winning the loyalty of smaller developing countries for the subsequent coalitions that emerged."
[72] Croome 1999, 107.   [73] Drake and Nicolaides 1992, 78–79.

could benefit from a services accord.[74] The Rajiv Gandhi administration in India and the Sarney and Collor administrations in Brazil were already crafting market-opening moves in their services sectors, especially in telecommunications.[75]

Meanwhile a spate of studies on trade in services, often reflecting industry positions or shaping them, continued to pour out of the developed world. The OECD Trade Committee, which had started working on services, released its report in March 1987. While pushing for services liberalization, it acknowledged that regulation was an essential part of services. But, an Office for Technology Assessment study in the United States acknowledged that while the country remained competitive in telecommunications and information technologies, its lead was declining in banking, finance, engineering and construction.[76] Maritime and shipping in the United States had always articulated a protectionist position. The US Treasury now began to lobby against liberalization of financial services.

The United States submitted its proposal to GNS in 1987, which asked for progressive and phased liberalization and for negotiation of a framework agreement that would allow for specific sectoral agreements to come in later. The proposal was hesitant in applying national treatment to all without reciprocity. Several other proposals followed, all of them arguing for tailoring services liberalization one way or another. By the end of 1988, there were thirty-five proposals to consider. No final agreement could be struck but there were broad enough agreements on the services agenda and principles for the GNS to prepare a draft text for Montreal "which included a fairly large number of open points ('square brackets'), none of which, however, seemed likely to give great difficulty."[77] At Montreal, these broad principles were honed down further and a negotiating timetable was set for the future.

From Montreal to Brussels

The next ministerial of GATT to bring the round to a close, before the Fast Track Authority of the US President expired, began on December 3, 1990, in Brussels. The services coalitions continued evolving as they already had been evolving before Montreal but with divisions in US service industries becoming entrenched. As developed countries' interests began to deviate from the evolving services agreement, those of the developing countries moved toward it. On intellectual property, the months between April 1989 and December 1990 were marked in agenda-setting

[74] Oxley 1990, 108–109.
[75] Singh 1999.   [76] Drake and Nicolaides 1992, 76–77.   [77] Croome 1999, 109.

terms by reformulation and fine-tuning of mini-agendas and the working of developing countries within the negotiating group to try to include issues of benefit to them. The shift in stance on IP issues after Montreal, when India and Brazil caved in to the IP agenda, is significant. For the purposes of this chapter, it is nonetheless important that the developing world was unable to limit the IP agenda or form effective coalitions until 1989. After that, developing countries did make marginal gains by forming coalitions (often with the EC and Japan) on particular issues.

Intellectual property: The acquiescence of hardline countries like India, Brazil, and Argentina and the silence of others like Korea and those of ASEAN had a lot to do with their inability to break the monolithic IP coalition ranks of the North, 301 pressures from the United States, and also expectations of gains in other areas. After agreeing to the April 1989 text, they worked within the negotiating group to effect gains.

Fifteen proposals came in by the end of 1989 as the negotiating group began to meet, the most significant being from the EC. It was almost as strong as that of the United States and signaled, again, that Europeans were behind the Americans.[78] Fourteen proposals came in from the developing world including those from India and Brazil. The Indian submission, in July 1989, continued to argue that many IP matters were sovereign or domestic issues though it did agree to discuss the issues at GATT. Brazil's submission argued for striking a balance between rights and responsibilities. Many developing countries also stated their preference for lodging the agreement at WIPO.[79] Developing countries looked for concessions on compulsory licensing, the related issue of patent protection in pharmaceuticals, phase-in periods, and recognition of their needs with respect to development.[80]

By late 1989, the stage was set for final concessions and trade-offs and, consequently the IP negotiating group was now somewhat ahead of others. "The main issues and proposals had all been explored, the points of difference (numerous by the count of a Secretariat checklist, more than 500 in all) were known, and there was every prospect that a very substantial agreement could emerge from the negotiations."[81] Developing

---

[78] Another motive was that by strengthening IP protections in commodities such as French wine, the EC might have been looking for concessions by the French on agriculture that had marred the mid-term review and continued to hold the round back.
[79] Watal 2001, 28.
[80] Croome 1999, 216–217. There are differences among observers on the level of expertise among developing country negotiators. Drahos (1995) notes that developed country negotiators treated their counterparts from the developing world as novices. Watal (2000: 32) notes that countries like India had brought in separate expert negotiators for industrial property, copyrights, and layout designs. Of course, the two positions are not mutually exclusive.
[81] Croome 1999, 217–218.

countries preferred to wait for progress in other areas before proceeding in intellectual property. Of particular interest to them were agriculture tariff reductions and the phasing out of the multifibre arrangement regime in textiles. This deadlock was broken in March 1990 when the United States, EC, Japan, and Switzerland submitted texts that could form the basis of a final treaty. A group of fourteen developing countries, with help from UNCTAD, put together the so-called 'Talloires text' (named after the town near Geneva where they met) or W/71 to counter the March proposals.[82] However, the Latin Americans did not want to be seen as hardliners and did not throw their weight behind this text. The text itself was not detailed enough in its provisions to really counter the other pro-posals. But it did yield minor gains by providing the basis for interpreting compliance (Articles 7 and 8 of TRIPS) and sovereign control of anti-competitive practices (Article 40).[83]

The draft of the TRIPS agreement was drawn up after the Talloires text submission with a group of 10 + 10 developed and developing countries. As with GNS, the collective brainstorming and participation in meet-ings seem to have yielded results. Watal notes several issue-based coali-tions that led to developing country gains.[84] India's request to merge government use and compulsory licensing in exchange for not putting any restrictions on these measures was supported by the EC, Japan, and Canada and made it into TRIPS.[85] This then formed the basis of the now famous Article 31 of TRIPS that in turn was the basis of the com-pulsory licensing concessions that developing countries received as the Doha Round opened. On other issues, the inability of the developed world in agreeing to specific language on copyright (Article 13) and patents

---

[82] The fourteen were: Argentina, Brazil, Chile, China, Colombia, Cuba, Egypt, India, Nigeria, Pakistan, Peru, Tanzania, Uruguay, and Zimbabwe.

[83] Watal 2001, 32.

[84] Ibid. An obvious way to build coalitions would be to take advantage of differences among developed countries. The best known differences were: appellations of origin important to wine producers in France; the first to file versus first to invent patent differences between the United States and many others; Canada's compulsory licensing procedures; Japanese resistance to extending copyright protections to software; European protection of moral rights of authors protecting their works from being changed or deformed by others; US recording industries' push for prohibiting rentals such as those of CDs in Japan (Devereaux 2002, 21). Furthermore, these pressures were most apparent in the last two years of the round when the North-South issues were more or less already settled.

[85] Based on interview with Jayashree Watal, World Trade Organization (November 5, 2004). India was told by Canada that US laws allowed for compulsory licensing for government use such as by NASA. US negotiator Mike Kirk had so far argued that the United States was not opposed to government use but he did so without using the language of compulsory licensing. Once India understood US law, it was able to argue for allowing for compulsory use whether or not it was for government purposes.

(Article 30) also leaves room for interpretation for the developing world. Developing countries also joined in with Commonwealth Countries in support of parallel trade measures (Article 6).

By mid-summer 1990, 10 + 10 had put together the five proposals into a 100-page "composite draft text," which was then edited for the Brussels meeting. No country was yet committed to this text and by the time of the meeting several important issues had not been decided including term-life of patents and phase-in periods. In the meantime, US 301 pressures continued citing developing countries on the watch list.[86] The Brussels meeting itself fell apart over agriculture and thus neither the outstanding issues nor those requiring high-level trade-offs could be negotiated.

Services: The preparedness of the GNS at the Montreal meeting helped to push its agenda into specific directions until the Brussels meeting. The four modes of supply and trade principles such as national treatment and market access were a fait accompli by now. Issues of sectoral coverage and application of MFN were key agenda items. Developing countries tried to define the agenda for both of these in their own favor while building coalitions of support. On one particular issue of importance to them, however, the cross-border movement of unskilled labor, they found little support. As before Montreal, the support for services negotiations continued to decrease in the United States and this was tied to the MFN issue, too.

With the framework of modes of supply and principles in place, GNS moved toward sectoral testing exercises, involving micro-agendas, in 1989. The sectors were: telecommunications, construction, transportation, tourism, professional services and financial services. This list was pared down from thirteen sectors and over one hundred sub-sectors. In general, these exercises revealed the limits of applying many of the GATS principles carte blanche to sectors covered. Second, specialists from these sectors got involved. In telecommunications, the support of the International Telecommunication Union (ITU) helped to resolve many technical matters but its involvement also might have allowed developing countries to resist moves toward cost-based pricing that the United States wanted (ITU supported the old pricing regime).[87]

Coalition building with developed countries allowed developing countries with beneficial outcomes. One of the debates that arose from sectoral exercises, and from the fifteen papers that were submitted by countries during Autumn 1989, concerned the scope of sectoral coverage. Here, the United States wanted a top-down approach of a negative list requiring countries to list sectors and sub-sectors that were not covered. This

---

[86] Ryan 1998.   [87] Singh 2002.

position was viewed as extreme by most of the developing world and parts of the developed one, mainly within the EC. The latter, supported by the developing world, wanted a bottom-up positive list covering only the sectors listed.[88] Furthermore, proposals by India and Brazil argued for support of infant industries and transfers of technology. By far, the most demanding proposal was that of the United States in October 1989, which asked for broad sectoral coverage as well as specific commitments.[89]

Subsequent evolution of this issue shows increasing concerns in the developed countries. The fifteen-page draft that GNS put together in November 1989 from these proposals was full of square brackets and major debates continued to flare up. There were crucial sectors or sub-sectors that the developed world wanted to exclude. One of the most famous of these is the French 'cultural exception,' which applied to audio-visual negotiations. But support for services in the United States was also coming undone. Maritime industries were opposed to giving up their protections, telecommunications and finance did not want to liberalize if others did not, and the airlines were hesitant. Significantly, the Coalition of Service Industries changed its position and denounced the services framework coming out of GNS. In July 1990, USTR announced that the United States would need to derogate from MFN in shipping, civil aviation, and basic telecommunications.[90] This was followed by USTR Carla Hills' announcement in November that the United States did not agree to unconditional MFN in services. The EC and developing countries were outraged. This was ironic, given that a little over three years earlier, developing countries had not even wanted to negotiate services.

On July 23, however, Felipe Jaramillo sent over to the Trade Negotiations Committee (TNC) his own proposed text for an agreement. Even as broad agreement still needed to be struck on sectoral coverage and MFN, the proposed text contained all the elements of the agreement that became GATS. Section One dealt with Scope and Coverage detailing the four modes of supply. Section Two covered General Obligations and Disciplines, which included principles such as MFN, transparency, and harmonization of regulations. Section Three, Specific Commitments, covered market access and national treatment. Section Four was concerned with Progressive Liberalization. In the Jaramillo text, Sections Five and Six, Institutional and Final Provisions, were incomplete. Issues of sectoral coverage and MFN continued to dog the negotiations and, by late 1990, it was clear that there was no time for negotiating specific commitments

---

[88] Preeg 1995, 104.
[89] The proposals from the United States, Switzerland, New Zealand and Korea suggested the name of the framework: the General Agreement on Trade in Services.
[90] Drake and Nicolaides 1992, 87.

that the United States wanted before the Brussels meeting. India, Brazil and Egypt had argued that the mandate of the GNS was only to negotiate a framework. In the Green Room discussions that followed, developing countries in particular were not willing to move the discussions further until issues such as textiles and agriculture were moved forward.[91]

Given the disagreements, the draft that Jaramillo forwarded in November 1990 on his own responsibility added to the six sections of the May draft a list of annexes (maritime, inland waterways, road transport, air transport, basic telecommunications, telecommunication services, labor mobility, and audiovisual services). The ministers at Brussels were both impressed as well as stymied by the scope, complexity, and the tentative language. An EC delegate noted that "the ocean of brackets" made it "well-nigh impossible to distinguish substantive political opinions from mere technicalities."[92] However, negotiations on services in Brussels were moving forward quite smoothly until the protests by 24,000 angry farmers and the agriculture impasse brought the ministerial to a close.

Brussels to Marrakesh

The TRIPS negotiations after Brussels were fairly straightforward and essentially completed by December 1991, although developing countries did manage to squeeze a few minor concessions from the North on transition periods and dispute settlement. Issue-based coalitions worked in these cases. The services negotiations dragged on into the early morning of December 15, 1993, the deadline to conform to the twice resanctioned Fast Track Authority of the U.S. President. The text was then forwarded for the Marrakesh meeting in April 1994.

After Brussels, the GNS continued to work as it was but the other fourteen negotiating groups were reduced to six; the groups on textiles, agriculture, and TRIPS were of immense importance to developing countries.

TRIPS: The final negotiations in intellectual property took place mostly between September and December 1991 with the last meeting of the TRIPS group taking place on December 18, 1991, when 95 percent of it was deemed negotiated.[93] Attempts by developing countries to try to reopen negotiations on issues that had already been negotiated (for example an attempt by the Andean Group on moral rights of authors) did not yield anything. However, developing countries did make a few

---

[91] Croome 1999, 214. Green Room refers to discussions among the most influential or concerned parties in GATT/WTO jargon, taking their name from a room that adjoined the Director General's office.
[92] Croome 1999, 215.   [93] Quoted by Croome 1999, 276.

gains on issues that had not been decided, as in the difficult negotiations over transition periods. With help from the EC, the transition period for developing countries on IP protection varied between five and ten years, less than the fifteen originally proposed. The US pharmaceutical industry was unhappy with this outcome.[94] The United States tried to dilute the leeway in transition periods by seeking pipeline or retroactive protection for products still in the course of research. An EC/India proposal countered by offering Exclusive Marketing Rights (EMRs) for five years once the product was introduced.[95] The 1991 draft text, which came to be known as the 'Dunkel Draft', then noted that countries not awarding patents had to institute EMRs for five years. For India, intellectual property had always been a make-it-or-break-it issue. The Dunkel Draft was thoroughly denounced and burned at several street demonstrations.[96]

By 1991, the coalition for intellectual property was one of the few supporting the Uruguay Round in the United States.[97] Thus, it was increasingly hard for the United States to make any concessions and it played tough. It kept up its 301 pressures on key developing countries. India was named a priority foreign country in April 1991 and Brazil in April 1993. China, not a member of GATT but an observer seeking accession, conceded to many of the US demands on IPRs in 1991. Thailand amended its patent laws in 1992.

The stiff opposition by civil society led India to try to negotiate concessions up till the end-game.[98] In December 1993, with Canada's help, it was agreed that certain TRIPS violation complaints would not be brought to dispute settlement for five years. Apart from this final concession, TRIPS was part of what Dunkel described as "final political trade-offs."[99] Brazil specifically called for decisions in agriculture and textiles.[100]

Services: The MFN issues in 1991–92 and the services sectoral commitment issues in 1992–93 dominated the round in many ways, apart from discussions in agriculture. The developing world did not need to make any concessions it did not want.

---

[94] Devereaux 2002, 25.
[95] As drugs can have R&D and trial periods of several years before introduction to the market, US firms wanted patent protection while they were still in the pipeline and also after they were introduced in the market. The EMR agreement, while not quite offering pipeline protection, did bar rival drugs from being sold even if they were developed.
[96] For example, at a November 1993 protest in Bangalore, India, half a million Indian farmers were addressed by both farm and non-farm organizations from Brazil, Ethiopia, Indonesia, Korea, Malaysia, Nicaragua, the Philippines, Sri Lanka, Thailand, and Zimbabwe (Brecher and Costello 1994, 7). At protests like these a familiar refrain was "Reject Dunkel, Reject Imperialism" (Tolan 1994, 20).
[97] Devereaux 2002, 24.   [98] Watal 2001, 34–35.
[99] Quoted in Croome 1999, 275.   [100] Croome 1999, 253.

72   *J. P. Singh*

MFN discussions took all of 1991 in the Group of Negotiations on Services. The United States had softened its stand on MFN in Brussels but was still afraid of according a general obligation with no restrictions, especially as its telecommunications and financial sectors were quite open already.[101] One set of countries in GNS wanted sectoral agreements on exemptions but others felt it would lead to widespread use of exemptions. The compromise in July was to ask countries to submit lists of activities or measures for which they would seek MFN exemptions rather than entire sectors. The United States kept the issue alive until mid-1992, insisting that it was not ready to give MFN to those countries making weak sectoral offers.

The TNC reviewed the 440-page Draft Final Act on December 20, 1991, and noted the lack of sectoral commitments in services. In January, a four-track approach toward the round emerged, with tracks one and two in goods and services, respectively. A March deadline was fixed for making commitments but only 47 offers had come in by April. The number increased to 54 covering 67 countries by the end of 1992.

Sectoral commitment negotiations continued into 1993. In telecommunications, India and Egypt opposed a measure proposed by the United States calling for cost-based pricing. The services group did not agree but the US delegation in December 1993 gave in. EC support was crucial here.[102] As a result of this and the complicated nature of telecommunications, it was agreed to continue negotiations in basic telecommunications (and also financial services) after the round closed. The agreement in telecommunications came about in 1997.[103] The most hotly contested issue, one that almost broke down the round at the last minute, was audiovisual. While this was mostly a US–EU issue, both India and Brazil would benefit from trade liberalization in the audiovisual area. However, India sided with the United States on this issue, while Brazil supported the EU. Quite a marked difference from the types of coalitions that came about in TRIPS!

Final analysis

The final outcomes for GATS and TRIPS are hard to predict without examining negotiation processes. Above all, the changing interests of the North and the South, that altered the win-sets of both parties, explain the two outcomes as well as the differences between them. The national interests themselves reflect not only the changing positions of domestic constituencies as the negotiations evolved but also the workings of

---

[101] Croome 1999, 271–272.   [102] Singh forthcoming, Chapter 3.   [103] Singh 2002.

negotiation tactics such as agenda-setting, coalition building, and unilateral threats.

Had the national interests of countries not changed during the negotiation process, GATS would have been heavily supported by the North and TRIPS might have had a limited scope. Both would have been opposed by the developing world though services would have garnered much more opposition than intellectual property. In reality, the interest in an expansive GATS, or in its key sectors, seemed to wane among developed countries while the developing world made an almost 180° turn in coming out in support of GATS. In intellectual property, the North's interest in an agreement on counterfeit goods changed to an interest in a TRIPS agreement covering an array of IP infringements. The South moved from barely being organized to oppose the IP agenda, to explicitly opposing the TRIPS outcomes at the end. It learned its lesson: the opening of the Doha Round was held up until the North made crucial concessions on intellectual property (see chapter 3, "Reframing the Issue").

The mobilization of domestic constituencies, and their changing interests, is one of the factors explaining the variability of win-sets during the negotiations. This chapter concentrates on the influence of domestic constituencies, mainly businesses, on negotiations. Before the Uruguay Round started, businesses in services and intellectual property in the North clearly favored strong agreements. The services coalition was quite monolithic while the coalition on intellectual property was still evolving. Over time, the IP interests strengthened and closed their ranks, but the services interests became divided. Among developing countries, the IP interests remained entrenched in their opposition to services, but whereas they were hardly mobilized at the beginning of the round, they presented almost a transnational coalition opposing TRIPS at the end of the round. In services, their national interests began to reflect the growing importance of services to their economies. In many cases, these services sectors were owned and controlled by the state but market liberalizations were underway as in telecommunications and banking. In other cases, important private sectors already existed such as financial services from the Caribbean, construction from East Asia, and audiovisual content from India or Brazil.

This chapter is concerned with explaining the differences in negotiation outcomes starting with interests of domestic constituencies and then building to national interests and their intersection with international negotiation processes. However, the origins of domestic interests themselves are important. In particular, the feedback loop between negotiation processes and the reorganization of domestic interests is not examined here but must be included to understand the overall role of negotiations.

An analogy might help: just as market transactions not only reflect but also shape consumer behavior, international negotiations as political markets or interactions also shape the interests of all actors involved at both international and domestic levels. Empirical analyses of such third image reversed influences, especially as they apply to the first and second images, are sorely needed.

This chapter examines the way negotiation tactics, a set of interactions at the systemic international level, alter the matrix of alternatives for the negotiating parties in general. Agenda-setting, coalition-building, and unilateral threats are examined in depth. In terms of agenda-setting, this chapter shows that paying close attention to agenda-setting in services before and during the Uruguay Round resulted in the inclusion of issues in such a way as subsequently to allow for concessions favorable to the developing world. In intellectual property, the agenda was not watched so closely, allowing the developed world to work toward an expansive TRIPS. Officials as well as scholars now acknowledge the lack of attention paid to the deliberately fuzzy language that allowed for the IP agenda to follow. It may be appropriate then to speak of a *negative delayed agenda formation effect:* delays in accepting agendas can result in a worse outcome if resources are not spent by the opposing side in countering or cutting the agenda. Such resources, as discussed in this chapter, may include paying close attention to the domestic interests of countries pushing the agenda, participation in agenda-setting meetings, and producing technical information supporting a counter-agenda and counter-frames. On the other hand, a *positive delayed agenda formation effect* can be identified for services in general or for intellectual property after 1989 when the developing world did pay close attention to agenda-setting with enormous resource costs incurred. For services, the two-track decision at Punta del Este that set the stage for other concessions on services later on resulted in part from agenda-setting by the developing world.

Agenda-setting is a necessary but not a sufficient condition for ensuring concessions to oneself in negotiations. Once an issue is on the agenda, other negotiation tactics must be used: these same tactics may be used to get items on the agenda, too. Coalition-building with important players or around particular issue-areas can effect concessions. Coalitions often require compromises and thinking strategically about one's interests and linking them with those of the others. Quite obviously, the coalition-building by the US on services and intellectual property paid off for getting these items on the agenda and with other concessions. However, in services the coalition showed divisions in ranks, mostly because of the differing nature of service industries backing national governments but also because coalitional interests changed as the differential impact of the evolving GATS framework began to be assessed by coalitional partners. Developing countries were able to use the divisions in ranks and also the two-track decision to keep building coalitions of support. The two-track decision itself, while an agenda-setting victory, also reveals coalitional influences: EC defection from the Prepcom meetings and the Jaramillo group was crucial here. Similarly, the other major victory, the inclusion of positive *and* negative lists as part of GATS resulted from similar processes. In intellectual property, the developing countries were unable to exploit any divisions in the ranks for coalition-building purposes when the round opened and, as noted above, came under unilateral pressures from the United States. Coalition-building around micro-issues after 1989 did allow them to effect concessions in phase-in periods and compulsory licensing.[104] However, by then the developed world already presented quite a monolithic coalition and thus only minor concessions were possible.

Based on the hypotheses and empirical evidence in this chapter, two additional observations about coalition-building can be made. First, moderate coalitions negotiate between extremes to try to break deadlocks, in what may be termed the "café au lait effect".[105] That a moderate coalition, the Jaramillo group, developed in services is interesting. Scholars of domestic politics, especially American government, are used to noticing moderate coalitions develop out of extreme ones to break deadlocks. That it happened in services but not in intellectual property is instructive for lessons on not only how to form moderate coalitions (as in services) but also on how to prevent them (as in intellectual property). The inability of a moderate coalition to form in intellectual property might be seen later in negotiation histories as a bit of an anomaly. It may even be argued

---

[104] "Given the relatively unified assault by the North against the largely weak and divided South, the achievements of developing countries in maintaining a certain balance between public interest and strengthened protection, were small but surprisingly significant . . . these results would not have been possible without the direct or indirect issue-based support from several developed countries." Watal 2000, 43.

[105] I am thankful to social movements theorist Cathy Schneider for noting that this is what social movement theory terms the 'positive radical flanks effect' (Haines 1984). However, I prefer the term 'café au lait effect' because it calls attention to an exemplar in negotiation history and also steers clear of any group being termed radical. Social movement theory also uses it to show how groups in the middle always draw the most support. In negotiation histories, the effect is more about breaking deadlocks while the extent to which they draw support is questionable. After all, while inclusion of services on the agenda might be due to the Jaramillo group, the two-track decision owes as much to the defection of the EC to the developing country hard-line group. I am instructed by the social movement literature, which notes that this effect may be positive or negative. Haines (1984) examines the funding of the civil rights groups from 1957 to 1970 to show that donors gave more to perceived moderate groups because of groups that got characterized as "too far out."

that the very reason that Brazil and India caved in in 1989 might be due
to the latent moderation or defection in the developing world ranks, the
latter featuring many of the same countries as in the café au lait group.
These East Asian and Latin American developing countries had by 1989
softened their opposition to intellectual property due either to their own
incipient strength in IT industries or due to punitive threats from the
United States in the form of 301 pressures. The "café au lait effect" is
consistent with the two coalition-building sub-hypotheses of this chapter;
such coalitions are particularly effective when they include important
players or when they form around sub-issue areas. This effect can then
be seen as one of the outcome variations specifying a new set of credible alternatives. Second, the interplay between micro (sub-issue) versus
macro coalitions is interesting. In either case, important players must lend
their support. However, the findings of this chapter only offer preliminary
conclusions regarding the choice between macro versus micro coalitions.
Quite clearly, the victories in services were due to macro coalitions while
those in IP were micro ones. It would seem that micro coalitions are only
good for chipping away at the margins. However, macro coalitions also
consume enormous resources.[106]

Counter-explanations may now be examined. International political
economy theories explain the outcomes in GATS and TRIPS, the current regimes in services and intellectual property, without much of a
look at negotiation theories or processes. Three of these explanations
are reviewed here via possible counterfactual arguments explaining the
outcomes.

1. *Interests specified* ex ante *can predict global outcomes*: There are two
variations to this argument, one coming from political scientists and
another from economists. Political scientists looking at global power distributions can note that the way power structures define interests can
predict negotiation processes.[107] In a hierarchical power distribution, the
interests of great powers prevail over those of the weak. This seems to be
the case with intellectual property. Why was this not the case in services?
The two cases examined here were picked precisely because the power
distribution could be held constant. However, the outcomes are different due to differences in the negotiations process. Furthermore, if initial
interests defined by an existing power distribution determine outcomes
then we should have expected the developing world to have made more
concessions in services than in intellectual property. The opposite turned

[106] A policy lesson about macro coalition-building and agenda-setting is then obvious: start early.
[107] Krasner 1991.

out to be the case. Interests themselves changed. Even in TRIPS, power had to be filtered through agenda-setting, coalition-building, and unilateral threats to be translated into an outcome. Quite clearly, both power structure and negotiation process matter.

A power distribution theorist could argue that the overall package still revealed gains in the North's favor and that these gains reflected the North's interests. While the answer lies beyond the empirical evidence presented in this chapter, three things may be mentioned. First, the developing world made the least number of concessions in an area most unfamiliar to them at the beginning of the round, namely services. This suggests that the developing world cannot be seen as totally disadvantaged in these 'high-tech' issue-areas that may be seen to be shaped by the North's interests. Second, this chapter finds no evidence that the developing world actually made the kind of trade-offs suggested by some in accepting an IP agreement in return for concessions in textiles. India agreed to the main tenets of the IP framework in 1989 without asking for anything in return. Other countries seemed to cave in to unilateral threats from the United States. In the end-game of the Uruguay Round, when such trade-offs could be made, the IP negotiations focused mostly on North-North issues.[108] Third, it is debatable if the overall final outcome of the Uruguay Round reflects only the North's interests. Winham calls the overall package "an acceptable outcome": "Developing countries as a group benefited from the agreements on agriculture, textiles and clothing, and safeguards, and they were probable, but uncertain, gainers on services. Developing countries were disadvantaged on balance by agreements on intellectual property and antidumping, and probable, but uncertain losers on subsidies."[109]

Economists look at national interests as an aggregation of domestic industry interests and then posit outcomes based on these interests. GATS and TRIPS can then be taken to reflect the underlying interests of industries that wanted these sectors liberalized. Again, this is too simplistic. As this chapter shows, the negotiation processes helped to change national interests. They may have even altered industry interests. Furthermore, even when domestic or national interests are well-specified, negotiation outcomes do not always reflect them. IP industries from the South did not get what they wanted; even many in the North thought TRIPS was too weak. In services the cases for the South and the North were the opposite. Negotiation processes then arbitrate and alter domestic and national interests. The lines between interests specified ex ante and negotiation outcomes are neither straightforward nor predictable.

---

[108] Sell 2004, 108–120.   [109] Winham, 1998, 117.

It is also argued that the developing world caved in or enthusiastically supported the GATS framework because the developing world coalition leaders like India and Brazil were already carrying out services liberalizations at home. They had domestic support for their positions.[110] However, this explanation is consistent with the conclusions of this chapter. There was nothing straightforward about this domestic support, which hardly created any wiggle room for these countries to accept the services agenda. In fact, developing countries remained opposed to the services agenda until 1986. Their biggest victories in services, the two-track proposal and the idea of combining positive and negative lists, came about before liberalizations had really been accepted as a fait accompli in the developing world. As Winham himself notes, India did not come around until 1991. Most of Brazil's services liberalizations were delayed until Cardoso came to power because of opposition from domestic groups. Developing country domestic industry until the mid-1990s was Janus-faced about services liberalization: it wanted liberalization but not for foreign service providers.

2. *The developing world's 'wins' at the Uruguay Round are linked to issues outside of GATS and TRIPS*: First, the minor wins in intellectual property could be explained by a prior convergence of interests, the special and differential (S&D) treatment provision, dating back to the Kennedy Round in the 1960s.[111] It has been argued that the longer transition periods accorded to the developing world at the Uruguay round honored the S&D provisions.[112] However, it is also pointed out that S&D was a controversial issue in the Uruguay Round and the developed world – especially the United States – was loathe to make such concessions, wanting developing countries to graduate instead. Oyejide argues that after a hard fought battle, the round reduced rather than expanded the scope of S&D provisions "to extended transition periods."[113] Arguably, then, the transition periods may not have been accorded, as the US pharmaceutical industry wanted, without agenda-setting and issue-based coalitions by the South toward the end of the round. Second, developing country gains in the two issues examined above extended to more than just transition periods, especially in services, and thus went far beyond the S&D provisions. Third, the oft-made claim that the developing countries

---

[110] Ibid. Winham (p. 112) also argues that Argentina produced a moderate text for services in 1989 when it defected from the developing world coalition opposing services, because it saw its main interest in not opposing the services but furthering the agriculture agenda. This text's provisions helped to define many features of GATS later. Argentina's move is consistent with the "café au lait effect" noted above.

[111] This idea was posed to me by Beth Yarborough.

[112] Pangestu 2002, 157–158.   [113] Oyejide 2002, 507.

made a Faustian bargain, trading away their fortunes in new issue-areas in return for concessions in the old ones, is belied by this chapter. No such thing happened in services. Even the caving in of India and Brazil to the TRIPS agenda in 1989 was followed by moves to improve the developing country gains in IP rather than some sort of blind acquiescence to this agenda. No trade-offs were made for concessions in textiles and agriculture at the time the deadlock on intellectual property was broken.

3. *Epistemic communities – groups with shared beliefs and ideas help to shape agendas.*[114] By this line of reasoning, the bigger the epistemic community, the more likely that an agenda will go through. Drake and Nicolaides use this explanation specifically for GATS. However, the TRIPS epistemic community was smaller and yet the developed North got more concessions from the developing South. Again, it was not just who supported and shared particular ideas but how these ideas were translated into agenda-setting and coalition-building that mattered. Cowhey's explanation is consistent with the conclusion of this chapter in noting that the 'small bang' of negotiation will push the work of the liberalization oriented epistemic community forward.[115]

A final caution might be to doubt the generalizability of this chapter's conclusions along two lines. First, one might note that the negotiation of new issues at the Doha Round is vastly different. Is it? The concessions received by the developing world in TRIPS at the beginning of the Round are consistent with paying close and early attention to agenda-formation and coalition-building. Second, one could even note that it is easier to gain concessions in new issue-areas than in old ones because the constituencies in the North and South are not so entrenched.[116] This is consistent with my claim that, contrary to received wisdom, developing countries may not be net losers in negotiating the global information economy in issues such as services. Beyond this, the issue needs further empirical investigation. There are plenty of entrenched constituencies in new issue-areas in both the North and the South: pharmaceuticals in India, maritime and aviation in the United States, and cultural industries in France and Canada are examples.

In conclusion, this chapter seeks to contribute to emerging theories dealing with the formation of national interests. It takes issue with rational choice accounts that take these interests as given but does not necessarily contradict the fact that actors are socialized into practicing strategic behaviors. With an eye toward social interactions, Keohane writes of empathic self-interests without giving us a theory of interactive

---

[114] Cowhey 1990; Drake and Nicolaides 1992.   [115] Cowhey 1990.
[116] This was pointed out to me by Sheila Page.

circumstances under which these types of interests may or may not arise.[117] Different types of national interest can lead to different types of empathic or strategic behaviors. The sources of the type of behavior practiced, where it is practiced, and the way it is practiced depend on the international environment. This chapter agrees with Katzenstein that social practices can change interests, though it does not get into the larger question of identity changes.[118] The analysis presented here, while using negotiation process variables, is also consistent with Peterson's recent work on 'situation definitions' in international negotiations where states' interests come out of understanding the parameters of each situation as each of them asks the question "what am I doing?"[119] This process, she argues, also leads to inclusion or exclusion of particular actors depending on the authoritative policy claims they make. While agreeing with critiques of rational choice theories, she takes issue with constructivist accounts in their failure to account for which actors are included or excluded in a negotiation. This chapter has shown that negotiation theories not only identify which actors make particular claims but also the micro processes that help them persuade others with those claims, namely via agenda-setting and coalition-building.[120]

We need to pay attention to negotiation theory to see how negotiation tactics allow for the *creation as well as alteration of interests* to accommodate or to exclude other parties' interests. Coase inched toward a theory of transaction costs by noting that if markets are so efficient, then why do firms exist? Williamson substantiated the same in positing the relationship between markets and hierarchies.[121] We may inch toward a positive theory of negotiations – rather than treating the latter as a residual variable – by asking the following: if power or markets are so efficient, then why do negotiations exist? They exist because power and markets provide ample wiggle room for the creation, alteration, and resolution of interests.

REFERENCES

Adlung, Rudolf, Antonio Carzeniga, Bernard Hoekman, Masamichi Kono, Aaditya Mattoo, and P. Chauvet. 2002. The GATS: Key Features and Sectors. In *Development, Trade, and the WTO: A Handbook*, eds. Bernard Hoekman, Aaditya Mattoo, and Philip English. Washington, DC: The World Bank
Axelrod, Robert. 1985. *The Evolution of Cooperation*. New York: Basic Books

[117] Keohane 1984.   [118] Katzenstein 1996, 21.   [119] Peterson 2004.
[120] For an article on negotiations, Peterson 2004 is curiously silent on negotiation processes and implicitly argues for the intrinsic value of claims rather than treating them as political processes.
[121] Williamson 1975.

Braithwaite, John, and Peter Drahos. 2000. *Global Business Regulation*. Cambridge: Cambridge University Press

Correa, Carlos M. 2000. *Intellectual Property Rights, the WTO and Developing Country: The TRIPS Agreement and Policy Options*. Penang, Malaysia: Third World Network

Cowhey, Peter F. 1990. The International Telecommunications Regime: The Political Roots of Regimes for High-Technology. *International Organization*. 34 (2):169–99

Croome, John. 1999. *Reshaping the World Trading System: A History of the Uruguay Round*. The Hague: Kluwer Law International

Devereaux, Charan. 2002. *Intellectual Trade Meets Intellectual Property: The Making of the TRIPS Agreement*

Drahos, Peter. 1995. Global property rights in information: the story of TRIPS at the GATT. *Prometheus* 13 (1): 6–19

Drake, William J, and Kalypso Nicolaides. 1992. Ideas, interests, and institutionalization: 'trade in services' and the Uruguay Round. *International Organization* 46 (1): 37–100

Evans, Peter, Harold K. Jacobson, and Robert D. Putnam, eds. 1993. *Double-Edged Diplomacy: International Bargaining and Domestic Politics*. Berkeley: University of Berkeley Press

Friedman, Jeffrey, ed. 1996. *The Rational Choice Controversy*. New Haven, Conn: Yale University Press

Gallagher, Peter. 2000. *Guide to the WTO and Developing Countries*. World Trade Organization and Kluwer Law International

Gorlin, Jacques. 1985. *A Trade-Based Approach for the International Copyright Protection for Computer Software*

Green Donald P., and Ian Shapiro. 1994. *Pathologies of Rational Choice Theory: A Critique of Applications in Political Science*. New Haven, Conn: Yale University Press

Grieco, Joseph M. 1982. Between dependency and autonomy: India's experience with the international computer industry. *International Organization* 36 (Summer): 609–632

Haines, Herbert H. 1984. Black Radicalization and the Funding of Civil Rights. *Social Problems*. 32:31–43

Hoekman, Bernard M. November 1993. New Issues in the Uruguay Round and Beyond. *The Economic Journal* 103 (421):1528–39

Hoekman, Bernard M. and Mitchell M. Kostecki. 1995. *The Political Economy of the World Trading System: From GATT to WTO*. Oxford: Oxford University Press

International Intellectual Property Alliance. 1985. *Piracy to US Copyrighted Works in Ten Selected Countries*. Submitted to USTR

Jackson, John H. 1997. *The World Trading System: Law and Policy of International Economic Relations*. Cambridge, Mass: The MIT Press

Jawara, Fatoumata, and Aileen Kwa. 2003. *Behind the scenes at the WTO: The real world of international trade negotiations*. London: Zed Books

Katzenstein, Peter, ed. 1996. *The Culture of National Security: Norms and Identity in World Politics*. Ithaca, NY: Cornell University Press

Keohane, Robert O. 1984. *After Hegemony: Cooperation and Discord in the World Political Economy*. Princeton: Princeton University Press

Keohane, Robert and Joseph Nye. 1977. *Power and Interdependence*. Boston: Little, Brown

1998. Power and Interdependence in the Information Age." *Foreign affairs*. 77 (5): 81–94

Keohane, Robert, and Helen Milner, eds. 1996. *Internationalization and Domestic Politics*. Cambridge: Cambridge University Press

King, Gary, Robert O. Keohane, and Sidney Verba. 1994. *Designing Social Enquiry: Scientific Inference in Qualitative Research*. Princeton, NJ: Princeton University Press

Krasner, Stephen. 1985. *Structural Conflict: The Third World Against Global Liberalism*. Berkeley: University of California Press

1991. "Global Telecommunications and National Power." *International Organization 43* (3): 336–66

Kuran, Timur. 1995. *Private Truths, Public Lies: The Social Consequences of Preference Falsification*. Cambridge, Mass: Harvard University Press

Mascus, Keith. 2000. *Intellectual Property Rights in the Global Economy*. Washington, DC: Institute for International Economics

May, Frederick W. 1992. Launching the Uruguay Round: Clayton Yeutter and the Two-Track Decision. Case 144. Institute for the Study of Diplomacy, School of Foreign Service, Georgetown University, Washington, DC.

Murmann, Johann Peter. 2003. *Knowledge and Competitive Advantage: The Coevolution of Firms, Technology, and National Institutions*. Cambridge: Cambridge University Press

Narlikar, Amrita. 2003. *International Trade and Developing Countries: Bargaining Coalitions in the GATT and WTO*. London: Routledge

Nelson, Richard R., and Sidney G. Winter. 1982. *An Evolutionary Theory of Economic Change*. Cambridge, Mass: Harvard University Press

Nye, Joseph. 1991. *Bound to Lead: The Changing Nature of American Power*. New York: Basic Books

Odell, John. 1985. "The Outcomes of International Trade Conflicts: The US and South Korea, 1960–1981," *International Studies Quarterly* 29:263–86

1993. International Threats and Internal Politics: Brazil, The European Community, and the United States. In *Double-edged Diplomacy: International Bargaining and Domestic Politics*, eds. Peter B. Evans, Harold K. Jacobson, and Robert D. Putnam, 237–64. Berkeley: University of California Press

2000. *Negotiating the World Economy*. Ithaca NY: Cornell University Press

2002. Bounded Rationality and the World Political Economy. In *Governing the World's Money*' eds. David M. Andrews, C. Randall Henning, and Louis Pauly. Ithaca, NY: Cornell University Press

Oxfam. March 2002. *Rigged Rules and Double Standards: trade, globalization and the fight against poverty*

Oxley, Alan. 1990. *The Challenge of Free Trade*. London: Harvester Wheatsheaf

Oyejide, T. Ademola. 2002. Special and Differential Treatment. In *Development, Trade, and the WTO: A Handbook*, eds. Bernard Hoekman, Aaditya Mattoo, and Philip English. Washington, DC: The World Bank

Pangestu, Mari. 2002. Industrial Policy and Developing Countries. In *Development, Trade, and the WTO: A Handbook*, eds. Bernard Hoekman, Aaditya Mattoo, and Philip English, 504–8. Washington, DC: The World Bank
Peterson, M. J. May 2004. Diverging Orbits: Situation Definitions in Creation of Regimes for Broadcast and Remote Sensing Satellites. *American Political Science Review* 98 (2): 277–91 .
Petrazzini, Ben. 1996. *Global Telecom Talks: A Trillion Dollar Deal.* Washington, DC: Institute for International Economics
Preeg, Ernest H. 1995. *Traders in a brave New World: the Uruguay Round and the Future of the International System.* Chicago: The University of Chicago Press
Putnam, Robert. 1988. Diplomacy and domestic politics: the logic of two-level games. *International Organization* 42 (Summer):427–60
Raghavan, Chakravarthi. 2002. *Developing Countries and Services Trade: Chasing a black cat in a dark room, blindfolded.* Penang, Malaysia: Third World Network
Rosenau, James N. 1990. *Turbulence in World Politics: A Theory of Change and Continuity.* Princeton: Princeton University Press
1997. *Along the Domestic-Foreign Frontier: Exploring Governance in a Turbulent World.* Cambridge: Cambridge University Press
Ryan, Michael. 1998. *Knowledge Diplomacy: Global Competition and the Politics of Intellectual Property.* Washington, DC: Brookings Institution Press
Sell, Susan K. 1995. Intellectual Property Protection and Antitrust in the Developing World: Crisis, Coercion, and Choice. *International Organization.* 49 (2):315–49
1998. *Power and Ideas: North-South Politics of Intellectual Property and Antitrust.* Albany: State University of New York Press
1999. Multinational Corporations as Agents of Change: The Globalization of Intellectual Property Rights. In *Private Authority and International Affairs*, eds. A. Clare Cutler, Virginia Haufler, and Tony Porter. Albany: State University of New York Press
2003. *Private Power, Public Law: The Globalization of Intellectual Property Rights* Cambridge, UK: Cambridge University Press
Sharma, Devinder. 1994. *GATT to WTO: Seeds of Despair.* New Delhi: Konarak Publishers
Singh, J. P. 1999. *Leapfrogging Development?: The Political Economy of Telecommunications Restructuring.* Albany, NY: State University of New York Press
2000A. "Weak Powers and Globalism: The Impact of Plurality on Weak-Strong Negotiations in the International Economy." *International Negotiation* 5(3):449–84
2000B. The institutional environment and effects of telecommunications privatization and liberalization in Asia. *Telecommunications Policy* 24:885–906
2002. Negotiating Regime Change: the Weak, the Strong and the WTO Telecom accord. In *Information Technologies and Global Politics: The Changing Scope of Power and Governance*, eds. James N. Rosenau and J. P. Singh, 239–72. Albany: State University of New York Press
Forthcoming. *Negotiating the Global Information Economy*
Sjostedt, Gunnar. 1994. Negotiating the Uruguay Round of the General Agreement on Tariffs and Trade. In *International Multilateral Negotiation:*

Approaches to the Management of Complexity, ed. I. William Zartman, 44–69. San Francisco: Jossey-Bass Publishers

Tolan, Sandy. July 10, 1994. "Against the Grain." *Los Angeles Times Magazine*

Tversky, Amos and Daniel Kahneman. 1986. Rational Choice and the Framing of Decisions. *Journal of Business*

United States Government. 1984. *U.S. National Study on Trade in Services: A Submission by the United States Government to the General Agreement on Tariffs and Trade*. Washington, DC: Government Printing Office

Watal, Jayashree. 2001. *Intellectual Property Rights in the WTO and Developing World*. The Hague: Kluwer Law International

2003. Implementing the TRIPS Agreement. In *Development, Trade, and the WTO: A Handbook*, eds. Bernard Hoekman, Aaditya Mattoo, and Philip English, 359–68. Washington, DC: The World Bank

Williamson, Oliver E. 1975. *Markets and Hierarchies. Analysis and Antitrust Implications: a Study in Economics of Internal Organization*. New York: Free Press

Williamson, Oliver, ed. 1983. *Markets and Hierarchies: Analysis and Anti-trust Implications*. New York: Free Press

Winham, Gilbert R. 1986. *International Trade and the Tokyo Round Negotiation*. Princeton: Princeton University Press

1998. Explanations of Developing Country Behaviour in the GATT Uruguay Round Negotiation. *World Competition and Law Review* (March):109–34

Wriggins, Howard. 1976. Up for Auction: Malta Bargains with Great Britain, 1971. In *The 50% Solution: How to Bargain Successfully with Hijackers, Strikers, Bosses, Oil Magnates, Arabs, Russians, and Other Worthy Opponents in This Modern World*, ed. I William Zartman. New Haven: Yale University Press

World Trade Organization. November 14, 2001. Declaration on the TRIPS Agreement and Public Health. Ministerial Conference, Doha, WT/MIN(01)/DEC/W2

Yoffie, David B. 1983. *Power and Protectionism: Strategies of the Newly Industrializing Countries*. New York: Columbia University Press

Zacher, Mark W. with Brent A. Sutton. 1996. *Governing Global Networks: International Regimes for Transportation and Communications*. Cambridge: Cambridge University Press

Zartman, I. William 1971. *The Politics of Trade Negotiations between Africa and the European Economic Community: The Weak Confront the Strong*. Princeton: Princeton University Press

Zartman, I. William, ed. 1987. *Positive Sum: Improving North-South Negotiations*. New Brunswick, NJ: Transaction Books

Zartman, I. William and Maureen R. Berman. 1982. *The Practical Negotiator*. New Haven, Conn: Yale University Press

Zartman, I. William and Jeffrey Z. Rubin. 2000. *Power and Negotiation*. Ann Arbor: University of Michigan Press

3   Reframing the issue: the WTO coalition on intellectual property and public health, 2001

John S. Odell and Susan K. Sell

Introduction

In November 2001 the World Trade Organization's ministerial conference in Doha adopted a Declaration on the WTO Agreement on Trade-related Aspects of Intellectual Property Rights (TRIPS) and Public Health. The process that led to this declaration is one of the most interesting episodes in recent international economic negotiations. A coalition lacking obvious power achieved significant, unexpected gains despite careful opposition from powerful transnational corporate firms and their home governments. This chapter seeks to explain this puzzling outcome and considers whether it suggests any generalizations that are likely to be useful in other cases.

Like all negotiation outcomes, this one has two dimensions: whether agreement was reached and the agreement's terms. Given the chasm between the two camps' perspectives, this agreement itself is surprising. Given the great power disparities, the gains of the developing countries are also surprising. These gains are defined relative to the status quo prior to the 2001 talks. The 1994 TRIPS agreement, whose origin is discussed in chapter 2 on the Uruguay Round, established obligations of WTO member states to comply with certain international rules protecting the rights of owners of patents and copyrights. Many national laws allow the government to violate patent rights under some conditions. Thus TRIPS too permitted countries to seize patents and issue compulsory licenses, for example authorizing a domestic firm to produce and

The authors are deeply indebted to participants in this negotiation and campaign who made time to speak to us on the understanding that their identities would not be divulged. Odell is grateful to USC, its School of International Relations, and its Center for International Studies for supporting his research, and to the Graduate Institute of International Studies, Geneva, for its hospitality while he conducted research in 2002. We benefited from comments on an earlier draft by Didier Chambovey, Heinz Hauser, Carlos Pérez del Castillo, Klaus Stegemann, an anonymous referee, other participants at our Geneva conference, and other members of our research team. None of these friends should be held responsible for use we made of their advice.

sell generic equivalents of a brand name drug without permission from the foreign inventor. Such licenses were subject to specified conditions including adequate remuneration to the right holder. Nevertheless, when Brazil, Thailand, and South Africa, facing the catastrophic HIV/AIDS pandemic, sought to avail themselves of these flexibilities, the United States and its global pharmaceutical firms brought intense coercive pressure to bear against their measures. Washington cited their obligations under the TRIPS agreement and implicitly threatened penalties against their trade. Although these complaints were eventually withdrawn, this pressure had a chilling effect on others who might contemplate using the exceptions.

In campaigning for the Doha Declaration a large coalition of developing countries sought explicit assurance that they would not be subject to WTO penalties under TRIPS for addressing health crises. Some of them probably also hoped to weaken the unpopular TRIPS agreement more generally. This bargaining coalition used what we call the mixed distributive strategy (defined in the introductory chapter). The United States, Switzerland, and their pharmaceutical firms defended against this initiative with a mixed distributive strategy of their own. They sought to ensure the narrowest possible interpretations of these flexibilities, lest developed country markets become flooded with cheaper generic versions of lucrative brand-name drugs. The final 2001 Declaration was much closer to the developing countries' initial position and, according to most observers, moved the WTO status quo significantly toward their objectives.[1]

This outcome was not readily predictable from simple international relations theories based on asymmetrical political or market power or political institutions. We conclude that this outcome was not inevitable because of exogenous conditions, but resulted instead from a sequence of rational choices that could also have gone in other directions. The negotiating process including those choices played a key role.

Our main specific point, stated as a possible generalization, will be that a developing country coalition seeking to claim value from dominant states in any regime will increase its gains if it captures the attention of the mass media in industrial countries and persuades the media to reframe the issue using a reference point more favorable to the coalition's position, other things equal. During the GATT's Uruguay Round, powerful transnational firms and their governments had framed intellectual property protection as a trade issue. They had argued that strong patent

---

[1] Abbott 2002; Charnovitz 2002; Garcia-Castrillon 2002; 't Hoen 2002; Love 2001; but see views of Elouardighi in Love 2001 and of Gillespie-White 2001.

protection promotes trade and investment for mutual benefit and that the alternative is tolerating piracy. More recently, TRIPS critics attempted to frame intellectual property protection as a public health issue, arguing that strong protection could be detrimental to public health provision. Reframing in this case was a tactic in a distributive strategy (for gaining at the expense of the United States and other property owners' positions.)[2] This case also suggests three additional hypotheses.

We use the single case study method, since our purposes are to interpret an interesting instance, to trace a process, and to generate hypotheses for wider investigation. This case of negotiation, like every case, was unique, and we do not claim that any instance can prove any theory decisively. Our purpose is not to test or prove a hypothesis. But uniqueness is not necessarily a barrier to generating new possible generalizations that are worthy of checking in other cases.

The next section lays out the reasoning behind four hypotheses. Subsequent sections use them to interpret this case through a chronological narrative. The chapter concludes by considering possible objections to these interpretations and looks beyond this case to others.

The main arguments

Our argument that outcomes will vary with reframing attempts builds upon the assumption – explained in the introductory essay – that human beings, including trade negotiators, legislators, newspaper editors, and constituents, make decisions using bounded rather than classic unbounded rationality. Their beliefs are influenced in part by the social milieus in which they move and are also malleable – subject to the influence of advocacy and persuasion, including framing tactics. People transform information into knowledge sometimes by employing different normative frames.[3] Frames have also been defined as "specific metaphors, symbolic representations and cognitive clues used to render or cast behavior and events in an evaluative mode and to suggest alternative modes of actions."[4]

WTO negotiators attempt to frame proposals to make them sound as favorable as possible. They attach rationales promising benefits and downplaying costs and they emphasize the negatives of rival proposals. Posing choices in this way calls for responses that are partly consequentialist and partly evaluative: the policy or agreement will have certain effects

---

[2] In other cases parties or mediators might promote a new frame to build support for an integrative outcome (in which all parties are better off or at least no worse off).
[3] Comor 20012001.   [4] Zald 19961996, 262.

and, at least implicitly, these effects will be good or bad. Explicitly ethical arguments can also be part of framing. According to Crawford, "ethical arguments are characterized by the use of prescriptive statements that rest on normative beliefs."[5] For example, patent rights should be upheld because it is wrong to steal. Alternatively, patent rights should be relaxed to prevent unnecessary deaths. Clearly these subjective frames of reference imply different policy responses. Much of the negotiation process is a contest of partisans trying to establish the dominant frame of reference.

Constructivist theorists of international relations offer insights that are consistent and can be integrated with a bounded rationality perspective. What constructivists refer to as "social construction" is also strategic.[6] "The concept of framing draws attention to the fact that power results not only from military and economic resources as Realists assume, but also, as constructivist approaches suggest, from the power to (re-)define and (de-)legitimize."[7] Thinking about preferences as malleable opens the door to more constructivist notions of argumentation[8] and persuasion.[9] The more a developing country coalition does to win this subjective contest to establish the dominant frame, the greater its negotiated gain will be, according to this first argument. Conditions when such attempts are less likely to succeed are discussed in the conclusion.

The second hypothesis is that in any regime, a developing country coalition will gain more if the coalition's internal bargaining prevents the group from fragmenting. This is part of a distributive strategy insofar as it is aimed at achieving maximum gain through credible threats. Outsiders with conflicting preferences can be expected to attempt to divide and rule, unless the coalition is regarded as insignificant. Whether any coalition remains united behind its common position depends, according to this hypothesis, on the negotiation process within the coalition. If a leader or others make offers or threats to fellow members to keep them from jumping ship, or if members offer arguments to persuade other members that their interests will be served better by rejecting these outside offers and threats, the group will gain more, other things equal, than groups that do not actively manage internal coalition dynamics.

The third hypothesis is simply that the larger the coalition, the less it will lose and the more it will gain, provided that it manages the fragmentation problem. In the WTO in particular, decisions are made by consensus. A consensus is defined to mean that every member either assents or remains silent. Even the weakest state has the theoretical authority to block a consensus, which could be a tactic for shifting the distributional outcome in

---

[5] Crawford 2002, 41.   [6] Sell and Prakash 2004; Finnemore and Sikkink 1998, 909–11.
[7] Joachim 2003, 269.   [8] Risse 2000.   [9] Crawford 2002; Müller in Fierke et al. 2001.

its favor. But alone, a weak state's credibility will be low, since all will be aware of its vulnerability to pressures inside and outside the organization and its need for agreement on other issues. Forming a coalition is a tactic supporting a distributive strategy because it increases credibility, and according to this hypothesis, credibility will rise with numbers, other things equal.

Fourth, a developing country coalition will probably gain more in any regime if it employs what we call a mixed-distributive strategy than if it adheres to a purely distributive one, other things equal.[10] The pure distributive strategy has been defined as a set of tactics that are functional for claiming value from others and defending against such claiming, when one party's goals are partly in conflict with those of others. It comes in both offensive and defensive variants. For delegates of a weak state surrounded by giants whose goals may conflict with theirs in part, it may often seem safest and most natural to act defensively to protect against claiming by the strong. Opening with a high demand, delaying concessions, and offering arguments to persuade others to make unrequited concessions are tactics belonging to a strict distributive strategy. It can at least buy time for learning more about one's interests, forming coalitions, and reducing or delaying losses. A stronger variant would also take others' issues hostage, threatening to block agreement on those issues if one's own position is not satisfied.

But the effect of any threat depends on its credibility, which is where the weak are at a disadvantage by definition. Giants generally have far better alternatives to an agreement, by virtue of their market size, technological lead, global corporations and strong domestic political institutions. A threat by the weak is less likely to be believed in general, at least considering these objective power indicators alone. And if a coalition forms but fragments prior to the end, an individual member will end up making concessions in return for nothing, unless its government is prepared to take the risks of blocking the entire WTO by itself. Having passed up opportunities to gain some concessions by offering others, it reaps only losses. If the coalition's threat is credible, another risk is that if the other parties also refuse to back down this will produce a stalemate with no gains.

But more generally, parties' objectives in international negotiations are almost never perfectly opposed. Often there are also opportunities for deals that will make multiple parties better off than before. Integrative tactics sometimes achieve gains by either discovering and exploiting common interests, or uncovering differences that can be exploited for mutual

[10] Odell 2000, chap. 7.

benefit, as in commercial trade itself. Adhering exclusively to distributive tactics works against this mutual-gains process. If party A refuses to engage in any integrative tactics, it encourages B and C to manipulate information, delay, take their own hostages, make threats, and develop alternatives to agreement with A. Party A discourages B and C from initiating integrative moves and fails to discover what gains for itself might be achieved through logrolling or reframing.[11] Even when A makes a credible threat and B and C are considering yielding, the odds of settlement would be higher, goes the argument, if A's strategy mixes in some integrative elements that give the others some gains to deliver to their frustrated constituents.[12] At least in common conditions if not all conditions, then, a developing country coalition is likely to gain more using a mixed-distributive strategy, one dominated by distributive tactics but diluted with integrative moves.

This chapter's analysis highlights choices that intervened during this process between initial preferences and power asymmetries on one hand and the outcome on the other, choices that were not fully determined by material conditions.

TRIPS, the AIDS pandemic, and a fight over access to medicines

The TRIPS agreement dramatically extended intellectual property rights and instituted a legally binding global regime for intellectual property protection. In the past, many countries had chosen not to offer patents for pharmaceuticals, in the interest of keeping down the costs of necessary medicines. The earlier multilateral agreement, the Paris Convention for the Protection of Industrial Property, offered generously permissive conditions for issuing compulsory licenses.[13] TRIPS changed this by requiring states to offer patent protection for pharmaceuticals and by restricting the conditions under which compulsory licenses could be granted. Many developing countries had previously adopted regulations stipulating that patents had to be "worked" in their countries, and mere importation of a patented item did not satisfy the requirement. Under TRIPS importation "counts" as working the patent, helping protect the owner against compulsory licensing. All these changes redounded to the benefit of the patent

---

[11] In a situation where the parties believe their objectives are completely opposed, we would not expect resort to integrative tactics since they can only expose the actor to exploitation. But any pair of states that value their long-term relationship have at least one common objective.

[12] This applies to powerful countries too. Quad negotiators also run the risk of forcing an impasse if they reject all integrative moves.

[13] Sell 1998, chap. 5.

holder and reflected the interests of the powerful lobby of global corporations based in the United States who sought a legally binding, enforceable global intellectual property agreement.[14] Pharmaceutical companies such as Merck and Pfizer actively participated in the process that led to TRIPS and had a significant hand in shaping the final provisions.

After the Uruguay Round these corporations pursued an aggressive campaign, with the help of the US Trade Representative (USTR), to ensure compliance with TRIPS, to speed its implementation prior to the negotiated deadlines, and in many countries to negotiate still higher levels of property protection (known as "TRIPS Plus").[15] This campaign resulted from several choices that could have gone otherwise.

One important component of the negotiating context was the rapidly spreading AIDS crisis. Responding to this crisis, Thailand and South Africa chose to make use of TRIPS articles 30 and 31 that permit compulsory licensing. When a state grants a compulsory license, rights to produce a product are licensed to another party without the patent holder's permission. Compulsory licensing allows states with manufacturing capacity to produce generic drugs that are more affordable. One of the conditions is that licenses must be used predominantly for supplying the home market rather than exporting.[16] Countries in the grip of the HIV/AIDS crisis also sought exceptions so that countries with generic capacity could export products produced under compulsory license, so the many countries with small domestic markets could also benefit from economies of scale.

In 1997 and 1998 after Thailand planned to produce a generic version of the AIDS drug ddI, US trade officials, on behalf of the US-based Pharmaceutical Research and Manufacturers Association (PhRMA), decided to threaten sanctions on core Thai exports. Thailand subsequently dropped its compulsory licensing plans.

In December 1997, South African President Nelson Mandela signed the South African Medicines and Medical Devices Regulatory Authority Act. The Medicines Act allowed the Minister of Health to authorize broad-based compulsory licensing to manufacture generic versions of HIV/AIDS drugs. Article 15c permitted parallel importing so that South Africa could take advantage of discriminatory pricing policies and import the cheapest available patented medicines. PhRMA was outraged and

---

[14] Sell 2003.
[15] "TRIPS Plus" refers to conditions that restrict options available under TRIPS, require particular forms of protection not mandated by TRIPS, or eliminate flexibilities afforded by TRIPS. See Drahos 2001.
[16] Maskus 2000, 178.

wrote to USTR Charlene Barshefsky and Commerce Secretary William Daley denouncing the South African Act.[17]

In February 1998, forty-two members of the Pharmaceutical Manufacturers of South Africa (mainly local licensees of global PhRMA) chose to challenge the Act's legality in Pretoria High Court. They maintained that the Medicines Act was unconstitutional because it violated constitutional guarantees of property rights.[18] They also argued that it violated TRIPS by authorizing uncompensated compulsory licensing. PhRMA saw South Africa as a bell-wether. It is PhRMA's most important African market, "where all the patents are,"[19] with 41 percent of the region's GNP, and a large population of HIV/AIDS patients. It also has generic manufacturing capacity and economies of scale. PhRMA feared South Africa's potential for becoming a competitive generic supplier undercutting PhRMA's markets. PhRMA also objected to parallel importing as "downright dangerous," not only risking public safety with counterfeit medicines, but also diverting low-priced medicines from low-income to high-income countries and thus diminishing profits available to finance new research.[20]

In its February 1998 submission to USTR, PhRMA recommended that South Africa be named a "Priority Foreign Country" and argued that the South African law posed a direct challenge to the achievements of the Uruguay Round.[21] In response, the USTR placed South Africa on the section 301 "watchlist" and urged the South African government to repeal its law. Throughout 1998, US government pressure intensified. In June 1998 the White House announced a suspension of South Africa's duty-free treatment under the US Generalized System of Preferences program.[22] While hindsight is 20:20, this aggressive campaign actually hastened the mobilization of opposition to it.

Northern NGOs, Northern attention, and reframing

In this case, it was Northern non-governmental organizations (NGOs) that chose to spearhead an effort to gain attention in Northern mass media. NGOs could have spent their efforts on other issues. States'

[17] *Washington Post*, May 21, 2000, A1.
[18] Visser in Warner et al. 2002, 721–22. *Pharmaceutical Manufacturers' Association of South Africa* v. *President of the Republic of South Africa*, Case No. 4183/98 (High Court of South Africa), available at http://www.cptech.org/ip/health/sa/pharmasuit.html.
[19] Love in Warner et al. 2002, 704.   [20] Finston in Warner et al. 2002, 727.
[21] Submission of the Pharmaceutical Research and Manufacturers of America for the 'Special 301' Report on Intellectual Property Barriers. February 23, 1998. Obtained from PhRMA and on file with authors.
[22] Bond 1999, 771.

Coalition on TRIPS and public health 2001 — page 93

exogenous material interests alone did not generate this element of the process. These organizations attempted to reframe the issue by advancing a different reference point for evaluating TRIPS. In the 1980s TRIPS advocates had framed it as an alternative to tolerating piracy of private property, and in that frame TRIPS looked like a clear improvement. Many developing country governments opposed adding these rules to the WTO, since they would shift money from South to North. But the United States and the European Union made TRIPS an inseparable part of the Uruguay Round package, and opting out of the whole would have had devastating trade consequences.

Now the NGOs compared TRIPS to a different reference point – saving the lives of poor people suffering from HIV/AIDS. In this new frame TRIPS as it applied to medicines was far more vulnerable to objection. The critics argued that medicines that could save or prolong lives were available, but their makers were refusing to sell them at marginal cost, choosing to let people die in order to hold up profit margins. Not only that, but Washington was also trying to use the WTO to discourage countries from exercising the exception to save lives. The moderate version of the argument acknowledged a public interest in protecting intellectual property rights in general but insisted that in a conflict, health must come first. While TRIPS' architects never intended for the agreement to lead to unnecessary deaths, post-1994 pressure on Thailand, South Africa, and Brazil provided opportunities for opponents to claim exactly that.

After 1997 Northern mass media greatly expanded their coverage of the AIDS crisis in Africa. Figure 3.1 reports a rough measure of this increase in international media attention.

Progressive activists who had always opposed TRIPS and the WTO astutely recognized popular attention to this crisis as an opportunity to force a wedge into this trade regime and perhaps discredit it more generally. The NGO campaign contributed to a sharp spike in media discussion of possible connections between patent protection and health problems in 2001 (Figure 3.2). As a result, Northern publics heard of TRIPS mostly for the first time, and heard of it framed as a threat to public health.

Critics used US Vice President Albert Gore's nascent presidential campaign in the summer of 1999 as an occasion to draw attention to the issues. Gore had been maintaining a PhRMA-friendly stance in part to attract PhRMA campaign dollars. NGOs called the AIDS Coalition to Unleash Power (ACT UP) Philadelphia and the Ralph Nader affiliated Consumer Project on Technology (CPT) repeatedly disrupted Gore's campaign appearances with noisemakers and banners that read "Gore's Greed Kills." These stunts gained media attention.

94   *John S. Odell and Susan K. Sell*

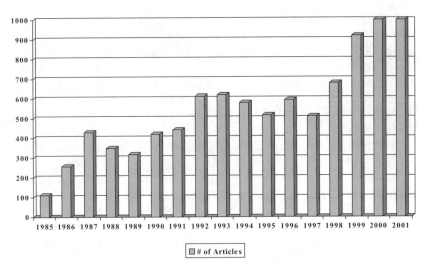

Figure 3.1: Number of Articles in Major Newspapers on "HIV" and "Africa," 1985 – 2001
Source: Sell and Prakash 2004. Articles as reported in Lexis-Nexis.

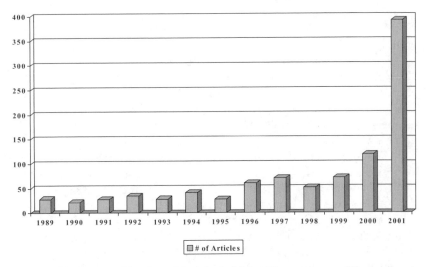

Figure 3.2: Number of Articles in Major Newspapers on "Patents" and "Public Health," 1989 – 2001
Source: Sell and Prakash 2004. Articles as reported in Lexis-Nexis.

The political results were nearly immediate. "The Clinton Administration withdrew two years of objections to the new South African law in June, the same week that Gore declared his intent to run for president and AIDS activists began tormenting his campaign."[23] In September 1999 the United States removed South Africa from its 301 watchlist. NGOs actively provided assistance to the South African government in the continuing private PhRMA litigation; for example, Love drafted some important affidavits on its behalf. Meanwhile the NGO coalition was growing and included, among others, Health Action International, OXFAM, Médecins Sans Frontières, ACT UP Paris, and Treatment Action Campaign.

South Africa remained steadfast in its refusal to alter its law despite the PhRMA litigation. The government had been careful to investigate the bill's legality under TRIPS prior to enacting it. During the trial it came to light that article 15c was based on a "draft legal text produced by the WIPO (the World Intellectual Property Organization) Committee of Experts," which undermined PhRMA's claims that the law was inconsistent with international law.[24] The South African case underscored that developing countries would need clarification of the interpretation of TRIPS flexibilities for public health, so that they could proceed confidently without the specter of political and legal challenge.[25] For Northern politicians the visible protests also raised the domestic political costs of supporting PhRMA's position.

Brazil also exercised leadership in the access to medicines issue. Despite relentless pressure from the United States and its pharmaceutical firms, in 1996 Brazil chose to pass a patent law that provided that "local working" of a patent is required for a patent holder to enjoy patent rights in Brazil. TRIPS stipulates that importation of a patented item constitutes "working", but Brazil's law states that only local production, not importation, satisfies the working requirement. Brazil's law permits the government to issue compulsory licenses for goods that are not manufactured locally within three years of receiving patent protection. Brazil maintained that the threat of compulsory licensing had helped it negotiate reasonable drug prices with global pharmaceutical companies; it used this threat effectively against Roche and Merck in the quest for affordable AIDS drugs. PhRMA saw the provision as a threat in so far as it could inspire other developing countries with pharmaceutical manufacturing capacities to follow suit and insist upon an interpretation of TRIPS Article 27(1) that would limit the rights they enjoyed on the basis of importation.[26]

[23] *Washington Post*, May 21, 2000, A1.   [24] 't Hoen 2002, 31.
[25] 't Hoen 2002.
[26] The issue in this dispute was the "working" requirement and not the separate health exception in Brazilian law.

Developing countries looked to Brazil as a beacon of hope in strategies to combat the HIV/AIDS crisis.[27] Brazil provided anti-retroviral therapy free to HIV/AIDS patients as a matter of public policy. For example the Brazilian generic manufacturer Far Manguinhos produced a version of the anti-retroviral Nevirapine that reduced mother-to-child transmission of HIV.[28] The Brazilian program dramatically cut the rates of infection and death from HIV/AIDS. The government stood firm in the face of US challenges. In February 2000 at the behest of PhRMA, USTR petitioned the opening of a panel against Brazil in the WTO for alleged violation of TRIPS Article 27(1) on importation and working the patent.

The Brazilian government mobilized extensive NGO support in defense of its policies, and the *New York Times* ran a magazine cover story praising Brazilian HIV/AIDS policy.[29] Brazil publicly offered to "support developing countries to help them increase manufacturing capacity by transferring technology and know-how. NGOs feared that the US action could have a negative effect on other countries' ability to accept Brazil's offer of assistance."[30] But Brazil's refusal to back down and the groundswell of support led the US ultimately to withdraw the case in June 2001. As US Trade Representative Robert Zoellick stated, "Litigating this dispute before a WTO dispute panel has not been the most constructive way to address our differences, especially since Brazil has never actually used the provision at issue."[31]

Brazil's policies and its commitment to extensive generic production helped to create a market for high quality generic drugs. The government had purchased HIV/AIDS drugs from Indian, Brazilian, Korean, and Chinese generic drug suppliers. The resulting competition between suppliers drastically reduced drug prices. In just three years the per-kilo price of 3TC, "the most patented anti-retroviral drug in Africa," dropped from $10,000 in 1999 to $700 in 2002.[32]

The Indian generic drug manufacturer Cipla was also an important player in altering the market. In September 2000 at an international meeting in Brussels, Cipla's CEO Dr. Yusuf Hamied "publicly stated the prices at which he could provide anti-retrovirals to developing countries . . . The pharmaceutical executives of major companies 'listened agog to Hamied's matter-of-fact price list for chemical equivalents of

[27] *New York Times* (Sunday magazine), January 28, 2001. Viewed on July 12, 2003 at www.nytimes.com/library/magazine/home/20010128mag.aids.html.
[28] Drahos with Braithwaite 2002, 9.
[29] *New York Times* (Sunday magazine) January 28, 2001.
[30] 't Hoen 2002, 33; Viana 2002, 311.
[31] *WTO Reporter*, June 26, 2001, viewed on June 6, 2003 at http://cptech.org/ip/health/c/brazil/bna6262001.html.
[32] Love in Warner 2002, 700.

Glaxo's Epivir, Boehringer's Nevirapine and Bristol-Myers' Zerit.'"[33] CPT and Cipla collaborated to make a dramatic offer; in early 2001 Hamied announced that Cipla would provide anti-retroviral drugs to Médecins Sans Frontières for $350 a year, or about $1 a day per dose. The February 7, 2001 announcement, featured on the front page of the *New York Times*, "shocked the world, and completely transformed the global debate on treatment for HIV in Africa. At this price it was clear that many would die needlessly, if steps were not taken to remove barriers to access to medicines."[34]

Changes in market conditions altered the firms' best alternative to negotiated agreement (BATNA). The Brazilian strategy created a large market, and generic competition spurred further price reductions. These market changes highlighted the benefits of pursuing developing countries' strategies to address public health emergencies, and fueled the increasing characterization of PhRMA as heartless and profit-hungry. PhRMA reacted by offering to supply certain drugs for free or at reduced prices to sub-Saharan Africa.

They also responded to this transnational campaign by repeating their original arguments, countering their critics' claims, and making another tactical retreat. Their dominant argument all along had been that enforcement of drug patents globally was essential to the process of discovering new medicines. They claimed that the cost of inventing a new drug averaged more than $400 million.[35] Pricing these products at only the marginal cost of producing each new pill would fail to recover development expenses and thus drain the well. The basic reason for all patents was to create an incentive for invention, in the public interest. It was not simply a matter of private greed. Undoubtedly these managers, like counterparts in other industries, resented companies in other countries copying and selling their inventions without compensating them.

The firms disputed critics' efforts to blame patents and TRIPS for poor people's lack of access to needed drugs. Many developing countries did not provide patent protection and under TRIPS were exempt from this requirement until 2005. India, to take a major example, did not enforce drug patents, a large generic industry produced copies of anti-retroviral drugs, and yet thousands of people were dying of AIDS every year in India. Obviously poor people face many obstacles to good health, from lack of clean water to lack of skilled caregivers and hospitals to the stigma that many societies attach to AIDS victims in particular. But the

---

[33] Drahos with Braithwaite 2002, 9.
[34] E-mail message from James Love, March 26, 2002 (on file with authors).
[35] Grabowski 2002, 851–52.

medicines campaign forced PhRMA to become defensive about intellectual property enforcement and its implications for the HIV/AIDS crisis. In May 2001, PhRMA posted a new item on its web site explaining all the activities it was undertaking to help poor countries facing the HIV/AIDS pandemic. PhRMA further argued that the WTO should instead focus on reducing developing countries' high tariffs and corruption in government procurement, which both raise drug prices there.[36] The firms objected that the NGOs were distorting the patent issue for their own political purposes by blowing it out of proportion. More quietly they complained that governments like Brazil and India were simply reflecting the economic self-interest of their own producers.

Meanwhile, however, in March 2001, PhRMA also chose to end its legal case against the South African government. PhRMA claimed it had always preferred a negotiated settlement and claimed victory in so far as South Africa pledged to abide by TRIPS and its own Constitution.[37] In view of the unanticipated political backlash, however, it was difficult not to see this suit as a major blunder from the firms' own standpoint. Choosing to file and aggressively pursue this case, even after USTR had backed off, exacerbated their public relations problem.

Forming a large Geneva coalition with a mixed distributive strategy

The US challenge to South Africa's medicines law catalyzed the formation of a bargaining coalition in the WTO to seek gains at the Doha ministerial.[38] First WIPO experts had advised that the proposed legislation was consistent with TRIPS, and then the US had said it was not. The African Group decided to lead a coalition seeking a ministerial interpretation in its favor. The African Group was a standing organization of forty-one WTO member states that had defended common positions in WTO talks since 1999. In 2001 Zimbabwe chaired the African Group as well as the WTO TRIPS Council. In April Zimbabwean Ambassador Boniface Chidyausiku requested a special TRIPS Council session on access to medicines. Chidyausiku argued that "the WTO could no longer ignore the access to medicines issue, an issue that was being actively debated outside the WTO but not within it."[39] Zimbabwe had led important

---

[36] *International Trade Reporter*, October 25, 2001, 1687.
[37] European Federation of Pharmaceutical Industry Associations. Pharmaceutical Industry Welcomes Amicable Settlement Reached by All Parties in South African Court Case: "Patients are the Real Winners." Press release, April 19, 2001, Brussels, viewed at www.efpia.org (archives) on June 7, 2003.
[38] Interview with an African leader of the coalition, Geneva, November 4, 2002.
[39] 't Hoen 2002, 38.

access to medicines efforts in the World Health Organization (WHO) and had been deeply involved in the issues at least since 1998.[40] Quickly other developing countries signed on and eventually the coalition numbered sixty member states – far too many to be ignored if they remained united. Brazil had been pressing the issue in the WHO and the UN Commission on Human Rights and became a leader of this WTO coalition especially at the end. India was particularly active at the technical level.[41] Brazil and India both had sizeable generic drug industries that stood to gain export revenue from free parallel imports. Other members included Pakistan, Bangladesh, Indonesia, Thailand, Sri Lanka, the Philippines, and eleven other Latin American and Caribbean states. Norway and the Netherlands also provided tangible support to the coalition. The TRIPS Council agreed to hold a meeting in June.

The coalition chose to aspire to a goal that it felt was feasible. At the outset, one coalition diplomat recalled, "We did not immediately visualize what we should demand, our objective. One possible outcome was a [ministerial] declaration but we were not sure what its content should be."[42] There was some thought of attempting to amend TRIPS formally, perhaps article 8, 27 or 31. But this would have required ratification by national legislatures including the American. "The price would have been pretty high, so little energy was spent on that."[43] If this coalition had chosen a more radical negotiating objective for Doha, its gains might well have been smaller, like those of the Like Minded Group of countries discussed in chapter 4.

The coalition also actively sought help in crafting its position. Before the June meeting, the African Group requested assistance from the Geneva-based International Centre for Trade and Sustainable Development (ICTSD) in preparation for the TRIPS Council meeting. ICTSD hosted an informal roundtable on TRIPS, biological resources and public health for the African negotiators based in Geneva. ICTSD also invited several experts, including NGO representatives, to speak about the topics.[44]

On the eve of the TRIPS Council meeting, Oxfam, Médecins Sans Frontières, and Malaysia's NGO, Third World Network, held a press conference and issued the following statement:

Governments need a permanent guarantee that they can put public health and the welfare of their citizens before patent rights, without having to face the kind

[40] Sell 2003, 148.
[41] Interview with a participating NGO representative, Geneva, November 13, 2002.
[42] Interview with a Latin American member of the coalition, October 21, 2002.
[43] Ibid.   [44] ICTSD 2001.

of legal pressures or threat of trade sanctions experienced by South Africa and
Brazil . . . People all over the world will be watching whether WTO member
countries meet the challenge of tackling the global health crisis, and demonstrate
their commitment to the prevention of further unnecessary deaths.[45]

In the TRIPS Council process the coalition's actions reflected an offensive distributive negotiating strategy. It was distributive in the sense of
claiming value from others' positions and offensive in the sense of representing the demandeur rather than the defender. In the June 20 meeting
Zimbabwe's delegation presented the Africa Group Statement proposing
that "members issue a special declaration on the TRIPS Agreement and
access to medicines at the Ministerial Conference in Qatar, affirming that
nothing in the TRIPs Agreement should prevent Members from taking
measures to protect public health."[46] The African Group plus Barbados, Bolivia, Brazil, the Dominican Republic, Ecuador, Honduras, India,
Indonesia, Jamaica, Pakistan, Paraguay, the Philippines, Peru, Sri Lanka,
Thailand, and Venezuela presented the lead paper.[47] It documented in a
"detailed and concrete way the difficulties that were created for Members
by various provisions of the TRIPS Agreement."[48] It included specific
concerns and presented concrete and detailed remedies.

For its part, the United States was caught somewhat off-guard. According to Abbott, "the US and the like-minded group (Australia, Canada,
Japan, and Switzerland), as well as the WTO Secretariat, appeared to
have underestimated the intense concern among developing Members
on this set of issues." The United States and its supporters' response can
be described as defensively distributive, advocating "policy positions that
sought to discount the fact that problems existed."[49] The US position
echoed PhRMA's standard response that poverty, not patents, are the
barrier to access. The United States focused on inadequate health infrastructure in developing countries and urged a "comprehensive approach"
to deal with health problems. The TRIPS Council agreed to reconvene
in July for further discussion.

At a July 25 follow-up meeting, the African Group presented a "Statement by the Africa Group: TRIPS and Public Health Informal Session
of the WTO TRIPS Council", expressing its displeasure with the US
efforts to deflect attention away from the role that TRIPS might play in
obstructing access to medicines. Referring to the US and like-minded
group's statement of June 20 urging a "comprehensive approach" the
statement read:

---

[45] Ibid., 63.   [46] Africa Group Statement in ICTSD 2001, 47.
[47] IP/C/W/296 in ICTSD 2001, 50–57.
[48] Abbott 2002, 481–82.   [49] Ibid., 482–83.

It is not within the mandate of the TRIPS Council to talk of the infrastructure in different countries, in terms of hospitals, doctors and nurses. Nor will [it] be useful for this forum to discuss the global funds and other initiatives for the purchase and distribution of medicines. These issues belong and are being addressed in their appropriate fora and institutions . . . We must be clear about the mandate and objective of our exercise in this forum; that is, to examine the various provisions of the TRIPS Agreement and issues of public health and access to medicines, and most importantly, to ensure that the implementation of the TRIPS Agreement does not amount to an obstacle to the promotion of access to affordable medicines and the protection of public health.[50]

Throughout the summer the coalition continued to seek the assistance of various experts in preparing their proposals. It worked on its positions in collaboration with a supportive World Health Organization, NGOs, and a number of legal and economic experts whose presentations were coordinated through the Quaker United Nations Office, the latter providing a venue for several important meetings, and posting relevant expert papers on its web site.[51] Developing country delegations made use of this research in preparing their proposals.[52]

By the time the coalition tabled its long joint proposal for a special ministerial declaration[53] on September 19, it was focused on its core negotiating objective. Coalition members wanted a separate declaration because they feared the issue would get too little attention if it were folded into the main declaration.[54] Paragraph 1 proposed that ministers establish the sweeping principle that "nothing in the TRIPS Agreement shall prevent Members from taking measures to protect public health." Its authors modeled this language on existing TRIPS provisions such as article 73 (b) that established a general exception for any measures a member feels are necessary for its security interests.[55] The Brazilian delegation argued consistently to their coalition colleagues that getting agreement to this first paragraph should be the top negotiating priority.[56] The objective was a political declaration that "was not legally binding but would have a legal effect."[57] It was expected to tip WTO panels and the Appellate Body to favor health goals when they were asked to apply the rules in particular disputes.

The proposal included numerous other technical demands as well, all of which would have tipped the regime more in favor of developing country health authorities and against foreign pharmaceutical firms. Several of these greater technical demands might have resulted from logrolling

[50] ICTSD 2001, 59.   [51] http://www.quno.org.
[52] Interview, African coalition delegate, Geneva, November 4, 2002.   [53] WTO 2001a.
[54] Interview, African coalition delegate, Geneva, November 4, 2002.   [55] Ibid.
[56] Interview, Latin American delegate, Geneva, October 21, 2002.   [57] Ibid.

among coalition members at the early stage. Or they might have been intended from the outset as elements of a mixed strategy, items that could be dropped during the endgame in return for US concessions on the top priority.[58] One provision would extend the transition period by another five years before developing countries would be required to provide patent protection. One of the most important specified that "a compulsory license issued by a Member may be given effect by another Member." This rule would seem to authorize India and Brazil to export generics to African countries lacking generic producers, overriding the TRIPS Article 31f qualification to the contrary. Paragraphs 4 and 8 of the proposal also look like ambitious efforts to amend TRIPS at Doha, in effect.

The same day a counter-coalition of the United States, Switzerland, Canada, Japan, and Australia tabled an alternative response to the public pressure. Objecting that the first proposal was too sweeping, their brief general draft[59] for the preamble of the main ministerial declaration would have had WTO ministers recognize the problem of poor peoples' access to medicines to treat pandemics, affirm in general the appropriateness of using the flexibilities already in TRIPS, and also affirm that the existing agreement is part of the solution, on the familiar argument that patent protection is a necessary incentive for research and development. This language was narrower in all respects. It restricted the issue to access to medicines, maintaining that language extending to public health in general "could be used to justify broad exemptions to TRIPS rules beyond what is needed to address health emergencies."[60] It referred to medicines needed to treat pandemics such as AIDS, malaria and tuberculosis only and not other diseases. And it would not have widened any exceptions or settled any disputes over the rules' interpretation.[61]

The European Union made an effort to play the mediator on this issue. They first proposed an alternative option to the United States, Japan, and Canada, who rejected it as too large a departure from TRIPS. The EU continued trying to offer an alternative to the US position, which probably encouraged the developing countries and made the US–Swiss coalition weaker than it could have been, according to one participant.[62]

The September 11 terrorist attacks in the United States added a dramatic change to the negotiating context. This context became significant because of the way in which negotiators actively linked it to the process.

---

[58] Interviews, WTO secretariat and delegates, November 2002.   [59] WTO 2001b.
[60] *International Trade Reporter*, October 25, 2001, 1686.
[61] *Inside US Trade*, September 28, 2001, 11.
[62] Interview with an EU official, Geneva, November 13, 2002; written communication from a Swiss official, January 2004.

In October, in what was presumed to be another terrorist attack, pow-
dered anthrax had been sent through the US mail, killing several postal
and media workers. Buildings on Capitol Hill were evacuated when traces
of anthrax were found. Some leaders in the US and Canadian governments discussed issuing compulsory licenses for ciprofloxacine (Cipro)
to ensure adequate emergency supplies of the drug. Ultimately these
countries negotiated steep price discounts with Bayer, just as Brazil had
done with Roche and Merck. The irony was lost on no one. Developing
country delegations also raised North American hypocrisy privately with
US negotiators in Doha face to face. One reported asking, "Why are ten
lives sufficient to [break a patent in your country] but one million lives
in developing countries not sufficient? What is the difference?"[63] Deftly
bringing this exogenous development into the negotiating process, the
coalition helped to shift the terms of the debate.

The coalition also faced, and effectively resisted, efforts to divide and
conquer. The United States attempted to tempt some of its members
with side payments. In the fall USTR Zoellick made two lesser offers to
subgroups presumably in the hope of splitting the coalition and bury-
ing their proposal. He offered to extend TRIPS transition periods for
pharmaceutical products until 2016 for least developed countries. This
would have practical and legal benefits for those countries but would do
nothing to increase supplies of medicines where they were lacking. And
it would not apply to Brazil, India, or eighteen African countries including the largest and most active in the WTO. Second, Zoellick offered to
observe a moratorium on TRIPS dispute actions against all sub-Saharan
African countries for measures they took to address AIDS.[64] The African
Group was the most prominent demandeur and this would address its
most pressing worry. If it accepted, the Bush administration could safely
veto the more sweeping coalition proposal, leaving exposed the Asian
and Latin American members including India and Brazil, and Egypt,
who had substantial pharmaceutical industries and domestic markets.[65]
In a boundedly rational world it was not obvious these moves would fail.

In Geneva, however, no coalition ambassador broke ranks. Ambassador Stuart Harbinson of Hong Kong–China, chair of the WTO General
Council, tried informally to craft a compromise and made some headway.
But neither side was willing to accept the other's language for the most
important paragraph. On October 27 Harbinson issued a single negotiating text on TRIPS and health that presented two options in square
brackets. Option 1 favored by the southern coalition read as follows:

[63] Interview, Latin American WTO negotiator, London, December 19, 2002.
[64] *International Trade Reporter*, October 25, 2001, 1687; *Financial Times*, October 25, 2001.
[65] *International Trade Reporter*, October 25, 2001, 1687; *Financial Times*, October 25, 2001.

Nothing in the TRIPS Agreement shall prevent Members from taking measures to protect public health. Accordingly, while reiterating our commitment to the TRIPS Agreement, we affirm that the Agreement shall be interpreted and implemented in a manner supportive of WTO Members' right to protect public health and, in particular, to ensure access to medicines for all.

In this connection, we affirm the right of WTO Members to use, to the full, the provisions in the TRIPS Agreement which provide flexibility for this purpose.

Option 2, favored by the United States and its supporters read as follows:

We affirm a Member's ability to use, to the full, the provisions in the TRIPS Agreement which provide flexibility to address public health crises such as HIV/AIDS and other pandemics, and to that end, that a Member is able to take Measures necessary to address these public health crises, in particular to secure affordable access to medicines. Further, we agree that this Declaration does not add to or diminish the rights and obligations of Members provided in the TRIPS Agreement. With a view to facilitating the use of this flexibility by providing greater certainty, we agree on the following clarifications.[66]

As before, Option 2 narrowed the declaration, and the phrase "does not add to or diminish the rights and obligations of Members" sharply circumscribed any possible legal effects. This language had been borrowed from the WTO's Dispute Settlement rules.[67]

Celso Amorim, the Brazilian ambassador, stayed focused on the coalition's core negotiating objective and made clear that Brazil and the coalition would prefer no declaration to one that excluded their sweeping general principle. Amorim had had long experience negotiating over TRIPS issues from the Uruguay Round and bilaterally with the United States, and he moved into a leading role for the coalition.[68] He reasoned that with all the popular attention to the issue in the North, the coalition would have a better chance with ministers at the political level than with Geneva ambassadors. He did not object to both options appearing in the single negotiating text, but threatened that if Harbinson omitted the coalition's version, Brazil would reopen the entire Doha package.[69] Evidently the threat was credible. Harbinson sent both to Doha.

The endgame in Doha

The 146 ministers got down to business on November 10, 2001. In Qatar, coalition negotiators fought off splitting tactics and maintained their unity, but also mixed some integrative tactics into their mostly distributive strategy to break the impasse and close the deal. The intense

---

[66] WTO 2001c.   [67] 't Hoen 2002, 42.
[68] Interviews with delegates and Secretariat officials, Geneva, November 2002.
[69] Interview with Celso Amorim, London, December 19, 2002.

activity surrounding the medicines issue prior to the November Doha meeting prompted Mike Moore, WTO Director General, to declare at the start of the meeting that "the TRIPS and health issue could be the deal-breaker for a new trade round."[70] Brazil signaled its determination by bringing its Health Minister (who was also a candidate for President) to participate; this was the first time that a developing country health minister had ever participated in a trade negotiation.[71] Moore appointed Luis Ernesto Derbez of Mexico to serve as mediator to facilitate a settlement on the TRIPS/health issue, in parallel with other mediators working on five other outstanding issues.

Just before going to Doha, the United States invited the African ministers to Washington, where they were again offered the moratorium. Reportedly Kenya's Trade Minister Nicholas Biwott, one of the most influential African leaders, was tempted to accept. But internal bargaining prevented him from defecting from the coalition. Biwott was serving at the time as head of another WTO coalition, the African–Caribbean–Pacific States. Geneva diplomats reportedly led by Zimbabwe had persuaded the ACP group to decline the moratorium offer – it did not apply to the Caribbean – and hold out for the more sweeping principle. This made it awkward for Biwott to take a different position, and in Doha he stayed within the fold.[72]

In Doha Derbez called a meeting in which some twenty-five countries participated. NGO representatives were busy outside the room. By now the US attitude reportedly had changed. Having failed to open any cracks in this large coalition and preferring an overall WTO deal, Zoellick chose to fall back and negotiate on the basis of Option 1[73] over the objections of his pharmaceutical industry. On the third day the United States and Brazil, representing the two camps, reached final agreement on language. The declaration included a slightly amended version of the coalition's top principle:

We agree that the TRIPS agreement does not and should not prevent Members from taking measures to protect public health. Accordingly, while reiterating our commitment to the TRIPS agreement, we affirm that the agreement can and should be interpreted and implemented in a manner supportive of WTO Members' right to protect public health and, in particular, to promote access to medicines for all.[74]

It affirmed members' rights to issue compulsory licenses and the freedom to determine grounds for such licenses. US efforts to limit the

---

[70] 't Hoen 2002, 42.   [71] Viana 2002.
[72] Interviews, two WTO ambassadors, Geneva and London, November and December 2002.
[73] Abbott 2002, 488; interview, London, 2002.   [74] WTO 2001d.

declaration's applicability to "pandemics" and "crises" failed; even the title of the declaration underscores the developing countries' preferred, broader reference to "public health." The United States agreed to drop the language proposed to limit the declaration's legal effects while still giving least developed members a ten-year extension of the deadline by which they must provide patent protection for pharmaceuticals.

The coalition, in exchange for this fallback favoring its top priority, agreed to fall back from several of its other demands, mixing integrative steps into their strategy. None of the most ambitious ideas in their formal proposal appeared in the final declaration. Perhaps the most significant retreat was to agree to postpone until 2002 discussion of how to resolve the problem of poor countries lacking drug production capacity. One coalition leader later said that at that time neither side's thinking about how to solve it was well advanced.

The outcome, the Doha Declaration on TRIPS and Public Health, reflects the coalition's core demand. "Our expectations were fully met," said Paolo Teixeira, Brazil's top AIDS official. "Even six months ago, this was unthinkable."[75] The Brazilian delegation was satisfied with its status as "soft law" that can guide dispute settlement panels.[76] Despite PhRMA's claims to the contrary,[77] it is difficult to imagine that a declaration that it fought so hard to prevent was a gain for PhRMA.

Of course events continued to unfold after the Doha conference, but at the time of writing it was too early to assess further any net effects of this case and later events. Almost nothing had been agreed in the multilateral round that Doha launched. The one definitive result to date was an August 2003 deal in the TRIPS Council to implement the public health declaration's paragraph 6. This deal provided authority for any member state that lacked sufficient medicine manufacturing capacity to import needed medicines from any other member state. This waiver of Article 31(f) was not restricted to any list of diseases or set of countries, as the United States had sought, but it did carry a set of procedural requirements, justified as needed to prevent diversion of low-cost medicines to more lucrative markets.[78] This decision was to be replaced

[75] *Wall Street Journal*, November 14, 2001.
[76] Interview with a WTO ambassador, London, December 19, 2002. The eventual value of this declaration will be determined as disputes are decided and policies and practices adjust. For diverse early assessments, see Abbott 2002: 489; Charnovitz 2002; García-Castrillon 2002; Horlick 2002; Schott 2002; 't Hoen 2002: 43–44; Wolff 2002.
[77] Pharmaceutical Research and Manufacturers of America (PhRMA), press release, WTO Doha Declaration Reaffirms Value of Intellectual Property Protection, November 14, 2001, viewed on July 7, 2003 at www.PhRMA.org/press/newsreleases/2001-11-14.310.phtml. Also see Rozek and Rainey 2001.
[78] The decision of the WTO Council on TRIPS is at IP/C/W/405. See Matthews 2004 for commentary.

by a permanent TRIPS amendment to be adopted by 2004. No such permanent amendment had been agreed by then, and developing countries were complaining that the 2003 arrangement was proving too cumbersome to solve the problem.

Advocates hoped the 2001 declaration might improve poor countries' leverage when negotiating with multinational pharmaceutical firms over prices during emergencies. During the following two years, observers did note some developing country successes in price negotiations.[79] Advocates hoped the declaration would encourage governments to exercise their rights and discourage the US from filing complaints when they do. But no legal disputes had yet shown how panels or the Appellate Body would use the declaration's soft-law guidance. And some critics worried that Washington was turning to bilateral free-trade-area negotiations and possibly investment treaties outside the WTO to shift intellectual property rules further in favor of owners at the expense of public health in developing countries,[80] at least for countries that signed such agreements. Most of these agreements also had yet to be tested.

In any case, in 2001 all sides agreed that the Doha declaration would be and was a significant change. The developing country coalition was clearly better off than before 2001 and it gained more than the Like Minded Group, whose outcome is described in the next chapter.

Conclusions

One possible objection to the preceding analysis might be that the outcome could be explained without referring to the negotiation process at all, by referring instead to prior preferences of the players, their relative power, or the nature of the international institution. We began, however, by showing that this outcome was surprising to such a perspective. If the dominant powers' preferences had been sufficient to determine the outcome, there would have been no WTO declaration at all, or one expressing sympathy for victims while reaffirming the status quo without qualification.

Any attempt to explain this outcome without reference to the negotiation process would miss much of the answer. We have highlighted several choice points where boundedly rational players could well have chosen differently, in which case the collective interaction probably would have proceeded along a different path. Developing country governments could easily have spent their extremely scarce trade negotiating resources on

---

[79] Benvenisti and Downs 2004.
[80] Correa 2004; Benvenisti and Downs 2004; Drahos 2004.

other issues. Obviously there would have been no WTO declaration if they had not proposed one, and almost certainly none had its supporters not organized a governmental coalition to promote it. The global firms could have chosen not to file complaints against Nelson Mandela and developing countries on three continents. If they had not, their NGO opponents probably would not have mobilized against them as widely in the world, as quickly and as noisily. And without the public reframing campaign, the coalition probably would not have had the domestic Northern support to achieve a WTO declaration as early as 2001. During the Geneva preparations, the developing country coalition could easily have been reluctant to threaten to hold the entire WTO round hostage – a relatively bold distributive tactic. If this coalition had not threatened or if it had been smaller and less credible, the mediator would have been more likely to lean toward the US position in drafting the single negotiating text that framed the discussions in Doha. If this coalition had not actively managed its internal dynamics as late as Doha, it could well have fragmented as the Like Minded Group did. In that scenario if all else had been as it was, the health outcome probably would have been lesser changes providing more limited benefits to some coalition members and not the more general change in soft law and the larger symbolic victory. On the other hand, had all else been the same except the coalition had adhered strictly to distributive tactics right to the end and refusing all offers at compromise short of its original proposal – as the Like Minded Group did – the Bush administration would have been much more likely to choose to accept a deadlock despite some public opinion costs at home. All this is not to say that bargaining is ultimately random. It is to say that researchers need to concentrate more theoretical and empirical work on discovering regularities in this process.

It is true that this coalition benefited from exogenous conditions that might be difficult to duplicate in the same combination elsewhere. Most obviously, few trade issues present anything as compelling as the horrifying AIDS pandemic to bring popular pressure to bear on dominant governments to make concessions. The anthrax scare and the quick North American consideration of breaking drug patents posed a timely opportunity to weaken the credibility of the US negotiating position in the WTO. The TRIPS/health coalition also enjoyed two institutional advantages in 2001 that might not always be present. The WTO had already suffered an embarrassing debacle in Seattle in 1999. Leaders of at least the larger trading governments believed that a second failure would be devastating for the organization's credibility and legitimacy, which probably lowered somewhat the 2001 reservation values for governments that valued the organization. Furthermore, the 2001 talks were designed only to launch a new round. At the end, positions might be firmer.

Yet none of this guaranteed that the trade ministers would hand developing countries a victory on health in 2001 regardless of what they and the NGOs did. External factors do not mean much unless negotiators make efforts to convert them into negotiating currency. Other crises – such as in Rwanda and Sierra Leone – have inflicted huge objective humanitarian costs but have not been followed by a significant agreed international response. What sometimes intervenes between exogenous conditions and outcomes are the processes of framing and reframing, mobilizing concern and support, and negotiating. In this instance developing countries deftly highlighted the magnitude of the crisis, solicited NGO support and underscored North American hypocrisy when the opportunity presented itself. There is no reason why analogous intervening processes could not operate to some degree on issues less dramatic than drugs to save the lives of dying people. Our claim is not that the negotiation process is the only thing that affects outcomes, but that it makes a significant difference and needs more attention.

A set of mostly weak states managed to gain significantly from a WTO negotiation despite the unfavorable power asymmetry they faced. They worked together as an explicit coalition, and made it larger than most, creating unusual credibility should they threaten to block the whole organization. They then did make such a threat and it was taken seriously. Through internal bargaining they decided to spurn lesser offers that could have undermined their common proposal and their threat credibility. This group followed a mixed-distributive strategy, one that attempted mainly to shift value from the United States and its friends but was also prepared to drop demands in return for concessions in order to close the deal. The Southern governments worked in tandem with a public NGO campaign to raise popular awareness of their problems in the North and reframe the existing regime in a manner more favorable to their proposal. In the public mind the NGOs framed the WTO rules in light of the AIDS disaster and raised the political cost for trade ministers who did nothing to help. Each of these aspects of this case suggests or applies a hypothesis about the negotiation process that is worth checking in a variety of regimes.

In a world of bounded rationality, much of the negotiation process is a contest of partisans trying to establish the dominant frame of reference. The more a coalition can do to prevail in this subjective contest, the larger its gains are likely to be. Reframing efforts may take forms other than an NGO campaign. Analyzing negotiations on this level shows that rationalist and constructivist insights are complementary and should be considered together more often. The case also has an implication for two-level games theory. It shows that reframing from abroad can widen the domestic win-set, in this case lowering the reservation value of the US negotiator.[81]

But reframing attempts sometimes fail; what are their limits? Generally, which arguments will prove to be persuasive, under which conditions? International relations scholars have not been able to establish much valid theory on this elusive issue. But we will conclude with speculations pertaining to ethical arguments in particular, about which some ideas are accumulating. Scholars agree about the general sequence of the process – problem definition, prescription, and politicization[82] – yet highlight different elements as being decisive in shaping outcomes. For example, Keck and Sikkink (1998) have argued that framing that emphasizes bodily harm to innocent or vulnerable individuals is more likely to be successful; other attempts face longer odds. Several[83] have argued that framing works best when advocates are able to graft a new policy item or perspective onto an existing policy frame or culture. In this vein, negotiators are more apt to fail when they push for something that is antithetical to an organization's mandate.[84] Sell and Prakash (2004) highlight political opportunity structures and the role of agency. Joachim (2003) focuses on organizational capacities and access to institutions. Albin (2001) and Muller (2001) examine framing and ethical argument as a way to discover joint gains. As Albin points out:

Negotiators are ultimately motivated . . . to act upon grounds which others can accept as justified so as to reach and maintain cooperative agreements. Their frequent endorsement of impartial notions, such as justice as a balanced settlement of conflicting claims, means that a widely respected agreement can be reached. It entails that the voices and interests of weaker parties are taken more into account than if such values had not operated.[85]

In this sense, analysis of ethical argument can be perfectly compatible with more utilitarian assessments of negotiation.[86] In a world of egoistic states in a condition of anarchy, negotiators must strive to make cooperation as self-enforcing as possible. When states need to rely on each other to achieve cooperative outcomes, "proposals which appear too self-serving and cannot be supported by some widely accepted principle rarely go far."[87]

---

[81] See Schoppa 1993 for a related argument.
[82] Crawford 2002, 102, 109; Joachim 2003, 268; Keck and Sikkink 1998; Price 1998; Sell and Prakash 2004.
[83] Odell 1982, 68; Hall 1989; Keck and Sikkink 1998; Price 1998.
[84] Ricupero 1996.   [85] Albin 2001, 229.   [86] Koremenos et al. 2001.
[87] Albin 2001, 227–28.

Constructivist theories of communicative action[88] also hold promise for negotiation analysis. These embrace a focus on process and reject the simplifying assumption of "mute" actors. Such theories allow "for the possibility that political actors may do things we expect of ourselves and of others in everyday life: allow ourselves to be convinced by a good argument, change our opinions, be able where appropriate to reconsider our goals, and not remain prisoners of established objectives and priorities."[89] "Arguments that mobilize logic, empathy, or analogy" can serve to delegitimize accepted practices.[90] For example, exposing hypocrisy or documenting unintended negative consequences of a policy can be powerful tools. Indeed, it is not even necessary that the negotiators themselves change their minds in the process. They may steadfastly cling to their original preferences, yet find the costs of acting on those preferences prohibitive if their counterpart's framing efforts have altered public perceptions of the meaning of those actions. By connecting patent protection to unnecessary death, the coalition and its NGO supporters made the USTR's BATNA increasingly unsavory.

By the same token, it is important to keep in mind that *all* is not argument and communicative action. Negotiations take place within a political, economic, cultural, and institutional context. Even the best arguments bump into irreducible material, political, or cultural realities that limit their impact. According to Coleman and Gabler, "engagement in truth-seeking or framing cannot always contain or change the tensions and severe social consequences that result from selecting, prioritizing, and acting upon one set of norms at expense of another."[91] These scholars examine the relationship between normative argument and institutional capacity and systematically begin to explore conditions under which communicative action will not result in change. This is promising work combining constructivist and materialist perspectives to arrive at general propositions. Negotiation analysis provides an excellent opportunity to combine these insights and expands opportunities to bridge analytical divides to explain important processes and outcomes in international politics.

REFERENCES

Abbott, Frederick. 2002. The Doha Declaration on the TRIPS Agreement and Public Health: Lighting a Dark Corner of the WTO. *Journal of International Economic Law* 5 (2): 469–505

[88] Risse 2000.   [89] Muller 2001, 174.
[90] Crawford 2002: 102. On analogies and abstract reasoning, see Breuning 2003.
[91] Coleman and Gabler 2002: 483.

Albin, Cecilia. 2001. *Justice and Fairness in International Negotiation.* Cambridge: Cambridge University Press

Benvenisti, Eyal, and George W. Downs. 2004. Distributive Politics and International Institutions: The Case of Drugs. *Case Western Reserve Journal of International Law* 36 (1): 21–51

Bond, Patrick. 1999. Globalization, Pharmaceutical Pricing, and South African Health Policy: Managing Confrontation with US Firms and Politicians. *International Journal of Health Services* 29 (4): 765–92

Breuning, Marijke. 2003. The Role of Analogies and Abstract Reasoning in Decision-Making: Evidence from the Debate Over Truman's Proposal for Development Assistance. *International Studies Quarterly* 47 (2): 229–46

Charnovitz, Steve 2002. The Legal Status of the Doha Declarations. *Journal of International Economic Law* 5 (1): 207–11

Coleman, William D., and Melissa Gabler. 2002. Agricultural Biotechnology and Regime Formation: a Constructivist Assessment of the Prospects. *International Studies Quarterly* 46 (4): 481–507

Comor, Edward. 2001. The Role of Communications in Global Civil Society. *International Studies Quarterly* 45 (3): 389–408

Correa, Carlos. 2004. Investment Protection in Bilateral and Free Trade Agreements: Implications for the Granting of Compulsory Licenses. *Michigan Journal of International Law* 26 (4): 331–53

Crawford, Neta. 2002. *Argument and Change in World Politics: Ethics, Decolonization, and Humanitarian Intervention.* Cambridge: Cambridge University Press

Drahos, Peter. 2001. BITS and BIPS: Bilateralism in Intellectual Property. *The Journal of World Intellectual Property* 4 (6): 791–808
    2004. Securing the Future of Intellectual Property: Intellectual Property Owners and Their Nodally Coordinated Enforcement Pyramid. *Case Western Reserve Journal of International Law* 36: 53–77

Drahos, Peter with John Braithwaite. 2002. *Information Feudalism: Who Owns the Knowledge Economy?* London: Earthscan Publications

Finnemore, Martha and Kathryn Sikkink. 1998. International Norm Dynamics and Political Change. *International Organization* 52 (4): 887–918

García-Castrillon, Carmen. 2002. An Approach to the WTO Ministerial Declaration on the TRIPS Agreement and Public Health. *Journal of International Economic Law* 5 (1): 212–19

Gillespie-White, Leslie. 2001. What Did Doha Accomplish? International Intellectual Property Institute, November 19, viewed at mail.iipi.org/db/views/detail.asp?itemID=21

Grabowski, Henry. 2002. Patents, Innovation and Access to New Pharmaceuticals. *Journal of International Economic Law* 5 (4): 849–60

Hall, Peter, ed. 1989. *The Political Power of Economic Ideas.* Princeton: Princeton University Press

Horlick, Gary. 2002. Over the Bump in Doha? *Journal of International Economic Law* 5 (1): 195–202

International Centre for Trade and Sustainable Development (ICTSD) 2001. *TRIPS, Biological Resources and Public Health: Documents and Discussion Papers*

Presented at the ICTSD – Africa Group Roundtable on 12 June 2001. Available at www.ictsd.org

Joachim, Jutta. 2003. Framing and Seizing Opportunities: The UN, NGOs and Women's Rights. *International Studies Quarterly* 47 (2): 247–74

Keck, Margaret and Kathryn Sikkink. 1998. *Activists Beyond Borders.* Ithaca, NY: Cornell University Press

Koremenos, Barbara, Charles Lipson, and Duncan Snidal, eds. 2001. The Rational Design of International Institutions. *International Organization* 55 (4): 761–99

Love, James. 2001. Views on the Draft Declaration on the TRIPS Agreement and Public Health (November 13, 2001), viewed on June 3, 2005 at http://www.focusweb.org/main/html/Article34.html

Maskus, Keith. 2000. *Intellectual Property Rights in the Global Economy* Washington, DC: Institute for International Economics

Matthews, Duncan. 2004. WTO Decision on Implementation of Paragraph 6 of the Doha Declaration on the TRIPS Agreement and Public Health: A Solution to the Access to Essential Medicines Problem? *Journal of International Economic Law* 7 (1): 73–93

Müller, Harald. 2001. International Relations as Communicative Action. In *Constructing International Relations: The Next Generation,* eds. Karin M. Fierke and Knud Erik Jorgensen, 160–78. Armonk, NY: M. E. Sharpe Inc.

Odell, John. 1982. *U.S. International Monetary Policy.* Princeton: Princeton University Press

2000. *Negotiating the World Economy.* Ithaca NY: Cornell University Press

Price, Richard. 1998. Reversing the Gunsights: Transnational Civil Society Targets Landmines. *International Organization* 52 (3): 613–44

Ricupero, Rubens. 1996. Integration of Developing Countries into the Multilateral Trading System. In *The Uruguay Round and Beyond: Essays in Honor of Arthur Dunkel,* eds. Jagdish Bhagwati and Mathias Hirsch. Ann Arbor: University of Michigan Press

Risse, Thomas. 2000. "Let's Argue!" Communicative Action in World Politics. *International Organization* 54 (1): 1–39

Rozek, Richard and Renee Rainey. 2001. Broad-based Compulsory Licensing of Pharmaceutical Technologies. *Journal of World Intellectual Property* 4 (4): 463–480

Schoppa, Leonard J. 1993. Two-Level Games and Bargaining Outcomes: Why *Gaiatsu* Succeeds in Japan in Some Cases but Not Others. *International Organization* 47 (3): 353–86

Schott, Jeffrey. 2002. Comment on the Doha Ministerial. *Journal of International Economic Law* 5 (1): 191–95

Sell, Susan K. 1998. *Power and Ideas: North-South Politics of Intellectual Property and Antitrust.* Albany: State University of New York Press

2003. *Private Power, Public Law: the Globalization of Intellectual Property Rights.* Cambridge: Cambridge University Press

Sell, Susan K. and Aseem Prakash. 2004. Using Ideas Strategically: The Contest Between Businesses and NGOs in Intellectual Property. *International Studies Quarterly* 48 (1): 143–76

't Hoen, Ellen. 2002. TRIPS, Pharmaceutical Patents, and Access to Essential Medicines: A Long Way From Seattle to Doha. *Chicago Journal of International Law* 3: 27–45

Viana, José M. N. 2002. Intellectual Property Rights, the World Trade Organization and Public Health: The Brazilian Perspective. *Connecticut Journal of International Law* 17: 311–17

Warner, Mark, Amir Attaran, Susan Finston, James Love, Robert L. Mallett, and Coenraad Visser. 2002. Boundaries of Access and Enforcement: Panel I: AIDS Drugs and the Developing World: The Role of Patents in the Access of Medicines. *Fordham Intellectual Property, Media & Entertainment Law Journal* 12: 675–751

Wolff, Alan. 2002. What Did Doha Do? An Initial Assessment. *Journal of International Economic Law* 5 (1): 202–206

WTO. 2001a. Proposal by the African Group, Bangladesh, Barbados, Bolivia, Brazil, Cuba, Dominican Republic, Ecuador, Haiti, Honduras, India, Indonesia, Jamaica, Pakistan, Paraguay, Philippines, Peru, Sri Lanka, Thailand, and Venezuela, for a Ministerial Declaration on the TRIPS Agreement and Public Health. IP/C/W/312 and WT/GC/W/450, October 4

WTO. 2001b. Preambular Language for Ministerial Declaration. Contribution from Australia, Canada, Japan, Switerland, and the United States. IP/C/W/313, October 4

WTO. 2001c. General Council. Preparations for the Fourth Session of the Ministerial Conference. Draft Declaration on Intellectual Property and [Access to Medicines] [Public Health]. JOB(01)/155, October 27

WTO. 2001d. Declaration on the TRIPS Agreement and Public Health, Ministerial Conference, Fourth Session, Doha. WT/MIN(01)/DEC/W/2, November 14

Zald, Mayer N. 1996. Culture, Ideology, and Cultural Framing. In *Comparative Perspectives on Social Movements*, eds. Doug McAdam, John D. McCarthy, and Mayer N. Zald, 261–74. Cambridge: Cambridge University Press

4 The strict distributive strategy for a bargaining coalition: the Like Minded Group in the World Trade Organization

Amrita Narlikar and John S. Odell

Developing country delegates in multilateral trade negotiations have become quite active in forming bargaining coalitions. But there has been little research concerning how this has been done, what the results have been, or what influences these results.[1] In tackling these questions, this chapter identifies strategy choices made by weak-state coalitions as possible influences on their outcomes, the outcome being the primary dependent variable.

Our method is to learn more about the multilateral negotiation process through a single case study and attempt to generate a potential generalization for further investigation in other cases. The Like Minded Group of countries (LMG) in the World Trade Organization illustrated what we call the strict distributive strategy in WTO negotiations from 1998 through the November 2001 ministerial conference in Doha, Qatar. This coalition put forward a number of detailed proposals that would have shifted value from North to South and denied any negotiating gain to the North until the North had first granted the group's demands. Despite a great deal of organized professional effort in Geneva, however, the group had by the time of the Doha conference, as we read the record, sustained a major loss and collected relatively small gains especially on their leading

The authors are indebted to participants in this negotiation who made time to speak to us on the understanding that their identities would not be divulged. Narlikar thanks the Center for International Studies, University of Southern California, for funding that enabled her to conduct research in Geneva for this paper. Odell is grateful to USC, its School of International Relations, its Center for International Studies, to the Graduate Institute of International Studies, Geneva, for its hospitality while he conducted research in 2002, and to Pablo Heidrich and Julia Witt for able research assistance. We benefited from comments on an earlier draft by Thomas Chadefaux, Esperanza Durán, Magdi Farahat, Urs Luterbacher, Tony Payne, Diana Tussie, participants at our Geneva conference and a seminar at the University of Sheffield, and members of our research team. None of these friends should be held responsible for use we made of their advice.
[1] Early studies on coalition formation in GATT and WTO negotiations include Hamilton and Whalley 1989; Kahler and Odell 1989; Tussie and Glover 1995. Narlikar 2003 is a recent book-length treatment.

issue compared with the status quo. The LMG did play a leading role in delaying what they regarded as another serious loss. But this coalition gained less at Doha than others such as the coalition concerned with TRIPS and public health, which used the mixed-distributive strategy, as shown in chapter 3.

The main generalization, in summary, is that for a developing country coalition, gains from the strict distributive strategy will diminish under two possible conditions. First, gains will be less likely to the extent that other parties regard the group's demand as worse than impasse, naturally. Second, gains from this strategy will fall to the extent that the group fragments and loses its credibility. The present case illustrates this second risk. The lower the likely gains from this strategy, the more attractive an alternative strategy becomes.

One caveat: we claim to have generated but not tested a hypothesis here. Qualitative methods such as the single case study and the comparison of a few cases are not designed to prove any general proposition conclusively. A larger number of cases selected neutrally would be needed for a proper test. Factors not emphasized here are likely to be important as well and every case will of course have unique features.

We begin the chapter with the reasoning behind our main argument. The next section describes the negotiating strategy and agenda of the LMG. Next we develop our argument by tracing the 1998–2001 negotiation process leading to the Doha outcome, which is described in the fourth section. The fifth section shows that the LMG's outcome was inferior to those of two other 2001 coalitions that followed mixed strategies. Next we briefly examine reasons why the Like Minded Group did not follow a more mixed strategy. We conclude by showing that some alternative explanations may be helpful but are not adequate for this case, and by highlighting the chapter's implications for researchers and negotiators.

1   The Logic behind the Main Argument

Any negotiation outcome will depend on how other parties play their cards, of course; any government is operating in a strategic interaction. But with this complex reality as a backdrop, it may still be possible to identify some useful rough generalizations about strategies and their effects, other things being equal.

The *strict distributive strategy* is defined as a set of tactics that are functional only for claiming value from others and defending against such claiming, when one party's goals are in conflict with those of others. It comes in both offensive and defensive variants. A *strict* distributive strategy is one that is not tempered by any integrative tactics, such as an offer to exchange concessions that would make each party better off than before. A *mixed strategy* includes distributive and integrative tactics in some proportion.

The strict distributive strategy can achieve major gains if the conditions are favorable, but many times conditions are not highly favorable, especially not for developing countries. One general risk of this strategy is impasse, when the coalition establishes a credible commitment to a point in the issue space but this point is more than the other side can accept – it is outside the zone of agreement. This can happen accidentally, when the coalition believes the other is bluffing but miscalculates because of incomplete information about the other's private reservation value. It might happen deliberately at a given stage in a negotiation if the coalition, aware the other side will not accept at this time, prefers a temporary impasse in hopes that sending a strong signal will prompt the other to yield later. Either way, if the outcome is impasse the strategy obviously gains nothing tangible for the coalition at that time. It also runs the risk that the other will decide to turn away to some alternative to agreement with this coalition rather than backing down. This paper does not document this first side of the logic, but one recent example might be the Group of 20 and the outcome at the WTO ministerial conference in Cancún in 2003.

The second unfavorable condition for this strategy is when the coalition loses its initial credibility because it later fragments during the process. One strong distributive tactic in WTO negotiations is a threat to block consensus. In the WTO a strong norm holds that agreements should be reached by consensus, which gives even the smallest delegation the authority to prevent agreement. But success with any threat depends on credibility, which depends on unity.

The unity of any WTO coalition will depend on five possible factors or challenges. One challenge facing coalitions everywhere is the familiar free-rider problem, which rises with numbers. A second common risk, also relevant for the strong as well as the weak, is that outsiders will attempt to split the group to undermine its credibility, a problem that choice of the strict distributive strategy can exacerbate. Faced with a coalition standing firm behind high demands and refusing to discuss any concessions, the other has three ways of responding. A) It can give in to the demands; B) it can accept no agreement; or C) it can attempt to divide the coalition through bilateral deals or threats and thus undermine its credibility. If the first two options are seen to be more expensive than the third, the outside party will resort to C.

Third, unity depends on how coalition members respond to others' attempts at divide-and-rule. Members theoretically can offer side payments to keep potential defectors in the fold, or attempt diplomatic persuasion to convince them the odds are better inside the group than outside. If members do not attempt such defenses or they are weak, unity suffers.

Fourth and specifically in trade affairs, the greater the heterogeneity of commercial interests among coalition members, the more opportunities others will have to tempt a delegation to defect with a separate offer or threat on an issue that is more important to that country than to its partners. Greater heterogeneity also makes it difficult for members to agree on which concessions to make if a coalition should consider some integrative bargaining with outsiders in the endgame.[2]

And fifth, the poorer the countries in the coalition, the more difficult it is to resist fragmentation. These pressures are well captured by Robert Jervis in his interpretation of Rousseau's Stag Hunt: "If the failure to eat that day – be it venison or rabbit – means that he will starve, a person is likely to defect in the Stag Hunt even if he really likes venison and has a high level of trust in his colleagues. (Defection is especially likely if the others are also starving or they know that he is.)"[3] If the country is small and poor, it is difficult to hold firm with the collective position, even if the latter is likely to yield higher gains (were the coalition successful). The large and wealthy countries generally have far better alternatives to an agreement, by virtue of their market size, technological lead, global corporations and domestic political stability. Less developed countries are also less able to afford to make side payments to potential defectors. Hence a threat by the poor is less likely to be believed in general. A threat by one small trader alone is especially unlikely to be believed. One ambassador from a small developing country contends that the authority to block the WTO is an illusion.

> The US can block a consensus but not [my country]. If you block, the entire weight of the organization comes down on you. The problem is that on other issues I need others to be flexible. If I block on this issue, I am in trouble on the other issue.[4]

Not only may this exclusively distributive strategy fail to claim value from others. Simultaneously it tends to undermine the process of identifying and realizing joint gains with outsiders. Parties' objectives in international negotiations are almost never perfectly opposed. Often there are also opportunities for deals that will make multiple parties, including

[2] Hamilton and Whalley 1989.   [3] Jervis 1978, 172.
[4] Interview with a trade negotiator from a developing country, Geneva, October 19, 2002.

Coalition A, better off than before. To be sure, these possibilities are often difficult to identify. Many rational negotiators are careful to conceal their capacities to fall back to true reservation values, to enhance the credibility of their positions when attempting to claim value from others. Many may also attempt to conceal their priorities across issues. But when parties' private objectives actually are partly consistent, integrative tactics sometimes elicit gains for A by either discovering and exploiting common interests, or uncovering differences that can be exploited for mutual benefit, as in commercial trade itself. Integrative tactics include asking other parties to identify their priorities, proposing an exchange of concessions, and proposing to redraw the issue space itself in a way that benefits some without costing others. These tactics require a minimal level of trust and a greater openness with information about one's own position. A mixed-distributive strategy is one dominated by distributive tactics but is diluted with integrative moves. A common mixture is sequential – beginning with the distributive and adding some integrative near the end.

If A refuses to engage in any integrative tactics, it encourages B and C to manipulate information, delay, take their own hostages, make threats, and develop alternatives to agreement with A. Party or Coalition A discourages B and C from initiating integrative moves and fails to discover what gains for itself might be achieved through logrolling or reframing.[5] Even when A makes a credible threat and B and C are considering yielding, the odds of settlement would be higher, goes the argument, if A's strategy mixes in some integrative elements that give the others some negotiating gains to deliver to their frustrated constituents. This reasoning applies to coalitions of powerful countries too. EU and US negotiators also run the risk of forcing an impasse if they reject all integrative moves.

In summary, Coalition A could bet everything on the strict distributive strategy, calculating that adversaries will fall back in the final brinkmanship. But if the coalition fragments, an individual member will end up making concessions in return for nothing, unless its government is prepared to take the risks of blocking the entire WTO by itself. Having passed up opportunities to gain some concessions by falling back from some of its demands, it reaps only losses. If either unfavorable condition or risk is likely, a mixed strategy including some integrative tactics might well gain more.

---

[5] In a situation where the parties believe their objectives are completely opposed, we would not expect resort to integrative tactics since they can only expose the actor to exploitation. But any two states that value their long-term relationship have at least one common objective.

120   *Amrita Narlikar and John S. Odell*

2   An example of a heterogeneous coalition and a strict distributive strategy

The LMG began as an eight-member coalition in the preparatory process leading up to the Singapore ministerial conference in 1996. India took the lead in forming the coalition,[6] whose original members were Cuba, Egypt, India, Indonesia, Malaysia, Pakistan, Tanzania, and Uganda. Its initial agenda was to block inclusion of the so-called Singapore issues of trade and investment, trade facilitation, transparency in government procurement and competition policy. The group helped forestall what they regarded as a loss in that the new issues were included in paragraphs 20–21 of the Singapore ministerial declaration only as part of a study program rather than actual negotiations.[7] Additionally, the LMG was vociferous in its opposition to the inclusion of labor standards in the WTO, and obtained a promise against this in the Singapore declaration, paragraph 4. Recognizing the importance of having a positive agenda rather than simply opposition to the Singapore issues, from the preparatory process for the 1998 Geneva ministerial onwards, the LMG began to focus on the problems that developing countries faced in implementing the Uruguay Round agreements. As a result of its activism, implementation issues were first accorded recognition in the Geneva ministerial declaration, in paragraphs 8, 9, and 10.

But the LMG really came of age in 1999 when discussion began for the possible launch of a new round at the Seattle ministerial. At this time the LMG expanded to include the Dominican Republic, Honduras, and Zimbabwe. It took a detailed and fairly consistent position in the debates on the launch of the Millennium Round. The group also became more institutionalized through weekly meetings. By the time of the Doha ministerial, the coalition included Sri Lanka along with Jamaica as permanent observer. Kenya too began to attend its meetings. While the group continued to meet after the Doha ministerial, this chapter focuses on the period from mid-1998 to 2001. During this phase the group was at its most active and its agenda was at its most evolved, to date. Additionally by focusing on these years we are able to observe a phase of negotiation that ended with an identifiable outcome.

This group fits our definition of a coalition, that is, a set of states that defend a common position in a negotiation through explicit coordination. These delegations met regularly in Geneva, divided the labor, and produced many joint proposals for this WTO negotiation. Not every

[6] Interviews, Geneva, 2002.   [7] WTO 1996.

delegation received clearance from the capital to sign every joint proposal, and so only the names of the signing countries, not the Group's name, appeared on their proposals. For this chapter, we identify the group's members through interviews and press sources, and classify as LMG proposals all those submitted by this set of countries unless more than three members are missing. We also exclude a proposal as an LMG proposal if LMG states constitute fewer than half the sponsoring countries.

Two readers of an earlier draft of this chapter objected that the LMG was not a true bargaining coalition, on the grounds that not all members signed all proposals, or that some members never intended to continue defending the common position they had signed through the end of the negotiation. It is conceivable that some governments planned from the beginning to abandon their partners. Our research during and after this period, however, indicates that many were serious about working together. This group met every week during the run-up to Doha, despite the crushing schedule of official WTO meetings during the same time, illustrating a remarkably high level of dedication and explicit coordination. A number of its delegates assured us convincingly before and after Doha that they took their common agenda seriously. They disagreed about priorities to some extent, naturally. But an intention to defect regardless of the intervening process would be difficult for any independent scholar to document. We believe there would be few coalitions to study if the operational definition excluded every candidate group for which it was impossible to document the absence of secret intentions to defect.

Coalition design

This coalition was relatively small in numbers, consisting of only 14 out of 142 member states at its high point. But in the aggregate the LMG accounted for about 5 percent of world imports, making it stronger in underlying power assets than some developing country trade coalitions.

It was heterogeneous economically and regionally. It brought together countries from different rungs of the development ladder, including Uganda and Tanzania as least developed countries, countries with different exports, and countries from Central America and the Caribbean, Africa, South Asia, and Southeast Asia, as shown in Table 4.1.

This diversity brought some advantages. It gave the group greater legitimacy within the developing world, and permitted an important sharing of resources. For instance, at least one LMG member would have representation in most small-group meetings involving developing countries,

Table 4.1 *The Like Minded Group: goods exports and income per capita (2001)*

Member state	Gross national income per capita	Goods exports	Leading goods exports	Share of world exports (%)
	Dollars	Million dollars		
Malaysia	8,340	87,921	integrated circuits computer parts	
Indonesia	2,940	56,321	textiles and apparel petroleum	
India	2,450	43,611	textiles and apparel diamonds	
Pakistan	1,920	9,242	textiles and apparel rice	
Dominican Rep	5,870	5,333	apparel medical apparatus	
Sri Lanka	3,560	4,817	apparel tea	
Egypt	3,790	4,128	petroleum cotton	
Kenya	1,020	1,945	tea cut flowers	
Zimbabwe	2,340	1,770	tobacco ferroalloys	
Cuba	n/a	1,708	sugar metallic residues	
Honduras	2,450	1,318	crustaceans bananas	
Jamaica (observer)	3,650	1,225	textiles and apparel aluminum	
Tanzania	540	780	coffee fish	
Uganda	1,250	457	coffee fish	
LMG combined		220,576		4.6
For reference:				
China	4,260	266,000		5.6
Japan	27,430	403,496		8.5
USA	34,870	730,803		15.4
European Union	n/a	874,100		18.4

Source: Gross National Income per capita 2001: PPP estimates, World Development Report 2003; Export data: 2001 WTO/UNCTAD Intl Trade Center on line

which meant that the LMG was kept abreast of all parallel research initiatives and negotiating positions.[8] Still, whether such underlying assets are converted into negotiating gain will depend on coalition strategy and its degree of unity. Heterogeneity became a problem at the end of this process.

Strategy

This coalition's actions during this period fit the definition of a strict distributive strategy. During these years three broad sets of issues dominated the LMG's agenda: implementation issues, other development issues, and process-related systemic concerns.[9] The group was best known for defining and championing the issue that came to be called implementation. This issue had two components. To the first category belong problems developing countries were having implementing their commitments under the rules, due to capacity constraints' especially in least developed countries. The second category referred to the alleged failure of the developed countries to implement promises of the Uruguay Round. Although the 1994 deal had been designed as a "Grand Bargain,"[10] developing countries had opened their markets quite significantly and accepted new rules favoring intellectual property owners while developed countries had not delivered equivalent commercial gains to developing countries. One LMG ambassador stated the indictment in the following terms:

The experience of the past five years with implementation of the Uruguay Round agreements has made it evident that the overall "package" of agreements covered by the "single undertaking" was inherently unequal. Moreover, several key agreements have been implemented in a manner that has eroded their spirit and compromised their objectives. Consequently, developing countries have not gained any meaningful increase in market access in the key areas where they have a clear comparative advantage, especially textiles and agriculture.[11]

[8] Interview with a WTO negotiator from an LMG country, Geneva, May 21, 2003.
[9] Note that there is often a close link, even an overlap, between implementation issues and development issues. But very broadly, implementation issues refer specifically to the problems of implementing the Uruguay Round agreements that apply to developing countries as a group; development issues bring in issues that have traditionally been missing in the GATT and WTO and often apply specifically to the Least Developed Countries (LDCs) and small and vulnerable economies.
[10] Ostry 2000 describes the "Grand Bargain" as "essentially an implicit deal: the opening of OECD markets to agriculture and labor intensive manufactured goods, especially textiles and clothing, for the inclusion into the trading system of trade in services (GATS), intellectual property (TRIPS) and (albeit to a lesser extend than originally demanded) investment (TRIMS). And also – as a virtually last minute piece of the deal – the creation of a new institution, the WTO, with the strongest dispute settlement mechanism in the history of international law."
[11] Akram 2001.

The LMG was at the forefront in raising the demand that until the imbalance of the Uruguay Round agreements was corrected, there was no question of beginning new negotiations in the WTO.

In raising implementation problems, the LMG went beyond simply opposing. They developed technical expertise and presented detailed proposals on a diverse set of WTO issues including TRIPS, TRIMS, agriculture including the net food-importing developing countries, accelerated integration of textiles, customs valuation, and implementation of recommendations of completed reviews and WTO disciplines. All called for concessions by developed countries without offering them any negotiating gain. For example, the coalition pointed out that while "S&D [special and differential treatment] prior to the WTO was in recognition of the special problems of development faced by developing countries, . . . the WTO only recognizes the special problems that developing countries may face in the implementation of the agreements."[12] The LMG argued that even this limited form of S&D (with an altered focus from enhanced market opportunities to the granting of transition periods and technical assistance) did not go beyond best-endeavor promises. As a result, the group emphasized that all existing S&D provisions in the different WTO agreements needed to be fully operationalized and implemented.

To improve the payoff from the Textile agreement the LMG called for importing countries to grant so-called "growth-on-growth" earlier rather than wait for it to take effect from January 1, 2002.[13] The group also called for a moratorium to be applied by importing countries on antidumping actions until two years after the entire textiles and clothing sector was integrated into the GATT.[14] In agriculture, the LMG called for the elimination of tariff peaks, tariff escalations and export subsidies by developed countries, a lowering of domestic supports, and the creation of a Development Box that would allow developing countries to deviate from their commitments to meet development and food security needs.[15] On TRIPS, the group presented an agenda similar to the coalition on TRIPS and public health in demanding that essential drugs of the

---

[12] WTO 2001a.

[13] "Growth-on-growth" refers to article 2 of the 1994 Agreement on Textiles and Clothing which provides that annual growth rates applied to quotas in the earlier Multifibre Agreement were to be augmented in three stages by 16, 25, and 27 percent respectively. "For example, an annual growth rate of 6 percent under the MFA would become 6.96 percent during the first three years of the ATC, 8.7 percent during the four years of the second phase, and 11.05 percent for the last three years," http://www.wto.org/english/thewto_e/minist_e/min96_e/textiles.htm. The LMG proposed that the importing countries apply the augmented growth rates for stage 3 with effect from January 1, 2000 instead of January 1, 2002, paragraph 17, WTO, 1999c.

[14] WTO 1999c, WTO 1999d.   [15] WTO 1999e.

WHO be included in the list of exceptions to patentability. It also raised several other demands under TRIPS such as the extension of the period of implementation, and extension of additional protection for geographical indications to products other than wines and spirits.[16] The LMG was also active in the area of general WTO rules and disciplines. On antidumping, for instance, the LMG proposed ways of restricting back-to-back investigations, and that the lesser duty rule be made mandatory when a developing country is the target of the duty. On subsidies, in the name of balanced implementation the LMG proposed among other things that non-actionable subsidies be expanded to include the subsidies that developing countries use for development purposes.[17] The group called for making mandatory the provision on extended time periods for developing countries for Sanitary and Phytosanitary measures (SPS) compliance, and appealed for a greater involvement of developing countries in all phases of standard setting under SPS and Technical Barriers to Trade (TBT). Throughout the period, the LMG pointed to the importance of technology transfer. It proposed the setting up of a working group to study the implications of the existing trade agreements on a commercial basis and ways of enhancing such transfer, particularly for developing countries.[18] Finally, the position of the LMG, even until November 2001, was consistent with its position at Singapore – that no new issues (including the Singapore issues) could be brought in until the imbalance of the Uruguay Round was corrected.

Second, going beyond implementation of past agreements, the coalition also took the lead in raising certain other issues and proposals to aid development, particularly to help the least developed countries, the small and vulnerable economies, and some highly indebted poor countries (HIPCs). It proposed that in the medium term, WTO agreements should be amended to provide an "enhanced, effective and binding S&D scheme" for developing countries. Bearing in mind the debt overhang of the HIPC countries, the LMG proposed the setting up of a working group to study the various implications of debt on the capacity of developing countries to take advantage of trade liberalization, and also to suggest remedial measures and appropriate flexibilities in the implementation of particular agreements countries facing high and specified levels of debt.[19] It also proposed the setting up of a working group for the study of the inter-relationship between trade and finance.[20]

Third, the LMG placed considerable emphasis on issues relating to the process of negotiation. It spent much time internally engaged in what one

---

[16] WTO 1999c, WTO 1999b.   [17] WTO 1999c; also WTO 1999a.
[18] WTO 1999f; WTO 2001b.   [19] WTO 2001d.   [20] WTO 2001c.

delegate described as "the educative mode." Lacking sufficient information and understanding of the issues and having extremely limited governmental resources for WTO negotiations, coalition delegates divided the labor of studying the issues and shared their ideas for joint positions.[21] And particularly in the aftermath of Seattle, the LMG and many others raised the call for institutional reform in the WTO to improve the participation of developing countries.

In sum, the tactics used by the LMG toward the developed countries during this period typify a strictly distributive strategy.[22] In this case the strategy was offensive in its demand for immediate redress of the implementation issues, development concerns and systemic issues. It was defensive in its resistance to the Singapore issues, labor, or the launch of a new round of negotiations before LMG concerns were addressed. The following specific LMG tactics illustrate this type of strategy.

- The members formed a coalition consisting of those who agreed to defend a central principle for claiming value from developed countries. The coalition strongly criticized developed countries for failing to keep their part of the Grand Bargain and gave them little credit for what they had done.
- The LMG contended that if fresh concessions to developing countries were made conditional on launching a new round or adding new issues, it would be tantamount to the developing countries paying two, three or even four times for what they had been promised and had paid for in past rounds. (This reasoning assumed that the new issues would bring net costs, not benefits, to developing countries.)
- The coalition began with an extremely ambitious opening position, circulating detailed demands covering a large share of the existing WTO rules. Its 1999 agenda implied renegotiation of many Uruguay Round agreements.
- The proposals offered no negotiating gain to the developed countries, in contrast for example to proposing a tariff-cutting formula designed to apply to all members. The predominant rationale as to why developed countries should make these concessions was presented not in terms of mutual gains but in terms of legitimacy, the correction of past injustices, and the exceptionality of the problems of developing countries.
- The coalition attempted to take others' priority issues hostage, a common distributive tactic. The LMG opposed proposals for issues that

---

[21] Interview with an LMG ambassador, Geneva, October 22, 2002.

[22] In practice a negotiator or delegation may not choose a strategy all at one time and in a self-conscious way. Some may choose one step at a time and accumulate a set of actions without considering them as a whole. But even if so, our premise is that it will still be useful to define strategies this way and classify actual behavior using these concepts, for purposes of research and improving general knowledge of negotiation.

were high priorities for the European Union, Japan and the United States, and threatened to block consensus on them unless LMG demands were granted.

- They placed the onus of correcting capacity-related constraints in developing countries at the systemic level, though some acknowledgement was made of the domestic limitations of developing countries in availing themselves of the benefits of liberalization in the proposals. Hence, for instance, the LMG demanded not only technical assistance to facilitate their participation in the multilateral trading system, but also enhanced market access and other forms of S&D from developed countries.

- Once the LMG had laid its proposals on the negotiating table, it limited itself exclusively to distributive tactics; as a group it never blended integrative tactics into its strategy, as some coalitions did. For instance, we have not found evidence of follow-up attempts, either in the form of concessions the coalition could consider making in return, or of willingness to introduce complementary measures at the domestic level to further their own agenda. We have not found evidence that the LMG prioritized its numerous demands or asked Quad countries (The European Union, United States, Japan and Canada) to identify their relative priorities – common steps in the process of identifying possible exchanges of concessions. The LMG did show a willingness to stagger some demands (e.g. its proposals on implementation issues identified some to be addressed before/after Seattle, and others to be addressed in the first year of the negotiations). But otherwise there was little indication of areas in which the LMG was willing to accept less or back down. All demands seem to have been presented as an all-or-nothing package in which everything was a deal-breaker, rather than a set of prioritized demands on which some negotiation was possible. Even within the group there appear to have been no collective fallback positions, no plan B on how to respond to pressures from the developed countries and negotiate settlements. While the "educative mode" constituted integrative tactics inside the coalition, the sharing of experiences and learning by the LMG with non-members was usually open only to developing countries.

3   The negotiation process, 2001

What, then, were the effects of this strategy on the negotiation process and its outcome? It seems to us that this coalition's choice of a strict distributive strategy, given prevailing conditions, helps account for a disappointing outcome for the LMG (described in section 4).

Consider a selective review of the process concentrating on the last half year. To summarize, given the LMG strategy of making high opening demands, the Quad had three options. The European Union and United States could allow the situation to build up to an impasse. But in the aftermath of the debacle at Seattle and imperatives generated by 9/11, another stalemate would have had significant costs for them. The second option – to give in completely to the offensive demands of the LMG – would have been even more costly in their eyes. So during 2001 the two giants chose a third option and began to mix some integrative elements into their own distributive strategies to try to negotiate compromises they would find acceptable. Some of these integrative moves were targeted towards specific countries or subgroups in and outside the LMG. When the LMG did not respond as a group to overtures toward compromise, these Quad carrots (and possibly sticks) had the effect of splitting the group. Eventually developing countries including some LMG members individually or in groups fell back from their own demands in order to capture at least some gains in Doha. By then the Like Minded Group had fragmented and with it, the credibility of its threat to block consensus.

In 2000 after the Seattle debacle, the WTO General Council, under the chairmanship of Norway's Ambassador Kåre Bryn, began to evolve a more transparent and inclusive process of negotiation to rebuild mutual trust. It was agreed to give serious consideration to implementation complaints and reach decisions by the end of that year. That fall developing country delegates remained quite disappointed with a lack of concrete results.[23] Yet by January 2001, according to an African WTO ambassador,

> The tone has changed. Developing countries have had their "mourning period" on implementation. Now people are talking about solutions. No one thinks industrialized countries will give developing countries more to "rebalance" agreements without something in exchange.[24]

In 2001 the EU began to water down the terms of the Singapore issues that it would accept. For instance, it would allow developing countries to opt out of a WTO agreement restricting policies toward foreign investment. As another integrative move, the EU offered its Everything But Arms initiative to least developed countries.

The new Republican administration in Washington dropped the labor rights issue and USTR Robert Zoellick met with numerous developing country ministers. He paid a visit to India in August. In late July the Indian newspaper *The Statesman* had written:

---

[23] *World Trade Agenda [WTA]*, November 20, 2000, 6.
[24] *Financial Times*, January 30, 2001. No one except perhaps the LMG.

The Doha WTO meeting, slated for November, will in all probability start a new round of trade talks . . . But perhaps, New Delhi's official posture is not so much a given stance as a bargaining tactic. That is, by saying it will not relent it is checking out how much parties in favour of a new round are willing to concede. If so, that is not necessarily a bad strategy, provided India is sure of its bargaining strength. Punching above our weight, as we did at countless international fora during the days of Nehruvian highmindedness, is likely to produce a knockout blow in trade negotiations where national interest is fought for with bare knuckle ferocity. India cannot sabotage Doha. So, we must be ready to concede at the right moment, having first made a realistic assessment of how much we can extract, and what we have to give up.[25]

While in India, Zoellick announced duty-free treatment on $540 million worth of Indian exports, in a clear move to induce India off its blocking position.[26] At that time *The Hindu* warned the government that many countries were deciding in favor of a round and that time was running out for India to influence the agenda.

The Government is continuing with its efforts to build and maintain a developing country alliance. But, as past events have shown, this can come apart at the last minute. The Government should not be caught in a position in Doha where it has to sign on the dotted line because in the end it finds itself alone.[27]

The Indian government continued to refuse any deals.

On September 26, WTO General Council Chairman Stuart Harbinson issued two single negotiating texts, draft ministerial declarations meant to express a possible consensus.[28] They were compromises and most delegations complained about items included or excluded. On October 13 and 14 Singapore hosted an informal meeting of twenty-one trade ministers from WTO countries to attempt to narrow gaps between them. Included were African countries that had been excluded from meetings in Seattle. After this meeting Singapore's Minister George Yeo reported that some degree of understanding had been reached on all the gaps and that the WTO was 75 percent of the way toward agreement to launch a new round. India's Minister Murasoli Maran was much less satisfied and continued to oppose a new round. But Pakistan "added to the view expressed privately by many delegates: that India has become increasingly isolated in its stance."[29] Pakistan's Minister Abdul Razak Dawood said, "We feel much more comfortable than two months ago. We are beginning to see a convergence of views on the main issues."[30]

---

[25] *The Statesman* (India), August 9, 2001.
[26] *Financial Times*, August 9, 2001; *The Statesman* (India), August 9, 2001.
[27] "Preparing for Doha," *The Hindu*, August 11, 2001.
[28] *International Trade Reporter [ITR]*, October 4, 2001, 1546.
[29] *ITR*, October 18, 2001, 1633.   [30] *Ibid.*

On October 16 the European Commission announced it had granted Pakistan a side deal improving access for Pakistani textiles and apparel. India was reported to be "hopping mad" over Pakistan's deal.[31] On October 27 Harbinson published second drafts of his two main single texts plus one on TRIPS and public health. The text on implementation did not meet all LMG demands. On the controversial new issues his text said "work" would proceed until the next ministerial conference after Doha, when decisions would be taken on "modalities" of negotiation. The Least Developed Country coalition rejected these drafts as imbalanced against their interests. Pakistan and India denounced Harbinson for planning to send the single text, omitting their dissenting positions, to ministers without a decision by the member states to authorize him to do so.[32] In Doha on the first day a large group of South Asian and African ministers repeated their blunt rejection of talks on investment or competition policy.[33]

Aileen Kwa (2003) cites evidence about other carrots offered and promised to individual members of the LMG to split them off. Regarding Pakistan she adds that the United States gave it a large aid package. One week after the Doha ministerial, the IMF and the World Bank agreed to debt service relief for Tanzania for US$ 3 billion under the HIPC Initiative. Jamaica and other countries of the Caribbean were given an aid package from the IMF after Doha for their post-9/11 tourism-hit economies. A week before Doha, she says, Japan signed a bilateral agreement on investment with Indonesia on the condition that Indonesia agree to an investment agreement at the ministerial. Our own research has not been able to confirm all these allegations. Nor is it clear that correlation, when it occurs, demonstrates causality, particularly since several of these payoffs seem to have been related more to support for the US war on terrorism than compliance with the Quad in the WTO.[34]

However, we too have found at least some evidence of carrots used to buy off individual LMG members. One coalition delegate reported that the Quad offered concessions that affected larger numbers of smaller countries, and in areas where there was no major trade impact (such as assurance of S&D), and in so doing managed to leave the concerns of the larger countries (such as India) unattended.[35] So, for instance,

---

[31] *WTA*, October 29, 2001, 8.
[32] *Bridges*, November 6, 2001, 3; interview, Geneva, fall 2002.
[33] *Bridges* Daily Update, November 13, 2001.
[34] It could be argued that the "War on Terrorism" itself affected the trade negotiations by creating new pressures for reaching agreement.
[35] Interview with a WTO negotiator from an LMG country, Geneva, May 20, 2003.

the African Group, including the African LMG members, accepted the TRIPS and Public Health Declaration and a WTO waiver for the African–Caribbean–Pacific (ACP) preferential arrangement with the EU. In return the African members dropped their opposition to negotiations over industrial tariffs, environment, and Singapore issues.[36] Promises of assistance for capacity building and development aid packages were important for the weakest members of the group.[37] The Egyptians are reputed to have been offered an aid package.[38] Pakistan was offered the US aid package and increased EU textiles quotas and is alleged to have tempered its position in the Textiles Monitoring Body in return.[39]

In addition to carrots, negotiators report that several sticks were also brandished. As one put it, adhering to the LMG position could have got us everything or nothing.[40] This was too big a risk to take, especially as some countries feared that they would lose even the little that they had gained on implementation.[41] Developing countries were told that if they did not agree on the new issues, the African, Caribbean, and Pacific group of countries' (ACP) waiver and the declaration on TRIPS and public health would be withdrawn. "The other source of pressure was that no minister was prepared to be blamed for the failure of Doha, and standing in the way of fighting terrorism."[42] Smaller countries were warned that if they continued with their opposition, their preferences would be withdrawn.[43] According to the accounts of LMG negotiators, threats extended to the balance of payments problems of developing countries, political issues, Free Trade Arrangements (FTAs) and the dependence of developing countries on the IMF.[44]

Several LMG delegates report that the Quad, recognizing the unity of the LMG at the Geneva level, decided to exercise pressures in their national capitals. Ministers were called and told that their ambassadors were standing in the way of consensus and should be ordered to concede or be recalled.[45] Some complied, given that many capitals were

---

[36] Interviews with delegates from developing countries, May 2003.
[37] Interview with a WTO negotiator from an LMG country, Geneva, May 22, 2003.
[38] Interviews, Geneva, May 2003.
[39] Interviews with delegates from developing countries, Geneva, May 2003.
[40] Interview with a WTO negotiator from an LMG country, Geneva, May 20, 2003.
[41] African delegate, quoted by Kwa, 2003, 29.
[42] Zimbabwe's Ambassador Boniface Chidyausiku, quoted by Kwa 2003, 31.
[43] Interview with a WTO negotiator from an LMG country, Geneva, May 23, 2003.
[44] Interviews with WTO negotiators from LMG countries, Geneva, May 2003.
[45] Such pressures were exercised not only on the smaller members of the LMG but also its more powerful members. For instance, Tony Blair is alleged to have called the Indian Prime Minister, Atal Behari Vajpayee, twice, who ultimately then asked Minister Maran to concede; reported in interview with a WTO negotiator from an LMG country, Geneva, May 20, 2003.

not as well-versed in the technical WTO issues as their diplomats, and the capitals, with their broader responsibilities, were also more susceptible to cross-issue linkages (e.g. development aid packages). In Doha itself, ambassadors were told that they could not speak on behalf of their ministers and were actively stopped from interjecting. In the past, ministers had had the discretion to call on their expert ambassadors to speak for them, and this change worked to the severe detriment of developing countries in general and the LMG in particular. As many ministers were not deeply familiar with the technical issues on the agenda, had little experience with the process in the WTO's Green Room, and some even lacked the necessary skills in English, they were in a weak position to oppose. After Doha three ambassadors are alleged to have been recalled from Geneva because of their hard-line stance.[46]

Once the process of fragmentation begins, it can be expected to have an important effect on the internal dynamics of the group as well as externally. Internally, when one defects, the value of the coalition for the remainder diminishes, making defection look more tempting for them as well, producing a domino effect. As one LMG ambassador explains: "Once it became evident to the other countries that some were falling off, then they had to consider if it was politically prudent for them to take up a stance of resistance.'[47] Another similarly admitted, "We were also afraid that if we continued to block, we would end up becoming the only country that blocks. Remember, India was completely isolated at Doha and few countries can take that risk."[48] Externally, declining unity of the coalition undermines its credibility to block, thereby further diminishing the likelihood of achieving the desired agreement with gains. This in turn may be expected to prompt further defections. A few may remain straggling along with the original group agenda, but they no longer pose a credible threat to block. These are also the countries that end up with neither a small bilateral deal nor the aspired collective gain.

The LMG maintained an active and coordinated position through much of the preparatory process. But by November 14 in Doha, India at the end stood alone in its resistance, according to our interviews. The united front had collapsed.

---

[46] Interview with a WTO negotiator from an LMG country, Geneva, May 23, 2003; Kwa 2003.
[47] Interview with a WTO negotiator from an LMG country, Geneva, May 21, 2003.
[48] Interview with a WTO negotiator from an LMG country, Geneva, May 22, 2003.

4   The 2001 outcome: little gain and a major loss for the LMG

The outcome was disappointing for the LMG as a whole and perhaps even more so for the countries that had not settled for bilateral deals. For the coalition the results of the Doha meeting consisted of relatively little tangible gain on their major issues and a major loss, as we read the record in light of the coalition's stated aims and the surrounding context.[49] On their signature issue, implementation, they gained almost nothing of tangible value by November 2001. And they suffered a major loss – the launch of a new round without prior rebalancing of the Uruguay Round's payoffs. The coalition could rightly point to certain other gains from this period, but these seem to be mostly less tangible or due partly to causes other than LMG efforts.

On the implementation issues, the Doha result was "almost a bare cupboard," in the words of the Pakistani representative.[50] The ministers folded some of these issues into the new round – meaning that developing countries could be compelled to pay or pay again through the single undertaking for any new concessions received. Getting some implementation concerns into the round's agenda was a gain compared with having them excluded altogether. But the ministers separated most implementation complaints from the main ministerial declaration, shunting them into a separate "decision on implementation-related issues and concerns."[51] Most of the points in this "decision" merely took note of a report, urged members to make best efforts, or referred a matter back to a WTO body for more talks. The much-discussed idea of improving the Textiles Agreement by applying more favorable "growth-on-growth" provisions was downgraded to a request to the Council on Trade in Goods to talk about it again. The main declaration set a deadline of end of 2002 for action on these matters.

We find a few small tangible gains on implementation. Some paragraphs in the decision defined the phrase "reasonable interval" in existing agreements to mean not less than six months. Paragraph 11 agreed that members would not initiate TRIPS complaints under the nullification and impairment provision while members examined modalities for such complaints. This paragraph also declared that the TRIPS Council

[49] This section does not attempt a comprehensive assessment of the Doha outcome for all parties. It only compares the stated demands of the Like Minded Group with the outcome on those issues. A more comprehensive assessment from a liberal economic standpoint, for example, would identify in the Doha deal considerable scope for achieving welfare gains through negotiating that is not highlighted here.
[50] Quoted by Panagariya 2002.   [51] WTO 2001e.

shall establish a mechanism for monitoring and implementation of previous obligations for technology transfer to the least developed. Otherwise, though, the strategy aiming to squeeze out gains before or during the Doha meeting had yielded little one could put in the bank.

Coalition members can point to certain other gains they had sought, but most of these seem less tangible or due partly to other causes. The Doha development agenda is unprecedented in the attention it accords to development concerns. The main ministerial declaration uses the expressions 'least developed' countries 29 times, 'developing' countries 24 times, and 'LDC' 19 times.[52] But many of these references still amounted only to lip service. And it seems likely that at least some of this emphasis should be attributed to demands many developing countries would have vocalized in some way even had there been no LMG. Northern support for this rhetorical emphasis probably owed something to the Seattle debacle, which was due to more than LMG strategy.

Regarding implementation we believe, though we lack concrete evidence to document it, that this coalition's public campaign did help delegitimate the Uruguay round deal in the eyes of many Northern trade policy experts. By the late nineties after also reading complementary publications by World Bank economists and others, many Northern observers privately seemed to recognize greater imbalance in the Grand Bargain than they had perceived in 1994.

In other matters of development, the main declaration included two provisions proposed by the Like Minded Group. The ministers established two new working groups on trade, debt and finance (Paragraph 36) and technology transfer (Paragraph 37). But these were agreements only to study the issues jointly rather than to negotiate over them, and recommendations from these talks were limited significantly to steps that might be taken "within the mandate of the WTO." Paragraph 44 reaffirms that the provisions of S&D "form an integral part of the WTO Agreements." References to S&D recur in all the declarations, both as a principle and in terms of its application to specific groups like the Least Developed Countries (LDCs) or the small economies. Paragraph 35 of the main declaration sets up a new work program under the auspices of the General Council, directed towards fuller integration of the small and vulnerable economies into the multilateral trading system. Paragraphs 42 and 43 are devoted specifically to the LDCs. Paragraph 42 states, "We commit ourselves to the objective of duty-free, quota-free market access for products originating from LDCs . . . We further commit ourselves to consider additional measures for progressive improvements in market

[52] Panagariya 2002.

access for LDCs." But the LDCs and the small economies respectively organized two coalitions of their own, parallel to the LMG, to work for these provisions. It seems natural to attribute these pieces of the outcome mostly to those other coalitions. References to technical assistance and capacity-building programs for developing countries recur throughout the declarations. But as we will show later, these were also a top priority demand of the African Group, which included many more members than the LMG and which made a credible threat to block the round if these promises were not part of the deal.

Regarding systemic issues, the LMG had been among the most vocal and consistent groups in calling for greater transparency. The process of decision-making at Doha was certainly more inclusive than it had been at Seattle. Mike Moore reports that of the twenty-two ministers present in the final negotiations at Doha, sixteen were from developing countries.[53] According to our interview sources, at least six of these were LMG countries. The open-ended pattern of consultation meetings in 2000 and 2001 was an important development beyond the less open processes at Seattle. However, it is difficult to attribute improvements in process solely or even primarily to the efforts of the LMG. Other factors may have played a significant part in precipitating change, including the Seattle collapse, general agreement even by the Quad that something had to change, initiatives by Chairs Bryn and Harbinson to help the parties evolve a more transparent process, and the active interest and proposals by NGOs and other groups.

The major loss was the launch of a new round without first getting more tangible gains to rebalance the Uruguay Round agreements. In addition, one environmental issue was even added to the Doha agenda at the last minute to the surprise of many, even though many developing members had consistently opposed it and it had never appeared in a chair's text. The outcome regarding the Singapore issues was ambiguous. The declaration said the ministers agreed to launch talks on these issues – a loss for the LMG – but only conditional on a subsequent decision at the next ministerial conference. Relentless opposition by India and partners managed to delay this loss for at least two more years.

Overall, however, the coalition probably was worse off after the Doha ministerial than before, judging from its collective goals. Nor did many demands of individual LMG members make their way into the Doha declarations in any substantive way. Pakistan's gains on textiles in the declarations were few. Malaysia's successes on non-agricultural market access involved little more than a few unenforceable promises. Uganda's

---

[53] Moore 2003.

concerns about studying the implications of tariff reductions for the
LDCs and the decline of preference margins went unnoticed. Mauritius
got a promise of a study program specific to the small and vulnerable
economies and recognition of the importance of S&D, but with no binding obligation beyond study. Above all, these countries were now faced
with an even more complicated set of issues to negotiate, to which their
original concerns are bound, and with a deadline of 2005 for completing
the round. B. L. Das, former Indian Ambassador to the GATT, writing
about a pattern seen over several multilateral negotiations, put his finger
on the risk in strategy choices like those made by the LMG in 1998–2001.
"The transition from the long period of determined opposition to sud-
den collapse into acquiescence at the end has denied these countries the
opportunity of getting anything in return for the concessions they finally
make in the negotiations."[54]

5   Fragmentation is not inevitable: LMG in a comparative light

Fragmentation is not inevitable, however. The result will also depend
on how coalition members respond to attempts at divide-and-rule. Two
different developing country coalitions responded during this same phase
by rejecting lesser offers and holding together behind their joint position:
the TRIPS/ public health coalition and the ACP.

In the case of the TRIPS/ public health coalition (chapter 3), the United
States offered deals appealing to subgroups. The LDCs were offered an
extension of TRIPS transition periods for pharmaceutical products until
2016. For sub-Saharan African countries, Zoellick proposed a moratorium on TRIPS dispute actions for measures they took to address AIDS.
But the coalition stood firm. Just before the ministerial, the US again
offered the moratorium to African ministers at a meeting in Washington.
But through internal bargaining efforts especially by Geneva diplomats,
the coalition managed to avert possible defection at ministerial level. In
Doha, the United States then agreed to negotiate on the basis of the
coalition's proposal. Having achieved this much, the coalition recipro-
cated with some integrative moves and closed a deal.

The case of the ACP 2001 was similar in the use of sequentially mixed
strategy distributive tactics initially, mixed later with integrative ones. On
the last day of the ministerial, six African ministers went to the Director
General and firmly threatened to block unless they were satisfied on two
issues: technical assistance and a WTO waiver for a new preferential

[54] Das 2003.

pact between the African, Caribbean and Pacific states and the European Union.[55] Others found this threat credible and the ACP got the waiver and the promise of assistance. In return for this concession, the ACP countries softened their stance on many other issues (including the LMG issues).

To be sure, there were differences between these two coalitions and the LMG besides their negotiation strategies. Activists on TRIPS/health saw an opportunity to make the emotional AIDS pandemic a factor in WTO negotiations to their advantage, and they allied with northern NGOs to reframe TRIPS as a public health question. This coalition represented a much larger share of the WTO membership – sixty states – including populous Brazil, India, and all of sub-Saharan Africa. The ACP was also a group with a large number of members and it too set more modest goals than the LMG. But each of these two also began with a distributive strategy, achieved and maintained a credible threat to block, but then shifted to a mixed-distributive strategy in the endgame in order to take home some gains.

Had the LMG coalition used a mixed strategy with a similar sequencing, it is quite possible it too would have reaped larger gains. Suppose the LMG had started with high opening demands but eventually asked whether the Quad would concede on some areas in return for LMG concessions on others, or responded to such feelers from the Quad. To take a hypothetical example, the LMG could have scaled down its demands on geographical indications in return for substantive commitments on antidumping from the United States. Another would have been to allow talks on investment but on the condition that an agreement would allow governments to screen investments in the pre-establishment phase and clearly specify the obligations of investors. In return the LMG would have held firm for something on its agenda. The Quad's integrative tactics suggest they were open to deals, at least up to a point. A prospect of reaping these greater gains on its collective agenda would in turn have reduced the temptation of coalition members to defect to separate bilateral deals, and thereby preserved the coalition's credibility in the areas where it stood firm.

6   Strategy Choice and Coalition Identity and Structure

But then why did this particular coalition not choose a mixed strategy? Why did the LMG not attempt to bargain more in the endgame rather than simply acquiescing?

[55] Interview with a participant in the meeting, Geneva, September 24, 2002.

A fundamental reason was that the identity and membership of this particular coalition worked against such a strategy. Coalitions are themselves results of an earlier phase in the negotiation process, and earlier choices can constrain later ones. In this chapter we concentrate on the 2001 LMG outcome and its observed external strategy, the most proximate variable, and do not attempt to explain thoroughly the prior process of negotiating coalition formation. It does suggest a fascinating agenda for future research.

In brief, the members chose to design this coalition's identity as states sharing a common principle – a Like Minded Group – rather than common specific commercial interests. One negotiator explained: "The LMG was really about the inherently unfavorable Uruguay Round. Its point was that only after these issues had been addressed would it engage in new discussions."[56] Another responded to this question saying:

We didn't engage in such trade-offs, and I would argue that we still shouldn't. After all, a major goal of the LMG has been to restore the balance of the Uruguay Round agreements. Why should we pay a second, third or fourth price for that? We felt that the issues we had raised were important in themselves and should be considered on their own merit.[57]

To pay for new gains by falling back from these demands would have been to renege on their defining principle, they felt.[58]

The Like Minded Group's, economic and policy heterogeneity inhibited internal agreement as to priorities[59] and exchanges of concessions with outsiders. Such internal agreements are likely to be challenging for any coalition; homogeneity is never complete.[60] But some LMG negotiators say it was almost impossible for the LMG to engage in trade-offs or even agree on a fallback position for this reason. Consider the diverse levels of development and specific export interests shown in Table 4.1. Thus while Pakistan and Malaysia could have fallen back on customs valuation, India could not agree. Honduras could have fallen back from the group's demands on textiles and clothing but these were central to Pakistan and

---

[56] Interview with a WTO negotiator from an LMG country, May 20, 2003.
[57] Interview with a WTO negotiator from an LMG country, May 22, 2003.
[58] Actually, our interviews found that some delegates in coalition countries personally adhered to this principle with less strength than others.
[59] When we raised the question about prioritization, some negotiators responded that the Quad has indeed made such demands from developing countries. They interpreted these demands for prioritization as part of a strategy of claiming value from them rather than creating joint gain. This would suggest possibly a new variable relating to the level of trust between the negotiating parties. It may also be possible to speculate that the level of trust will increase if the two parties attempt to use mixed strategies.
[60] Hamilton and Whalley 1989.

others. Least developed members had difficulties with Malaysia's preference for aggressive tariff cutting on industrial goods. In fact, according
to one interview, LMG members in 2001 did not even try to agree on
fallback positions. They had expected to block if their demands were not
met, did not anticipate that members would defect, and so did not plan for
damage control.[61] Once a position was arrived at, the LMG would stick
to it relentlessly, and thereby also increase the temptation of members to
defect for smaller but more certain gains.

A special reason for the strategy choice in the LMG case might be
domestic hostility toward the WTO in India, the coalition's most active
member. There the WTO was widely condemned and few firms or politicians spoke in favor of additional WTO agreements, especially not more
agreements like TRIPS. Rigid opposition was believed to be more popular with the public and parliament than a more flexible strategy involving
concessions, even if the former meant losses and the latter meant some
gains for India.[62] It has also been argued that the fact that India had a
coalition government during this period further lowered the odds the government would take the risk of offering concessions before force majeure
made them seem unavoidable.[63]

Clearly not all weak-state coalitions need to be structured as the LMG
was. The TRIPS/health coalition, in contrast, brought together countries
with similar preferences focused on a single main issue. Those formed
with a more homogeneous structure in the first place will probably be less
inhibited from using a mixed strategy. Nor are they necessarily prevented
from using principles to some extent. Negotiators in bilateral as well as
multilateral talks commonly present their positions draped with a principle in the hope of legitimating the position and turning opinion in its
favor. Often they compromise later in ways not entirely consistent with
the framing principle. And if other conditions and tactics are favorable
enough, a delegation or coalition sometimes can generate a consensus to
use its principle to define the agreement. The TRIPS/public health coalition in 2001 began with a claiming principle couched in ethical terms
(linking the issue of TRIPS with the highly emotive issue of the AIDS
pandemic). But once the broad principle had been accepted, the coalition

[61] Interview, WTO negotiator from an LMG country, May 20, 2003.
[62] This hypothesis raises two questions for future research. The first relates to the
counterfactual: had India proposed the use of a mixed strategy, would the LMG have
been able to implement the use of such a strategy, with some very different results? And
second, what have been the domestic and international sources of India's traditional
proclivity to "Just Say No" in international trade negotiations? The latter is research in
progress; Narlikar presented an early draft at a conference in Brasília on *Order, Hegemony,
and Global Counter-Hegemonic Coalitions*, April 14, 2005.
[63] Interview, Geneva, December 2002.

also agreed to compromises including the slight amendment of the coalition's top principle.

7   Alternative Explanations

Several alternative explanations for this case's outcome come to mind, but after examination they seem inadequate by themselves. One familiar set of answers would appeal to power differences. One variant in this set would assume that coalitions with larger market sizes are likely to gain more than coalitions limited to the small. The Quad countries should gain more than any coalition limited to developing countries, and coalitions that involve large market developing economies will gain more than those that comprise small developing economies. Several examples support such a hypothesis. The TRIPS and public health coalition, for instance, had the support of India besides the active leadership of Brazil and South Africa. But having large members is neither necessary nor sufficient. The LMG also had India as a leading player and comprised about 5 percent of the world's imports – a larger share than many other coalitions of developing countries enjoyed at the time, such as the small and vulnerable economies, LDCs and ACP countries – and yet its gains at Doha were disappointing in comparison to the gains of these other coalitions.

Another structural variant might argue that coalitions with a larger number of members can make a more credible threat to block in the WTO and hence are likely to gain more than coalitions with a smaller number of members. In support of this hypothesis, we have the examples of the 2001 TRIPS and public health coalition and the ACP coalition that were both about four times larger than the LMG. But large groups are also associated with the greater costs of free-riding and may be more difficult to hold together due to greater heterogeneity that can result from large membership. Several large coalitions, such as the Informal Group of Developing Countries, have been far less successful. Some smaller groups have gained more. The Cairns Group in the Uruguay Round comprised only fourteen members at its inception, exactly the same size as the LMG at Doha, and yet the former recorded significantly greater gains. Similarly, the G-20 developing countries managed at least to retain their cohesion in Cancún in 2003. If expanding membership helps credibility, it also increases the danger of fragmentation and may not be necessary.

A different additional view has predicted that a coalition's gains will diminish the more its demands diverge from the organization's culture, an element of the context. The Cairns group appealed to the basic norm of market liberalization, arguing it should be extended to agriculture and this coalition gained something in the Uruguay Round;[64] the Like Minded Group during this period met even more resistance because they sought to reopen Uruguay Round agreements that had been signed and ratified by all member states. This hypothesis seems on first glance to add to an understanding of the present case. But this idea might benefit from further research and refinement to disentangle the effects of a regime's culture or norms and its rules. The LMG opposed some of the formal rules adopted in the previous round and the norm of liberalization, but did so partly by appealing to other informal regime norms – that agreements should be balanced, and that developing countries are entitled to positive discrimination. The norm of special and differential treatment was accepted by many but contested by many others. The African, Caribbean, and Pacific group won renewal of a waiver for their preferential Cotonou agreement during this same period. The TRIPS and public health coalition succeeded while demanding a ministerial reaffirmation of an exception to a norm – protecting property rights – but this exception was already written into the rules. What counts as an organization's culture needs more precise consideration than we can give here. Conformity with its culture or norms may also help but such conformity may not be necessary for gains, which probably also vary with how the parties play their cards within that culture. Generally, shortcomings of these alternative explanations in accounting for evidence suggest that the negotiating process – including decisions made when designing coalitions – may have a crucial role to play in influencing outcomes.

8   Conclusion

The use of a strictly distributive strategy by the Like Minded Group in the WTO was a significant contributor to its disappointing outcome in 2001, leaving it perhaps worse off after Doha than before, according to its own stated collective objectives. Faced with their high demands and distributive tactics, the European Union and the United States attempted the cheaper alternative of buying off individual members and succeeded. Had the coalition not fragmented, several of its negotiators believe it would have gained more in Doha. But as soon as the coalition began to fragment, its credibility was undermined, thereby increasing the vulnerability of remaining members to bilateral pressures. As a result, collectively the LMG got little, while the few countries that adhered to the collective position until the end left empty-handed or worse.

---

[64] Ricupero 1998 suggests this hypothesis.

These cases have implications for researchers and negotiators more generally. They suggest that a mixed strategy is likely to gain more for a weak-state coalition than the strict distributive strategy, at least under common conditions. To implement a mixed strategy, coalition members should attempt to negotiate among themselves over priorities and joint fallback positions. These are only a few cases, however; more research is needed to check these propositions and explore their limits.

Our argument also identifies conditions or ways in which the strict distributive strategy will gain more than it did here. Regarding fragmentation, any coalition can expect to gain more if it corrals free-riders and fends off splitting tactics. The odds of doing so will be greater if the coalition is structured in the first place to have greater homogeneity. A single-issue coalition may have less difficulty in practicing a mixed strategy, though that type of coalition also faces other significant problems.[65] Second, assuming some heterogeneity, the odds will be greater if some member or members make side payments to other members to offset the attraction of defection. Doing so may have political costs, however, if the side payment takes the form of a commitment to open the home market. Few developing countries have the resources for financial side payments. Less costly are diplomatic efforts to persuade other members to reject outside offers, by arguing that remaining loyal to the group promises greater gain for that country than defecting. We need more research, however, on which persuasive efforts tend to be more effective in such negotiations.[66]

The second risk is impasse. If an outsider believes it has an alternative to a WTO agreement that is equal or superior to the coalition's terms, the outsiders may well prefer no deal with the coalition. What matters most is how parties perceive their alternatives at a particular time. Studies of the "power of the weak" identify tactics for influencing these perceptions.[67]

Looking beyond a given negotiation episode, it could be argued that taking a strong stand and demonstrating unified willingness to accept a breakdown at one stage will increase the credibility of the threat to walk away in future episodes. But in a boundedly rational world, it is also difficult to know what alternatives others will perceive at that future time. Another risk is that breakdowns will encourage other parties to improve their alternatives, or that trade negotiators will lose control of the process at home to powerful politicians with other agendas.

In sum, low-income and middle-income countries face daunting obstacles to success in WTO negotiations whatever strategies they choose. But

---

[65] Narlikar 2003.
[66] See chapter on the TRIPS and public health coalition for ideas.
[67] See references in the introductory chapter and case studies in other chapters.

one of the things they control is how they negotiate. The implication is that their own choices make some difference to their outcomes. Greater research attention could deepen and widen our understanding of this and other aspects of the economic negotiation process.

REFERENCES

Akram, Munir. 2001. Implementation Concerns – a Developing Country Perspective. *South Bulletin*, No. 6, 15 February, viewed at http://www.southcentre.org/info/southbulletin/bulletin06/bulletin06.htm on June 10, 2005.

Das, Bhagirath Lal. Strengthening Developing Countries in the WTO. Trade and Development Series, No. 8. Third World Network, www.twnside.org.sg/title.td8.html; accessed on May 13, 2003

Jervis, Robert. 1978. Cooperation under the Security Dilemma. *World Politics* 30 (2): 167–214

Kahler, Miles and John Odell. 1989. Developing Country Coalition-building and International Trade Negotiations. In *Trade Policy and the Developing World*, ed. John Whalley, 149–66. Ann Arbor: University of Michigan Press

Kwa, Aileen, 2003. *Power Politics in the WTO*. Bangkok: Focus on the Global South

Hamilton, Colleen, and John Whalley. 1989. Coalitions in the Uruguay Round. *Weltwirtschaftliches Archiv* 125 (3): 547–56

Moore, Mike. 2003. *A World Without Walls: Freedom, Development, Free Trade, and Global Governanace*. Cambridge: Cambridge University Press.

Narlikar, Amrita. 2003. *International Trade and Developing Countries: Bargaining Coalitions in the GATT and WTO*. London: Routledge, 2003

Odell, John, 2000. *Negotiating the World Economy*. Ithaca NY: Cornell University Press, 2000

Ostry, Sylvia. 2000. The Uruguay Round North–South Grand Bargain: Implications for Future Negotiations. Political Economy of International Trade Law, University of Minnesota. September; available at http://www.utoronto.ca/cis/ostry.html; accessed on 10 June 2005

Panagariya, Arvind. 2002. Developing Countries at Doha: a Political Economy Analysis. *World Economy* 29 (9): 1205–33; also available at http://www.columbia.edu/~ap2231/Policy%20Papers/Doha-WE-2.pdf; accessed on June 10, 2005.

Ricupero, Rubens. 1998. Integration of Developing Countries into the Multilateral Trading System. In *The Uruguay Round and Beyond: Essays in Honor of Arthur Dunkel*, eds. Jagdish Bhagwati and Mathias Hirsch, 9–36. Ann Arbor: University of Michigan Press

Tussie, Diana and David Glover, eds. 1995. *The Developing Countries in World Trade: Policies and Bargaining Strategies*. Boulder: Lynne Rienner

WTO. 1996. Singapore Ministerial Declaration. WT/MIN(96)/DEC, December 18

WTO. 1999a. Agreement on Subsidies and Countervailing Measures. Communication from Cuba, Dominican Republic, Egypt, El Salvador,

Honduras, India, Indonesia, Nicaragua and Thailand. WT/GC/W/164/Rev.2, June 14

WTO. 1999b. Agreement on TRIPS, Proposal Regarding Extension of Protection of Geographical Indications under Paragraph 9(a)(i) of the Geneva Ministerial Declaration. Communication from Cuba, Dominican Republic, Egypt, Honduras, India, Indonesia, Nicaragua and Pakistan. WT/GC/W/208, June 17, 1999

WTO. 1999c. Implementation Issues to be addressed before/at Seattle. Communication from Cuba, Dominican Republic, Egypt, El Salvador, Honduras, India, Indonesia, Malaysia, Nigeria, Pakistan, Sri Lanka and Uganda. WT/GC/W/354, October 11

WTO. 1999d. Implementation Issues to be addressed in the First Year of Negotiations. Communication from Cuba, Dominican Republic, Egypt, El Salvador, Honduras, India, Indonesia, Malaysia, Nigeria, Pakistan, Sri Lanka and Uganda. WT/GC/W/355, October 11

WTO. 1999e. Agriculture: Proposal under Paragraphs 9(a)(i) and 9(a)(ii) of the Geneva Ministerial Declaration. Communication from Cuba, Dominican Republic, Egypt, El Salvador, Honduras, Sri Lanka, Uganda and Zimbabwe. WT/GC/W/374, October 15

WTO. 1999f. Transfer of Technology Provisions in the WTO Agreements. Communication from Cuba, Egypt, Honduras, India, Pakistan and Malaysia. WT/W/GC/327/Add.1, September 28

WTO. 2001a. Proposal for a Framework Agreement on Special and Differential Treatment. Communication from Cuba, Dominican Republic, Honduras, India, Indonesia, Kenya, Malaysia, Pakistan, Sri Lanka, Tanzania, Uganda and Zimbabwe. WT/GC/W/442, September 19

WTO. 2001b. Proposal for the Establishment of a Working Group for the study of the inter-relationship between Trade and Transfer of Technology. Communication from Cuba, Dominican Republic, Honduras, India, Indonesia, Kenya, Malaysia, Pakistan, Sri Lanka, Tanzania, Uganda and Zimbabwe. WT/GC/W/443, September 18

WTO. 2001c. Proposal for the establishment of a Working Group on the inter-relationship between trade and finance. Communication from Cuba, Dominican Republic, Honduras, India, Indonesia, Kenya, Malaysia, Pakistan, Sri Lanka, Tanzania, Uganda, and Zimbabwe. WT/GC/W/444, September 18

WTO. 2001d. Proposal for the establishment of a Working Group on the inter-relationship between trade and debt, Communication from Cuba, Dominican Republic, Honduras, India, Indonesia, Kenya, Malaysia, Pakistan, Sri Lanka, Tanzania, Uganda, and Zimbabwe. WT/GC/W/445, September 18

WTO. 2001e. Decision on Implementation-related Concerns. WT(MIN)/01/17, November 20

5 Learning in multilateral trade negotiations: some results from simulation for developing countries

Cédric Dupont, Cosimo Beverelli and Stéphanie Pézard

Introduction

Whereas there are still many gaps in our understanding of negotiation processes, one well-established pattern is that the way negotiators communicate and interpret information does matter. It codetermines both the process and outcome of bargaining. In the study of international negotiations, authors have particularly focused on how actors behave when they have, at the beginning of the process, limited information regarding the resources, resolve, and domestic context of their negotiating partners. A large body of literature has explored such situations with the use of formal game-theoretic analytical tools, making use of so-called incomplete information models to see how limited information can influence actors' strategies. Incomplete information about domestic politics has been a particular focus of study, especially since the advent of the two-level game metaphor,[1] which gave a new start to an older research tradition on domestic politics and international negotiations.[2] Authors have paid particular attention to the influence of domestic feasibility sets, win-sets in Putnam's words, on international negotiations,[3] starting from the assumption that negotiators can never, or at least very rarely, exactly

This article is built around simulation exercises conducted within the programs of the Training Institute of the WTO. We thank the WTO for allowing us to observe those exercises for research-related purposes and Gilbert Winham for allowing us to interfere in the exercise that he designed. An earlier version of the chapter was presented at a conference on Developing Countries and the Trade Negotiation Process at UNCTAD in Geneva, November 6–7, 2003. We are most grateful to John Odell for valuable comments, suggestions and support on the various drafts of this chapter, to John Cuddy and Magdi Farahat for discussing our paper during the conference, and to Christoph Zulauf for valuable research assistance. We also benefited from comments from other contributors to this book and from the financial support of the Geneva Academic International Network (GIAN).

[1] Putnam 1988.   [2] Schelling 1960; Iklé 1964.
[3] See for instance the work of Iida 1993; Milner 1997; Milner and Rosendorff 1997; Mo 1994 and 1995; Pahre 1997; Dupont 1994a and 1994b; Dupont and Sciarini 1995 and 1998.

know the domestic constraints of their counterparts, and may also have difficulty with their own constraints. While such recent formal work has helped to better determine the conditions of applicability of Schelling's famous theory of strength in (domestic) weakness, that question remains problematic, to say the least, for many analysts, observers and practitioners of international negotiations. We see two main reasons for this. A first one is linked to what Allan and Dupont call the lack of robustness of most game-theoretic models that use advanced solution concepts (relying on refined criteria for unexpected behavior) for reducing indeterminacy in complex settings.[4] Particularly problematic are the rationality demands placed upon negotiators who are assumed to be very sophisticated maximizers who carefully update any piece of information that they get. There is a kind of sophistication to the square. Actors are assumed to form sophisticated beliefs about the state of the world and to change them in sophisticated fashion. A second reason is that game-theoretic models have almost uniquely looked at bilateral bargaining processes,[5] mostly due to the technical limits, or deficit, of game theory for situations of multiple actors.

One response to these problems has been to rely on less demanding formal tools, in particular those stemming from the negotiation analytic tradition pioneered by Howard Raiffa.[6] As John Odell's study shows,[7] those tools connect better to empirical developments than most game theoretic constructs. Yet, on the particular issues of limited information and multilateralism, they are far from convincing, as Odell acknowledges in his concluding chapters. The focus remains mostly on two actors, and beliefs are not rigorously explored.

Another response has been the development of evolutionary game theory based on the extensive experimental literature on coordination games.[8] Taking inspiration from the early work of Simon,[9] this literature has developed and tested various "learning mechanisms." Relaxing some restrictive conditions of standard game theory[10] – no fixed number of players, no hyper-rationality, and a less demanding updating of beliefs – has helped produce more realistic models of convergence toward an outcome. Yet, communication is strikingly absent in this literature. Coordination remains a tacit process based on probabilistic estimates of the others' behavior. There has not been much response in the literature to the question of how individuals process information and how this leads them gradually to an outcome.

---

[4] Allan and Dupont 1999.
[5] For exceptions see Bueno de Mesquita 1990; Morgan 1994.
[6] Raiffa 1982.   [7] Odell 2000.
[8] Crawford 1990 and 1995; van Huyck, Battalio, and Beil 1990, 1991, and 1997.
[9] Simon 1955 and 1959.   [10] Young 1998; Foster and Young 2003.

There is thus a fundamental need for further work that would help design analytical tools that could simultaneously model multiple actors with endogenous beliefs. Such a goal will remain elusive if one does not accept a range of simplifying assumptions. Advanced mathematics will not be a solution without those assumptions, unless one is willing to accept large-scale indeterminacy. The question is therefore to determine what are, and should be, the appropriate simplifications. While some could be theoretically derived, we claim that careful and precise empirical observations are necessary. There has been so far a striking lack of data collection for assessing the influence of beliefs on negotiation processes. Studies using formal tools have either remained mostly abstract or have focused on a few case studies as plausibility probes for the hypotheses derived from game-theoretic models. Furthermore, there has been a clear emphasis on developed countries, in particular the United States and European countries. In our view, such a bias has to be remedied, not only for improving our understanding of how developing countries fare in negotiation processes but also for our general understanding of the impact of limited, or biased, information in international negotiations.

Indeed, within the context of the work cited above, a focus on developing countries may allow significantly different lessons to be drawn. There are at least three reasons for this: (a) developed countries tend to have more transparent domestic political systems, making them "easier" cases for two-level games, and therefore tend to skew the analytical focus on beliefs about domestic political constraints; (b) developed countries can "afford" to carefully process and update information during negotiation processes simply because they have the required expertise and staff; lacking such an expertise and such a staff, developing countries may simply pay less attention to information problems. From a positivist perspective, this implies that it is misleading to try to use beliefs to explain developing countries' negotiation behavior. From a normative, prescriptive (policy-science) perspective, this could mean that there is urgent need for developing countries to acquire expertise in information processing and updating; (c) generally speaking, developed countries tend to be stronger actors who, in the context of game-theoretic models, discount future agreements to a lesser extent; existing models reveal a clear difference between such actors and weaker ones in terms of both negotiation offers, content and timing of agreement.[11]

In order to begin sorting out these different issues systematically, this chapter provides preliminary evidence from simulated worlds. This evidence will be connected, when and where relevant, to the partial findings

---

[11] See in particular Dupont 1994a and 1994b.

148   *Cédric Dupont, Cosimo Beverelli and Stéphanie Pézard*

of the case studies that appear elsewhere in this collective book. The chapter makes use of simulation exercises conducted by the Training Institute of the World Trade Organization (WTO) for participants from the developing world. The approach borrows from the tradition of laboratory experiments for negotiation processes,[12] while being closer to reality because individuals who participate in simulated trade negotiations are officials from member states, and therefore very likely to participate in similar real negotiations in the future. In fact, several of them already have some practical experience from real negotiations. Furthermore, in contrast to standard laboratory experiments that rarely last more than one hour, the simulation exercises run over several days and they are not under the permanent control of observers. Apart from a few pre-fixed meetings, participants are free to organize the negotiations the way they judge most appropriate. In practical terms, this has made observation more difficult, and more time consuming, but also empirically richer than in standard laboratory experiments.[13]

The chapter first describes the basic features of the simulation exercise and the research questions that it helps explore. It then turns to the results obtained from a first series of experiments from December 2002 to June 2003. We first address the question of whether there is indeed some learning by actors during the negotiation. Then we turn to the learning dynamics and in particular the factors that can be expected, according to the literature, to have an impact on the process of learning. We conclude with a summary of our main results and with suggestions for the continuation of our work.

1   Features of the simulated world and research questions

1.1   Simulation protocol

We conducted our observations on an existing simulation exercise, the Trade Negotiation Simulation Exercise (TNSE) as used at the WTO Training Institute. The TNSE, initially designed by Gilbert Winham at Dalhousie University, features the participation of four fictional countries. Two of them, Alba and Tristat, have developed economies, whereas the other two, Medatia and Vanin, have developing economies. The TNSE consists of two nested exercises: a negotiation over tariff reductions and the redaction of a subsidy code.

[12] See in particular Roth 1987 and 1988; Roth and Murnighan 1982. See the recent survey and its applications to international relations in McDermott 2004.
[13] For a discussion of the limits of laboratory experiment, see McDermott 2004, 24–30.

For each country the team includes a minister, an ambassador who usually acts as chief negotiator, a tariff expert, a non-tariff expert, and at least one counsellor. Participants approach the TNSE with a reasonable amount of information. They know the characteristics of their own country, as well as those of the others, both in terms of levels of development (i.e. GDP) and existing trade policies. In addition, cabinet orders distributed to ministers contain knowledge about: a) the products/sectors in which tariff concessions can be granted by their own country; b) the products/sectors in which their own country is asking trade partners to liberalize their tariff policy; c) the negotiating guidelines for the subsidy code. Ministers are free to decide which pieces of information they want to pass on within their respective teams. Cabinet orders are usually not communicated to other teams, although there is no formal restriction to do so in the simulation protocol.

The participants to the TNSE are diplomats from developing countries enrolled in a course at the WTO Training Institute prior to this exercise.

Several features of the exercise work towards making it as realistic as possible:

- Strict "cabinet orders", serving as negotiating guidelines and constraints, which Ministers transmit to their negotiating teams;
- A certain freedom in the organization of teams, where the ambassador can be either a mere coordinator or the leader of negotiations;
- Strong time pressure, for the agreement, if agreement there is, must be concluded within three days.[14] Teams are constantly reminded of the deadline (strictly enforced) during the course of the exercise;[15]
- The high level of stress inherent to any serious negotiation can also be found in the exercise, despite the fact that the interests at stake are fictional. We have observed evidence of high emotional commitment to the performance of one's team (arguments, tears).
- The exercise ends with the responses of ministers to their cabinet, in which they report the details of the agreement reached and their ability – or inability – to respect the cabinet orders they had been given. Even though there is no actual cabinet involved in the game, this formality aims at establishing a two-level game logic;

---

[14] This time pressure is also highlighted by the results of the debriefing questionnaires on the estimated sources of inefficiencies in the negotiation: the proposition "Lack of time to explore further negotiating opportunities" was consistently mentioned as one such source of inefficiency (no. 2: 8 yes, 6 no; no. 3: 13 yes, 5 no; no. 4: 12 yes, 1 no; this question did not appear in the exercise no. 1).

[15] For instance, the date and hour at which the agreement must be signed is constantly written in big letters on the whiteboard of the room where all multilateral meetings take place.

- According to the exercise guidelines, all countries believe in the virtues of free trade, but they have different economic, social and political interests and different levels of development, which leads to major clashes during the course of the negotiations;
- There is a president who acts as an "honest broker", facilitating the sharing of information among teams and chairing a few multilateral meetings. The secretariat (staff from the WTO Training Institute) helps with technical aspects and logistics.

Despite all these elements, the TNSE remains a simulation that falls short of the real negotiations such as the ones studied by the other contributors to this volume. Differences between the simulated and real worlds are particularly important on the following dimensions:

- Obviously, the interests at stake are fictitious. Thus, participants' identification with their "national interest" cannot be compared with what would happen in real negotiations;
- Ministers, who normally remain behind the scenes, and most of the time in their capitals during real rounds of negotiations, have a tendency in the TNSE to get involved in the process, and can sometimes be found to participate actively in the talks;
- There seems to be an implicit understanding that an agreement *must* be reached almost by any means. This may derive from the way the exercise is structured, through pressures by the secretariat, or from elementary psychological dynamics by which the subject of an experiment wants to "succeed" and not make the whole exercise (whose purpose is to reach a multilateral agreement) fail. All these elements account for the fact that, among the numerous exercises that have been performed (including those we did not observe), few of them have resulted in failure to reach an agreement. This means that in a way the exercise artificially increases the cost of no agreement, lowering the participants' "best alternatives to a negotiated agreement" (BATNAs) and forcing them to go beyond cabinet orders more than they would be willing to do in real circumstances. This is not to say that nothing like this exists in real life (on the contrary, one can reasonably claim that negotiators always prefer success to failure), but in the TNSE the trade-off between the "happy ending" of the exercise and the preservation of the national interest leans much more towards the first element.
- The fact that, as noted above, there is no real cabinet behind the cabinet orders aggravates the tendency to try to reach an agreement at any cost, since there are no considerations of accountability. In other words, all the ministers know that whatever they accept in the name of their country in the negotiations, there will be no one to fire them once they are back in their fictional capitals.

• Finally, the simulation includes four countries bargaining over a restricted set of tariffs lines, which is obviously a much less complex exercise than a multilateral round of negotiations with more than 140 countries, many issue areas and many trade policy tools.

1.2   Data set

With all these limitations in mind, we observed and studied a series of four TNSEs between December 2002 and June 2003.[16] These simulations involved 99 individuals from developing countries and countries in transition. Individuals were grouped in country teams of five or six members. In each exercise, participants elected one chairperson for the whole process.

We carefully observed the four exercises and collected data in different ways. First, we conducted daily interviews with the ambassadors and ministers of each country (32 individuals in total). The questionnaires[17] aim at systematically tracing the evolution of the negotiation from the perspective of the participants.[18] Most questions focus on informational issues and the way they affect the negotiation process. To avoid interfering too much with the process, interviews were meant to be very short.

Second, we distributed at the end of each exercise a debriefing questionnaire to collect overall impressions of the exercise. And third, we sat in rooms where participants were negotiating when these rooms were located in the building of the WTO. We took notes of the offers and requests made by countries and of the arguments behind them. For practicality reasons, the results that we discuss in the next section mostly use data from the questionnaires (with some complements coming from direct observation) and focus on the tariffs negotiations.

We had no control over the selection of participants, nor on the composition of groups of negotiation. Although this may become a problem at a later stage of our research (impossibility to trace some possible variations depending on the origins of participants), it has the advantage of avoiding any intentional bias on our part. And we did get variation in

---

[16] These four TNSEs were respectively included in a Special Course on Negotiations (December 2–13, 2002), two three-month Trade Policy Courses (English and French-speaking, January 13 – April 4, 2003), and a Special Course on Negotiations (June 16–27, 2003). For the sake of brevity they will be labeled no. 1, 2, 3 and 4 in the rest of this chapter.

[17] Copies of the questionnaires can be obtained from the authors on request.

[18] Due to our effort to improve the interview questions and the debriefing questionnaires, some elements have sometimes been changed from one exercise to the other, which explains why the results of some questions can only be analyzed for two or three exercises instead of four.

terms of geographical origins (all the continents represented), in terms of training/education (economics, law, social sciences), in terms of gender, in terms of current professional status and in terms of experience in the field of trade negotiations.[19]

1.3   Research questions

Our purpose in studying the different TNSEs is to get as close as possible to the negotiators (who are not forbidden to speak because of matters of secrecy, as they could be in a real negotiation) in order to grasp their understanding of the role they see themselves playing, of the strategies that are available to them and of the way they perceive other countries. Negotiators must approach the talks with a more or less defined knowledge of the interests of the country they represent, and with the clearest possible knowledge of the other(s). In that context, we are interested in answering the following two sets of questions:

1. Do actors learn during the negotiation process? Do we see any evidence that dealing with partners has changed their initial apprehension of the bargaining situation?
2. How are the initial information and knowledge updated and translated into new beliefs and tactics? Do negotiators follow some preestablished cognitive heuristics, or do they react to the tactics adopted by other teams? What does this suggest about likely outcomes as a result of choosing specific strategies and tactics?

These are the questions we will try to explore in this chapter, using our own observations of the bilateral and multilateral meetings, as well as the feedback from the participants we were able to gather. Although simple, prima facie, this simulation setting is already quite complex as far as beliefs are concerned. Indeed, there is a dual problem of incomplete information, both within and between parties. The setting combines features of agent-principal models as well as bilateral bargaining models. Given that there are four parties that can bargain either bilaterally, or multilaterally (on three or four sides), information diffusion, through signaling,

---

[19] Participants in the first and fourth exercises tend to be higher ranked diplomats or civil servants, most accustomed to a strategic approach to negotiations. From the answers given in the debriefing questionnaire to the question: "Have you ever participated in or observed any real negotiation?" we observe that 31 participants, over a total of 67 returned questionnaires, have prior negotiating experience (this represents 46 percent of those who responded and 31 percent of the participants). According to the existing literature we should expect individuals to learn through experience. Bazerman, Magliozzi and Neale 1985; Neale, Huber and Northcraft 1987; Neale and Northcraft 1986.

can also be quite varied.[20] In short, this is a very interesting setting for collecting data. As we will show below, it brings results that complement several of the findings of the case study analyses by other contributors to this book.

2   Evidence

As previous exercises using the same protocol had already showed, the simulation led to different final outcomes. Countries came out with different average tariff cuts, different bilateral agreements, different sector agreements, as well as different texts on subsidies. Agreements followed more or less the cabinet orders. This clearly indicates that the simulation itself is not predetermined: cabinet orders are not precise or strict enough to dictate the outcome of the game. The negotiating process therefore does determine the outcome. Our focus here is on information exchange and the evolution of actors' perceptions and knowledge. Our discussion considers general trends with minimal attention paid to anecdotal evidence. We first present data that uncover a learning curve among actors and then analyze potential reasons behind particular learning patterns.

2.1   Evidence of learning

To uncover some learning attitude, we look at whether participants improve and refine their information as the simulation proceeds through time. We focus on three interrelated aspects: bottom lines of negotiating partners, the zone of agreement and the cooperative attitude of other countries.

2.1.1   Getting to know others' bottom lines   During the tariff negotiation process, consisting primarily of a number of bilateral discussions aiming at negotiating tariff cuts sector after sector, or product after product, countries reveal progressively their position and their bottom line becomes progressively clearer for their partners. We should expect this "revealing" process to be the main source of improved knowledge.

In order to assess the learning aspect of the exercise, we ask the ambassadors in their daily questionnaire to evaluate, on a scale from 1 (minimum) to 5 (maximum), their knowledge of the maximum concessions that other countries could make. The answers were recorded for each

---

[20] The multiple actors setting allows for an empirical exploration of what Lohmann calls "player linkage," that is, strategies that "control" some actor through its links with other actors in the system (here in the negotiation process): Lohmann 1997.

Table 5.1 *Change in negotiators' perceived knowledge of others' bottom lines*

	From day 1 to day 2 (N=48)	From day 2 to day 3 (N=48)	From day 1 to day 3 (N=48)
Increase	16	21	16
Same	8	13	6
Decrease	11	6	8
Missing	13	8	18

Note: number of cases for each column corresponds to three perceptions by country times the number of exercises, that is, 3 × 4 × 4. Last column looks at change between day 1 and day 3 without taking into account the situation in day 2

of the three days of the TNSE, allowing us to compare the levels of knowledge (as given by the ambassadors) over time. Table 5.1 provides a detailed account of how the perceived knowledge of maximal concessions by ambassadors changes in the negotiation process.

Abstracting from relative movements, it appears that perceived knowledge of the opponents' maximum concessions does increase as the negotiation goes on. Whereas 33 percent of responses (16/48) on day 2 indicate an increase of perceived knowledge, the proportion goes up to 44 percent (21/48) on day 3. Furthermore, one should note a decrease in the number of actors who cannot or do not want to respond (27 percent for the day1–day2 transition, 17 percent for day2–day3). Yet, given the small number of observations, these trends do not meet acceptable levels of statistical significance.

We also asked ambassadors to evaluate other ambassadors' knowledge of the maximum concessions that their own country could make.[21] This allows us to check whether the evaluation by the ambassador of country X of country Y's bottom lines corresponded (matched) with the evaluation by the ambassador of country Y of Country X's knowledge about Country Y's bottom lines. Consistent (matching) evaluation by both sides can be considered as an indication of smooth and efficient flow of reliable information. On the other hand, a mismatch would signal the presence of a difficulty in bypassing biases, communication problems or simply misunderstandings. The first row of Table 5.2 summarizes the evidence. It can easily be seen that matching is not the rule: it happened only in 36 cases out of a total of 144 (25 percent) while in 38 pairs at least one ambassador answered that he could not tell. Yet, one can see a higher rate of matching as the negotiation proceeds. For the third day, we observe

[21] The question was: "On a 1 to 5 scale, 5 being the maximum, how would you evaluate X's knowledge of the maximum concessions that you can make?".

Table 5.2 *Mismatch and perception of bottom lines*

	Day 1 (N=48)	Day 2 (N=48)	Day 3 (N=48)	Total (N=144)
Matching answers	8	11	17	36
Difference of 1	10	19	11	40
Difference of 2	6	8	5	19
Difference of 3	6	2	2	10
Difference of 4	0	1	0	1
Incomplete	18	7	13	38

Note: matching is defined as a situation in which the perceived knowledge by actor A of actor B's bottom lines has the same coding as the perception by B of actor A's knowledge of B's bottom lines

17 cases of matching out of 35 pairs (48.6 percent). This percentage is significantly higher than the one observed during the first day (8 out of 30 cells, 26.6 percent) or the second day (11 out of 41 cells, 26.8 percent). This could be an indicator that parties, as the negotiation goes on, come to converge on their evaluation of the context.

One possible objection here could be that the source of mismatch is the content and wording of the questionnaire. For instance, interviewees may not give the same weight to the different values of the scale. Two ambassadors could both think they have a very good knowledge of the concessions that the other can make, but that for one "very good knowledge" deserves a 4 (on the 1 to 5 scale) while for the other it deserves a 5. For this reason, we refine the above analysis by looking not just at the existence of mismatches but also at the size of those mismatches. Table 5.2 reveals that most of the mismatches are small ones. It also shows that the downward trend observed in Table 5.1 from day 1 to day 2 may be misleading. The overall increase in the number of mismatches between those two days is uniquely due to the increase in the number of small mismatches, other ones decreasing. Another objection, more radical, may also be the absence of statistical significance of the learning trend, which in our view should not be interpreted on too strict an econometric standard.

2.1.2 Viewing a zone of agreement The ambassadors' daily questionnaires contain a question on whether they think there is a zone of agreement with negotiating partners (three possible answers: "Yes," "No" or "Don't know"). Logically, based on the evidence from the previous questions, one should expect a convergent process here too. Table 5.3 summarizes the data.

Table 5.3 *Answers to "Do you think that there is a zone of agreement with X?"*

	Day 1 (N=48)	Day 2 (N=48)	Day 3 (N=48)
Yes	22	28	33
No	5	6	4
Do not know or no answer	21	14	11

Note: number of cases is the product of three answers times four countries times four exercises for each day

Table 5.4 *Dyadic evaluations of the zone of agreement*

	Day 1 (N=24)	Day 2 (N=24)	Day 3 (N=24)
Yes-Yes	8	8	13
No-No	0	0	0
Yes-No and No-Yes	2	3	1
At least one no answer	14	13	10

Note: number of cases is the product of six bilaterals times the number of exercises for each day

Very clearly, negotiators seem to become more optimistic about the existence of a zone of agreement as the process goes on. Not only the number for "Yes" increases, but also the numbers for "Don't know" and "No" decrease.

As for our discussion of bottom lines, we now assess the question of the zone of agreement on a dyadic basis, rather on an individual basis. Specifically, for each pair of countries we examine whether both countries come up with the same answer (either Yes–Yes or No–No), with an opposite answer (Yes–No or No–Yes) or simply an incomplete answer (one of them at least not answering the questions).

As in the case of the evaluation of maximum concessions, Table 5.4 shows that the incidence of mismatch is lowest on the third day of negotiations, indicating the progressive acquisition of common knowledge. Parties very rarely come up with a different assessment of the existence of a zone of agreement and never mutually come up with a negative answer. In addition, the number of "Don't knows" or missing answers diminishes with time. It is also relevant to point out that only in one case did we observe more than one mismatch in the same bilateral relationship: this was Medatia–Vanin in exercise no. 3, where Medatia's optimism was contrasted by Vanin's reiterated pessimism about the prospects of reaching a bilateral tariff agreement.

2.1.3 Cooperative attitude Change was also perceptible in the answers to the questions: "Which country do you find the most cooperative? Which country do you find the least cooperative?" Looking at the time series for each country across the four exercises (32 observations), 56 percent (18) of them show change, 22 percent (7) no change at all and 22 percent (7) are incomplete. So clearly negotiators modify their evaluation of their partners across time.

Another, less straightforward, way to uncover change on that dimension is to check if there is an increasing number of dyads with mutually compatible evaluation, that is, dyads in which both actors declare each other as the most or the least cooperative. Such a trend does emerge, albeit slightly, from the observed simulations, in particular if we contrast it to dyads with diametrically opposed evaluations.[22] Indeed, during the interviews on the first day, there were three matching pairs and three non-matching pairs. On the second day, there were five matching pairs and three non-matching pairs. On the third day, there were still five matching pairs, but no non-matching pair.

Overall, the results derived from the daily interviews with the ambassadors indicate that there seems to be a learning process that operates during the course of the exercise: actors gain new information about their negotiating partners – an information that progressively tends to become common knowledge – and update their beliefs according to it. Our data seem to suggest that with time negotiators' views converge in a threefold manner: a) there is a narrowing of differences between perceived knowledge of maximum concessions and evaluations of that (actual) knowledge by the opponent; b) we see an increase in number of pairs of negotiators agreeing on the existence of a zone of agreement; c) there is an increase in pairs mutually designating each other most/least cooperative.

Hence our results so far seem on the one hand to give empirical credit to models or theories that posit that actors learn throughout a negotiation process. Moreover, as indicated in some game-theoretic models (standard or evolutionary types), learning is not a smooth process. Actors may update in different directions or may simply continue not to update for quite some time. On the other hand, the evidence seems to contradict some of the results obtained in laboratory experiments. For instance, we do not so far have any clear evidence that when negotiators hold beliefs

---

[22] We could not use data from exercise 1 because the questionnaire did not include the relevant questions.

they tend to ignore information that disconfirms those beliefs, as shown in work in laboratory experiments.[23] Similarly, we cannot affirm that negotiators exhibit cognitive closure, as a way to simplify their negotiation behavior.[24] One could object that the high number of missing answers may in fact give support to those laboratory results. Yet, this could only be the case if there were some consistency in actors' missing answers, which we did not find. It thus appears that our work may differ quite significantly from prior work using simulated worlds, and yields trends more in line with some formal, abstract models.

2.2   Information transmission and patterns of change

The data, presented above, suggests that the convergence process is on the one hand not smooth, and on the other hand is sometimes hard to discern. The aim of this section is to uncover factors that can affect patterns of learning and link them to strategic or tactical choices by actors. We structure our discussion along factors that have been extensively assumed or researched in other work. We begin with the relevance of signals, then turn to the imprint of initial expectations, continue with potential problems of transparency and the influence of biases and country specific features, and lastly we discuss the importance of truthfulness.

2.2.1   A signalling game?   We have not found explicit evidence that actors have as sophisticated an interpretative attitude towards signals as assumed in most theoretical models of bargaining. However, we can confidently argue, on the basis of our qualitative observations, that the exercises do contain features of signalling games, in which actors send pieces of information about their "type" to negotiating partners and in which partners show a capacity to decipher the meaning of signals. To give one specific example, in exercise no. 4 for instance, during the preliminary discussions (before the starting of bilateral meetings), Alba proposed a formula approach that implicitly aimed at getting a drastic reduction in Tristat's agricultural tariff peaks, as high as 120 percent for one product. This strong "signal" was well understood by Tristat's Ambassador, who declared to his team: "Our position in agriculture is going to be extremely uncomfortable."

As assumed in formal models, the interpretation of signals is a difficult, contingent exercise in particular when countries resort to bluffing tactics. This is the case, for example, with Alba vis-à-vis Medatia in exercise no. 1.

---

[23] Lord, Ross, and Lepper 1979.
[24] De Dreu, Kool, and Oldersma 1999; Kruglanski and Webster 1996.

On the second day of negotiations, Alba initiated a new tactic by asking all tariffs to be bound at the applied rate. Alba's Ambassador was well aware that this request was way beyond what Alba's cabinet orders instructed him to accept from Medatia, so we can safely claim that the request was a bluff. Interestingly, Medatia's reaction was not to change anything in its assessment of the zone of agreement but it did change its evaluation of Alba's knowledge about its own bottom lines. Tough bargaining requires credibility, as for instance when one chooses a distributive strategy.[25]

As an evidence of the difficulty to signal, we observed, in some cases, inconsistencies between tactical moves and the related signals. In exercise no. 3, for instance, Alba issued a very generous offer of tariff reductions to Medatia but the ambassador, due to poor negotiating skills, was not able to send a consistent signal of generosity.[26] Alba's ambassador's conduct had a very negative impact on Medatia's ambassador's assessment of Alba. During the interview that followed the episode, he pointed at Alba as the least cooperative partner (while on the first day Alba was the most cooperative partner for Medatia). He also evaluated that a zone of agreement between Medatia and Alba no longer existed. Finally, he gave Alba a 2 on the truthfulness scale, while on the first day Alba had scored 3. The situation improved significantly on the last day of negotiations. Medatia's Ambassador estimated that there was again a zone of agreement with Alba; he also gave Alba a 4 on the truthfulness scale, which is the highest score given by him during the three daily interviews. This example is a good example of how hard it can be to get the right credit from giving concessions. Ortiz's study on NAFTA negotiations reveals that one way to force a partner to value a concession rightly is to simultaneously ask for concessions from the other.[27] Or when others fail to acknowledge the value of concessions, the only solution may be to try to reframe the negotiation context.[28]

More generally, this discussion is a good indicator of the complexity of signals. In particular, it is hard for negotiators to determine which pieces of the interchange between parties are relevant signals. To put it into the context of game-theoretic models, how can negotiators determine a "revealing" signal? Our observations so far are not sufficient for elaboration on that topic but it is clear that signals are rarely clear enough. A particular offer or request needs to be carefully communicated and explained

---

[25] Narlikar and Odell, chapter 4 in this volume.
[26] Of course, the evaluation of generosity is subjective. In this instance, Alba offered reductions on fifteen products out of a total of thirty. Moreover, this was an unconditional offer, also in the sense that it did not respond to any request by Medatia. Third, it was very close to the offer contained in the final bilateral agreement, indicating its closeness to Alba's bottom line.
[27] Ortiz, chapter 6 in this volume.   [28] Odell and Sell, chapter 3 in this volume.

so as to have the expected effect on or elicit the expected answer from the receiver.

2.2.2   *Importance of initial beliefs and expectations?*   Initial opti-

mism seems to be a characteristic of participants in the simulations. When asked "Are you satisfied with the advancement of negotiations up to now?" on the first day, ambassadors generally express a moderate or high level of satisfaction – even in cases where bilateral meetings have not yet formally begun, and the teams are still involved in the process of elaborating their "offers" and "requests" and/or agreeing on negotiating modalities.[29] Similarly, few ambassadors replied negatively on the first day to the question of the existence of a zone of agreement,[30] even though it is very likely that very few of them (if any) had a clear idea of the right answer at this point in the negotiation.

Turning to the explanation for such optimism, overconfidence might be at work. Negotiators tend to overestimate their ability to control uncontrollable events.[31] In this context, it has been argued that a reason parties cooperate in one-shot prisoner dilemma games is the illusion that their own cooperation will create cooperation in the other party.[32]

However, it is also possible that the large number of positive replies is a consequence of ambassadors' expectations that the TNSE is constructed in such a way as to allow for bargaining zones. Both explanations may be directly linked to a problem of information, which would require specific efforts from negotiators, as we discuss next.

2.2.3   *Illusion of transparency?*   Whereas the simulations reveal

a convergence process, they also reveal, through the large number of questions unanswered, that actors have anything but a clear perception of others. Prior work using laboratory experiments points, as a potential explanation, to possible biases in the estimation by any negotiator of other negotiators' knowledge. For instance, one study, measuring negotiators' perceived transparency with regard to their objectives, finds that negotiators overestimate the transparency of their objectives, in particular when those goals have a high salience and when they can easily resort

---

[29] The level of satisfaction ranges from 1 (least satisfied) to 5 (fully satisfied). On the first day, there was one 5 (6.25 percent of the total of 16 answers), five 4 (25 percent), seven 3 (43.75 percent), two 2 (12.5 percent) and just one 1 (6.25 percent). Interestingly, the lowest scores were recorded in the exercise no. 3, which ended with full agreement, well before the deadline.

[30] no. 1: 2 Yes, 6 Don't know, 1 No (3 No answer); no. 2: 5 Yes, 0 No, 7 Don't know; no. 3: 6 Yes, 4 Don't know, 2 No; no. 4: 9 Yes, 1 Don't know, 2 No.

[31] Crocker 1982; Miller and Ross 1975.

[32] Morris, Sim, and Girotto 1998; Shafir and Tversky 1992.

to communication.[33] Another study finds that negotiators who were told to conceal their preferences were overestimating their partners' ability to detect these preferences but did only do so at the end of the negotiation after 30 minutes.[34]

As regards the reasons for these biases, prior research highlights that negotiators' overestimation of their partners' ability to discern their preferences stems from both the downsides of knowledge (tendency to project one's knowledge onto others / overestimating the availability of whatever they themselves know) and an illusion of transparency (overestimating the extent to which their own characteristics and goals "leak out" and are known by others).

Put into the perspective of the TNSE, such research would indicate that negotiators' perception of their opponents' knowledge of their resistance point is biased towards overestimating that knowledge and even more so as time passes. In the four exercises we clearly see an increasing trend. In 15 cases out of 48, estimations increase in contrast to only 3 cases of decrease. But we also observed 11 cases without any change and 19 cases with missing or incomplete responses.

Going back to the data presented in Table 5.2 above, we do not see much evidence of the illusion of transparency either. Counting the number of times that the perception of knowledge of one party coincides with the estimation of that knowledge by the other party, we find a total of 36 cases of matching, 38 invalid answers (where at least one party did not answer), 24 cases where the latter party overestimates the knowledge of the first party and 46 cases where that knowledge is underestimated.

This seems to go in an opposite direction from the bias of an illusion of transparency.[35] The evidence may instead confirm previous work that reveals that people tend to perceive themselves as being better than others on desirable attributes and have unrealistically positive self-evaluations.[36]

---

[33] Vorauer and Claude 1998.   [34] Van Boven, Gilovich, and Medvec 2003.
[35] To further test this interesting result we would need, however, to include new, and more specific, questions in the interviews. For instance we could ask ambassadors to estimate their opponents' maximum concessions sector by sector. This would be compared with the cabinet instructions and maybe partly with that party's own perception to find out the accuracy of the negotiator's judgment. Finally, negotiators would also be asked to give an estimation of the correctness of their judgments on the opponent's preferences and resistance point. The perceived knowledge would consequently be compared to actual knowledge to find out if negotiators are indeed overconfident of their judgments. Similarly one could test the illusion of transparency. Another interesting question would be to ask negotiators if they are aware that their opponent is overestimating their knowledge on their preferences and maximum concessions. However, a question asking the negotiator to estimate the perceived knowledge of the second negotiator on the preferences and resistance point of the first instead of estimating his actual knowledge could make negotiators realise the answer implicitly (overconfidence).
[36] Messick, Bloom, Boldizar, and Samuelson 1985; Svenson 1981; Brown 1986.

In our view, the ability to find out and process information on opponents is one such desirable attribute. Indeed, if one asks an ambassador whether he has found out what the other party's resistance point is, we expect him to be more likely to inflate his skills rather than admit that he was unable to find out this information.

Clearly, our discussion in this subsection and in the previous one on overconfidence underlines the gains that could be gained from relying upon third parties for obtaining better or additional information on others, as demonstrated in the case of NAFTA negotiations.[37] The same study also shows that access to multiple channels of information about others is also useful. Overcoming overconfidence and illusions is particularly crucial for actors who face stronger partners, as shown in the study of the TRIPS and services during the Uruguay Round.[38]

2.2.4   Too quick or oversimplified tactical choices?   Unduly fixed visions of what the others can give and what they should do can be a serious obstacle to learning. As some literature has shown, individuals sometimes have the tendency to ignore the cognitions of others and the contingent process of negotiation.[39] An example of this attitude in the TNSE is to adopt the following approach: "I am strictly following cabinet orders, and will not grant any further concession". Normally, it takes some time for negotiators to fully understand that their cabinet orders are mutually incompatible. Some of them simply never come to this understanding, thus making the process fail.[40] Usually, this happens only to isolated participants. For example, Tristat's counsellor in exercise no. 4 had a major argument with his ambassador and other team members about the opportunity to include the agricultural sector in any bilateral deal. Interpreting the cabinet orders as a strict rule, he preferred failure in the negotiations to making any concessions.

To simplify the game, participants could use other rules of thumb. One would be to search for an agreement at any cost, based on the understanding that it is the purpose of the exercise and that reaching an agreement is the outcome expected by the secretariat. To avoid clashes with cabinet orders, the ability of negotiators to reframe the bargaining context becomes crucial, something which is nicely documented in the TRIPS and public health episode prior to the Doha declaration.[41] Countries also use their knowledge of the power relations that exist among themselves:

---

[37] Chapter 6 this volume.   [38] Chapter 2 this volume.
[39] Samuelson and Bazerman 1985; Caroll, Bazerman, and Maury 1988.
[40] This happened in a TNSE we did not observe, except for the debriefing session, in which the problem emerged.
[41] Chapter 3 this volume.

they know that they have different BATNAs, and that some of them are more in need of an agreement (either in the tariff negotiation, the non-tariff negotiation, or both) than others. We can see from the debriefing questionnaire given in exercises no. 3 and 4 that most participants can think of an answer when they are asked: "Regarding tariff negotiations, which do you think was the country that was most in need of striking a bilateral agreement with your country?".[42] The same question on non-tariff negotiations yielded similar results.[43] This is all the more remarkable since each team has a number of its members involved either in the tariff negotiations, or in the non-tariff negotiation. This means that experts in tariffs, for instance, are unlikely to know much about what is happening in the non-tariff negotiations, and are therefore not expected to be able to reply to every question in the debriefing questionnaire.

Such behavior would imply that negotiators do not rely on the details of offers and requests to elaborate their strategy and tactics: they are convinced that they know the "rules of the game" perfectly and who will give up most in the end. We observed it in the case of Alba's ambassador, in exercise no. 1. He understood very well the strengths and weaknesses of the others' positions, and after issuing his last offer to Tristat he advised his delegation not to meet members from Tristat's delegation, so that Tristat would have to come to Alba and not the other way round. Alba's ambassador, who was a highly skilled negotiator, knew that Tristat needed the agreement more than Alba, who had a better BATNA. He plainly told Tristat's ambassador that "If we cannot sign, we will not sign", pushing Tristat quickly to accept the last offer. Obviously this rule of thumb can only be something for skilled and experienced negotiators (who are well-experienced in the dynamics of negotiations), such as Alba's Ambassador in exercise no. 1. But more than experience, one also needs power to be able to follow such a rule of thumb. Developing countries in our simulation and in the real world are not vested with such power and their signals are therefore often "ignored" from those who have it. Yet, the case studies in this book show that power imbalance can be partially reduced through resort to legal argument,[44] coalitions,[45] or issue linkage.[46]

2.2.5 Self-serving bias? The absence of a bias related to previous negotiating "rounds" does not rule out the possibility that actors

---

[42] Exercise no. 2: 11 answers and 4 no answers; exercise no. 3: 13 answers and 5 no answers.

[43] "Regarding non-tariff negotiations, which do you think was the country that was most in need of striking a multilateral agreement? Why?"; exercise no. 2: 9 answers and 6 no answers; exercise no. 3: 12 answers and 6 no answers.

[44] Chapter 7 this volume; Chapter 8 this volume.

[45] Chapter 4 this volume; Chapter 3 this volume; Chapter 2 this volume.

[46] Chapter 6 this volume.

develop one or more biases during the process. Due to the short time-span in which the exercise takes place, this phenomenon can best be observed ex post, looking at the results of the debriefing questionnaire. The purpose of the debriefing questionnaire was to enable the participants to reflect on the exercise that had just been completed and to make them share their perceptions of the main features of the game, namely its conformity with reality (or lack thereof), the negotiating strategies that were pursued, and the major problems that slowed down the reaching of an agreement.

The results show that participants have a very different assessment of the relevance of a possible problem depending on whether it originates from their team or from others. When asked "Do you think lack of flexibility from other countries was a major problem in the negotiating process?" the answers are overwhelmingly positive.[47] On the other hand, when asked "Do you think lack of flexibility from your own minister was a major problem in the negotiating process?" the responses are just as overwhelmingly negative.[48] We find parallel results when we compare two other potential problems that mirror each other: a majority of participants found that "unrealistic initial requests from other countries" constituted a major problem in the negotiation process, while "unrealistic ministerial instructions for your team" did not. Individuals tend to blame others' personal traits (e.g. lack of flexibility) rather than situational characteristics for failure.

These results reflect a fairly strong self-serving bias, i.e. a natural tendency to take credit for success but blame the situation (or the others) for failure. The participants attribute the difficulties encountered in the course of the negotiations not to their own gaps, but to the others', even though it seems quite absurd to believe that only the other Ministers' toughness slowed down the negotiations, and not one's own. This bias is, in the case of teams, reinforced by the common tendency to favor one's in-group against the out-group. More specifically, the constitution of teams, however arbitrary, has the effect of developing cohesion with members of the same team (in-group) and prejudice towards the other teams (out-group).[49] This tendency develops with time, as the different teams get to know (and confront) each other. In exercise no. 4, we asked parallel questions in the debriefing questionnaire (i.e. at the end of the exercise) on the performance of the teams:[50] more people invoked "lack

---

[47] no. 2: 14 Yes, 1 No; no. 3: 16 Yes, 2 No; no. 4: 9 Yes, 4 No (1 no answer).
[48] no. 2: 1 Yes, 12 No (2 no answer); no. 3: 0 Yes, 16 No; no. 4: 2 Yes, 12 No.
[49] See Muzapher Sherif's experiment on group competition. Sherif 1967.
[50] The question on "lack of skill of other negotiating teams" did not exist in the questionnaires of the three previous exercises.

of skill of other negotiating teams" as a problem in the negotiation than "poor performance of your own negotiating team".[51]

A previous study has elaborated further the self-serving bias by combining it to the notion of *fairness*; according to that study, parties to a negotiation tend to confuse what is fair and what benefits them; in other words, they assess fairness in a way that serves their interests.[52] We also observed such reactions in the TNSEs in two dimensions, one reflecting the type of country, and the other reflecting individual, sector specific interests.

The four countries of the TNSE represent the whole of world trade, with varying levels of development across them. Even though the exercise is structured not to favor any particular country or group of countries, participants tend to think that developing countries should be granted special treatment due to their socio-economic condition. In the course of simulations, developing countries tried to explain to their developed partners that exchanging one concession for one concession was not a fair deal because a developing country would lose much more than a developed country. In other words, "one concession" did not have the same weight for the two types of country, and developing countries should therefore be given more than they themselves gave. Developed countries, on the other hand, were willing to follow strictly their cabinet orders and not give any extra benefit to developing countries based on their condition. Not only did they think that their behavior was fair, they also considered that the simple fact of negotiating with developing countries was a demonstration of good will. This is all the more striking in that some participants coming from developing countries tend to "overplay", in the sense that they are more demanding towards developing countries than actual developed countries would be (this was for instance the case with Alba's Ambassador in TNSE no. 3).

The existence of individual (or sector specific) self-serving bias can also be observed in the TNSE. Countries have different "sensitive" sectors, i.e., protected sectors in which cabinet orders mandate to limit concessions, because of domestic concerns. A recurrent example can be found in negotiations between Alba and Tristat over the four TNSEs we observed. These two countries are both developed ones, so that considerations of fairness cannot be related to a development gap. Alba's most sensitive sector is textiles whereas Tristat's is agriculture. The major difference

---

[51] To the question: "Do you think the following were major problems in the negotiating process?" we got the following results for "Poor performance of your own negotiating team": 1 Yes, 11 No and 1 no answer; for "Lack of skill of other negotiating teams", we got 5 Yes, 8 No and 1 no answer.
[52] Babcock and Loewenstein 1997.

between the two countries is that the former applies much lower tariffs in the textiles sector than the latter in the agricultural one. This means that the same percentage reduction would bring down Tristat's agricultural tariffs more dramatically than Alba's textiles tariffs.[53] Any offer of reciprocity in tariff cuts is usually presented as fair and balanced by Alba, but is perceived as unfair by Tristat. This happened, for example, in exercise no. 4. At first, Tristat tried to exclude agriculture from the talks; later, when it understood that there would not be any deal if agriculture were to be excluded, it argued in favor of special and differential treatment based on the notion of multifunctionality. Whereas this last example again shows the importance of framing in getting out of a difficult situation,[54] the importance of biases in preventing learning processes calls for the help of third parties in the negotiation processes. Besides information providers (see above), third parties may bring technical advice,[55] or may help deeply reframe the terms of the bargaining.[56]

2.2.6 Country characteristics and individual learning Our discussion of self-serving bias suggests some differences across countries. Do we find additional evidence of variations in negotiation behavior that may come from country characteristics? Generally speaking it is difficult to infer a particular pattern in the answers to the question of the cooperativeness of countries. Asked about the most and least cooperative countries, some ambassadors name the same most or least cooperative country three days in a row, while some others change their assessment every day (see Table 5.5). In exercise no. 2, for instance, Medatia and Tristat consistently cite Alba as "most cooperative" during the three days of the TNSE, but in the exercise no. 3 they never mention the same country twice. When countries change their mind and name a different country from the one they had the day before, they do not do it simultaneously, and they rarely change to the same country. This means that the assessment of cooperativeness is not multilateral at all: it depends on how the bilateral meetings go. A turbulent bilateral with one country is often sufficient to have its name mentioned in the "least cooperative" category.

However, over the four TNSEs a slight pattern seems to appear as can be seen in Table 5.5. Alba is cited 17 times as the most cooperative country

---

[53] For example, if both Tristat and Alba would cut their tariff peak by 30 percent, Tristat's tariff on dairy products would be reduced from 120 to 84 percent, while Alba's tariff on t-shirts would only be reduced from 20 to 14 percent.
[54] Chapter 3 this volume.   [55] Chapters 7 and 8 this volume.
[56] Chapter 3 this volume.

Table 5.5 *Number of mentions as most or least cooperative country*

	Most cooperative (Max=36)	Least cooperative (Max=36)
Alba	17	3
Medatia	10	7
Tristat	11	19
Vanin	9	11

Note: Each country can be named at most three times per day by its partners as the most or least cooperative, yielding a maximum number of citations of 36

over a maximum number of 36, while others are cited between 9 and 11 times only. For the least cooperative country, it is Tristat who is cited more often than the other countries (19 times over a maximum of 36). One reason could be that Alba is the most developed of the developed countries, with the understanding that it might be easier for a developed country to grant generous concessions. Another relevant element is the content of the cabinet orders: a country may be consistently cited as most cooperative if it has more lenient orders. Tristat, as we argued above, has an extremely difficult negotiating position in agriculture because of very high tariff peaks (up to 120 percent); its concern even with cuts of less than 1 percent is a sure recipe for making other teams upset.[57] As we mentioned above, getting out of this situation often requires an ability to reframe the situation, something that is still needed for farm products in the Doha Round.

However, one should take these results carefully. In fact, in exercise no. 3, accounting for a relevant part of the cases where Tristat is listed as least cooperative one, Tristat's team was significantly underskilled in comparison to the other teams (not even being able to issue offers and

---

[57] For example, in exercise no. 1 the relationship between Tristat and Vanin were empoisoned by this factor. We report an excerpt from the bilateral meeting on the last afternoon of the exercise:

VANIN: "We have to think of other strategies because this is not working. You are just talking about decimals. We are thinking of withdrawing our position on subsidies negotiations as well. We have been very serious, we have made efforts. But 0.6, 0.4 percent . . ."

TRISTAT: "But it is important!"

V: "No, you are playing with these percentages. This is meaningless"

T: "It is not a point of reducing. It is the relative amount of reduction from base rate"

V: "It is meaningless"

T: "It is meaningless for your country, but it is meaningful to mine. We are not going any further".

requests, and thus organize bilateral meetings). It is therefore not surprising that other teams constantly pointed at Tristat. More observations would be needed to detect any recurrent pattern.

Another feature linked to the way in which ambassadors evaluate the cooperativeness of other countries is the personality of the negotiators. It is difficult, for instance, not to relate the fact that Alba was cited 6 times out of 11 in exercise no. 1[58] and only 2 times out of 12 in exercise no. 3[59] to the personalities of Alba's ambassadors conducting these particular negotiations. In exercise no. 1, he was a very experienced, articulate and skilled diplomat, while in no. 3 he was a more difficult character, with a contemptuous and derogatory attitude towards other negotiators and in particular towards developing countries. In this aspect again the TNSE appears as a realistic simulation: the clash of personalities can undermine negotiations and threaten the obtaining of a final agreement.

So, in sum, even though there is here some additional evidence that country features may systematically influence individual behavior, we can hardly describe this evidence as overwhelming.

2.2.7   Truthfulness and learning   The importance of truthfulness is the last issue that we would like to discuss in this chapter. Clearly, truthfulness should facilitate information exchange and thus should help to secure the convergence process.[60] Even though negotiators are usually not naive enough to believe that the expression: "this is the maximum I can give" is always to be taken at face value, it usually helps a negotiation move forward if they know that the other person is not making exaggerated demands. From that perspective, ambassadors were asked every day the following question: "How would you evaluate the truthfulness of the others' claims?" The results show interesting trends. First, a large number of answers show stability in the assessment of others' truthfulness (14 answers out of 36). Second, we find an upward trend in the evaluation of others' truthfulness (9 answers out of 36) and almost no decreasing trend (3/36). In the remaining ten cases ambassadors were either not able or not willing to say anything.

The upward trend is therefore not dominant, contrary to what was found on the question on knowledge. The emphasis on the stability of the perception of others' truthfulness seems to indicate that the trust building phenomenon is less salient than the building of knowledge. It seems as if once a country has an idea of how much someone's claims can

---

[58] In exercise no. 1, Alba was never cited as least cooperative country.
[59] In exercise no. 3, Alba was cited 2 times over 8 as least cooperative country.
[60] Thompson 1991.

be trusted, it sticks to this opinion and this opinion is quite resistant to change (i.e. it is not significantly updated as new information comes in). One reason could be that trust has more to do with issues of personality than knowledge. Evaluation of truthfulness may have more to do with the personality (friendly or deceptive) of negotiators as perceived on the first day than with the subsequent development of the negotiations. This means that changing such evaluation cannot simply rely on the exchanges occurring strictly within the bargaining process but should be part of a larger strategy of information gathering and exchange. Ortiz's study[61] of NAFTA demonstrates how crucial such a strategy was for Mexico's ability to influence the negotiation outcome.

It is interesting to see whether there is a correlation between countries' assessment of each other's cooperativeness, and their evaluation of the level of truthfulness of their claims. For exercises no. 2 and 3, we observed that the two questions entail similar answers: the country that is deemed as the most cooperative is always the one that scores highest on the question "How would you evaluate the truthfulness of others' claims?" Conversely, the country that is said to be the least cooperative is always the one with the lowest score in terms of truthfulness. This happens in 100 percent of the 33 instances observed in these two exercises (18 for most cooperative and 15 for least cooperative). Results are different in exercise no. 4: in 6 instances over a total of 24, we observed discrepancy in the relation "most cooperative" – "most truthful" or the opposite "least cooperative" – "least truthful." However, if we look closer at the discrepant results of exercise no. 4, we find out that the truthfulness scores of the most truthful country and of the most cooperative country (that was, in other exercises, also the most truthful) are usually quite close: we note a difference of one point in 5 cases out of a total of 6, and two points in the last case. Overall, there seems therefore to be a correlation between the level of truthfulness and the level of cooperativeness. We need more observations to strengthen that point, but it seems that ambassadors tend not to differentiate between the two concepts.

Conclusion

Information exchange is a central feature of international negotiations. As a large body of literature from different fields and using different research methods has showed, information transmission and interpretation can have an important influence on the bargaining outcome whether actors use distributive or integrative strategies. Yet, there are still many

---

[61] Or, if some countries share the same highest score, one of them.

gaps in our understanding of the uses individuals make of information, particularly of changing information. Formal models assume some information processing rules, descriptive studies tend to come up with post hoc claims, and previous laboratory experiments seriously question learning. Our chapter brings some new preliminary evidence using simulation exercises designed to be close to real world negotiations (both in time and complexity) and involving individuals with either prior experience in trade negotiations or with likely future involvement in such negotiations. Furthermore, simulations involve participants from the developing world (or countries in transition), in contrast to most existing studies so far.

The first major finding of our work is that there seems to be a consistent pattern of convergence of perception and knowledge among negotiators. Individuals revise their initial beliefs and expectations as the negotiation proceeds. In short, individuals show what we could call a learning attitude. On that account, formal models of the negotiation process, in particular signaling models, do seem to make valid assumptions. And the experimental literature may look too pessimistic.

The chapter brings home a second set of more specific findings as regards patterns or dynamics of information processing by individuals. Overall, these findings reveal that learning is difficult and can be derailed by a host of factors. Signals are both difficult to define and interpret especially when bluffing is a recurrent tactic and truthfulness difficult to establish. Overconfidence seems to be at work both with regards to the ability to uncover others' characteristics and constraints and with regard to the ability to reach an agreement. Self-serving biases and some other forms of cognitive closure affect the narrowing of differences between the bargaining positions. Different country characteristics may also interfere, although to a lesser extent. These results pose two big challenges to the literature using formal game-theoretic models with Bayesian updating of information. First, the "common knowledge" assumption in models of incomplete information seems to assume far too much. Indeed, the so-called "illusion of transparency" shows that players do not share others' beliefs about them. Second, the variety of refinements to the Bayesian Nash Equilibrium (and other solution concepts for games of incomplete information) may capture the skewed updating observed when negotiators have self-serving biases or show some degree of cognitive closure. But models standardize the behavior of all players, something that runs against the evidence collected during the TNSEs.

In contrast, these findings on learning behavior are indicative of the difficulties facing negotiators in real settings and call for solutions. The other contributions to this book provide useful avenues. To begin with, moves at the bargaining table should be complemented with intense and multiple exchanges between negotiation partners, as shown in the case of NAFTA negotiations between Mexico and the United States.[62] Whereas overconfidence and other types of biases seem to be "the name of the game" in multilateral trade negotiations,[63] there are ways to overcome them. First, negotiators may choose to be helped by third parties that steer them away from preconceived ideas and inadequate tactical behavior through the provision of additional information,[64] or technical advice.[65] Second, negotiators may be pushed to open their eyes through public opinion trends under the influence of the civil society and the media.[66] In both cases, getting out of a deadlock is easier if the frame of the negotiation is changed. Yet, as powerful as framing can be,[67] it remains relatively rare because quite demanding in terms of conditions for success. Lastly, regular encounters between individuals should mostly aim at establishing truthfulness as a critical facilitator for learning and smoother negotiation processes. Clearly, on that account, it may be easier to negotiate among a small group of Geneva-based diplomats than among elected politicians who meet occasionally. From this perspective, the institutional set-up of the negotiation may play an important facilitating role. This role underlies the creation of the WTO as a permanent forum for multilateral trade negotiations.

We end with some caveats and some avenues for further work. The evidence we present in this chapter is based upon a limited number of individuals (roughly 100) who did a simulation exercise with a specific design (GATT/WTO) and whom we observed mostly on tariffs negotiations. One clear drawback of the chosen design is that we were not able to gain much about learning in multilateral settings. In a GATT/WTO tariff world, bilateral meetings drive the process and thus learning mostly follows the bilateral route. A last, and important, caveat relates to the impossibility to contrast our findings with exercises done by participants from the developed world. The fact that our findings differ in several respects from results obtained in laboratory experiments in developed countries' universities with students mostly coming from the developed world may hint at possible interesting variations. There are, however, too many potential differences between our sample of students and the samples in the relevant literature. Conclusions are therefore speculative at this stage.

The caveats clearly outline the three most important avenues for future work. First, we aim to expand the number of observations using the same

---

[62] Chapter 6 this volume.
[63] Expression used by Magdi Farahat, Geneva, 7 November 2003.
[64] Chapter 6 this volume.   [65] Chapter 8 this volume.
[66] Chapter 3 this volume.   [67] Ibid.

design and same data collection methods. This will allow us to conduct a more specific analysis of individual variations. Second, we would like to run the same experiment with participants from the developed world. Third, we will try to run a different experiment with a more multilateral flavor. Clearly the last two extensions raise difficult challenges but ultimately they will be the only way to test the robustness of the general trends reported here.

REFERENCES

Allan, Pierre and Cédric Dupont. 1999. International Relations Theory and Game Theory: Baroque Modeling Choices and Empirical Robustness. *International Political Science Review* 20 (1), 23–47
Babcock, Linda and George Loewenstein. 1997. Explaining Bargaining Impasses: The Role of Self-serving Biases. *Journal of Economic Perspectives* 11(1): 109–26
Bazerman, Max H., T. Magliozzi, and Margaret A. Neale. 1985. Integrative Bargaining in a Competitive Market. *Organizational Behavior and Human Performance* 34(3): 294–313
Brown, Jonathan D. 1986. Evaluations of Self and Others: Self-enhancement Biases in Social Judgment. *Social Cognition* 4(4): 353–76.
Bueno de Mesquita, Bruce. 1990. Multilateral Negotiations: A Spatial Analysis of the Arab–Israeli Dispute. *International Organization* 44(3): 317–40
Caroll, John S., Max H. Bazerman, and Robin Maury. 1988. Negotiator Cognitions: A Descriptive Approach to Negotiatiors' Understanding of Their Opponents. *Organizational Behavior and Human Decision Processes* 41(3): 352–70
Crawford, Vincent P. 1995. Adaptive Dynamics in Coordination Games. *Econometrica* 63(1): 103–43
Crawford, Vincent P. and Hans Haller. 1990. Learning How to Cooperate: Optimal Play in Repeated Coordination Games. *Econometrica* 58(3): 571–95
Crocker, Jennifer. 1982. Biased Questions in Judgment of Covariation Studies. *Personality and Social Psychology Bulletin* 8(2): 214–20
De Dreu, Carsten K. W., Sander L. Koole, and Frans L. Oldersma. 1999. On the Seizing and Freezing of Negotiator Inferences: Need for Cognitive Closure Moderates the Use of Heuristics in Negotiation. *Personality and Social Psychology Bulletin* 25(3): 348–62
Druckman, Daniel. 1977. Social–Psychological Approaches to the Study of Negotiation. In *Negotiations. Social–Psychological Perspectives*, ed. Daniel Druckman, 15–44. Beverly Hills: Sage
Dupont, Cédric. 1994a. Domestic Politics and International Negotiations: A Sequential Bargaining Model. In *Game Theory and International Relations*, ed. Pierre Allan and Christian Schmidt, 156–90. Cheltam: Elgar Publisher
1994b. Domestic Politics, Information and International Bargaining. Comparative Models of Strategic Behavior in Non-Crisis Negotiations. Ph.D. diss., Graduate Institute of International Studies, Geneva

Dupont, Cédric and Pascal Sciarini. 1995. La négociation agricole Etats-Unis–Communauté Européenne dans l'Uruguay Round: une difficile convergence. *Revue suisse de science politique* 1(2–3): 305–52
1998. Seeds of Conflict. Unpublished manuscript, Graduate Institute of International Studies, Geneva; European Institute, Florence
Foster, Dean P. and H. Peyton Young. 2003. Learning Nash Equilibrium. The Santa Fe Institute Working Paper
Iida, Keisuke. 1993. When and How Do Domestic Constraints Matter? *Journal of Conflict Resolution* 37(3): 403–26
Iklé, Fred C.. 1964. *How Nations Negotiate.* New York: Harper and Row
Kruglanski, Arie W. and Donna M. Webster. 1996. Motivated Closing of the Mind: "Seizing and Freezing". *Psychological Review* 103(2): 263–83
Lohmann, Susanne. 1997. Linkage Politics. *Journal of Conflict Resolution* 41(1): 38–67
Lord, Charles G., Lee Ross, and Mark R. Lepper. 1979. Biased Assimilation and Attitude Polarization: The Effects of Prior Theories on Subsequently Considered Evidence. *Journal of Personality and Social Psychology* 37(11): 2098–109
Messick, David M., Suzanne Bloom, Janet P. Boldizar, and Charles D. Samuelson. 1985. Why We Are Fairer Than Others. *Journal of Experimental Social Psychology* 21(5): 480–500
Miller, Dale T. and Mike Ross. 1975. Self-serving Biases in the Attribution of Causality: Fact or Fiction? *Psychological Bulletin* 82(2): 213–25
Milner, Helen V. 1997. *Interests, Institutions, and Information.* Princeton: Princeton University Press
Milner, Helen V. and B. Peter Rosendorff. 1997. Democratic Politics and International Trade Negotiations. *Journal of Conflict Resolution* 41(1): 117–46
Mo, Jongryn. 1994. The Logic of Two-Level Games with Endogenous Domestic Coalitions. *Journal of Conflict Resolution* 38(2): 402–22
1995. Domestic Institutions and International Bargaining: The Role of Agent Veto in Two-Level Games. *American Political Science Review* 89(4): 914–24
Morgan, T. Clifton. 1994. *Untying the Knot of War. A Bargaining Theory of International Crises.* Ann Arbor: University of Michigan Press
Morris, Michael W., Damien L. H. Sim, and Vittorio Girotto. 1998. Distinguishing Sources of Cooperation in the One-round Prisoners' Dilemma: Evidence for cooperative decisions based on the illusion of control. *Journal of Experimental Social Psychology* 34(5): 494–512
Neale, Margaret A. and Max H. Bazerman. 1991. *Cognition and Rationality in Negotiation.* New York: Free Press
Neale, Margaret A., Vandra Huber, and Gregory Northcraft. 1987. The Framing of Negotiations: Contextual Versus Task Frames. *Organizational Behavior and Human Decision Processes* 39(2): 228–41
Neale, Margaret A. and Gregory B. Northcraft. 1986. Experts, Amateurs, and Refrigerators: Comparing Expert and Amateur Negotiators in a Novel Task. *Organizational Behavior and Human Decision Processes* 38(3): 305–17
Odell, John S. 2000. *Negotiating the World Economy.* Ithaca NY: Cornell University Press

Pahre, Robert. 1997. Endogenous Domestic Institutions in Two-level Games and Parliamentary Oversight of the European Union. *Journal of Conflict Resolution* 41(1): 147–74

Putnam, Robert D. 1988. Diplomacy and Domestic Politics: The Logic of Two-level Games. *International Organization* 42(3): 427–60

Raiffa, Howard. 1982. *The Art and Science of Negotiation*. Cambridge Mass: Belknap Press of Harvard University Press

Roth, Alvin E. 1988. Laboratory Experimentation in Economics: A Methodological Overview. *Economic Journal* 98(393): 974–1031

Roth, Alvin E. and J. Keith Murnighan. 1982. The Role of Information in Bargaining: An Experimental Study. *Econometrica* 50(5): 1123–42

Rubin, Jeffrey A. and Bert R. Brown. 1975. *The Social Psychology of Bargaining and Negotiations*. New York: Academic Press

Samuelson, W. F. and Max H. Bazerman 1985. The Winner's Curse in Bilateral Negotiations. In *Research in Experimental Economics*, ed. V. Smith, 105–37. Greenwich Conn: JAI Press

Schelling, Thomas C. 1960. *The Strategy of Conflict*. Cambridge Mass: Harvard University Press

Shafir, Eldar and Amos Tversky. 1992. Thinking Through Uncertainty: Nonconsequential reasoning and choice. *Cognitive Psychology* 24(4): 449–74

Sherif, Muzapher. 1967. *Group Conflict and Cooperation*. London: Routledge

Simon, Herbert A. 1955. A Behavioral Model of Rational Choice. *Quarterly Journal of Economics* 69(1): 99–108

Simon, Herbert A. 1959. Theories of Decision-making in Economics and Behavioral Science. *American Economic Review* 49(3): 253–83

Svenson, Ola. 1981. Are We Less Risky and More Skillful than Our Fellow Drivers. *Acta Psychologica* 47(2): 143–51

Thompson, Leigh L. 1990. The Influence of Experience on Negotiation Performance. *Journal of Experimental Social Psychology* 26(6): 528–44

Thompson, Leigh L. 1991. Information Exchange in Negotiation. *Journal of Experimental Social Psychology* 27(2): 161–79

Van Boven, Leaf, Thomas Gilovich, and Victoria Husted Medvec. 2003. The Illusion of Transparency in Negotiations. *Negotiation Journal* 19(2): 117–31

van Huyck, John B., Raymond C. Battalio, and Richard O. Beil. 1990. Tacit Coordination Games, Strategic Uncertainty, and Coordination Failure. *American Economic Review* 80(1): 234–48

——— 1991. Strategic Uncertainty, Equilibrium Selection Principles, and Coordination Failure in Average Opinion Games. *Quarterly Journal of Economics* 106(3): 885–910

van Huyck, John B., Raymond C. Battalio, and Frederick W. Rankin. 1997. On the Origin of Convention: Evidence from Coordination Games. *Economic Journal* 107(442): 576–96

Vorauer, J. D. and S. Claude. 1998. Perceived Versus Actual Transparency of Goals in Negotiation. *Personality and Social Psychology Bulletin* 24(4): 371–85

Young, H. Peyton. 1998. *Individual Strategy and Social Structure*. Princeton: Princeton University Press

Part II

Regional negotiations

6   Getting to "No:" Defending against demands in NAFTA energy negotiations

Antonio Ortiz Mena L. N.

On August 12, 1992 Mexico, the United States and Canada finally completed the negotiations for the North American Free Trade Agreement (NAFTA), which had started more than a year earlier.[1] They were unprecedented trade negotiations in that they posed Mexico, a developing country, against the world's sole remaining superpower in an attempt to establish a deep integration agreement.[2] There was little precedent to fall back on, and it was largely expected that the United States would virtually dictate the agreement, given the huge power asymmetries between the negotiating parties.

During NAFTA negotiations, Mexico[3] was loath, because of the nationalization of the oil industry in 1938 and the weighty symbolic importance oil still had (and has) in Mexican politics, to permit US participation in Mexico's oil industry.[4] For its part, the US government was

I would like to thank John Odell for inviting me to participate in the project out of which this chapter came. I am extremely grateful for the generosity and earnestness with which he contributed to the improvement of this chapter. All shortcomings must remain my sole responsibility. I would also like to thank Jesús Flores, Chip Roh, Jaime Serra, and Jaime Zabludovsky for sharing their thoughts on NAFTA energy negotiations. It is no exaggeration to say that without their help it would not have been possible to venture into this topic. Finally, the comments I received from participants at the conference on Developing Countries and the Trade Negotiation Process held at UNCTAD in November 2003, and from my colleagues at CIDE, were also most helpful.
[1] This chapter emphasizes the Mexican side of the story. Likewise, it deals with Mexico-US negotiations and only tangentially touches upon Canada's role, given that NAFTA energy negotiations were largely of a bilateral nature and carried out by the former two countries (author's interview with Charles E. "Chip" Roh, Deputy Chief NAFTA negotiator, USTR. Washington, DC, September 30, 2004). When reference is made to US negotiation results, it should be understood that they also apply to Canada.

[2] Lawrence might argue that NAFTA is not a deep integration agreement. While it is a free trade agreement and not a customs union or common market (which are regarded as deep integration agreements by Lawrence), the scope and coverage of NAFTA went well beyond most previous free trade agreements. See Lawrence 1996; Hufbauer and Schott 1993 offer a summary of NAFTA.

[3] When reference to "Mexico" is made throughout this text, it is to be understood that it stands for the Mexican government and the Mexican NAFTA negotiation team.

[4] See Meyer and Morales 1989; and Ortiz Mena L. N. 1993.

very interested in gaining access to Mexican oil reserves in terms of foreign investment access and supply guarantees. It was a complicated negotiating situation for Mexico, to say the least. As Jagdish Bhagwati stated, "If I were a consultant for Argentina or Brazil, I would tell them not to join NAFTA, because that is where the United States plays the game as they want to . . . just look at Mexico. They are sweating tears . . . because now the United States have started to negotiate free trade agreements with other countries. The advantages they [Mexico] had have disappeared and the concessions they made to achieve the agreement will stay in place, like the rights for oil exploration and intellectual property rights. . . . The United States is using all its lawyers and all its lobbyists to impose subtle barriers, above all in bilateral agreements. And developing countries sometimes do not have either the time or the resources to follow all these developments."[5]

Well, not exactly. While the adverse effects of preference erosion for Mexico are all too real, Bhagwati has got the story wrong. Mexico did not grant the United States any rights pertaining to oil exploration. In fact, under NAFTA "basic energy remains immune to free trade."[6] How was Mexico able to successfully defend itself against distributive strategies by the United States?[7] Did it have to pay a dear price for its success? Are there any lessons from Mexico's experience in negotiating with the United States that may be used by other developing countries facing unwanted demands?

This chapter examines the role played by Mexico's strategy choice and the actions it undertook to offset biases and bolster the credibility of its position on oil (among other factors) in the successful defense against distributive strategies by the United States during NAFTA energy negotiations. It proceeds as follows: the first section deals with Mexico's negotiating position in a number of energy related issues, and the outcome of negotiations in each of these issues; the second section assesses available explanations; the third section applies ideas from negotiation analysis as developed by Odell[8] to interpret this new case; and a final section

---

[5] "Argentina y el ALCA: los Consejos de un Gurú," *Clarín*, Argentina, July 27, 2003. Free translation from the Spanish by the author. Available at: http://www.clarin.com/suplementos/economico/2003/07/27/n-00215.htm. Accessed July 5, 2005.

[6] Hufbauer and Schott 1993, 5.

[7] Canada's main concern was that Mexico submit to energy supply commitments, as Canada did in its bilateral free trade agreement with the US. Author's interviews with Jaime Serra Puche, Mexican Trade Minister 1988–1994, Mexico City, August 19, 2003; Jesús Flores Ayala, Chair (Mexico), NAFTA Energy Negotiation Group. Mexico City, June 14, 2004.

[8] See Odell 2000 and the introduction to this volume.

considers the extent to which the lessons derived from Mexico's experience in NAFTA can be applied to other situations where defense against demands is a central part of the negotiation process.

1   The facts on energy: Mexico's negotiating position vs. negotiation outcomes

In terms of the whole NAFTA negotiation Mexico had very specific offensive and defensive aims, which were made public by President Carlos Salinas (1988–1994) and Trade Minister Jaime Serra Puche.[9] Offensively, Mexico wanted to achieve untrammeled market access to the US and Canadian markets, a faster tariff liberalization by those two countries than that carried out by Mexico, and the establishment of an effective dispute settlement system to deal with unfair trade practices (subsidies and dumping). Defensively, Mexico wished to maintain strict limits to foreign participation in the energy sector and did not want to undertake any energy supply commitments. Its defensive position on energy was set out in five "Nos," which are discussed below.

Mexico had vast oil reserves, and the United States was the world's major oil importer. As such, it wanted to have access to Mexico's oil, both for business-related purposes and to secure access to Mexican oil during times of energy shortages. For its part, Mexico badly needed investment in its oil sector to keep up with domestic demand and to make the most out of its oil export earnings. The United States in turn had a surplus of natural gas and Mexico a growing deficit.[10] This was a classic case of comparative advantage, and there seemed to be a very wide positive zone of agreement.

However, for domestic political reasons Mexico did not want to include energy in NAFTA negotiations.[11] It initially proposed an outright exemption of energy and basic petrochemicals from NAFTA negotiations and did not want to establish a working group on energy. The United States was against this position, and insisted on establishing a working group on energy.[12] While Mexico in the end acquiesced to the establishment of an energy working group, it did not flinch from its specific positions regarding energy.

[9] See Salinas 2000, 76; Serra 1994, and Ortiz Mena L. N. 2001, 316–23.
[10] Hufbauer and Schott 1993, 34.
[11] See Mayer 1998, 117–119; for an overview of oil and nationalism in Mexico see Meyer and Morales 1989.
[12] Maxfield and Shapiro 1998, 98.

The main issues where Mexico did not want to yield to US pressures were investment in energy-related areas and energy supply commitments. These concerns were expressed in the following five "Nos" regarding the role of energy in NAFTA negotiations:[13]
  (i) There will be no foreign investment in the exploration, exploitation and refining of oil in Mexico. These areas are to remain under state control.
  (ii) There will be no risk-sharing contracts with payment in oil reserves.
  (iii) There will be no energy supply commitments.
  (iv) There will be no liberalization of gas imports; all imports must be done through PEMEX.
  (v) There will be no foreign retail gasoline outlets.
In addition, Mexican President Carlos Salinas publicly stated that all "strategic" economic sectors covered by Article 28 of the Constitution (basic petrochemicals, railroads, and electricity, among others) would remain under state control.[14]

Given that energy negotiations in NAFTA covered a wide array of topics, for ease of discussion they are classified in four areas: investment, trade, energy supply commitments, and other issues. In each area Mexico's position is set out, and then compared with the negotiation outcome.

1.1   Investment

Three of the five "Nos" refer to investment-related commitments. Investment, together with energy supply commitments (discussed under "other issues," below), was the most contentious issue of NAFTA energy negotiations, if not of all NAFTA negotiations. Mexico's position on foreign investment in its oil industry was clear cut: no foreign ownership of oil reserves, no foreign production of primary petrochemicals,[15] no foreign participation in the exploration, exploitation, and refining of oil

[13] As will be seen in the next section, these issues, which were non-negotiable in Mexico's view, were made public on many occasions by President Salinas (see Salinas 2000, 39–157 passim). Trade Minister Jaime Serra also made frequent mention of these "Nos" (author's interview with Jaime Serra Puche, Mexican Trade Minister 1988–1994, Mexico City, 19 August 2003).
[14] Arriola 1994, 401. Serra also insisted on several occasions that the constitutional limits to foreign participation in the oil sector were non-negotiable. See Serra 1994, 537, 558, passim.
[15] Primary petrochemicals, also called basic petrochemicals, are produced directly from oil, while secondary petrochemicals are produced from primary petrochemicals. Some secondary petrochemicals may also be classified as primary due to their "strategic" nature. This distinction has been used by the Mexican government to determine which petrochemical products are out of bound for private investment (i.e. primary petrochemicals). In addition, final petrochemicals are those utilized by end users.

and natural gas, no risk-sharing contracts,[16] and no foreign participation in the retail gasoline market.[17]

In electricity, Mexico's position was not as steadfast as in oil, although it did not envisage significant privatization of the former industry. Both areas fall within the purview of Article 28 of the Constitution, which provides for state control over "strategic" sectors of the economy.

The United States "pushed for as much liberalization as possible in primary and secondary petrochemical production and in the exploration, drilling and refining of oil and natural gas. The United States, furthermore, wanted immediate, rather than phased-in concessions."[18]

In the end, US gains in investment were limited in electricity, and negligible in oil and gas: "Mexico succeeded in keeping its hydrocarbon industries closed to foreign participation. NAFTA specifically reserves to the Mexican state the right to control all activities and investment in the exploration, exploitation, refining, transportation, storage, and distribution of crude oil and natural gas, as well as the production, transportation, storage, and distribution of artificial gas, primary petrochemicals, and all other goods obtained from the refining of crude oil and natural gas."[19] In addition, risk-sharing contracts were not allowed, nor was foreign participation in the retail gasoline market. The United States did not attain its goals in key investment areas in the oil and gas sectors.

It did gain greater access to investment in petrochemicals. Basic petrochemicals were reclassified; fourteen of the nineteen basic petrochemicals that were present at the outset of NAFTA negotiations were liberalized, although three new basic petrochemicals were included in the list, so that eight products remained off limits to foreign investors. A 40 percent cap on foreign investment in secondary petrochemicals was lifted gradually. Majority foreign investment in final petrochemicals had been unilaterally liberalized since 1989.

Electricity was also liberalized. Under NAFTA, US and Canadian investors are able to acquire, establish and operate electric generating facilities for their own use or for cogeneration. Nonetheless, all sales of surplus power must be done through CFE.[20]

Coal was not regarded as a strategic sector when it came to making exchange of concessions. The 40 percent limit to foreign investment in coal mines and facilities was lifted after a three year phase-out period.

---

[16] Risk-sharing contracts stipulate that companies jointly engaged in oil exploration will have joint ownership of any oil reserves found.
[17] Author's interview with Jaime Serra Puche, Mexican Trade Minister 1988–1994, Mexico City, August 19, 2003.
[18] Maxfield and Shapiro 1998, 99.   [19] Ibid., 99.
[20] CFE is the Comisión Federal de Electricidad, the government owned electricity monopoly (Federal Electricity Commission).

1.2   Trade

Cross-border trade in gas and electricity was also a subject of interest in NAFTA negotiations. Mexico wished to maintain control over cross-border trade in gas and electricity, while the United States wanted a strong degree of liberalization.

NAFTA did liberalize trade in gas and electricity, but with severe restrictions. While it allows for US suppliers to negotiate contracts with and sell gas and electricity to end users in Mexico, all sales must be approved by PEMEX[21] and CFE, respectively, and their infrastructure must be used to make the transfer. The Mexican government thus retains a veto over cross border sales of gas and electricity.

A much less contentious issue was trade in coal. Mexico had a 10 percent tax on coal. The United States requested the elimination of the tariff, and Mexico acquiesced.[22]

Finally, trade in energy related equipment was also the subject of negotiations. Mexico treated it as a non-strategic issue, and negotiated sales of US equipment to Mexico. There were discussions on rules of origin and tariff phase-out calendars, but the end point was clear so that, at the latest, ten years after the entry into force of NAFTA all energy equipment sales to Mexico would be tariff-free.

1.3   *Energy supply commitments*

The United States and Canada, as members of the International Energy Agency, had signed an agreement in 1974 setting out the terms under which energy supplies to each other could decrease, and reaffirmed their commitment in the Canada–United States Free Trade Agreement (CUS-FTA), which had entered into force in January 1989.

Mexico stated publicly, at the outset of negotiations, that it would not make any commitments regarding energy supplies ("No" number 3). The United States and Canada "pushed adamantly for a Mexican commitment not to restrict energy exports to the other NAFTA countries during times of energy crisis."[23] Mexico steadfastly refused to accept such a provision and remains unbound by commitments in this area.

1.4   *Other issues*

Procurement   Mexico stated at the outset that, regarding procurement, everything was on the table. The United States had great interest

---

[21] PEMEX (Petróleos Mexicanos) is the state oil monopoly.
[22] Hufbauer and Schott 1993, 36.   [23] Maxfield and Shapiro 1998, 100.

in participating in PEMEX and CFE contracts (Mexico is not a signatory to the WTO Government Procurement Agreement). As a result of NAFTA, a threshold of US $250,000 was established, so that federal government enterprises not exempted from the Public Procurement chapter would open all tenders over this amount to North American competition. PEMEX and CFE were not exempted. Foreign participation in PEMEX and CFE contracts was fully liberalized after a ten-year transition period.

Performance contracts While Mexico objected to risk-sharing contracts ("No" number 2) and its objection was recognized under NAFTA, it was not opposed to using performance contracts as a bargaining chip. Under performance contracts, a service provider may earn a bonus if it exceeds certain pre-specified contract targets. The United States was interested in getting Mexico to accept performance contracts in the energy sector and Mexico acquiesced, although bonuses can only be paid in cash and not in kind.

Preferential energy prices The issue at stake was that Mexican firms were getting lower oil and electricity prices than their foreign competitors in Mexico. Mexico was not unduly concerned about this issue and in any case was gradually reducing subsidies across the board, so it acquiesced to US demands that it end preferential energy prices.

In short, Mexico had a clear stance in energy negotiations. It spelled out its five "Nos" and the fact that its Constitution would not be amended to accommodate NAFTA.[24] In principle everything else was amenable to negotiation. Despite strong and consistent US pressures to liberalize investment in the oil sector and subscribe to energy supply commitments, Mexico was able to fulfill its basic defensive aims in the NAFTA negotiations. How it managed to do so is examined in the following two sections.

2 Available explanations

The empirical puzzle can be restated in a succinct manner: how was Mexico able, despite extremely strong US insistence and most political pundits' expectations, to keep the energy sector largely out of NAFTA negotiations, to avoid concessions in terms of energy security when both

---

[24] Out of the five "Nos" three of them (those covering foreign investment in the energy sector, risk contracts, and trade in energy) could ostensibly be viewed as being covered by the Mexican Constitution under Articles 25, 27, and 28. The remaining two "Nos" (on energy supply commitments and on foreign retail gasoline outlets) may have been politically sensitive issues, but there were no constitutional prohibitions on the matter.

the United States and Canada "pushed adamantly" to make Mexico acquiesce, and at the same time still achieve its main offensive goals?

The outcome is a puzzle if one gives pride of place to Realist explanations that hinge on power disparities[25] and on the specific needs of the United States in terms of energy security, with its southern neighbor possessing vast oil reserves and the precedent of having recently obtained energy supply commitments with Canada under the CUSFTA. There are, of course, other strands of thought regarding the effects of asymmetry. For instance, Keohane argues that the interaction between stronger and weaker states need not necessarily lead to asymmetrical results, partly as a result of differences in preference intensity.[26] However, unless we can account for preference intensity independently of negotiation results, this approach may lead to a *post hoc ergo propter hoc* explanation. Given very intense preferences, weaker states must also be able to translate them into the desired outcome, and thus an examination of the negotiation process may still be apposite.

Likewise, analyses of NAFTA negotiations that look at initial positions and outcomes and conclude that the results show that Mexico gave precedence to sectoral aspects of the negotiation while the United States favored trade principles[27] also run the risk of post-hocery, unless careful attention is paid to the process that led from initial positions to eventual outcome.

Finally, pundits in Mexico pointed to the fact that Mexico would have to pay dearly to obtain its offensive and defensive aims in NAFTA, and that in any case the relative dearth of experience in international trade negotiations of the Mexican team would mean that US negotiators would ride roughshod over them. Throughout the negotiation process, several Mexican newspapers reported that Mexico had "given in" on the energy issue, and simply thought it would be impossible to conclude a satisfactory negotiation for Mexico in terms of market access without relenting on energy.[28]

From a theoretical perspective, the case can shed light on the way in which weaker states negotiating with stronger states can defend themselves effectively against unwelcome demands by the latter. Specifically, it illustrates the way in which different process-related variables affect the likelihood of successful defense against distributive strategies. The focus is on the options available to a weaker state defending against offensive distributive strategies. Before turning to the role that the negotiation

---

[25] See Krasner 1990.   [26] See Keohane 1990.   [27] See Maxfield and Shapiro 1998.
[28] The Mexican daily *El Financiero* stuck to this line of reasoning throughout the negotiations. Among the pundits expecting Mexico to "give away the shop" were two prominent left-leaning intellectuals, Adolfo Aguilar Zínser and Jorge G. Castañeda.

process played in NAFTA energy negotiations, I deal with alternative explanations.

Stephen Krasner[29] holds that cooperation and the ensuing creation of international institutions is difficult when states with very different power capabilities interact, as a result of both stronger state and weaker state incentives. Stronger states will prefer to act unilaterally and not to be bound by restrictive accords with weaker states. The latter will be hesitant to negotiate agreements that will increase their interactions (and thus vulnerability) with stronger states and will not be able to effectively resist non-compliance by the stronger state while they themselves will have to comply. They will experience weakened autonomy, and will in any case have a better option in bargaining multilaterally, where coalitions are possible. These considerations led Krasner to conclude in the late 1980s that a trade agreement between Mexico and the United States, similar to the one established between Canada and the United States, was extremely unlikely.

Krasner's prediction was not borne out, for NAFTA was signed just two years after publication of his article. One might argue, following an earlier work by Krasner,[30] that US national security interests are the driving force behind its behavior in the world political economy, and that security concerns explain why it chose to be bound by a restrictive accord instead of acting unilaterally in its relations with Mexico. However, the fact that investment in the oil sector and energy supply commitments, which were dear to US negotiators, were left out of the agreement, raises questions about whether national security concerns were so influential in shaping US negotiators' aims, and even more importantly, the results of negotiations.

Mexico secured an agreement where it obtained its main offensive and defensive aims, and where one of the offensive aims was precisely compliance guarantees through legalized dispute settlement. This means that an approach to economic interaction among states of different power capabilities that leaves out process has difficulty in accounting for a key NAFTA outcome: energy negotiations.[31]

Keohane[32] does not expect necessarily asymmetrical results from asymmetrical interaction, nor does he see great impediments to international cooperation under this setting. He argues that in some issue-areas

---

[29] See Krasner 1990.   [30] See Krasner 1978.
[31] See Ortiz Mena L. N. 2001 for coverage of compliance concerns and dispute settlement in NAFTA negotiations. The model developed there attempts to account for symmetrical outcomes under conditions of asymmetrical bargaining by redefining conceptions of power and vulnerability, while still leaving out process.
[32] See Keohane 1990.

(such as migration and drugs) it is difficult for stronger states to achieve their policy goals on a unilateral basis, so they have incentives to cooperate. Regarding weaker state leverage in international negotiations, he argues that preference intensity can sometimes compensate for the effects of power asymmetry, as can the fact that it is possible for weaker states to strike alliances with domestic groups in the stronger country, as part of its negotiating strategy.[33] While Keohane does contemplate the possibility of weaker states striking bargains with stronger states that are not the mere reflection of stronger state interests, his framework does not allow for a systematic analysis of the conditions under which weaker states may perform best in their negotiations with stronger states. In particular, a focus on preference intensity can lead to tautological reasoning. We need to understand what makes for weaker state influence, beyond generalities such as preference intensity and their ability to play the domestic politics game in the stronger state.

In terms of specific analyses of NAFTA negotiations, the works are relatively few. Most of them deal with negotiation outcomes, and the pros and cons of the bargains struck,[34] rather than with the reasons for the observed gains and losses reflected in the legal text. Maxfield and Shapiro, Mayer, and Cameron and Tomlin are among the few works that deal with the reasons behind the negotiation outcomes.[35] Following a sectoral analysis, Maxfield and Shapiro attempt to assess who "won" and "lost" each sector. Regarding oil, their assessment is that the United States made some gains given the inclusion of energy in the negotiations despite initial opposition from Mexico and by the mere fact that there is an energy chapter in NAFTA, but lost on foreign participation, made only limited gains in market access, and made no headway on energy exports in times of crisis. They conclude that "On balance, Mexico came out ahead in this chapter of the NAFTA negotiations."[36]

Their explanation for the observed outcome is, however, not fully satisfactory. They focus on initial preferences and negotiation outcomes, and largely leave out the negotiation process. They note that the United States tended to win in matters of trade law and principles (such as intellectual property rights and dispute settlement), while Mexico tended to win in sectoral issues, such as oil and agriculture, and conjecture that this may be the result of trade politics being more principle-based in the United States and sector-based in Mexico.

---

[33] See also Odell 1980 on the use of transnational coalitions with domestic groups in the United States regarding US–Latin American trade negotiations.

[34] See Hufbauer and Schott 1993; Léycegui and Fernández de Castro 2000; and Borja 2001, inter alia.

[35] See Maxfield and Shapiro 1998; Mayer 1998; and Cameron and Tomlin 2000.

[36] Maxfield and Shapiro 1998, 101.

This conjecture, however, is yet to be validated and there is considerable evidence that can yield opposite conclusions. Classics such as Schattschneider and Lowi, and more recent work with nuanced analyses such as Destler, O'Halloran, and Mayer point to the continuing importance of interest groups in the formulation of US trade policy.[37] Mexico opened up its economy on a unilateral basis during the 1980s and 1990s without strong pressure group action in favor of free trade, while a significant number of groups clamored for continued protection.[38] In this view, US trade politics should be portrayed as sector-based and Mexico's as principle-based, *contra* the formulation of Maxfield and Shapiro's, who suggest that research dealing with the relative insulation of trade policymakers and business preferences may shed some light on the NAFTA bargain.

A better understanding of negotiation outcomes thus requires, at a minimum, a closer analysis of the role played by domestic politics, and that is precisely what Mayer sets out to do.[39] Following Putnam, he argues that the United States was interested, from a business perspective, in having Mexico open up its energy sector, which would benefit US oil companies and their suppliers; from a national security perspective, secure energy supplies from Mexico would mean less reliance on "insecure" Middle Eastern supplies. Both of these considerations "weighed in" on key Texan political figures who were to play an important part in NAFTA negotiations: President George H. W. Bush, Secretary of State James Baker, Secretary of Commerce Robert Mosbacher, and Senate Finance Committee Chairman Lloyd Bentsen.[40]

While Mexico needed foreign investment to modernize its inefficient oil infrastructure, domestic politics played a significant role in determining its negotiating position. Since the 1938 nationalization of the oil industry (largely affecting US and UK interests), oil had become a symbol of national sovereignty. In the end, domestic politics and the symbolic importance of the oil industry outweighed purely economic considerations, and at the outset of the negotiations the Mexican government spelled out its five "Nos" regarding energy.

---

[37] See Schattschneider 1935; Lowi 1964; Destler 1986; O'Halloran 1994; and Mayer 1998. Interestingly, Maxfield and Shapiro do mention Schattschneider, but do not follow up his arguments.

[38] Ortiz Mena L. N. 2004a.

[39] Mayer uses three levels of analysis (international, domestic, and individual), and three modes of politics (rational choice, regime theory, and symbolic response), depending on the negotiation issue and aspect to be analyzed (Mayer 1998, 13–28). For the specifics of NAFTA negotiations (as opposed to the decision to negotiate, the fast track renewal negotiations, or the ratification), he largely focuses on domestic politics, or more precisely on a two-level bargaining model based on Putnam 1988.

[40] Mayer 1998, 117–18.

Following comments by US Deputy Chief Negotiator Charles E. "Chip" Roh on the logic behind Mexico's stance, and the reasons for the position taken by US oil firms, Mayer ventures that the strong position taken by Mexico may have been the result of advice given to them by Canadians, regarding the importance of stating explicitly at the outset of negotiations what is off limits, for otherwise the United States "will beat you and beat you again." In addition, the strategy may also have been designed to play a role in Mexican domestic politics, so Mexican negotiators could say that they had been tough on oil, and thus the rest of the deal would look more palatable. The United States implicitly understood this, and countenanced from the outset that it could "come short" on oil, but expected to compensate with gains in other areas. Finally, the US oil industry had a clear sense of the possible and did not exert undue pressure after an initial try.[41]

In interpreting the outcome given these incompatible preferences, Mayer notes that for the United States one of the initial appeals of NAFTA had been improved access to Mexican oil, both in terms of investment and secure supplies, and that energy had been a most difficult issue from the outset of negotiations. Despite Mexican protestations, US negotiators were not convinced that Mexico would not budge on the issues of foreign investment in the energy sector and on energy supply guarantees. Near the end of the negotiations, Mexican Trade Minister Serra threatened to walk away if the United States insisted on the oil issue, and the message was also conveyed to the US delegation by President Salinas' chief of staff. The United States relented when it realized that Mexico would not budge. The United States was by then in a hurry to wrap up the negotiations. It opted to make some gains in the energy procurement area instead.

In Mayer's view, then, two factors were key in determining the outcome of the energy negotiations: Mexico's domestic political constraints and domestic political developments in the United States, which put pressure on Bush to wrap up the negotiations. The political costs that would have been borne in Mexico by acquiescing to US demands on investment in oil and energy security would have been so high that no issue linkage (concession) by the United States would have compensated for it, and the United States finally came to understand this.[42]

As the November 1992 US presidential election approached, Bush's approval ratings continued to deteriorate, and Republican political operatives decided it would be important for Bush to announce the successful

---

[41] Ibid., 119. The quotes in this paragraph refer to Charles E. "Chip" Roh's views, as transcribed by Mayer.
[42] Ibid., 152–54.

conclusion of NAFTA negotiations during the Republican National Convention due to take place in mid-August. They viewed the agreement as a political asset for Bush, that at the same time could be used to pressure candidate Bill Clinton to stop fudging on the issue and support NAFTA, lest he be accused of pandering to special interests (such as labor). With that aim in mind, a negotiating session in the infamous Watergate complex started on July 29, and ended shortly after midnight, August 12. Energy was one of the issues not settled until the final stretch.[43]

Mayer's account of the energy negotiations is not inadequate, but rather incomplete. With his detailed analysis of domestic politics in the United States and Mexico, and how they played into the international negotiations, he goes further than is possible with Krasner and Keohane's basically systemic approach, and his explanations do not have a post hoc tinge, as is the case with Maxfield and Shapiro. However, several important questions are left unanswered.

For instance, why was it that Mexico's domestic political constraints were not taken as credible by the United States at the beginning of negotiations but were so taken at the end? Did the urge to wrap up the negotiations make it relent on the issue, or did its conception of Mexico's reservation value actually change? Why was it not able to convince Mexico that its own reservation value demanded an agreement that included greater access for US investors in the Mexican energy sector, energy oil supply guarantees, or both? Was not Mexico also under pressure to conclude the agreement, and if so why did the United States not use that fact to force Mexico into granting additional concessions in this key sector? More generally, when will a domestic political constraint be credible, and how can it override otherwise substantial power differentials among negotiators? If Mexico did manage to exclude a significant part of its energy sector from NAFTA negotiations, did it have to pay a high price for this in terms of negotiation trade-offs? Before turning to these issues seen through a negotiation process framework, I assess how well Cameron and Tomlin deal with them.[44]

Cameron and Tomlin provide a very detailed account of NAFTA negotiations by focusing on several key junctures in the process, and analyze the events through various approaches which include Neo-realism, Neo-liberalism, two-level game theory and their own "integrated" argument, which encompasses elements of the previous three approaches and negotiation theories. The key additional ingredient that is incorporated in the integrated approach is the notion of subjective utility attached by the negotiators to their non-agreement alternatives at any given point in the

[43] Ibid., 139–40.   [44] See Cameron and Tomlin 2000.

negotiation, which is in turn affected by the degree to which negotiators are risk averse. These considerations lead Cameron and Tomlin to make predictions for three issues, which are compared to the predictions made for those same issues by Neo-realism, Neo-liberalism, and the two-level game approach.

They expect that cooperation under anarchy among asymmetrical players will not necessarily lead to asymmetrical results, the reason for this being that the weaker state may have a better non-agreement alternative than the stronger one, and it may also have a lower discount rate. In terms of domestic politics, they expect negotiators of stronger states to be less responsive to weaker state demands vis-à-vis the stronger state's domestic constituents, and vice versa. They also expect a bargaining process in which the lower the subjective utility awarded to its non-agreement alternative, the more a given country will perceive the agreement in terms of gains over its best alternative to a negotiated agreement (BATNA), the more risk averse it will be to achieve those gains, the less willing it will be to risk the agreement by withholding concessions, and the more concessions it will offer in order to obtain an agreement (and vice versa).[45] How well does the Cameron and Tomlin approach allow us to understand the outcome of NAFTA energy negotiations?

Regarding asymmetry, their approach yields equivocal results. They state that Mexico was the demandeur and wanted NAFTA "very badly,"[46] and that "the most important asymmetry lay in the fact that Mexico needed the United States much more than the United States needed Mexico. The Mexicans had examined the alternatives and had already decided that they preferred NAFTA to anything else available to them."[47] While they recognize that at the end of the negotiations in August 1992 the United States was in a rush to conclude in order for Bush to present NAFTA as an important achievement, in an attempt to bolster his flagging ratings shortly before the November presidential election, it is not immediately clear whether the United States had more to lose than Mexico from a failure to conclude negotiations successfully. Their focus on the effect of each party's BATNA on negotiation strategies and outcomes is correct, but the ex ante specification of BATNAs to allow clear predictions is very difficult. If only the asymmetry strand of their argument is contemplated, it does not explain why the United States relented on oil.

What is surprising is that the United States pushed for a liberalization of investment in the energy sector throughout the negotiations, while US oil companies did not exert undue pressure either on US negotiators or directly on Mexican negotiators. "The major oil companies

---

[45] Ibid., 15–32.   [46] Ibid., 165.   [47] Ibid., 124.

were . . . 'pretty sophisticated' . . . in that they wanted to open up Mexico's energy sector but knew that Mexico would not do this at the behest of the United States."[48] Thus, the United States pushed hard on liberalization without undue pressure from US interests, and then relented in the face of steadfast Mexican opposition. A strict focus on domestic politics would have predicted less pressure on the investment issue, and cannot account for US attitudes on energy supply commitments, for no specific interest group was pressing for it. By and large, US negotiators were not acting on behalf of interest groups, and relented in the face of the weaker state's position on all major issues.

The third strand of their argument, on the bargaining process, can be seen as an extension of their parsimonious hypothesis regarding asymmetry. They give ample evidence to bolster their claim that Mexico was very risk averse and, as mentioned above, badly wanted NAFTA. According to Cameron and Tomlin, during the Dallas plenary meeting held in February 1992 Mexico caved in too soon and gave away concessions to the United States (basically in financial services) in order to push along negotiations to an early conclusion.[49] While Mexican behavior at Dallas coincides with Cameron and Tomlin's expectations, subsequent behavior does not, especially in the energy area. Mexico's high degree of risk aversion should have meant that it would not be willing to put the whole agreement at risk by withholding concessions.

However, in the final stretch of negotiations which took place at the Watergate Hotel the Mexicans were "stubborn in their continued refusal to guarantee energy export levels to the United States during times of shortage . . . , leading Canada to indicate that should Mexico prevail, they would seek to change the [CUS] FTA provisions on this issue."[50] With Mexico additionally adopting a maximalist position on procurement regarding PEMEX (it wanted to reserve all contracts for Mexican companies), trilateral discussions were suspended.

In the end, Mexico managed to get away with its five "Nos" (its main defensive aims), and at the same time to attain its main offensive interests in the negotiation: to ensure full market access to the US and Canadian markets, to have a tariff reduction schedule that recognized asymmetries (the United States and Canada liberalized faster than did Mexico), and to establish an effective dispute settlement mechanism.[51] Mexico attained all its negotiation aims without apparently paying too high a price for them. How was this possible, when the United States should have had the upper hand, given asymmetry, domestic politics, and negotiation advantages? Both Mayer, and Cameron and Tomlin, give partial

---

[48] Ibid., 89–90.   [49] Ibid., 113–19   [50] Ibid., 161–62.   [51] Salinas 2000, 76.

answers to this question, but ultimately cannot explain how Mexico was able to defend successfully against demands by the United States. In what follows, I examine the issue through the negotiation process framework.

3   The role of the negotiation process in successful resistance against US demands

There is much we still have to understand about successful defense against an offensive distributive strategy. Several cases have been examined (Brazil defending against the United States on instant coffee, Mexico defending against US antidumping actions on Mexican tomatoes, Japan defending against the United States on exchange rate adjustments, and on beef), but as Odell notes "the defending side will . . . want to tailor its tactics to the particular situation."[52]

Mexico's strategy choice was not sufficient on its own accord to successfully defend against demands. It had to be coupled with measures to guard against informational biases, actions in both the US and Mexican domestic political scene, and the reduction of potentially adverse effects from an unfavorable evolution of markets that were beyond its control to achieve the results detailed in the first section of this chapter.

3.1   *Mexico's sequentially mixed strategy and its framing tactics*

Mexico's strategy choice suggests that choosing a mixed strategy, rather than a strict distributive one, may gain more or lose less under some circumstances, even when negotiators believe their main strategies are in conflict, and that sometimes sticking exclusively to a defensive distributive strategy does not produce adequate results.[53] The importance of framing as part of the negotiation also stands out.

One key reason for the successful defense against US demands in energy negotiations is that Mexico displayed a sequentially mixed strategy, opening with mostly distributive moves and mixing in some integrative ones near the end. There is a vast array of actions available to weaker states when they wish to defend against an offensive distributive strategy; a defensive distributive strategy is just one of the alternatives, and not always the best one, as demonstrated by the 1969 Brazilian instant coffee case.[54]

---

[52] Odell 2000, 210. The discussion is divided according to analytically separate concepts to clarify the argument, but it must be borne in mind that their interaction is in reality quite complex.

[53] Ibid., 185–86.   [54] Ibid., 141–47.

During the pre-negotiation phase (from the announcement in early 1990 that an FTA between Mexico and the United States might be negotiated until the formal start of negotiations in June 1991) Mexico basically adopted a defensive distributive strategy. It maintained that strategy during the early phases of NAFTA negotiations, and when they neared the end Mexico turned to a mixed strategy. The decision to mix strategies in a sequential manner was decided from the outset of negotiations.[55]

NAFTA negotiations started, albeit informally, earlier than is commonly known.[56] In November 1988 President Bush met with President Salinas. Bush proposed an FTA to Salinas, but Salinas declined. During his campaign, Salinas had made no mention of the need to negotiate a free trade agreement with the United States. On top of his doubts about the intrinsic convenience of striking such a deal, he was worried that Mexico was about to start negotiations over Mexico's foreign debt with the United States and did not want to mix debt negotiations with trade negotiations, fearing that possible gains for Mexico in the debt area would be countered by concessions in trade.[57]

In March 1990, a month after Mexican Trade Minister Serra had proposed the negotiation of a bilateral free trade agreement to the USTR's Carla Hills, Canadian Prime Minister Brian Mulroney traveled to Mexico City and mentioned to Salinas that, in his dealings with the United States during the recently concluded CUSFTA, he had learned that it was very important to make it absolutely clear to them at the outset of negotiations what was simply non-negotiable, in order to avoid unpleasant surprises.[58]

Salinas heeded Mulroney's advice. At an economic cabinet meeting in May it was decided that oil would be excluded from the negotiations, according to the precepts of the Mexican Constitution. Thus, a negotiation tactic would be that Mexico's constitution would not be reformed to accommodate NAFTA negotiations, so Mexico's limits regarding concessions were clear cut. This decision was conveyed to Brent Scowcroft, Bush's National Security Advisor. At the same time, Serra had insisted that intellectual property rights (IPR) be kept as a negotiating card for future use.[59]

Despite Mexico's communications with top Bush advisors, the United States kept up the pressure to include oil in the negotiations even before they had formally started. For instance, in August 1990 US Commerce Secretary Robert Mosbacher gave an interview to ABC News, where he

[55] Author's interview with Jaime Serra Puche, Mexican Trade Minister 1988–1994, Mexico City, August 19, 2003.
[56] Please refer to the appendix to this chapter for a chronology of NAFTA negotiations.
[57] Salinas 2000, 12.   [58] Ibid., 60.   [59] Ibid., 67.

stated that oil would be in the negotiations, and specifically the issue of oil supply guarantees.[60]

The Mexican government realized that it would have to be prepared to counter US pressures in the negotiations, and specifically on the oil issue. Accordingly, Salinas established an inter-ministerial commission, where all NAFTA-related issues would be discussed and cleared before any public airing of views.[61] He also established the NAFTA Negotiation Office (which was highly centralized and answered directly to the president himself), kept recalcitrant members of the Foreign Ministry "out of the loop,"[62] and favored the creation of COECE, the Foreign Trade Business Organization Council, which coordinated all private sector actions in relation to NAFTA negotiations.[63]

Once the institutional structure for the negotiations was created, specific guidelines for negotiators were set out. In terms of defensive aims, at this stage it was deemed insufficient to simply rely on the assertion that the Constitution was not part of the negotiations. Thus, the five "Nos" were dictated to the negotiating team with instructions to stand absolutely firm regarding those issues throughout the negotiations. They would simply state and restate the position, and not engage in any arguments about it. The defensive aims were at the same time coupled with offensive aims (market access that recognized asymmetries between the Mexican economy and that of its future NAFTA partners, and the establishment of an effective dispute settlement mechanism).

These guidelines allowed the possibility of striking a deal with the United States, given the very wide range of issues that were subject to negotiations, through cross-sectoral trade-offs – IPR and foreign direct investment (FDI) liberalization, together with investor-state dispute settlement, were of paramount importance to the United States. Mexico was also interested in getting agriculture on the table, even though it was extremely vulnerable in some areas, above all corn.[64] Radical transformation of Mexican agriculture was required anyway, and it was used as a bargaining chip; current levels of domestic support for agricultural products were simply unsustainable, and something had to give. In addition, Mexico could make important gains in terms of market access. If Mexico requested exceptions, it would be inundated with requests from Mexican interest groups, and US groups would soon start to follow suit. The basic

---

[60] Ibid., 71.   [61] Ibid., 72.
[62] Schiavon and Ortiz Mena L. N. 2001.   [63] Ortiz Mena L. N. 2004b.
[64] The majority of Mexico's corn producers are very inefficient. Most of them are quite poor self-subsistence farmers.

tenet was that under NAFTA liberalization would be for real, and the negotiations would decide the "how" and "when," not the "if."[65]

Even the strict limits set out for oil still allowed some compromises; while the five "Nos" indeed posed significant restrictions on what was clearly non-negotiable, there was room for a deal regarding foreign investment in secondary and final petrochemicals, electricity generation, international trade in oil and gas, performance contracts, and procurement. In addition, the sectors that were off limits from the negotiations were among the most politically volatile, so it was relatively easy to strike deals on the somewhat less politicized issues that were on the table.[66]

While the Mexicans were preparing for negotiations, the United States continued to press Mexico on oil. In November 1990, a key meeting between Salinas and Bush took place in Monterrey, Mexico. Salinas asked Bush to include migration in the trade talks, but Bush replied that the US Congress would not ratify the agreement if it encompassed migration. Salinas then acquiesced in excluding migration from the talks, but stated that oil would accordingly also be excluded. The reservation values had been clearly posited, although Bush noted that the ratification of the agreement without the inclusion of oil would not be easy. US negotiators kept up the pressure on oil until the end of negotiations.[67]

Mexico no longer insisted on including migration, and used similar integrative strategies to counter US pressures. It did not attempt to offset defensive with offensive aims. The negotiation strategy was to offset its defensive distributive strategy with its partners' own defensive distributive strategy; otherwise it may have been under great pressure in terms of foregoing offensive aims or acquiescing to US offensive aims in order to maintain its energy sector off limits. The costs of exclusion may have been prohibitively high.[68]

Specifically, at the first preparatory meeting the Mexican team defended its demand to exclude petroleum by arguing that it was only fair, since the United States had decided to exclude maritime transportation,[69]

---

[65] Author's interviews with Jaime Zabludovsky Kuper, Deputy Chief NAFTA negotiator, Mexico's NAFTA Negotiation Office, Mexico City, August 15, 2003; Charles E. "Chip" Roh, Deputy Chief NAFTA negotiator, USTR. Washington, DC, September 30, 2004.

[66] Author's interview with Jaime Serra Puche, Mexican Trade Minister 1988–1994, Mexico City, August 19, 2003.

[67] Author's interview with Charles E. "Chip" Roh, Deputy Chief NAFTA negotiator, USTR. Washington, DC, September 30, 2004; Salinas 2000, 83–84.

[68] Author's interview with Jaime Serra Puche, Mexican Trade Minister 1988–1994, Mexico City, August 19, 2003.

[69] The US exclusion involved section 27 of the 1920 Merchant Marine Act, known as the Jones Act.

and Canada excluded (against strong US objections) cultural industries. Given that each party had items that were off limits from the negotiations, Mexico argued that there was fairness in the position each had taken.[70]

Mexico also understood that Canada would threaten to demand a modification of CUSFTA provisions on energy supply commitments should Mexico not accept a similar commitment, which in turn would generate incentives for the United States to press Mexico hard on the issue. Accordingly, an additional integrative strategy used was that each country was to reserve a strategic sector: for Canada, in addition to cultural industries, it was its vast freshwater reserves. If Canada had exempted water from the CUSFTA, Mexico was entitled to exempt oil from NAFTA.[71]

Once formal negotiations got under way, Mexico started with a defensive distributive strategy: it refused to discuss the energy issue, and was opposed to the creation of an energy working group as part of NAFTA negotiations.[72] Later on it acquiesced to US Chief Negotiator Carla Hills's demands for the creation of an energy working group, but Mexico insisted it be called an energy and petrochemicals working group, given there was space for negotiation on petrochemicals, but none on investment and energy supply guarantees.[73]

This set the basis for the tactic used by Mexico whenever oil resurfaced in the discussions: it held fast to the five "Nos", tirelessly repeating them and entertaining no arguments about them; it offered to discuss energy related issues that were not contemplated in the "Nos", and it also stated that a violation of the five "Nos" would not only shoot down the whole agreement but that if the United States pushed too far and too hard the whole issue would blow up in Mexican domestic politics with grave consequences for both countries.[74]

While Mexico stuck to a defensive distributive strategy throughout the negotiations in terms of its five "Nos", it did offer some flexibility in other energy areas (such as secondary petrochemicals, trade in gas and electricity, and procurement) and in other NAFTA issues like IPR and investor-state disputes. If its strategy had consisted of defensive demands in a vast number of areas, the room for maneuver would have been scant and the possibility of striking a deal low. By allowing bargains to be struck

---

[70] Author's interview with Jaime Serra Puche, Mexican Trade Minister 1988–1994, Mexico City, August 19, 2003.
[71] Salinas 2000, 90.   [72] Cameron and Tomlin 2000, 83.
[73] Author's interview with Jaime Zabludovsky Kuper, Deputy Chief NAFTA negotiator, Mexico's NAFTA Negotiation Office, Mexico City, August 15, 2003.
[74] Author's interview with Jaime Serra Puche, Mexican Trade Minister 1988–1994, Mexico City, August 19, 2003. Section 3.2 elaborates on the way in which Mexico's threat of domestic political instability was made credible.

in other areas (creating a positive zone of agreement), it was easier to successfully defend against demands.

As has been noted, the mixed strategy was facilitated by the fact that energy negotiations were embedded within the larger NAFTA negotiation, so cross-sectoral deals could be struck. It was also possible to develop a mixed strategy within the energy area by, for example, naming the working group "energy and petrochemicals" and bringing petrochemicals into the discussion, and by including PEMEX and CFE in procurement negotiations. This was especially important for the US negotiators, in so far as they would find it hard to explain why the energy negotiations had been a complete washout.[75] Thus, Mexico needed to offer a mixed strategy not only across sectors, but also within the energy sector itself. In addition, the mixed strategy was also created by dividing the negotiation process into stages, so principles were agreed upon first (the creation of a working group), and the details were left for later. This helped to break the impasse on energy, and concurs with suggestions to break impasses offered by Odell.[76]

Negotiating over the trade-related issues encompassed by NAFTA helped Mexico defend against demands, but there was also a lesson in avoiding other types of issue-mix, as was the case of debt and trade negotiations. Mexico might have paid a high price for the exclusion of the energy sector by obtaining a worse deal on its debt renegotiations than it actually did. By keeping these issues separate, it was able to secure a good deal on both of them. The lesson here is not that mixing or separating issues is good or bad per se, but that the decision must be made on a case by case basis, and that even when issues are separated it may still be possible to find a way to generate a mixed strategy.

The Mexican case suggests that it is best to use a defensive distributive strategy against another defensive distributive strategy, and not against an offensive distributive one. By positing that an exclusion should be counteracted by another state's exclusion, a positive zone of agreement is created, and the weaker state is no longer compelled to offset its exclusion against its own offensive aims. If Mexico had enticed the United States into negotiations by hinting that a deal on energy was possible, but baulked at the end, this might have generated a great deal of confusion and the construction of a winning coalition of votes in the US Congress would have been severely hampered.

---

[75] Author's interview with Charles E. "Chip" Roh, Deputy Chief NAFTA negotiator, USTR, Washington, DC, September 30, 2004.
[76] See Odell 2000, 212.

The framing of the issue also had an important impact on the success of the defense against demands. Mexico started to play off its exclusions against US exclusions even before formal negotiations started, as when Salinas proposed the inclusion of migration in the talks, and when Bush refused, giving Mexico a reason to exclude oil without any concessions: it had already accepted the exclusion of migration. This tactic was followed in the negotiations when Mexico argued that the exclusion of oil was equivalent to the exclusion of maritime transportation by the United States (even though Mexico had no overriding interest in amending the Jones Act), and when it framed Mexico's oil exclusion as equivalent to Canada's water exclusion, so as to make equivalent Mexican energy supply commitments with Canadian water (and not energy) supply commitments. The specifics of the strategy relied on imagination in terms of how to frame an issue differently, to be able to offset an exclusion with another exclusion.

The sequential mixed strategy, as opposed to a simultaneous mixed strategy also worked well in defending against an unwanted claim. The sequential nature of the offer helped Mexico play for time, so the United States had to decide during the last stages of the negotiation if it wanted to accept the tokens offered by Mexico in energy. If the offer had been simultaneous, the United States would in any case have taken the tokens for granted and kept on asking for more. Just as not having to offset Mexico's defensive distributive strategy against the counterparts' own defensive distributive strategy could have translated into much higher costs of exclusion for Mexico, a simultaneous offer could also have translated into unnecessarily higher costs of exclusion.

Finally, setting out in public the offensive and defensive aims at the outset of negotiations and sticking to that position throughout the negotiations was of great help in bolstering the credibility of Mexico's position; other countries have dithered, thus creating expectations in the United States that are difficult to back out from once they are in the air, and weaker countries typically find it very costly to walk out from negotiations once they have started.[77]

3.2   *Mexico's actions to offset biases and bolster the credibility of its position on energy*

Mexico's actions to avoid biases, discussed below, appear to bear out the expectation that "If negotiators are subject . . . to cognitive judgment

---

[77] Author's interview with Charles E. "Chip" Roh, Deputy Chief NAFTA negotiator, USTR, Washington, DC, September 30, 2004.

biases, then gains and losses from a strategy will vary directly with the extent to which the negotiator uses tactics designed to compensate his own biases."[78] The Mexican team's actions in exploiting the advantages of the decentralized US political system were important in this regard, as well as in bolstering the credibility of its reservation value on energy.

The long NAFTA negotiation process turned out to be a blessing in disguise. The Salinas administration's experience in dealing with the Bush team started with its debt negotiations of 1988–1989. During those negotiations, they learned that the US delegation was not monolithic, that some officials could be played off against others, and that when negotiations reached delicate points it was both possible and useful to have Salinas speak directly to Bush, who would then exert pressure on his own team. The Mexican team was no longer under the impression that its US counterpart was invulnerable.[79]

Fast track negotiations also helped the Mexican team learn about US preferences. In order for President Bush to obtain a renewal of fast track negotiating authority, a major lobbying effort by both Mexico and the United States had taken place. In December 1990 Mexico opened a branch of its NAFTA negotiation office in Washington. Mexican officials of the Washington office made a concerted effort to establish close links with both US legislators and US interest groups to aid in fast track approval. The contacts and knowledge derived from the fast track negotiations proved invaluable for the subsequent negotiations. The "intelligence" work conducted by the Washington office was very sophisticated and useful for Mexican negotiators. For instance, they were able to make assessments with a high degree of certainty on how different configurations of rules of origin for a given sector would affect congressional votes at the time of ratification.[80]

In addition to establishing the Washington office, Mexico hired a team of lobbyists and lawyers. Among the firms hired were Burson-Marsteller, Charls Walker and Associates, and Manchester Trade. Robert Herzstein, who had been a top US trade official during the Carter administration and was one the leading legal experts on unfair trade practices,[81] led a team of lawyers from Shearman & Sterling that closely advised Mexican negotiators throughout the process. Mexico also hired several former USTR officials. In all, it spent approximately US $35 million on lobbyists and legal advice throughout the three-year NAFTA process.[82]

---

[78] Odell 2000, 184.   [79] Salinas 2000, 9–37.   [80] von Bertrab 1996, 109, 118.
[81] In the 1970s he had helped Mexico successfully defend itself against US AD actions on Mexican tomatoes, see Odell 2000, 102–104.
[82] Salinas 2000, 93–94.

An important action taken to avoid biases was the hiring of lobby-ists and lawyers, and having them interact with members of the Washington NAFTA negotiation office. They helped Mexico understand the United States' reservation value on a number of issues, and thus to design a negotiation strategy that ensured there was a winning coalition as a result of Mexican offers. It also meant that Carla Hills could not cred-ibly bluff in order to extract concessions from Mexico. Under a biased information scenario, it is possible to imagine an outcome where the United States could credibly state that an agreement without liberaliza-tion of oil investment rules and commitments on energy supply would not be approved by the US Congress, or where the costs of exclusion were unnecessarily high.

Foreign advisors aided Mexico in revealing correct information about US preferences, and also helped it avoid making costly mistakes in appar-ently small details when negotiators' agreements were translated into legalese. The negotiations were undertaken in English, and the first legal text was in English, so Mexicans had to be extremely careful that what they thought they had agreed upon was effectively what the legal text stated. Likewise, after the end of negotiations there still remained a phase where Congress had to issue implementing legislation for NAFTA, and it was also possible to lose some gains that were made at the negoti-ation table in the process of turning NAFTA into US domestic law. The lesson to be learned here is that while Mexico's negotiators were extremely capable economists, an area of vulnerability lay in the different nature of the US legal system and its great complexity.[83] If a country is to defend against demands by the United States in economic negotiations, it seems that the most valuable foreign advisers may be not economists but lawyers.

The success of Mexico's actions during NAFTA negotiations can be compared to the failure of the gas pipeline negotiations between Mex-ico and the United States in the 1970s, when the Director General of PEMEX had made a public commitment in terms of the minimal accept-able outcome for Mexico (much as with the five "Nos"), but given his biased information the whole project fell through and proved to be very costly for Mexico.[84]

The US political system is complex given its decentralized nature, but it is also very transparent when it comes to interest group politics. This fea-ture allowed Mexico's NAFTA office, together with its myriad advisors, to

---

[83] Mexico uses a Roman law system, while the US has a common law system.
[84] See Odell 2000, 94–107.

do a thorough job of detecting legislator positions on each issue throughout the negotiations, and to make calculations on the required winning
coalition (218 votes in the House and 51 in the Senate)[85] for NAFTA
ratification.[86]

The decentralized nature of the system also allowed the Mexican team
to use the counterpart it thought best at any given point in time. Salinas
met with Bush several times during the negotiations, reiterating Mexico's
position on oil. The "Texan" group (James Baker, Robert Mosbacher,
and Lloyd Bentsen) was also approached during negotiations; they had
the "big picture" of NAFTA negotiations and did not let specific issues
get in the way of the deal, whereas Carla Hills was focusing exclusively
on trade issues and in fact was not keen on NAFTA, at least at the outset.
Specifically, Serra found it very useful to have two counterparts: he would
deal with Hills most of the time, but he also dealt directly with Commerce
Secretary Mosbacher as the need arose. The United States did not have
that advantage, in that there was no division between politicians and
negotiators, and Serra was the sole leader of negotiations.[87]

The knowledge of congressional positions also made it very difficult
for Hills to bluff in terms of how much room for maneuver she had
from interest group pressures; the Mexican team had virtually the same
information as did USTR. Her threats were for the most part not credible,
and in any case Mexico could counter them via direct contacts with the
relevant legislators and interest groups.[88]

Mexico had an apparent handicap in that Salinas (and the top negotiators) could not credibly state that Mexico's Congress would not approve
certain concessions, for the president effectively controlled Congress.[89]
However, this was overcome in several ways.

First, the opacity of the Mexican political system meant that Mexico
possessed an informational advantage over the United States in terms
of the potential domestic political consequences of certain concessions

[85] Some opponents of NAFTA argued that a qualified majority of 67 votes in the Senate
were required to ratify NAFTA (61 Senators voted in favor of NAFTA).
[86] Author's interview with Jaime Zabludovsky Kuper, Deputy Chief NAFTA negotiator,
Mexico's NAFTA Negotiation Office, Mexico City, August 15, 2003. Following congressional positions proved difficult, for shortly after the end of the negotiations the
House was renewed and the negotiation of labor and environmental side agreements
took place, forcing Mexico to continue with its lobbying and intelligence efforts. See von
Bertrab 1996, 180–254.
[87] Author's interview with Jaime Serra Puche, Mexican Trade Minister 1988–1994, Mexico
City, August 19, 2003.
[88] Ibid.
[89] See Martin 2000 for current theories on executive–legislative relations, foreign policy,
and the credibility of commitments.

(such as investment in oil, or the failure of NAFTA ratification), whereas Mexico was at no such disadvantage regarding US politics.

Second, Salinas made public pronouncements in Mexico regarding the fact that the constitution would not be modified, and repeatedly stated the five "Nos". It would have been extremely difficult to backtrack on such clear public statements.

Third, small incidents were magnified to bolster the credibility of Mexico's stance on oil. When a member of the US negotiating team made a public remark stating that oil was in the negotiations, Serra forcefully complained to Hills, and the negotiator was pulled out of the team. Likewise, when a Mexican Trade Ministry official casually remarked that energy would somehow have to be addressed in the negotiations, he was summarily sacked. On one occasion, Serra asked Zabludovsky to head the working group on energy; this was extremely rare as Chief and Deputy Chief Negotiators did not head working group sessions. Incidents such as these were used by Serra to send a signal both to his negotiating partners and to the domestic political establishment in Mexico in order to bolster the credibility of Mexico's position on oil.[90]

Fourth, vociferous opposition to NAFTA negotiations, and specifically the inclusion of oil, was favorable for Mexico's negotiators. Four of NAFTA's most outspoken critics (former presidential candidate Cuauhtémoc Cárdenas – the son of General Lázaro Cárdenas, who had nationalized the oil industry in 1938 – leftist intellectuals Jorge G. Castañeda and Adolfo Aguilar Zínser, and José Ángel Conchello, Senator from the right of center National Action Party) made their views amply known. Aguilar and Castañeda even testified before the US Congress. Critics such as these helped convey to the United States the difficulty of liberalizing investment in the oil sector and undertaking supply commitments, given the strong opposition to such measures in both leftist and rightist circles in Mexico.[91]

Finally, Mexico's stance regarding the five "Nos", and the general nature of the offensive aims, meant that they would be the reservation value in terms of which the whole agreement would be judged domestically. It is worth noting that in the press conference offered by Serra on August 12, 1992 just after the end of negotiations the first thing he mentioned, after the compulsory acknowledgement to all those involved in the negotiations, was that the Constitution was respected and the five "Nos" had prevailed in the negotiations; only then did he turn to the

---

[90] Author's interview with Jaime Zabludovsky Kuper, Deputy Chief NAFTA negotiator, Mexico's NAFTA Negotiation Office, Mexico City, 15, August 15, 2003.
[91] Salinas 2000, 84, 88, 122–26.

offensive aims and state how asymmetries had been recognized in terms of the pace of market liberalization.[92]

The five "Nos" also allowed Mexico to sidetrack any political opposition in Mexico regarding NAFTA ratification, so while it toiled hard to maintain its stance throughout the negotiations, in the end it greatly facilitated the politics of ratification in Mexico. The Mexican negotiating team went so far as to demand that article 601 of chapter VI (the energy chapter), state that the Mexican Constitution would be respected. It seemed like stating the obvious, given that NAFTA would have to comply with each country's constitution, but it was inserted anyway. It is the only place in NAFTA where there is an explicit mention of the Mexican Constitution.[93] Mexico's exemption from energy supply commitments was also clearly spelled out in the same chapter.[94]

Defending against demands by the United States has some advantages. The pluralistic and transparent nature of its political system means that, while it is a very difficult (might one say expensive?) endeavor to follow the positions of key legislators, it is nevertheless possible to do so. Apart from the informational component that can be derived from the particulars of the US political system, it is also possible to act within it. Mexico effectively lobbied both legislators and interest groups during NAFTA negotiations and the subsequent ratification phase. In comparison, defense against demands may be harder against the European Union, given that it now encompasses twenty-five countries, and some issues are dealt with by the European Commission while others are reserved to the nation states. Mexico's experience in negotiating with both the EU and the United States in free trade negotiations indicates that this may in fact be the case.[95]

In addition to lobbying with legislators and business groups, Mexico made use of contacts with top members of the Bush cabinet and, as

---

[92] Serra 1994, 635–37. In terms of offensive aims and the recognition of asymmetries, Mexico made great strides when it convinced the United States to bind Mexico's GSP tariffs at zero upon entry into force of NAFTA. At the time, Mexico was the most important user of US GSP concessions (author's interview with Jaime Serra Puche, Mexican Trade Minister 1988–1994, Mexico City, August 19, 2003).

[93] Author's interviews with Jaime Zabludovsky Kuper, Deputy Chief NAFTA negotiator, Mexico's NAFTA Negotiation Office, Mexico City, August 15, 2003; Jaime Serra Puche, Mexican Trade Minister 1988–1994, Mexico City, August 19, 2003.

[94] Author's interview with Jaime Serra Puche, Mexican Trade Minister 1988–1994, Mexico City, August 19, 2003.

[95] Author's interview with Jaime Zabludovsky Kuper, Deputy Chief NAFTA negotiator, Mexico's NAFTA Negotiation Office, Mexico City, August 15, 2003. Zabludovsky was also Mexico's Chief Negotiator for the trade component aspects of the Mexico–European Union Partnership Agreement. See also Schiavon and Ortiz Mena L. N. 2001, and Armendáriz 2000.

required, with President Bush himself, so negotiations were not circumscribed to what was taking place at the negotiating table. Multiple points
of contact with US officials were used to convey credibility to Mexico's
position of defense against US demands on oil. Salinas reiterated Mexico's position personally to Bush. As such, it was difficult for the United
States to view the position as mere tactical positioning at the negotiating
table.

Mexico also used domestic politics as leverage against US pressures,
closely following the expectation that "As constituents in a target country
raise the political cost of compliance for their government, gains from
[an offensive distributive strategy] will diminish."[96] NAFTA's opponents
actually helped negotiators by stating their steadfast opposition against
the inclusion of energy in the negotiations. This effect was amplified by the
fact that opposition came from both the left and the right of the political
spectrum and that it was conveyed directly to the US audience, including
congressional hearings. Thus, an apparent handicap that Mexico had in
the inability of Salinas to credibly threaten that his legislature would not
approve certain energy concessions was countervailed (inadvertently) by
NAFTA's opponents.

Salinas had also repeatedly stated in public that the Constitution would
not be amended as a result of NAFTA negotiations, and that the agreement would have to abide by the five "Nos". Going public helped Mexico
bolster the credibility of its defense against demands, and set political limits to what was acceptable. The specificity of Mexico's defensive distributive strategy also helped its successful defense; if the defensive distributive
strategy had resided solely in the fact that the Constitution was not up
for negotiation, there could have been several ways to circumvent it. The
more specific the defensive distributive strategy, the easier it was to use
public pressure to support it.

As has been noted, out of the five "Nos" only those pertaining to foreign investment in the energy sector, risk contracts, and trade in energy
can be construed as being covered by the Mexican Constitution; there
are no explicit constitutional prohibitions on energy supply commitments and foreign retail gasoline outlets. Nevertheless, the five "Nos"
were always treated as an indivisible grouping of items that were nonnegotiable.

The public commitment that the Constitution would not be amended
to accommodate NAFTA negotiation needs was maintained for the
energy sector, but in fact the Constitution suffered sixty-one amendments

[96] Odell 2000, 184.

during NAFTA negotiations and ratification (January 1990 to January 1994).[97] It is difficult to ascertain whether some of those amendments were derived from NAFTA negotiations, but the main point is that Mexico's successful defense against US demands in the energy sector did not reside in the simple recipe that the Constitution was not up for negotiation and that, given Mexico's constitutional prohibitions on energy, the result was easily derived from the negotiating premise. The fact that not all five "Nos" were covered by the Mexican Constitution, and that the Mexican Constitution was amended on numerous occasions concurrently with NAFTA negotiations, casts doubt on this simplistic explanation.

The non-democratic nature of the Mexican political system at the time also played in Mexico's favor, for its negotiators had a better notion of what Mexico's reservation values were than did the United States. Mexico could thus somewhat magnify the supposed potential negative consequences of the United States going too far in its offensive demands, so that uncertainty regarding Mexican domestic politics tended to favor Mexico.

The "theatrical" use of small incidents, such as the public sacking of a Mexican Trade Ministry official for even hinting that oil would be in the negotiations, also bolstered the credibility of threats regarding the defensive distributive strategy. Thus, a non-democratic state may, in some circumstances, still be able to make credible threats and even use the non-transparent nature of its political system in its favor.

3.3   Guarding against adverse market conditions

Odell's ventures that "The worse the alternative the relevant market . . . presents to the government negotiator, the lower his reservation value inside the talks, hence the softer his [offensive distributive strategies] and the smaller his gains and vice versa."[98] While the evolution of markets is beyond the control of trade negotiators, Mexican negotiators took certain actions to minimize the adverse effects of market developments and a possible worsening of Mexico's BATNA.

Given that NAFTA was a multi-issue negotiation, not only the oil market was relevant in worsening or improving each country's BATNA. Mexico was additionally concerned about the evolution of certain

---

[97] Calculation by the author based on López Ayllón 1997, 281–315. It is true that some primary petrochemicals were reclassified as secondary during this time, but the practice had been ongoing since the early 1980s, and those changes did not require constitutional amendments.
[98] Odell 2000, 183.

indicators of market expectations, such as the exchange rate and the Mexican stock market index. In terms of US market developments that affected negotiations, Mexico was concerned about a worsening US recession, which was a difficult environment under which to contemplate trade liberalization, and political calendars, if they can be considered a market in so far as they entail a context over which negotiators have no control. US presidential (and congressional) elections were slated for November 1992 and Mexico did not want to deal with a political setting for NAFTA ratification different from that for negotiations. Even less did they want negotiations to be carried out with two different administrations.

Mexico's BATNA worsened as NAFTA negotiations progressed. Whereas no business group in Mexico had requested that Mexico negotiate an FTA with the United States, once negotiations got under way a self-fulfilling prophecy started to take place, whereby significant business groups asserted that the failure to achieve a successful negotiation would generate great market uncertainty and possibly spell serious economic trouble for Mexico.[99] The Mexican team did what it could to protect itself from market developments. In late 1990 it spent considerable resources buying oil futures, with the aim of being able to count on a minimum amount of income for public coffers should oil prices fall. Throughout NAFTA negotiations pressures on the peso and capital flight were on the increase, so that by the end of negotiations the exchange rate was close to the upper band.[100] Oil prices did decrease, but due to the futures trading their impact on public finances was minimal.

While negative market developments could be used by US negotiators to pressure Mexico, the fact that Mexico was already the United States' third trade partner meant that if market dislocations were extreme, the United States would also be affected by negative externalities.[101] To offset market pressures to which Mexico was subject, but which might also affect the United States and Canada, early on in the negotiation process the three Ministers responsible for negotiations struck an agreement whereby none of them would publicly commit to a specific date for the end of negotiations. The mantra was that substance would drive pace, and not the other way around.[102] Attempts to keep the political calendar out of the negotiation process nonetheless proved futile. During the Dallas "jamboree" Mexico had precipitated into granting concessions too

---

[99]   Author's interview with Jaime Serra Puche, Mexican Trade Minister 1988–1994, Mexico City, August 19, 2003.

[100] The exchange rate regime followed under Salinas was that of a band.

[101] Author's interview with Jaime Zabludovsky Kuper, Deputy Chief NAFTA negotiator, Mexico's NAFTA Negotiation Office, Mexico City, August 15, 2003.

[102] Author's interview with Jaime Serra Puche, Mexican Trade Minister 1988–1994, Mexico City, August 19, 2003.

early, wanting to wrap up negotiations quickly in order to avoid becoming entangled with the US presidential election, but the United States was still playing for time and Mexico realized it would not be possible to secure an early agreement.[103]

Paradoxically, in the end US delaying tactics and the US recession ended up helping Mexico. While the recession made for a hostile environment for trade negotiations, it also gradually eroded Bush's popularity, which had been extremely high after the US victory in the Gulf War in early 1991. After the blunder it had committed in Dallas, Mexico learned to be more patient and played for time when it realized Bush's reelection was at risk. Indeed, "U. S. haste in August [1992] was one factor that contributed to Mexico's ability to avoid concessions in energy, even at the very end of negotiations."[104] The most delicate moments in terms of economic market developments for Mexico actually came after the end of negotiations, during the ratification phase. Trade-offs and negotiations continued even after the NAFTA text had been signed by the chief negotiators in San Antonio in October 1992, with Salinas, Bush, and Mulroney as witnesses.

In September 1993 Finance Minister Pedro Aspe noted at an economic cabinet meeting that, should NAFTA fail to be ratified, Mexico's economic policy would be unsustainable. In November, Miguel Mancera, the Central Bank governor, expected serious exchange rate disruptions if NAFTA was not ratified. The members of the economic cabinet argued that help from the US Treasury would be required in case of defeat, and planned on asking Treasury Secretary Bentsen for help when the moment came.[105] The Mexican government asked its pollster for a survey on public perceptions should NAFTA fail, and found out that there would be no undue irritation, if there were no exchange rate impact. It then proceeded to prepare investment agreements with Germany, the United Kingdom, Spain and Japan, proposed changes to the Foreign Investment Law, intensified its lobbying efforts to join the OECD and finalized the details of the financial rescue package that would be presented to Bentsen. A worst case scenario was planned for, just in case ratification fell through.[106] In the end NAFTA was ratified, but ratification had been far from a foregone conclusion. A great deal of arm twisting and pork had been required to secure the deal.[107]

---

[103] Cameron and Tomlin 2000, 101–105.   [104] Ibid., 234.

[105] By this time Lloyd Bentsen had left the Senate to become the US Secretary of the Treasury.

[106] Salinas 2000, 176–186.

[107] For accounts of the politics of NAFTA ratification, see Salinas 2000, Chapter 5; von Bertrab 1996, Chapter 4; Cameron and Tomlin 2000, Chapter 9; and Mayer 1998, Section III.

In multiple issue negotiations such as NAFTA, several market forces may affect negotiations. In terms of the energy negotiations, the United States was concerned about ensuring secure energy supplies from Mexico, as demonstrated by Mosbacher's pronouncements shortly before the start of the Gulf War. This meant that the more the United States decided to stop relying on oil supplies from the Middle East, the greater the value of securing an oil supply agreement with Mexico. Ceteris paribus, this should have translated into bargaining leverage for Mexico.

However, given that under no circumstances would Mexico entertain granting supply guarantees to the United States, greater political instability in the Middle East worked against Mexico for it enticed the United States to make strong offensive demands in an issue that Mexico was not willing to negotiate. In the end, the Gulf War did conclude successfully from a US perspective, and oil prices remained at acceptable levels for the United States. It is worth pondering what would have happened in the negotiations had oil prices continued to rise as a result of continued instability in the Middle East. At an extreme, it is possible to envisage that an adamant demand from the United States on energy supply commitments might have derailed the whole agreement.

The oil market posed an additional problem for Mexico, given the reliance of public finances on oil exports.[108] Should oil prices decrease (as they in fact did), the government's fiscal stance would be in a delicate position, and US negotiators could press hard at the negotiating table knowing the Mexicans needed an agreement to calm down markets. A lesson from this case is that Mexico bought oil futures and thus had control over the worst possible scenario regarding oil prices. In other words, it saw the potential damage from certain adverse market developments, and acted accordingly. In other issues, such as pressures against the exchange rate and capital flight, there was less the government could do except to try to secure a good trade agreement and hope it was done before markets started discounting the possibility of a deal being reached.

Mexico was prepared for the failure of negotiations, and did not contemplate caving in on energy to avoid such a scenario. The sort of measures taken by Mexico to prepare for the failure to have NAFTA ratified (such as drafting investment agreements with several European countries and the design of a financial rescue package which would be requested to the United States) are a necessary counterpart to an effective defense against demands. Should there be no contingency plans, success in defense against demands can turn into a pyrrhic victory if an agreement

---

[108] Approximately one-third of the federal government's income derives from PEMEX earnings.

falls through and markets react accordingly. By buying oil futures and designing contingency plans, Mexico improved its BATNA.[109] Obviously, not all of these measures should be made public, lest they generate a moral hazard, but countries defending against demands would do well to have contingency plans and not improvise should negotiations fail.

The evolution of the US economy also played into the negotiations, but paradoxically the worse the situation of the US economy, the greater the leverage it gave to Mexican negotiators. This goes against the accepted wisdom that protectionist pressures tend to resurface during a recession, and that it is not the best economic environment under which to conduct trade liberalization negotiations. During NAFTA negotiations, the negative evolution of the US economy greatly affected Bush's standing in the polls and his probability of being reelected. As the election approached, Bush needed NAFTA to show an important "presidential" achievement, which meant that the deteriorating economic situation worsened the United States' BATNA more than it did Mexico's and helped close the deal without the inclusion of oil. It is ironic that Mexico had been the demandeur, and at the end of negotiations the United States apparently wanted NAFTA at least as badly as Mexico did. Had the US economy been in good shape, it is probable that Bush could have expected a relatively easy reelection, and would not have been in a rush to conclude the agreement. Under a better US BATNA, Mexico would have had to struggle harder to keep energy out of the negotiations.

In short, the lessons regarding markets while defending against demands are to take action in those market segments where it is possible to limit their effect on worsening your own BATNA, and to have contingency plans should all else fail. Likewise, apparently negative market developments can turn out to be positive in the end, so it is important not to prejudge a situation; tactics should be adjusted accordingly.

4 Lessons on defending against demands in trade negotiations

The preceding section shows how Mexico displayed a wide array of actions in order to successfully defend against demands by the United States during NAFTA energy negotiations. To what extent can other states follow a similar course of action? Are there some general lessons to be applied, or are the actions germane only to NAFTA negotiations?

---

[109] Odell presents an analogous lesson in the comparison of the strategies followed by Kennecott and Anaconda in the face of possible conflicts with the Chilean government. Kennecott had alternative plans for a "worst case" scenario, while Anaconda did not. See Odell 2000, 209–10.

It is difficult to ascertain the relative importance of all the factors that affected the outcome from a single case study, but is it possible to envisage a situation where, in the absence of the negotiation strategy described in section 3, NAFTA would not have come to fruition as a result of Mexico's refusal to liberalize investment in the energy sector and provide energy supply guarantees, or where the costs of a successful agreement would have been higher for Mexico in terms of foregone offensive aims.

One may object to this assessment, by saying that it was in fact Mexico's position as the United States' neighbor and US bottom-line disinterest in securing gains in energy that determined the negotiation outcome, and that the negotiation process had little bearing on the result. Being a neighbor in fact cut both ways: while the top US leaders were interested in securing a deal with its southern neighbor, it was precisely Mexico's geographic position that generated incentives for the United States to seek energy supply commitments.[110]

Nor does it seem that US demands in energy were bluffs to be discarded in return for other gains; it genuinely sought gains in the energy sector and especially in supply commitments. Substantively, the United States thought it could get participation contracts (with payment in oil reserves), and was disappointed when it was unable to do so. It was truly disappointed when it was also unable to secure supply guarantees, given that Canada had granted them and they had nothing to do with foreign investment. US negotiators also reasoned that such a commitment would not mean treading new ground for Mexico, given that it had already assumed a general commitment on the matter as a result of GATT rules on supply restrictions.

An issue that merits further research is the virtual absence of US oil companies from NAFTA negotiations. According to Odell, "The more that constituents inside a threatening country express opposition to implementing the threat, the more they will diminish overseas gains from the offensive distributive strategy".[111] Had these companies pressed hard for liberalization and lobbied before Congress, Mexico would have had a more difficult US domestic political environment to contend with and would have faced a harder time in defending against US demands. Cameron and Tomlin posit that the oil companies had a better understanding of Mexico's reservation value, and opted to make gains in ways other than direct confrontation.[112] Serra was surprised in that he did not

[110] Author's interview with Charles E. "Chip" Roh, Deputy Chief NAFTA negotiator, USTR, Washington, DC, September 30, 2004. The relevant GATT rules are GATT 1994 Articles XI, XII, XIII, XIV and XVIII.
[111] Odell 2000, 184.   [112] Cameron and Tomlin 2000, 89–90.

receive any pressures from US oil interests during the negotiations.[113] If weaker countries face unwelcome demands from a stronger country, where both the stronger country's government and its industries have very strong preferences on the issue, the challenges faced by the weaker country will be greater than those that Mexico had to address.

Likewise, financial and human resource limitations will make it difficult for weaker countries to carry out a major lobbying effort and to receive top-flight legal advice. Nonetheless, subject to these caveats the negotiation strategies described below can be applied by countries when facing unwanted claims by a stronger state. Other actions, such as those carried out to counteract biases, to use domestic politics for negotiation ends, and to counteract the potentially adverse effects derived from market developments, may be applied in general, and not only when defending against unwanted claims.

- *Do not stick exclusively to a defensive distributive strategy as a response to unwanted claims. Mix integrative elements into your strategy to keep the game interesting to partner states.* If Mexico's negotiators had used only defensive distributive moves in a vast number of areas, the room for maneuver would have been scant and the possibility of striking a deal low. Instead, the Mexican negotiators used a mixed strategy in general. In the energy sector, the strategy consisted of improved market access via trade in energy, while maintaining limits on foreign investment and excluding energy supply commitments. This strategy made the overall game worthwhile for Washington and Ottawa and discouraged them from walking away from the table if they did not achieve all their demands.
- *When defending against an offensive distributive strategy use a sequential, as opposed to a simultaneous, mixed strategy.* The sequential nature of the offer, whereby Mexico stood by its defensive distributive strategy on investment and energy supply commitments throughout the negotiations and only near the end offered a mixed strategy regarding trade in energy, allowed it to successfully defend against an offensive distributive strategy. Had Mexico presented its mixed strategy at the outset of negotiations, the United States most probably would have kept on asking for more concessions from Mexico.
- *If a defensive distributive strategy is to be used, offset defensive demands against the other state's defensive demands, not against your own offensive claims.* Mexico, instead of "paying" for the right to exclude its energy sector from liberalization by giving up some of its offensive demands,

[113] Author's interview with Jaime Serra Puche, Mexican Trade Minister 1988–1994, Mexico City, August 19, 2003.

argued that its exclusions only matched US exclusions (in maritime transportation) and Canadian exclusions (in cultural industries). Having each side presenting its deal-breaker issues at the outset of negotiations also avoided unpleasant surprises and brinkmanship that could have resulted in the breakdown of negotiations.

- *If partner states make no defensive demands against which to match your request for exclusion, add an issue so this strategy may be put to work.* Before the formal negotiations started Mexico intimated that it wanted to include migration in the agenda. When the United States steadfastly refused, Mexico replied that this US exclusion meant that Mexico would have to exclude energy without paying any concessions.
- *Consider hiring lobbyists from the partner country to help avoid the effects of biases.* Mexico's hiring of US lobbyists allowed it to have firsthand and reliable information on the US reservation value on a number of issues, and thus to design a negotiation strategy that ensured there was a winning coalition as a result of Mexican offers. It also meant that the United States could not credibly bluff in order to extract concessions from Mexico. Under a biased information scenario, it is possible to imagine an outcome where the United States credibly stated that an agreement without liberalization of energy investment rules and commitments on energy supplies would not be approved by the US Congress, or where the costs of exclusion were higher than they in fact were. Admittedly, the high cost of foreign lobbyists and advisors could be a problem for poorer countries.
- *Get top-flight level legal advice about the partner country's laws, and if necessary sacrifice expensive foreign economic advice.* While it is likely that any well-trained economist will understand the economic impact of negotiation commitments in his or her home country, a small mistake by lawyers regarding long and complex texts can have dire consequences. This is likely when negotiating with countries with a different legal system than your own. At the end of NAFTA negotiations, the agreements struck by the negotiators had to be transformed into implementing legislation by the US Congress, so it was possible for Mexico to lose some gains that were made at the negotiation table in the process of turning NAFTA into US domestic law. The lesson here is that while Mexico's negotiators included extremely capable economists, an area of vulnerability lay in the different nature and complexity of the US legal system. If a country is to defend against an offensive distributive strategy by the United States in economic negotiations, it seems that the most valuable foreign advisers are not economists but lawyers.
- *Exploit opportunities offered by your partner's political system to monitor and change its negotiating positions.* The pluralistic and transparent nature of the US political system means that it is possible, though onerous, to

follow the positions of key legislators. In addition, Mexicans effectively lobbied US legislators and interest groups during NAFTA negotiations and the subsequent ratification phase. Mexican negotiators were thus able to assess with a fair degree of certainty whether they had a "winning coalition" of backers in the US Congress according the package of offers presented by Mexico.

- *Use multiple points of contact in the partner country's government, not only their trade negotiators.* Mexico made use of contacts with top members of the Bush cabinet and, as required, with President George Bush himself, so negotiations were not limited to what was taking place at the negotiating table. These multiple points were used to emphasize the credibility of Mexico's refusal to concede on energy. Other top US politicians were urged to pressure their own negotiators, so that no single issue would derail the whole negotiation, which was important for the Unites States from a political and not only an economic perspective.

- *Try to limit or offset potential market developments that could adversely affect your bargaining leverage.* Given the reliance of Mexican public finances on oil exports, a significant decrease in oil prices would have put them under strain. US negotiators could then press hard at the negotiating table knowing the Mexicans needed an agreement to calm down the markets. Near the outset of negotiations Mexico bought oil futures and thus had some control over the worst possible scenario regarding oil prices.

- *Prepare for the failure of negotiations: develop an alternative to agreement.* Mexico did not contemplate caving in on energy to avoid a breakdown. The government drafted investment agreements with several European countries and designed a financial rescue package that would be requested from the United States. By buying oil futures and designing contingency plans, Mexico improved its alternative to a NAFTA agreement and thus strengthened its negotiators' hands. Obviously, not all of these measures should be made public lest they generate a moral hazard, but notifying the partner delegation that you have alternatives could reinforce the credibility of your negotiating position.

Appendix: NAFTA negotiation highlights

1988

November	Bush proposes FTA to Salinas; Salinas rejects it

1990

February	Serra proposes FTA to Hills
March	Bush gives go-ahead for FTA with Mexico
August	Mosbacher publicly states that energy will be in the negotiations

September	Bush requests fast track authority renewal
November	Bush and Salinas meeting in Monterrey, Mexico; energy discussed

1991

January	Beginning of Gulf war
February	End of Gulf war
	Canada joins FTA negotiations
May	Fast track authority renewed
June	Official start of NAFTA negotiations, Toronto (first ministerial negotiating session)
August	Second ministerial negotiating session, Seattle; Mexico states five "Nos"
October	Third ministerial negotiating session, Zacatecas

1992

February	Fourth ministerial negotiating session, Chantilly (VA) Dallas "jamboree" (chief negotiators and working groups negotiating sessions). Working group on energy established; Mexico states Constitution will not be modified
April	Fifth ministerial negotiating session, Montreal
July	Sixth ministerial negotiating session, Mexico City
August	The Watergate sessions (Seventh ministerial negotiating session), successful end of NAFTA negotiations
October	NAFTA negotiators initial the Agreement in San Antonio
November	US presidential election, Clinton defeats Bush

1993

January	Clinton sworn is as US 42nd President
February	Start of NAFTA side agreements negotiations (labor and the environment)
August	End of side agreements negotiations
November	Negotiations on sugar and citrus (arm twisting and pork sessions)
	NAFTA ratified by United States House and Senate

1994

January	NAFTA entry into force

REFERENCES

Armendáriz, Manuel. 2000. Antecedentes de la Nueva Relación México–Unión Europea: el Acuerdo de Asociación Económica, Concertación Política y Cooperación (1997). (Background of the new relationship between Mexico and the European Union: the Economic Association, Political coordination and Cooperation Agreement (1997)) *El Mercado de Valores* LX (6): 20–35

Arriola, Carlos (Selected by). 1994. *Tratado de Libre Comercio de América del Norte: Documentos Básicos* (North American Free Trade Agreement: basic Documents). Mexico City: Secretaría de Comercio y Fomento Industrial

Bertrab, Hermann von. 1996. *El Redescubrimiento de América: Historia del TLC* (The rediscovery of America: a history of the Free Trade Agreement). Mexico City: Fondo de Cultura Económica

Borja, Arturo, coord. 2001. *Para Evaluar al TLCAN (Assessing NAFTA)*. Mexico City: ITESM-Miguel Ángel Porrúa

Cameron, Maxwell A. and Brian W. Tomlin. 2000. *The Making of NAFTA: How the Deal was Done*. Ithaca, NY: Cornell University Press

Destler, I. M. 1986. *American Trade Politics*. Washington, DC: Institute for International Economics

Hufbauer, Gary C. and Jeffrey J. Schott. 1993. *NAFTA: An Assessment* (revised edition). Washington, DC: Institute for International Economics

Keohane, Robert O. 1990. El Concepto de Interdependencia y el Análisis de las Relaciones Asimétricas (The concept of interdependence and the analysis of asymmetric relations). In *Interdependencia: ¿Un Enfoque Útil Para el Estudio de las Relaciones México-Estados Unidos?* (Interdependence: a useful framework for the study of Mexico–United States relations?), ed. Blanca Torres, 63–75. Mexico City: El Colegio de México

Krasner, Stephen D. 1978. *Defending the National Interest: Raw Materials Investment and US Foreign Policy*. Princeton: Princeton University Press

1990. Interdependencia Simple y Obstáculos para la Cooperación entre México y Estados Unidos (Simple interdependence and obstacles for Mexico–United States cooperation). In *Interdependencia: ¿Un Enfoque Útil Para el Estudio de las Relaciones México-Estados Unidos?* (Interdependence: a useful framework for the study of Mexico–United status relations?), ed. Blanca Torres, 45–61. Mexico City: El Colegio de México

Lawrence, Robert Z. 1996. *Regionalism, Multilateralism, and Deep Integration*. Washington, DC: The Brookings Institution

Léycegui, Beatriz and Rafael Fernández de Castro, coords. 2000. *¿Socios Naturales? Cinco Años del Tratado de Libre Comercio de América del Norte* (Natural partners? Five years of the North American Free Trade Agreement). Mexico City: ITAM-Miguel Ángel Porrúa

López Ayllón, Sergio. 1997. *Las Transformaciones Del Sistema Jurídico y los Significados Sociales Del Derecho en México: La Encrucijada Entre Tradición y Modernidad* (Transformations of the judicial system and the meanings of law in Mexico: the crossroads between tradition and modernity). Mexico City: Universidad Nacional Autónoma de México

Lowi, Theodore J. 1964. American Business, Public Policy, Case Studies and Political Theory. *World Politics* 16 (4): 677–715

Martin, Lisa L. 2000. *Democratic Commitments: Legislatures and International Cooperation*. Princeton: Princeton University Press

Maxfield, Sylvia and Adam Shapiro. 1998. Assessing the NAFTA Negotiations: US–Mexican Compromise on Tariff and Nontariff Issues. In *The*

Post-NAFTA Political Economy: Mexico and the Western Hemisphere, ed. Carol Wise, 82–118. University Park: Pennsylvania State University Press

Mayer, Frederick W. 1998. *Interpreting NAFTA: The Science and Art of Political Analysis.* New York: Columbia University Press

Meyer, Lorenzo and Isidro Morales. 1989. *Petróleo y Nación (1900–1987): La Política Petrolera en México* (Oil and the Nation (1900–1987): Oil Policy in Mexico). Mexico City: SEMIP-PEMEX-El Colegio de México-Fondo de Cultura Económica

Odell, John S. 1980. Latin American Trade Negotiations with the United States. *International Organization* 34 (2): 207–28

——— 2000. *Negotiating the World Economy.* Ithaca, NY: Cornell University Press

O'Halloran, Sharyn. 1994. *Politics, Process, and American Trade Politics.* Ann Arbor: University of Michigan Press

Ortiz Mena L. N., Antonio. 2001. The Politics of Institutional Choice: International Trade and Dispute Settlement. Ph.D. diss. University of California, San Diego

——— 2004a. Mexico's Trade Policy: Improvisation and Vision. In *The Strategic Dynamics of Latin American Trade*, ed. Vinod Aggarwal, Joseph Tulchin and Ralph Espach, 213–31. Stanford, and Washington, DC: Stanford University Press–The Woodrow Wilson International Center

——— 2004b. Mexico: A Regional Player in Multilateral Trade Negotiations. In *Trade Policy Reform in Latin America*, ed. Miguel Lengyel and Vivianne Ventura Dias, 47–73. London: Palgrave–MacMillan

Ortiz Mena L. N., Tania. 1993. Políticas Petroleras en México (Oil policies in Mexico). B.A. diss., Universidad Iberoamericana (Mexico)

Putnam, Robert D. 1988. Diplomacy and Domestic Politics: The Logic of Two-Level Games. *International Organization* 42 (3): 427–60

Salinas de Gortari, Carlos. 2000. *México: Un Paso Difícil a la Modernidad* (Mexico: a difficult step into modern times). Barcelona, Catalunya: Plaza & Janés Editores

Schattschneider, Elmer Eric. 1935. *Politics, Pressures, and the Tariff*. New York: Prentice Hall

Schiavon, Jorge and Antonio Ortiz Mena L. N. 2001. Apertura Comercial y Reforma Institucional en México (1988–2000): Un Análisis Comparado del TLCAN y el TLCUE (Trade liberalization and institutional reform in Mexico (1988–2000): a comparison of the North American Free Trade Agreement and the Mexico–European Union Free Trade Agreement). *Foro Internacional*, 41 (4): 731–60

Serra Puche, Jaime. 1994. (Several speeches), in *Tratado de Libre Comercio de América del Norte: Documentos Básicos* (North American Free Trade Agreement: basic documents). Mexico City: Miguel Ángel Porrúa and Secretaría de Comercio y Fomento Industrial

Part III

WTO Dispute Settlement Negotiations

7 Do WTO rules create a level playing field? Lessons from the experience of Peru and Vietnam

Christina L. Davis

Introduction

Scholars of international relations and the NGO groups protesting on the streets of Seattle in 1999 share a common assumption. Both believe that less developed countries are at a disadvantage when negotiating with more powerful counterparts. Smaller market size makes it ineffective for developing countries to use threats of retaliation in order to combat discrimination against their goods. In contrast, retaliation measures taken by larger economies can easily cause severe damage to a smaller economy. This leaves developing countries vulnerable to discriminatory trade policies adopted by their major trade partners.

In spite of their apparent lack of bargaining leverage, however, in some negotiations developing countries have been able to achieve positive outcomes – even the overturn of protectionist measures against their exports by the United States and EU. Simply evaluating the relative market power of the two sides in an economic negotiation is inadequate. As Odell argues, the strategies used in the negotiation process matter as much as the material resources of each participant.[1] In addition, the institutional context of the negotiation can generate pressure for liberalization.[2] For trade negotiations, the institutional context is shaped by the General Agreement on Tariffs and Trade (GATT) and its successor the World Trade Organization (WTO). The GATT/WTO system upholds trade rules that apply equally to rich and poor countries alike and are enforced by a third party adjudication process to settle disputes. The WTO dispute settlement procedures provide developing country

The author thanks Marc Busch, Thomas Cottier, Joseph Damond, Judith Goldstein, Eduardo Perez Motta, and John Odell for comments on this chapter, and thanks Anbinh Phan and Courtenay Dunn for valuable research assistance. The research benefited greatly from interviews with officials involved in the negotiations, who have not been cited by name at their request. The author is also grateful for funding support from the University of Southern California Center for International Studies.

[1] Odell 2000.   [2] Davis 2003.

members with a distributive tactic that helps them to negotiate the reduction of trade barriers against their products.

This chapter argues that the use of legal adjudication allows developing countries to gain better outcomes in negotiations with their powerful trade partners than they could in a bilateral negotiation outside of the institution. There are four mechanisms that are important: a guarantee for the right to negotiate, a common standard for evaluating outcomes, the option for several countries to join a dispute, and incentives for states to change a policy found to violate trade rules. Developing countries that use these institutional mechanisms by initiating complaints based on a strong legal case and in cooperation with other states will improve their capacity to gain concessions from other states. In contrast, developing countries that are not WTO members, or members that do not use the dispute settlement system, will often be unable to negotiate any concessions from more powerful states.

The first section of the chapter addresses the ways in which legal adjudication provides additional bargaining leverage for developing countries, and it also reviews studies on how developing countries have fared within the dispute system. The next two sections present case studies of negotiations with a small developing country demanding an end to protectionist regulations by a major trade partner. Using the approach of controlled comparison, the case studies were selected as negotiations that raise similar trade interests for two pairs of countries with roughly parallel positions in the international economy. Membership in the WTO is the key variable of difference.

The first case represents the options available to a developing country WTO member. Facing European labeling policies that discriminated against its scallops and sardines exports, Peru participated in two WTO disputes that brought about changes in the problematic policies. The second case represents the situation of a developing country that cannot appeal to WTO rules for leverage. As a non-WTO member, Vietnam must negotiate to maintain access for its catfish exports to the US market on the basis of the Bilateral Trade Agreement. Ultimately, Vietnam was unable to prevent the United States from adopting a labeling regulation and antidumping suit that discriminate against Vietnamese catfish. The two cases are useful to illustrate contrasting kinds of negotiations under conditions of asymmetric power.

The labeling cases raised similar strategies pursued by the United States and EC to protect against fish imports that threatened influential producer groups. The cases are also parallel in that both Vietnam and Peru offered an initial compromise solution that was rejected. Of course, there are important differences between the two pairs of negotiating countries.

The economic interests and political institutions of the United States and EC are likely to influence their negotiating behavior. Nevertheless, there is little reason to expect that the EC is substantially more favorable to free trade or more supportive of the WTO than the United States – both represent major trade powers that have a large stake in the multilateral trade system, and both have adopted policies that could be challenged as violations of the WTO rules.[3] One could also question whether Peru and Vietnam are comparable. Politically Peru shifted from dictatorship to democracy in 2001 with the election of President Alejandro Toledo, while Vietnam has remained in the hands of the communist leadership even as the government has loosened state control over some sectors of the domestic economy. Vietnam and Peru are both poor countries, but Vietnam at $430 per capita income is ranked by the World Bank as a low income country while Peru at $2050 per capita income is ranked as a lower middle income country.[4] Yet both clearly lack the market power to counterbalance the United States or Europe and are dependent on access to these valuable markets for their goods. Looking at power alone would lead one to expect that Peru and Vietnam would be unable to prevail over the EC or United States, which were determined to protect their domestic producer interests.

The examination of labeling policy is important because internal non-tariff regulations are among the most problematic trade barriers. Food labeling in particular has become controversial. A new set of agricultural trade disputes has arisen regarding the use of geographical indications to recognize regional specialties as distinct products. Trade talks about genetically modified products and food safety have also come down to a debate over appropriate labeling policies. Indeed, concern about implications for this broader set of food labeling issues heightened interest in the two WTO disputes discussed in this chapter.

1   Legal framing as a source of bargaining leverage

The creation of common rules is the key mechanism by which the multilateral system of trade rules reduces the importance of market power. The trade rounds in which members negotiate new rules rely on consensus procedures that allow any country to hypothetically exercise a veto over the content of the rules. In practice, however, the major powers

---

[3] Over the period from 1995 to 2003, 81 complaints have been filed against the United States and 47 complaints have been filed against the EC (with another 15 complaints against individual member states).

[4] World Bank, Gross National Income per capita 2002 (Atlas Method, US dollars), http://www.worldbank.org/data/databytopic/GNIPC.pdf accessed July 28, 2003.

have tended to dominate in this setting.[5] As a consequence, developing country priority areas such as agriculture and textiles have been the slowest to liberalize. This is a major source of inequality in the gains from the free trade system. Nevertheless, some progress is possible – the linkage between negotiations on multiple sectors and issue areas during trade rounds has brought some agricultural liberalization.[6] As has been witnessed at the Brussels meeting in 1990 during the Uruguay Round and at the Cancun meeting in 2003 during the Doha Round, developing countries can use their veto power to influence progress during trade rounds. Once a new GATT/WTO agreement has been adopted, developing countries can appeal to the rules system for fair treatment and hold other countries to fulfill the commitments they have made. Further, by working together in coalitions developing countries have shaped the agenda-setting process and set limits on agreements.[7] Chapters 2, 3, and 4 explain how coalitions can help developing countries do better in negotiations despite the power imbalance.

The strength of the trading system lies in its ability to bring states to comply with most of the rules most of the time. The main enforcement mechanism of the WTO is the adjudication process set forth in the Dispute Settlement Understanding (DSU), which strengthened the earlier GATT dispute settlement procedures. All members have the right to file a complaint and have a panel of trade experts rule on whether a policy measure represents a violation of the rules. The proceedings go forward according to a schedule with time limits, but there is always the option to negotiate a mutually agreed upon settlement. Indeed, more than half of disputes are settled before a ruling. When cases are not settled early, then the panel rules whether the policy is a violation. Yet even then, compliance is elective. Since there is no police enforcement for an international court, states have the choice to change their policy, offer compensation, or accept the likelihood that other states will retaliate against their goods.[8] Voluntary compliance occurs through negotiations about whether and how a state will change a policy that has been ruled a violation. In the case of a failure to satisfy the complainant, there may be further panel proceedings and eventual authorization of sanctions. The state may still refuse to comply with the ruling. The legal procedures encourage compliance by shaping incentives for different policy choices, but filing a complaint does not deterministically produce a particular outcome.

Legal framing describes the degree to which "the negotiation occurs within the bounds of formal rules and appeals to third party mediation."[9]

---

[5] Steinberg 2002.   [6] Davis 2004.   [7] Ricupero 1998.
[8] Bello 1996, 417.   [9] Davis 2003, 50.

The key distinction lies in the impartial standard to evaluate the policy according to rules accepted by all participants. The choice of an institutional context for adjudication of disputes frames the negotiation to give priority to legal arguments over political criteria. This kind of framing arises from procedural constraints, as distinct from the psychological framing discussed in chapter 3. In the WTO dispute settlement process, legal framing is highest during the adjudication phase conducted by the panel and following its ruling, but legal framing characterizes the entire dispute settlement process both during the consultation phase before establishment of a panel and during settlement talks between parties at any point later in the process.

The decision to file a legal complaint under the WTO dispute procedures represents a distributive tactic because the complainant demands a unilateral policy change from the defendant. Since the complaint itself responds to a perceived failure by the defendant to fulfill its obligations under the WTO, however, this move often represents a defensive rather than aggressive trade policy. For developing countries, the dispute mechanism offers an alternative recourse when bilateral negotiations fail to resolve a trade problem. While the United States and EU have unilateral policy options, developing countries often lack the power to even bring a larger country to the negotiating table to seriously address their concerns.

There are four ways in which legal framing helps developing countries counter discrimination against their exports by more powerful countries. First, the option to file a legal complaint allows developing countries to force a developed country to come to the negotiating table and discuss their request. Second, the DSU makes international trade law the standard for reaching an agreement. Third, use of shared legal rules facilitates finding allies with related interests to support the case. Fourth, the long-term economic interest in supporting the rules encourages compliance with rulings. Without the framework provided by the dispute settlement process, a developing country is likely to encounter refusal to negotiate by powerful countries, arbitrary standards, limited interest from third countries in their trade problem, and lack of leverage to bargain for concessions.

Simply getting a wealthy trade partner to agree to talk about its protectionist trade barriers is difficult for a developing country. Clearly, developed countries will have the upper hand in a negotiation that resorts to retaliation and counter-retaliation. Moreover, developed countries can use side-payments to bribe weaker countries to overlook their use of unfair trade barriers for their sensitive products. Since developing countries have less economic and political resources to provide side-payments of their own, they will be unable to persuade developed governments to change existing policies without some external leverage. Filing a complaint obligates the two sides to engage in bilateral consultations, and the DSU guarantees WTO members the right to a panel. As a result, members cannot simply adopt a unilateral position and refuse to discuss a trade problem. In contrast, this is all too often the case when a developing country makes a request at the bilateral level.

The adjudication process not only focuses the negotiation on the single issue, it also forces both sides to make a consistent argument based on existing law. This prevents the kind of moving target that occurs when there is no agreed standard for evaluating different arguments. In a legal dispute, the narrow focus on the single issue and the use of established principles reduce the flexibility for choosing among different negotiation tactics. Since developing countries lack the power to issue threats and side-payments or to unilaterally determine the standard of evaluation, in practice this constraint binds the developed country more than the developing country.

The use of multilateral rules for adjudication of a bilateral dispute also facilitates the formation of coalitions around a legal complaint. Because the individual case will hold a precedent for similar policies, the set of states participating in a case will include both those with a material interest in the immediate trade issue as well as those concerned about the legal implications of the case. The DSU agreement allows different levels of participation by multiple states.[10] Often states join consultations, with an average of three members requesting to join consultations for individual disputes. States with a substantial interest in the matter can also participate in the panel stage of the dispute process as a third party, which grants them the right to submit views to the panel. Out of the 98 panels that have issued reports to date, all but eight included third party participants.[11] While typically only a few members join as third parties, some cases will draw much wider interest. For example, nineteen members ranging from Japan and Canada to Belize and Suriname were third parties in Ecuador's complaint against the EU banana import regime. In other cases, a state may decide to file a complaint on the same issue after another state has filed a complaint. The filing of multiple complaints has become quite common, with a leading recent example being the nine cases against US steel safeguards.[12]

---

[10] DSU Article 4.11 allows other members to request to join consultations. Articles 9 and 10 establish procedures for multiple complainants and third parties.

[11] http://www.worldtradelaw.net/dsc/database/partiespanel.asp accessed January 19, 2004.

[12] The EC, Japan, Korea, China, Chinese Taipei, Brazil, Norway, New Zealand, and Switzerland all filed cases under the heading "United States – Definitive Safeguard Measures on Imports of Certain Steel Products." The EC was the first to file a case (DS248) on March 7, 2002.

For developing countries that may be hesitant to sue their major trading partner, following after another country has initiated a complaint reduces the legal and political cost. In a kind of legal bandwagoning, a developing country can join a case with a developed country and benefit from the legal arguments and bargaining influence of the other complainants. As a third party, developing countries can learn how the process works with little investment. As a co-complainant with a developed country, a developing country gains both legal advice and enforcement power if the dispute ends up going all the way to sanctions.[13] Disputes with multiple complainants and third parties add collective pressure against the respondent. In the case against the EC banana import regime, Latin American governments were helped by the United States being another complainant that issued sanctions when the EC did not change its policy following the ruling (see chapter 8 for a fuller account of this dispute case).[14] In addition to the greater market power for enforcement, a broader group of complainants diffuses the political damage to any particular bilateral relationship.

The institutional context of the negotiation shapes the negotiation process for bringing compliance. Many perceive retaliation as the means to enforce dispute rulings. If true, developing countries with small markets would be unable to inflict sufficient pain to enforce rulings in their favor. Indeed, one of the demands for reform of the DSU put forward by developing countries in the Doha Round calls for a right to collective retaliation for cases that involve developing country complainants. Such reforms may prove helpful, but nevertheless underestimate the enforcement power that exists independent of retaliatory capacity. Hudec emphasizes that authorized retaliation almost never occurred under the GATT rules and yet most complaints filed were resolved to the satisfaction of the complainant.[15] The WTO agreement strengthened provisions for retaliation (Article 22.2), but requests for authorization of retaliation remain infrequent – only 15 of 305 disputes since 1995 have led to a request for retaliation authority.[16] Moreover, some of the most outstanding

---

[13] Both third parties and co-complainants receive the submissions of other parties to the dispute. Informal consultations among interested parties regarding the case are also a source of advice on tactics.

[14] Ecuador, Guatemala, Honduras, Mexico, and the United States stood as complainants in the case, "European Communities – Regime for the Importation, Sale, and Distribution of Bananas" (WT/DS27). After the policy was ruled a violation of WTO rules in 1997 and a revised policy was also found to be in violation of the rules, the complainants were authorized to issue sanctions in 1999. Even then, however, a mutual agreement was not reached until April 2001.

[15] Hudec 1993.

[16] http://www.worldtradelaw.net/dsc/database/retaliationrequests.asp accessed January 23, 2004.

compliance failures are cases where retaliation by the United States or EC was authorized.[17]

While the mere potential for retaliation certainly shapes the negotiation process, incentives unrelated to retaliation are also at work. Many scholars have concluded that the need to uphold the overall credibility of the rules system leads countries to comply with rulings.[18] Either trade interests, or a sense of "shaming" could account for an independent compliance pull from international rulings.[19] When compliance is not motivated by the actual retaliation from the individual participant to the dispute, then market size becomes unimportant – even small states are able to use rules to shame and punish bigger states. There have been several cases in which developing countries have used the rules to gain compliance from developed country governments.[20]

This compliance pressure from a violation ruling operates through domestic politics.[21] Leaders need a justification to give to their domestic regulatory agency and lobby groups before they can change policies that were adopted to protect sensitive sectors. Small countries cannot afford side-payments to sweeten the deal or threaten retaliatory consequences. Thus their demands are all too easy to ignore for a developed country. Why would leaders choose to face political backlash at home with nothing in return? The need to comply with international law, however, provides political cover for making such difficult policy reversals. Refusal to change the policy would damage a rules system that brings gains from free trade for many other sectors while compliance with the ruling represents fulfillment of international obligation to support the international trade system.

On the other hand, some aspects of the dispute process disadvantage developing states. Many have pointed out that developing countries lack representation in Geneva and legal resources to adjudicate cases. The increasing number of legal reviews under the strengthened procedures of the new WTO dispute rules places a "premium on sophisticated legal argumentation" that may work against developing countries.[22] Ostry warns that the new dispute settlement system is so technical and evidence intensive that it requires "a level of legal expertise rare in non-OECD countries and therefore pots of money to purchase

---

[17] Since the Community Pillar has authority for economic policies, following WTO practice I will refer to the European Community (EC) when referring specifically to trade policies.
[18] Kovenock and Thursby 1992, Jackson 1997, Hudec 2002.   [19] Johnston 2001.
[20] In one example in the early years of the WTO, Costa Rica filed a complaint, "United States – Restrictions on Imports of Cotton and Man-made Underwear" (WT/DS24/1). After panel and appellate body rulings in favor of Costa Rica, the United States agreed to end its quotas restricting the import of cotton underwear from Costa Rica.
[21] Davis 2003.   [22] Busch and Reinhardt 2002, 467.

Northern legal services."[23] Even US and EC trade authorities rely on extensive private-sector support for trade disputes that is unlikely to be available in developing countries.[24] The comparative advantage in legal skills held by countries such as the United States augments the power disparity.

Since legal services can be purchased, the question is whether developing countries can afford to do so. The expense and difficulty of managing a complicated legal case clearly inhibit many developing countries from even filing a complaint. It is notable that least developed countries have initiated only one WTO dispute while the more advanced developing countries such as India and Brazil have been frequent users of the dispute system. Developing countries as a group have initiated 36 percent of the 304 complaints notified to the WTO by December 2003.[25] Of these cases, 54 complaints were issued by lower income developing countries, with 30 of these being against high income members.[26] Some have relied on their own legal counsel while others have hired leading international law firms. Since 2001, developing countries have also had the option to receive legal training or hire legal counsel from the Advisory Centre on WTO Law, which was established to provide discounted legal services for developing countries. A report by the Mexican delegation to the WTO on the problems of the DSU for developing countries concluded that "Financial aspects of engaging in a WTO dispute do not seem to be at the core of the problem." The report cites the availability of low cost legal assistance from the Advisory Centre on WTO Law and the relative insignificance of legal fees relative to the value of export losses from a trade barrier.[27] While legal costs may reduce the number of cases initiated by developing countries, they are not insurmountable for many governments.

The historical record provides mixed evidence about whether developing countries have fared better or worse in legalized disputes than other countries. Some find that economic weight has not been a major factor influencing the conduct of dispute settlement.[28] Others emphasize that

[23] Ostry 2002, 288.   [24] Shaffer 2003.
[25] WTO, "Update of WTO Dispute Settlement Cases," WT/DS/OV/18 (23 December 2003) p. 2.
[26] Lower income refers to the low income and lower middle income categories of the World Bank, which would include both Vietnam and Peru. Of the 30 disputes representing asymmetric power conditions, 13 were initiated by low income members and 17 were initiated by lower middle income members. http://www.worldtradelaw.net/ dsc/database/classificationcount.asp accessed January 19, 2004.
[27] "Diagnosis of the Problems Facing the Dispute Settlement Mechanism: Some Ideas by Mexico," Proposal presented to the WTO DSU Body, Geneva (November 2003) p. 5–7.
[28] Horn, Mavroidis, and Nordstrom 1999; Goldstein and Martin 2000; Busch 2000; Guzman and Simmons 2002.

228   *Christina L. Davis*

larger states gain better trade outcomes in dispute settlement through the leverage they gain from their market size.[29] Busch and Reinhardt show that there is a gap in the ability of developing countries to gain positive outcomes compared to developed countries.[30] In an evaluation of 380 GATT/WTO dispute outcomes from 1980 to 2000, Busch and Reinhardt show that developing country complainants were able to gain partial or full concessions for 63 percent of their complaints in comparison with the record of developed countries, which gained partial or full concessions for 72 percent of their complaints.[31] This is a disturbing sign for it shows that the playing field is not entirely level, yet it also indicates that developing countries do surprisingly well to hold their own despite their weaker economic position. More importantly, Busch and Reinhardt argue that developing countries do poorly during the early consultation period, rather than because of bias in rulings or difficulty to get concessions after a favorable ruling. Their statistical analysis shows that once a panel has been established, income does not have a significant effect on outcomes. If developing countries are in a weaker position in the informal negotiations that precede establishment of a panel, then one must wonder, how do they fare in their bilateral negotiations outside of the dispute settlement process? Looking more closely at the negotiation process will help to reveal whether and how GATT/WTO dispute settlement improves outcomes for developing countries relative to the alternative of negotiations outside the WTO.

2   Peru takes on European food labeling policies

The EC has erected formidable barriers to protect its primary sectors from imports. This has pitted it not only against the United States, but also developing countries. A report by Oxfam placed the EC at the top of their list for holding double standards with its trade barriers against agricultural imports from developing countries.[32] While some developing countries benefit from preferential trade agreements with Europe, most cannot penetrate the high tariffs that protect the European market or compete with the subsidized European products in world markets. At other times EC regulations act as trade barriers, as happened when two labeling regulations harmed Peruvian exports of scallops and sardines to Europe. This section will discuss how skillful use of legal tactics and joint effort with other WTO members helped Peru to prevail on the EC to change its labeling regulations.

---

[29] Bown 2004.   [30] Busch and Reinhardt 2003.
[31] Busch and Reinhardt 2003, 725.   [32] Oxfam 2002, 98.

Governments frequently regulate labeling policies for the sake of providing the consumer with accurate information. For example, regulations may require specification of contents and product names or the addition of health warnings. The challenge for international trade law is to distinguish between policies that legitimately regulate labeling policies and those that act as trade barriers. The legal framework for labeling policies relates generally to the GATT principles of non-discrimination and national treatment (Articles 1 and 3 of GATT 1994). These rules stipulate that the products of one state shall not be treated less favorably than the products of another state or than domestic products. More specific rules for such regulations are found in the Agreement on Technical Barriers to Trade (TBT).[33] Too many standards or arbitrary procedures for setting standards would indirectly or directly impede trade. Labeling policies represent one kind of non-tariff barrier that could be used to discriminate, such as by reserving the common marketable name for domestic products. The TBT Agreement stipulates that technical regulations should not have the effect of creating unnecessary obstacles to international trade (Article 2.2), and encourages members to use relevant international standards as a basis for their technical regulations whenever possible (Article 2.4). For example, the Codex Alimentarius Commission establishes guidelines that are accepted as the benchmarks for international standards on food regulations. Its standards are based on recommendations from scientific committees that are approved by members. However, since the TBT Agreement recognizes national governments' right to choose higher levels of protection for legitimate objectives to protect public welfare and the environment, there is much room for interpretation.

When changes in the application of regulations regarding labeling standards harmed Peru's exports to the EC market, it used the above rules framework to demand that the EC change its regulations.

Convincing the French that a scallop is a scallop

One of the first disputes initiated under the new WTO dispute settlement rules and TBT Agreement related to a French regulation for the labeling of scallops. In May 1995, Canada requested consultations with the EC regarding the French government order laying down official names and trade descriptions of scallops. The regulation prohibited Canada from marketing its particular species of scallops under the description "noix de

---

[33] First established in the 1973–79 Tokyo Round, the TBT was extended and clarified in the Uruguay Round.

coquille Saint-Jacques," by which name scallops are traditionally known in France. Instead Canadian scallops were designated to be labeled simply as "petoncles," a less esteemed word used for scallops.[34] Canadian exporters reported a substantial decrease in the volume of exports after the labeling change went into effect. The Canadian government had negotiated a temporary solution in bilateral talks, but after France subsequently annulled this agreement, Canada formally requested consultations under the rules of the WTO DSU. The EC represents the member states in WTO negotiations, so even though it was a French regulation, Canada filed its complaint against the EC and subsequent talks were engaged in by EC negotiators. In its complaint, Canada stated that Canadian scallops were being given less favorable treatment than the like national product with the result that Canada suffered nullification of its rights under the WTO agreement, and it claimed the French measure was not consistent with the TBT Agreement.[35]

Since the regulation also applied to scallops from Peru and Chile, they requested to join Canada in its consultations with the EC. These consultations were held on June 19, 1995 and were a chance to reach a negotiated solution. When no mutually acceptable agreement could be found, Canada requested establishment of a panel on July 10, 1995. At this stage Peru and Chile were closely following the Canadian lead and initiated independent requests for consultations. As was to be expected given Canada's experience, no compromise was found during Peru and Chile's consultations with the EC. In September, Peru and Chile each sent a request to establish a panel and specifically asked that it should be convened of the same panel members as served on the panel between the EC and Canada.[36]

The case illustrates the advantages of legal bandwagoning for developing countries. Peru knew that the Canadian delegation had evaluated the legal case as strong enough to justify filing a complaint. As co-complainants, Peru and Chile were able to view the Canadian written submissions and be present during the Canadian presentations to the panel, and the Canadian negotiating team also offered legal advice on the issues. Moreover, since the same panel would see both cases, the legal arguments made by the Canadian delegation would be referenced for the Peruvian and Chile cases. If the EC had refused to change the policy

---

[34] *Financial Times*, July 21, 1995.
[35] Request for Consultations by Canada, "European Communities – Trade Description of Scallops" WT/DS/7/1 (May 24, 1995).
[36] DSU Article 9.3 calls for the same persons to serve as panelists in cases with multiple complainants on the same matter.

after a violation ruling, Peru would not have been alone in trying to bring about compliance.

The adjudication process went forward with meetings in October and December of 1995, and a concluding session in February 1996. During this stage there was little room for negotiation as each side presented their legal case. Panelists are expected to judge the legal status of the policy rather than to mediate a compromise solution. The panel issued its interim ruling on March 14, 1996. This opened the period for comments by the participants on the ruling before it would be made public.

The period between the interim ruling and its public release represents an opportunity for a return to negotiation among the parties. Only they know the contents of the ruling, and they have the option to go forward with its public release or to reach a mutually agreeable settlement without any public release of the panel report. In the first five years of the WTO, nearly one-fourth of the panels established never issued a ruling (62 of the 80 panels issued rulings).[37] In this case, the negotiations were quite extended, and the parties requested three postponements of the final report. Finally on May 10, the parties announced a mutually agreed settlement. In accordance with Article 12.12 of the DSU, the panel then released a description of the case and solution but not the panel's legal evaluation of the policy. The announced solution included an exchange of letters in which the EC representative said the French government order would be replaced by a new order that would allow marketing of scallops under the name "noix de coquilles Saint-Jacques" as long as the scientific name of the species and country of origin were also indicated.[38] The new draft order was included with these texts and would take effect within two months. A Peruvian negotiator said early settlement was possible because the ruling favored Peru, and the EC then "gave in completely."[39]

The solution that seems so obvious was only possible when the negotiation took place directly after release of the ruling. The French government had backed out on the earlier bilateral settlement reached with the Canadians, and the EC had refused compromise during consultations with Canada, Peru, and Chile when it faced the certain initiation of a panel. The direct prospect of a negative ruling, however, persuaded the EC to compromise. At that stage, the EC had to offer enough of a concession to satisfy Canada, Peru, and Chile because any one of the participants could have insisted on release of the panel report that favored their position. Since this was the first case regarding the TBT Agreement, EC officials

[37] Busch and Reinhardt 2002, 468.
[38] Notification of Mutually Agreed Solution, "European Communities – Trade Description of Scallops" WT/DS12/12, WT/DS14/11 (July 19, 1996).
[39] Official of Peru's delegation in Geneva. Telephone interview by author. July 30, 2003.

may have been reluctant to have a precedent set with broader implications for other policies that contained potential violations of the TBT.

Going all the way on sardines

A similar food labeling policy was used by the EC against imports of sardines from Peru. The EC Regulation (Council Regulation 2136/89) adopted June 21, 1989 forbade marketing of fish under the name sardine, unless it was the species common to Sardinia and found in the Atlantic ocean and Mediterranean Sea (*Sardina pilchardus Walbaum*). The regulation had not been enforced, and Peru had developed a market niche in Germany for its sardines under the label of "Pacific sardines." The problem arose in 1999, when the European Commission began to enforce the regulation by refusing to allow the import of the Peruvian fish under that label. EC officials suggested that the species from Peru (*Sardinops sagax sagax*) should instead be marketed as "pilchards" or "sprats," in order to protect consumers and avoid confusion.[40] Peru declared that this was simply a disguised effort by Europe to protect its local fishermen.

Peru first initiated bilateral negotiations with the EC. Peru offered to label the fish Pacific sardines or Peruvian sardines, but the European response was that this still allowed market confusion because different species would be sold under the name sardines. A Peruvian government official involved in the dispute said that for two years Peru tried to reach a negotiated settlement through bilateral contacts at all political levels.[41] The EC would not compromise on its position that the product name sardines must be reserved exclusively for the European species.

Unable to reach agreement through bilateral negotiations, Peru formally filed a complaint to the WTO and requested consultations. This forced the EC to the negotiating table. Consultations presented the EC with an opportunity to make a compromise and avoid the panel process.

Peru had a strong legal basis for its complaint. Not only could it appeal to the more general principles of the GATT and TBT Agreements, but it also had grounds to appeal to TBT Article 2.4, which calls for members to use existing international standards as a basis for their technical regulations. The Codex Alimentarius Commission has a standard for canned sardines and sardine-type products that clearly lists the Peruvian species among several others in its definition of sardines. This standard, which had been adopted in 1978, called for the European species to be called by the name sardines alone, while other species should be labeled

---

[40] *Financial Times*, June 17, 2002.
[41] Official of Peru's delegation in Geneva. Telephone interview by author. July 30, 2003.

"X sardines" with the modifier indicating the country, geographic area, species, or common name of species in country where sold.[42] In its request for consultations filed with the WTO, Peru referred to this standard to claim that the European regulation represented an unjustified barrier to trade.[43] An official of the WTO secretariat said "From the beginning, it was clear what direction this case would take – the EC regulation was a trade barrier. I am surprised it went to a panel."[44]

Despite the high probability of a legal ruling in favor of Peru, the EC would not compromise early. The Peruvian official described the European position: "It was clear during the consultations that we must go forward with our complaint. They offered to use only the scientific name without allowing the use of sardines in the label, and they were not moving on this point."[45] Peruvian exporters said the scientific name was not marketable.

An official of the EC delegation agreed that the sardines issue seemed like a case that should have been settled early. He said, "The threat of a panel clearly gives impetus to find a solution," but also commented that it depends on the political reality in the community whether the threat of a panel will be sufficient.[46] In this case, fisheries represent a sensitive sector, and among members, Spain, France, and Portugal had sardine producers that compete with Peru and could be expected to oppose the change. The original policy was a Council regulation so that there was the question of whether member approval would be necessary to change the policy. Moreover, the major exporter of sardines to EC markets that competed with Peru was Morocco. Morocco stands as a beneficiary of special economic relations with the EC, already holding an association agreement with the EC that lowers trade barriers and having nearly completed the process of concluding a free trade agreement.[47] As a result of the political difficulty to compromise on these interests, the EC continued to uphold its position that the name sardines must be reserved for the one species.

Peru was at a disadvantage because it lacked experience and trade law expertise. One of the lead negotiators for Peru said, "We are a small delegation and this was my first case. It is hard because we are competing in

---

[42] Codex Standard for Canned Sardines and Sardine-Type Products (CODEX STAN 94–181 Rev. 1995), www.codexalimentarius.net/standard list.asp accessed July 25, 2003.
[43] Request for consultations by Peru, "European Communities – Trade Description of Sardines" WT/DS231/1 (April 23, 2001).
[44] WTO official. Interview by author. Geneva, May 7, 2003.
[45] Official of Peru's delegation in Geneva. Telephone interview by author. July 30, 2003.
[46] Official of EU delegation in Geneva. Interview by author. Geneva May 5, 2003.
[47] http://europa.eu.int/comm/trade/issues/bilateral/regions/euromed/index en.htm accessed July 31, 2003.

an unfair situation – they have cases all year long and have specialists on every aspect of trade law."[48] Fortunately, Peru's delegation received the help of the Advisory Centre on WTO Law, which had been established in 2001 as an independent intergovernmental organization to provide a low cost alternative for developing countries that need legal expertise in order to participate in the dispute settlement system. For a membership fee, developing countries gain access to low-cost legal services rather than paying the fees of a private law firm, which can easily reach $300,000 for a WTO case.[49] Fees are based on relative income of the member, so that Peru was charged only US$100 an hour for legal services.[50] Peru's legal counsel admitted that without these services, they would not have been able to manage the case on their own.[51] At every stage, from the selection of panel members, to the preparation of the legal briefs and response to questions from panelists, to the negotiation of possible settlement options, Peru's delegate was accompanied by a lawyer from the Centre.

Peru also benefited from the contribution of interested third parties. Although Peru was the only country to file a complaint, Canada, Chile, Colombia, Ecuador, Venezuela and the United States all participated in the process as third parties. The United States presented an oral statement that supported Peru's argument that the EC measure violated TBT Article 2.4: "There is ample evidence indicating that the EC measure, if anything, undermines the EC's objectives, since European consumers have in fact come to know the Peruvian product as a form of sardine, and will likely be confused by the use of other names. Indeed, the use of a proper descriptor prior to the term 'sardine,' as provided for in the international standard, appears to be a very effective means of assuring transparency and protecting the consumer."[52] The US official also responded to questions from the panel that several sardine species were sold by US fishermen to many parts of the world but were not exported to the EC because of the restrictive labeling requirements, and that these same fish could be sold in the United States under the name sardines.[53]

[48] Official of Peru's delegation in Geneva. Telephone interview by author. July 30, 2003.
[49] *Financial Times*, October 24, 2002.
[50] The rates range from $25 for least developed countries to $200 for the highest income developing country members. http://www.acwl.ch/ accessed January 20, 2004.
[51] Shaffer and Mosoti 2002, 15.
[52] USTR, Oral Statement of the United States at the Third Party Session with the Panel (November 28, 2001), "European Communities – Trade Description of Sardines" (DS231). http://www.ustr.gov/enforcement/2001-11-28_USoral.pdf accessed July 31, 2003.
[53] USTR, Responses of the United States to Questions from the Panel From the Third Party Session (December 7, 2001), "European Communities – Trade Description of Sardines" (DS231). http://www.ustr.gov/enforcement/2001-12-07 QA.pdf accessed July 31, 2003.

Finally, meeting later before the Appellate Body review of the panel decision, USTR Associate General Counsel Dan Mullaney neatly rebutted
a central claim of the EC legal defense: "The EC claims that its Sardine Regulation is based on this international standard, because it adopts
the first part of the standard, even though it contradicts the second
part. If the EC's assertion is correct, then a regulation that permits *only*
non -European species to be marketed as kinds of sardines – and prohibits
European sardines from being marketed as sardines at all – would also
be based on the international standard. Even the EC would presumably
agree that this would be the incorrect result."[54]

NGO groups also played a supportive role. The UK Consumers' Association worked with a UK law firm to prepare a ten-page letter, which
Peru attached to its panel submission. The letter referred to the EC regulation as "base protectionism in favour of a particular industry within
the EC" that "clearly acts against the economic and information interests
of Europe's consumers."[55] Since the EC argument was primarily justified in terms of avoiding consumer confusion, the support of a European
consumer organization was especially helpful for Peru. Indeed, the WTO
panel cited the letter in its ruling.

After the panel released its interim ruling, Peru and the EC tried to
negotiate an early settlement. The EC offered to change the regulation so
that it would allow the species of sardines included in the Codex regulation to be labeled as sardines as long as the scientific name of the species
and country name were also included on the label. This would meet the
Codex standard suggestions for one way to modify "X sardines." For
Peru, however, this was still short of its first choice to be able to label the
fish as "Pacific Sardines." In light of their legal victory, it would have been
difficult for the Peruvian government to justify to their domestic industry
why they chose to settle for a compromise. In addition, Peru's delegation
hoped that having the ruling accepted by the Dispute Settlement Body
would help them for future cases of a similar nature. A Peruvian negotiator said that they might have accepted early settlement if allowed to call
the fish "Pacific Sardines," but that the EC officials said they could only
offer the option that added the scientific name. The Peruvian negotiator
said, "If we were to settle at interim stage and not have the ruling become
public, then they must give us what we want and not just what they want –
we are giving away something and can't do that for free."[56] The stronger

---

[54] USTR, Statement of the United States at the Oral Hearing (August 13, 2002), "European Communities – Trade Description of Sardines" (DS231). http://www.ustr.gov/
enforcement/2002-08-13-eusardines-oralst8.pdf accessed July 31, 2003.
[55] Shaffer and Mosoti 2002, 16.
[56] Official of Peru's delegation in Geneva. Telephone interview by author. July 30, 2003.

legal case encouraged Peru to push harder with its distributive strategy to demand full concessions from the EC.

Why did the interim negotiation fail for the sardines case when it had succeeded in the earlier scallops case? One difference in the two cases was that Codex has only established specific standards for salmon, sardines, tuna and bonito and has more general standards for all other fish and shell fish. Thus the ruling on scallops was based on Article 2.2 that regulations should be "no more trade-restrictive than necessary." The Codex standard for sardines made Peru's legal case even stronger than it had been for the scallops dispute where no such specific international standard existed. This made Peru less willing to compromise. At the same time, having the panel ruling based on Article 2.4, which states that technical regulations should be based on international standards, made the precedent less far-reaching. In a politically savvy legal strategy, Peru had urged the panel to follow judicial economy and make a ruling on its first legal claim about Article 2.4 if this was sufficient, and only address its other legal claims related to Article 2.2 if necessary. The panel followed this request, and found the case sufficiently strong to rule the EC measure inconsistent with TBT Article 2.4 because it was not based on the existing international standard. This reduced the EC concern about the precedent of the ruling, so it had less need to offer a major concession at the interim stage and avoid public release of the panel report.

Indeed, the public release of the ruling may have been necessary for EC trade officials to justify to the Fisheries Commission that the regulation would have to be changed.[57] Political opposition made early concessions difficult, but the ruling strengthened the argument that change was necessary. In the scallops case, only French interests were at stake because it was a French regulation. This may have made it easier to reach internal agreement to compromise early in order to prevent a precedent harmful to all members. The sardines policy, however, directly affected the interests of several members. The greater difficulty to reach an internal agreement in the sardines case prevented the EC from offering an early settlement – a negative ruling was necessary to overcome opposition to changing the policy.

The panel released on its ruling on May 29, 2002. The report found the EC regulation inconsistent with Article 2.4 of the TBT Agreement and recommended that the Dispute Settlement Body request the EC to bring its measure into conformity with the TBT Agreement. The EC decided, however, to appeal the panel ruling. After further legal proceedings, the judges of the Appellate Body released their ruling on September 26, 2002. The Appellate Body ruling upheld Peru's arguments on every major point,

---

[57] Official of EU delegation in Geneva. Interview by author. Geneva May 5, 2003.

with a few exceptions that had no substantive impact for the case.[58] The Appellate Body respected Peru's request to only evaluate the legal merits of the case based on Article 2.4, and responded to the EC objection to parts of the panel ruling that held implications for an interpretation of Article 2.2 – these references were struck from the panel report and declared to be without legal effect.[59]

After the legal process concluded, the participants still had to reach a mutually acceptable agreement. On the one hand, the ruling set the parameters for what was expected of the EC. It had to change its regulation to conform with the TBT Agreement. The exact form of the new regulation, however, was left to the discretion of the EC. If not satisfied by the new regulation, Peru had the option to file for an Article 21.5 implementation panel. In the months that followed, officials negotiated everything from whether the name sardines would be followed or preceded by the country name or the scientific name to the size of type to be used on the labels. The original deadline for EC compliance came in April, but a request for an extension until July was granted. Peru's officials were satisfied when the EC officials offered a proposal that would allow the use of the name sardines, followed by the scientific name of the species in small italics.[60] The Commission published the new regulation (EC no 1181/2003), which would allow those species recognized by the Codex standard to be labeled as sardines joined together with the scientific name of the species.[61] Peruvian exporters were disappointed that they would have to append the scientific name rather than use simply the name "Peruvian Sardines" or "Pacific Sardines," but the EC had the right to choose any option that complied with the TBT standard and Peru's officials felt that the outcome was a success on the main point to be allowed to use the word sardines on the label.[62]

Peru's officials said that the ruling had provided the basis for their ability to get a good outcome from the EC. "We have to have a panel ruling or we get nothing. Winning the panel ruling opens space for negotiation and strengthens our position."[63] A second official concurred that the WTO case was essential to getting the outcome given that the EC had shown no signs of compromise during bilateral negotiations or during the

---

[58] The Appellate Body allowed the submission of *amicus curiae* briefs from an individual and from Morocco, although declaring that the contents were not necessary for deciding the appeal. This latter decision has been viewed as controversial for members, and was protested by Peru during the proceedings and by many others afterwards.

[59] "European Communities – Trade Description of Sardines" WT/DS231/AB/R (September 26, 2002): 95.

[60] Official of Peru's delegation in Geneva. Interview by author. Geneva, May 5, 2003.

[61] European Commission, OJ L165, July 3, 2003, 17–18.

[62] Official of Peru's delegation in Geneva. Telephone interview by author. July 30, 2003.

[63] Official of Peru's delegation in Geneva. Interview by author. Geneva, May 5, 2003.

consultation phase of negotiations after filing a complaint. Moreover, the costs were low so that officials were confident that the market gains would easily recoup the financial cost of pursuing the WTO case. The Advisory Centre on WTO Law clearly played an important role in reducing legal costs and managing the case. Peru appears not to have suffered from any adverse political costs. During the dispute there were no threats of significance issued against Peru and officials did not feel that there had been any damage to bilateral relations.[64]

With the help of discounted legal advice, and contributions from UK consumer groups and third party opinions, Peru was able to win a major case and bring about compliance by the EC. The case serves as an example to other developing countries that the dispute system can help a small country get a fair hearing and reach a satisfactory outcome.

3   Vietnam and the catfish dispute

In order to consider the counterfactual of a developing country that faces a similar problem but cannot choose a strategy of WTO adjudication, I next examine a negotiation by a non-WTO member, Vietnam, against the United States. This case highlights the disadvantages faced by developing countries that do not have recourse to WTO adjudication when facing discrimination against their exports. The dispute revolved around unilateral policies by the United States taken against imports of Vietnamese catfish.

The US–Vietnam Bilateral Trade Agreement

The institutional framework for US–Vietnam trade relations is based on a bilateral treaty concluded as part of the process of normalization in diplomatic relations between the two countries. Until 1994, the United States and Vietnam did not have any trade relations due to the trade embargo imposed since the end of the Vietnam war. The lifting of the embargo by President Clinton only opened the way for a trickle of bilateral trade. Since Vietnam still lacked most-favored-nation status, goods from Vietnam faced substantially higher tariffs than those from other countries.[65] The path to full normalization of relations involved lengthy

---

[64] Official of Peru's delegation in Geneva. Telephone interview by author. July 30, 2003.
[65] The Trade Agreements Extension Act of 1951 suspended MFN treatment for communist countries. By the time that the United States granted MFN status to Vietnam starting in 1998 (on a provisional basis with the need for annual renewal of the Jackson–Vanik waiver), only six countries did not receive MFN treatment.

negotiations for a bilateral trade agreement. Concerns about full accounting for prisoners of war and human rights in Vietnam made the return to
normalization politically sensitive in the United States, while it was also
a major step in the market-oriented *doi moi* reforms being undertaken by
the Vietnamese Communist leadership.

The US–Vietnam Bilateral Trade Agreement (BTA), signed on July
13, 2000 and entering into effect in 2001, was a comprehensive agreement that brought far-reaching internal reforms in Vietnam and produced a doubling of bilateral trade in its first year. With MFN recognition, Vietnam gained access to US markets on the same terms as
WTO members. Average US tariffs on imports from Vietnam fell from
around 40 percent to around 3–4 percent. In exchange, Vietnam agreed
to lower its own trade barriers by 25–50 percent on goods, grant market access for services, and provide regulations to protect intellectual
property rights. This involved major overhaul of domestic policies and
the legal system, and decisions that would expose weak sectors such as
banking and telecommunication industries to competition. An official of
the Vietnamese Embassy in Washington DC described the reforms as a
revolution, and said that the prospective gains from the agreement had
been important to overcome opposition from those who would lose out.[66]
The US negotiators saw the rising economic potential of Vietnam and
demanded these comprehensive reforms with the view that this moment
was "the best leverage we'll ever have" and could be used to get Vietnam
to open their market.[67] At the same time, supporters of the agreement in
both the United States and Vietnam could sell the liberalizing policies as
a stepping stone towards Vietnamese accession to the WTO.

The BTA is closely modeled on the WTO agreements. Many sections
such as those on national treatment and intellectual property protection
are directly taken from the relevant passages in the WTO agreements.
Most importantly for the questions that later arose regarding labeling
policy for catfish, the text from TBT Article 2.2 is adopted in Article
2:6b of the BTA text.[68] The United States and Vietnam committed not
to have regulations that would create unnecessary obstacles to trade.

One major exception to the parallel structure of the BTA and WTO
agreements, however, is the lack of a formal dispute settlement mechanism. While the WTO and even some regional agreements such as

[66] Official of the Vietnamese Embassy to the United States. Interview by author. Washington, DC, July 11, 2003.
[67] Former USTR official. Interview by author. Washington D.C., July 15, 2003.
[68] Agreement Between the United States of American and the Socialist Republic of Vietnam
on Trade Relations. Mimeograph available at USTR Reading Room, 1724 F St, N.W.,
Washington, DC.

NAFTA provide for adjudication of trade disputes, the BTA simply establishes a "Joint Committee on Development of Economic and Trade Relations" that is given a mandate to serve as a forum for consultations over problems regarding implementation of the agreement (Chapter VII Article 5).

Therefore, when in the first months after the start of the agreement Vietnam faced an unexpected protectionist measure by the United States against its catfish exports, there was nowhere for Vietnam to turn for third party mediation. The BTA reduction of tariffs and the growth of a promising industry for Vietnam resulted in a surge of Vietnamese catfish into US markets – increasing from 5 million pounds of frozen fillets in 1999 to 34 million pounds in 2002, and capturing 20 percent of the US market.[69] Declining prices intensified the difficulties for US producers, who in 2001 experienced a 30 percent drop in the average earnings from a kilogram of catfish.[70] The US Association of Catfish Farmers of America (CFA), representing the catfish farmers concentrated in a few southern states of the United States, soon lobbied for measures to restrict the import of Vietnamese catfish. Although the US catfish market is a mere $590 million, in both countries the dispute over catfish exports has taken on larger political significance and influenced how both sides view the bilateral trade relationship.

The labeling dispute

The first stage of the "catfish war" involved a US decision to change a labeling policy and its refusal to negotiate any compromise of that regulation. The US industry had invested in developing high-quality, farm-raised catfish and dramatically increased sales through a skillful marketing campaign. When Vietnamese catfish began making inroads into the US market, with some being sold as "Cajun Delight Catfish" or other such names, the domestic industry struck back with its own advertising campaign against the Vietnamese fish. They claimed that the Vietnamese fish were lower quality because they were raised in "Third World rivers." Representative Marion Berry from Arkansas even referred to the danger that Vietnamese catfish were contaminated by lingering Agent Orange sprayed by the United States during the war.[71] Such xenophobic advertising did not prevent 30 percent of US seafood restaurants from serving Vietnamese catfish.[72] Next, the CFA demanded that Vietnamese catfish should not be sold as catfish.

---

[69] *Washington Post*, July 13, 2003.   [70] *Far Eastern Economic Review*, December 6, 2001.
[71] *New York Times*, November 5, 2002.
[72] *The Far Eastern Economic Review*, December 6, 2001.

When the labeling issue first arose, USTR officials went to technical experts at the Food and Drug Administration (FDA) for advice. The FDA officials said that they could not revoke the right for Vietnam to use the catfish label with a modifier such as "Vietnamese catfish," since the Vietnamese product was a kind of catfish. At the time, "The Seafood List, FDA's Guide to Acceptable Market Names for Seafood Sold in Interstate Commerce 1993" listed twenty different kinds of fish including the Vietnamese species as eligible for marketing with a label including the word catfish. Vietnam had readily agreed to any labeling policy requiring it to identify country of origin and/or use "Mekong Catfish" on labels.[73] FDA inspectors who visited Vietnam confirmed that quality standards complied with FDA requirements, and the US Embassy in Vietnam reported that it had found "little or no evidence that the US industry or health of the consuming public is facing a threat from Vietnam's emerging catfish export industry."[74] The matter would have ended there if it had been up to the USTR and FDA.

Determined to maintain their hold on the domestic market, the CFA engaged southern politicians to legislate a change in US regulations to prevent Vietnam from being able to sell its fish as catfish. Their central claim held that the basa and tra catfish (*Pangasius bocourti and Pangasius hypothalmus*) from Vietnam were a different product from the US channel catfish (*Ictaluridae*). There was not a specific international standard regarding the labeling of catfish. The *Saigon Times Weekly* (January 26, 2002) quotes Carl Ferraris, a researcher from the California Academy of Sciences, to support the Vietnamese claim that the basa and tra fish are catfish – among over 2,500 kinds of catfish around the world known by that name. The fish database of the International Center for Living Aquatic Resources Management with sponsorship from the FAO lists over seven hundred fish species with "catfish" in the name.[75] The CFA and its supporters, however, argued that only the one species, *Ictaluridae*, should be called catfish.

In the closing days of debate on an appropriations bill, southern representatives inserted an amendment to change the FDA regulation. The

[73] Indeed, the marketing controversy was less the result of Vietnam's exporters than about the American wholesale retailers and supermarkets that were adding labels they thought would make the product sell better. Former USTR official. Interview by author. Washington DC, July 15, 2003.
[74] US Embassy report cited in Senate debates. Agriculture, Conservation, and Rural Enhancement Act of 2001, Senate debate December 18, 2001 [S13427].
[75] http://www.fishbase.org accessed July 28, 2003. Specific reference for entries on *Pangasius bocourti* and *hypophthalmus* are from T. R. Roberts and C. Vidthayanon (1991). "Systematic revision of the Asian catfish family *Pangasiidae*, with biological observations and descriptions of three new species" Proceedings of the Academy of Natural Sciences, Philadelphia. 143: 97–144.

amendment would prevent the FDA from processing fish labeled as cat-fish unless it was of the species *Ictaluridae*. One Vietnamese negotiator who had tried to urge reconsideration, said the issue was decided "purely by domestic politics – we have no leverage."[76] Their best effort was to contact the Congressmen who had helped to support the BTA and the normalization of US–Vietnam relations, such as Senators John McCain and Phil Gramm. These senators spoke out strongly against the mea-sure when the bill came up before the Senate. McCain condemned the amendment and the process by which it had been passed:

In fact, of the 2,500 species of catfish on Earth, this amendment allows the FDA to process only a certain type raised in North America – specifically, those that grow in six Southern States. The program's effect is to restrict all catfish imports into our country by requiring that they be labeled as something other than catfish, an underhanded way for catfish producers to shut out the competition. With a clever trick of Latin phraseology and without even a ceremonial nod to the vast body of trade laws and practices we rigorously observe, this damaging amendment . . . literally bans Federal officials from processing any and all catfish imports labeled as they are – catfish. . . . It patently violates our solemn trade agreement with Vietnam, the very same trade agreement the Senate ratified by a vote of 88 to 12 only 2 months ago. The ink was not dry on that agreement when the catfish lobby and its congressional allies slipped the catfish amendment into a must-pass appropriations bill.[77]

Despite such impassioned speeches, the measure was adopted as part of the 2002 Farm Act.[78]

There was some effort by the Senators who opposed the amendment to use the WTO cases on labeling to strengthen their argument. Both the scallops and sardines disputes were mentioned as a similar labeling restriction that the United States had opposed when it was European policies harming US producers. The Southern representatives claimed that the difference between the fish species at hand was much greater than the related WTO cases.[79] The comparison was even made that the US and Vietnamese fish were as different as a yak and a cow. Unlike Peru, however, Vietnam could not file a complaint to the WTO and have a more neutral source decide what should count as a catfish. Given no

[76] Official of the Vietnamese Embassy to the United States. Interview by author. Washing-ton, DC, July 11, 2003.
[77] Agriculture, Conservation, and Rural Enhancement Act of 2001, Senate debate Decem-ber 18, 2001 [S13426].
[78] The provisional measure became permanent in Section 10806 of the 2002 US Farm Act, which became law May 13, 2002 (Public Law 107–171).
[79] Agriculture, Conservation, and Rural Enhancement Act of 2001, Senate debate Decem-ber 18, 2001 [S13429].

choice but to accept the measure, Vietnamese exporters labeled their fish
as basa and tra.

The antidumping determination

When even the food labeling barrier did not restrain imports, the US
catfish industry switched tactics to file a petition in June 2002 requesting antidumping measures against the imports from Vietnam. The CFA
petition claimed that Vietnam was selling its fish in US markets at prices
below the cost of production with injurious effects on the US industry.

Dumping is considered a threat to fair trade conditions and competitive markets when an exporter sells goods at a higher price in its home
market while disposing of surplus capacity in foreign markets at lower
prices. Domestic laws to counter dumping predate international trade
rules, and have been recognized by the GATT and now the WTO rules.[80]
The United States accepts petitions from industries that claim to suffer
from foreign dumping of like products, and undertakes two parallel investigations before making a final determination. The first investigation is
supervised by the International Trade Administration within the Department of Commerce (DOC), which evaluates the normal price of the foreign product in order to determine whether it has been sold below price in
US markets. The ruling of dumping, however, must also be accompanied
by a finding of injury. The International Trade Commission (ITC) hears
evidence from both sides on whether the imports have caused damage
to the domestic industry. Positive findings in both investigations result in
the application of antidumping duties on the foreign product.

Problems arise, however, when antidumping policies become an alternative form of protection for weak import-competing industries. Given
that the investigation of dumping and industry damage occur under the
auspices of domestic law and national administrative officials serve as
the judge in a dispute between a national and foreign industry, there is
the possibility for bias in favor of the home industry. The initiation of an
investigation alone can help the domestic industry and harm the exporter
by creating market uncertainty about future trade (when imposed, duties
are retroactive such that importers may become hesitant to buy from an
exporter under investigation).[81] Cooperation with the investigation also
imposes considerable administrative costs on the export firms that must
provide detailed information about their business operations.

---

[80] GATT Article 6 allows use of antidumping duties when there is evidence that dumping
causes material injury to competing domestic industries.
[81] Palmeter 1996, 279.

After having declared that the Vietnamese product was fundamentally different from US catfish, now the antidumping suit depended upon defining the same fish to be a like product. According to US law, an antidumping petition must be initiated by a domestic industry that produces a like product with the imported good subject to investigation. This determination of like product, however, is made on a case-by-case basis when the petition is first accepted and again later when officials evaluate the injury to domestic industry from imports. As such, the definition of like product is often a matter of disagreement.[82] The President of the American Seafood Distributors Association said during a hearing about the antidumping case that "changing the name of Vietnamese catfish to basa should have been sufficient grounds to protect the market name of the domestic catfish producers and thus give them the product differentiation that should have ruled out the need to pile on with a dumping suit as well. The fact that we are here today to perform the alchemy of turning basa back into catfish strikes me and the organization that I lead as nothing short of a convoluted action to serve only one master. It's protectionism."[83]

After the CFA filed their petition, Vietnamese officials tried to prevent initiation of an investigation. Contacts with the US government were pursued at all levels. The DOC, however, was obligated by law to initiate the investigation so long as the CFA petition met their checklist as a valid claim (e.g. petitioners account for more than 50 percent of production of domestic like product, present evidence of injury from imports with data for calculation of estimated dumping margin, and follow necessary procedures). The petition from the CFA, which estimated that there should be a finding for a 144–190 percent dumping margin on the Vietnamese fish, was found to meet these standards.[84] Neither requests from Vietnam's officials nor letters from senators expressing concerns about broader relations could be taken into consideration at this stage.[85] The DOC approved the start of an investigation, referring to the case as concerning "certain frozen fish fillets from Vietnam" in light of the naming controversy.

The first hurdle for Vietnam was to try and prove that prices in Vietnam should be used in the calculation of normal prices. The CFA requested

[82] Palmeter 1996, 268.
[83] US International Trade Commission. Hearing report for Investigation no. 731-TA-1012 in the matter of certain frozen fish fillets from Vietnam. June 17, 2003.
[84] Department of Commerce "Initiation of antidumping Duty Investigation: Certain Frozen Fish Fillets From the Socialist Republic of Vietnam." *Federal Register* vol. 67 no. 142 (July 24, 2002): 4837–40.
[85] Department of Commerce official. Interview by author. Washington DC, July 11, 2003.

that Vietnam should be considered a non-market economy, which would mean that a surrogate country would be used for pricing calculation under the assumption that real prices could not be estimated in a state-controlled economy. This judgment was made on an economy-wide basis rather than through examination of the specific sector.[86] As a result, even though the catfish producers in Vietnam are a group of companies and small-scale farmers that generally operate by market principles, and there was no evidence to show they had received government subsidies or price directives, the economy was judged to be a non-market economy.[87] The non-market finding pushed the investigation into the realm of hypotheticals – Brink Lindsey of the Cato Institute condemned the process for determining non-market economy prices: "Basically, you can come up with any dang number you want to."[88] In the case of Vietnam, prices from Bangladesh were used to estimate what it would cost to produce fish in Vietnam if it operated on market principles.

Vietnam found itself forced to wage a legal fight in US trade courts. This being the first antidumping case for Vietnam, they were completely lacking in expertise. DOC officials had weekly meetings with officials from the Vietnamese embassy and traveled to Vietnam to offer a seminar to help the companies that were required to submit extensive surveys on their business operations. The complexity of antidumping procedures, however, required legal expertise. The Vietnamese government hired a US law firm to represent their interests in consultations regarding the case, while the Vietnamese exporters represented by the Vietnam Association of Seafood Producers (VASEP) hired another law firm to present their case before the DOC and ITC.

Proceedings went forward as an administrative investigation run strictly according to US antidumping laws. The DOC made its preliminary determination for dumping duties in January 2003. Based on the DOC calculations, which drew on a regression wage rate for Vietnam's labor costs and Bangladeshi prices for inputs and pricing of fish, the DOC determined that 38–64 percent antidumping tariffs should be applied.[89] The lower rate would apply to the large companies that had cooperated with the investigation by providing information, while the higher "Vietnam

---

[86] The DOC antidumping manual lists provisions regarding a market-oriented industry that might have been appropriate for the case. Vietnam unsuccessfully tried to prove the more general claim that the entire economy was market-based.
[87] Official of trade industry association. Interview by author. Washington DC, June 11, 2003.
[88] *Washington Post*, July 13, 2003.
[89] Department of Commerce. "Notice of Preliminary Determination of Sales at Less Than Fair Value," 68 FR 4986 (January 31, 2003).

wide" rate would apply to all of the small Vietnamese catfish producers who had lacked the information or resources to participate in the
investigation. These smaller producers, who compose 40 percent of all
those employed in the catfish industry in Vietnam, are the most market driven and least likely to be able to afford selling products below
price.[90]

The next phase opened a window for negotiation. Vietnam requested
to negotiate a suspension agreement, which is an effort by the government of the industry that is charged with dumping to reach a settlement
with the DOC. Although infrequent, such agreements have been reached
by means of fixing import prices to an agreed level and/or administering
a quota similar to a voluntary export restraint. The DOC then would
suspend the dumping investigation and not issue a final determination
on dumping. In this case, the officials from the Vietnamese delegation
and the DOC could not reach a mutually acceptable agreement on the
price level and quota size. An official from the Vietnamese side said that
the DOC took an inflexible approach, starting off with a high price and
low quota, and only agreeing to increase the quota if the price was also
increased. The Vietnamese side had begun with a request for a relatively
low price and high quota, and then came back having modified their
own offer slightly to include a higher price. After another failure to reach
agreement, the Vietnamese came back with a more substantial concession from their original proposal. DOC officials, however, had hardly
changed their original position and agreed that the first offer had been
the final offer. Since the Vietnamese side estimated that the DOC offer
would be equivalent to 60–80 percent tariffs, they rejected it and let the
antidumping investigation continue.[91]

DOC officials said that the negotiations for a suspension agreement
were undertaken in good faith and that the legal obligations of US antitrust law requires that any suspension agreement must stop the undermining of prices that causes the domestic industry damage. They must also
worry about a suspension agreement that leaves the petitioning domestic
industry dissatisfied, because then it could launch an appeal. An earlier
suspension agreement with Russia on hot-rolled steel was appealed by the
domestic industry. In that case, the DOC agreement was upheld. If an
agreement were overturned, however, it would be a bureaucratic night-
mare to roll back the provisions of an agreement that had already begun

---

[90] Official of trade industry association. Interview by author. Washington DC, June 11,
2003.
[91] Official of the Vietnamese Embassy to the United States. Interview by author. Washington DC, July 11, 2003. Official of trade industry association. Interview by author.
Washington DC, June 11, 2003.

implementation. Fear of an appeal from domestic industry restrained the DOC from considering any concessions. In the end, there was no overlap between their offer and what Vietnam was willing to accept.[92]

In contrast, a US antidumping investigation against imports of fresh tomatoes from Mexico provides an example of a successful negotiation to reach a suspension agreement. After the DOC initiated the investigation on April 18, 1996, Mexico filed a request for consultations under the WTO dispute settlement procedures with a complaint that the US investigation violated its WTO commitments.[93] The WTO case never advanced to the panel stage, however, since Mexico and the United States reached a suspension agreement three months later.[94] This agreement provided for reference prices and was accepted by the Mexican exporters. The right to file a WTO complaint represents one tactic that may be useful to challenge dumping charges with a weak factual basis and even to gain leverage during negotiation of a suspension agreement.

Vietnam considered using threats to gain leverage in the dispute. The *Economist* reported that Vietnam was threatening to launch an antidumping suit of its own against the subsidized imports of US soybeans.[95] In the end, however, threats were rejected as not serving Vietnam's own interests – there seemed little point in harming industries such as Cargill when the government was trying to encourage more foreign investment by such industries. Moreover, it was unlikely that the United States would be moved by threats from a country with such a tiny market. In 2002, US exports to Vietnam had a total value of $580 million, which is tiny relative to US total exports of $693 billion and relative to its exports to other countries in the region (US exports to China that same year were $22 billion, and its exports to Thailand were $4.9 billion).[96]

The DOC and ITC issued their final positive findings of dumping and injury after further hearings to evaluate the arguments presented by both sides. In its defense against the dumping charges, the Vietnamese side tried to use the earlier Congressional debate to argue that basa and tra fish were indeed different products from US catfish and were not any more responsible for the troubles of the catfish industry than were exports of other fish species like sole. Statistical evidence was presented to show that

---

[92] Officials of the Department of Commerce. Interview by author. Washington DC, July 11, 2003.
[93] Request for Consultations by Mexico, "United States – antidumping Investigation Regarding Imports of Fresh or Chilled Tomatoes from Mexico." WT/DS49/1 (July 8, 1996).
[94] Federal Register (61) 56617 [A-201–820] (November 1, 1996).
[95] December 14, 2002.
[96] Foreign Trade Division http://www.census.gov/foreign-trade/balance/ accessed July 30, 2003.

248 *Christina L. Davis*

imports of Vietnamese catfish did not influence US catfish prices. This was countered by the CFA legal team, which argued that the labeling policy had not prevented basa and tra from competing with US catfish, and offered its own statistical analysis to show that imported Vietnamese fish did have an impact on domestic catfish prices.[97]

One of the most strongly contested points in the legal briefs regarded whether valuation of the factors of production should be based on an integrated process of raising fish or on the purchase of a whole fish. The Vietnamese producers claimed their use of an integrated process was a source of comparative advantage, and that their actual factor inputs and production process should be used in the calculation of the normal price.[98] Instead, the DOC used the cost of whole fish purchase in Bangladesh along with the cost of other inputs – including water costs. The DOC justified this as necessary in order to find comparable data in Bangladesh for the construction of surrogate prices. The DOC explanation also questioned the degree of integration in the Vietnamese production of catfish.[99] The DOC calculations produced an estimated normal price much higher than the price at which Vietnamese catfish were sold in the United States. The final determination issued in July 2003 called for dumping duties of 37–64 percent.[100]

Vietnam's government protested the outcome, saying the case against it had been groundless.[101] Press reports in both Vietnam and the United States mocked the notion that Vietnamese catfish farmers or the Vietnamese government had the money to engage in dumping its fish below cost.[102] A US trade expert who had followed the case said it was unfathomable that Vietnam was dumping fish in the US markets, but that the determination was possible because "reality was thrown out" when the DOC constructs prices for non-market economies.[103] The use of figures from Bangladesh that were calculated with different years according to data availability and the use of data from India when there was inadequate data from Bangladesh contributed to the sense that the dumping margins

---

[97] US International Trade Commission. Hearing report for Investigation no. 731-TA-1012 in the matter of certain frozen fish fillets from Vietnam. June 17, 2003.

[98] Ibid.

[99] International Trade Administration. Final Decision Memorandum (June 16, 2003) p. 41 (copy of public memo on file in DOC records room).

[100] Department of Commerce. "Notice of Final Antidumping Duty Determination of Sales at Less Than Fair Value and Affirmative Critical Circumstances: Certain Frozen Fish Fillets from the Socialist Republic of Vietnam." FR 68, no. 120 (June 23, 2003): 37116–121.

[101] *Financial Times*, July 24, 2003.

[102] *New York Times*, July 22 and 25, 2003; *Vietnam News Agency*, July 10, 2002, http://www.vietnamembassy-usa.org/news/newsitem.php3?datestamp=20020710154153.

[103] Former USTR official. Interview by author. July 15, 2003.

had been determined arbitrarily. After the final decision, Vietnamese officials protested that it had been unfair to ignore the efficiency gains from their integrated production process that allowed them to sell the fish at a lower price.

There was little doubt about the devastating effect of the outcome for Vietnamese exporters. After the preliminary duties were imposed in January, the export of Vietnamese catfish to the United States had been down 30–40 percent, and the announcement that these duties would now be permanent is expected to deal the final blow to effectively close off the market.[104]

Release of the final determination was the end of the case from the perspective of US law, and there was no opening for Vietnam to negotiate the outcome. It could file an appeal for review by the Court of International Trade, but this remains a US Court that places the burden of proof on the challenging party to show the determination is not based on substantial evidence – the court will not overturn the agency's statutory interpretation so long as it could be conceived of as a permissible construction of the law.[105] For Vietnam, further legal bills with little hope for a change in the regulation made the option of appeal unattractive.

This contrasts with the option for WTO members to file a complaint and force the government that has applied antidumping duties to defend its decision as meeting WTO standards. The Antidumping Agreement specifies rules and procedures for application of antidumping duties, such as what facts are necessary to make a finding of dumping and injury.[106] Dispute settlement has been used to challenge cases where the methodology to calculate dumping or injury was questioned. Since 1995 there have been 51 separate requests for consultations regarding antidumping.[107] Indeed, the same day that the determination was made on Vietnam's catfish, the ITC also approved antidumping duties on semiconductors from Korea. The Korean government immediately announced it would appeal the decision to the WTO.[108] While antidumping laws are legal under international trade law, states can also be held accountable to justify the application of their antidumping laws' procedures in any given case. Dispute panels have often ruled against antidumping policies where rules of thumb used by administrative authorities in calculating margins fail to

---

[104] *Financial Times*, July 24, 2003.   [105] Palmeter 1996, 277.
[106] Jackson 1997, 255–57.
[107] This total represents requests for consultations under the Antidumping Protocol listed at http://www.wto.org/english/tratop_e/adp_e/adp_e.htm accessed January 23, 2004.
[108] *Financial Times*, July 24, 2003.

hold up before an international standard of review.[109] For example, when India filed a complaint against EC antidumping duties applied to imports of bed linen from India, the panel ruled against the EC measure on several grounds, such as inconsistencies in the calculation of the amount for profit in its construction of the normal price.[110] Following the ruling, the EC amended its antidumping duties according to the recommendation of the panel ruling.

For WTO members, the option to legally challenge an antidumping finding in the WTO may even deter the imposition of antidumping duties against their products. One study of US antidumping activity from 1980 to 1998 finds that GATT/WTO membership reduces the likelihood of the US government making a positive decision to impose antidumping duties, when controlling for other economic factors likely to influence the antidumping finding.[111] Members that actively use the dispute system are even less likely to be targeted. This would mean that non-members face the double disadvantage that they are more likely to face antidumping duties against their products and they will have no recourse to challenge these duties.

One can only speculate about whether Vietnam would be able to win a ruling against the US measure in this case if it were able to file a complaint. There might be grounds for Vietnam to contest the like industry definition as well as the methodology of calculation. Virginia Foote, the president of the US–Vietnam Trade Council, said, "I think that if Vietnam was a WTO member, it could bring the case to the WTO and we would see if Vietnam was considered dumping its products in the US market according to international standards."[112] Whether or not Vietnam could have used WTO dispute proceedings successfully in this case, there is a perception that Vietnam is more vulnerable because it does not have this option. One Vietnamese negotiator said that not being able to appeal to the WTO put them in a weaker position, and added that if Vietnam had been a WTO member, the CFA would still have filed its petition, but·Vietnam would have had more tools with which to negotiate.[113] One consequence of this case was a renewed urgency to join the WTO. Demetrios Marantis, chief legal adviser to the US–Vietnam Trade Council in Hanoi, said that the government had accelerated its effort to join the WTO after this case in

---

[109] Hudec 1993, 345.
[110] Report of the Appellate Body, "European Communities – Antidumping Duties on Imports of Cotton-type Bed Linen from India" WT/DS141/AB/R (March 1, 2001).
[111] Blonigen and Bown 2003, 266.
[112] Nguyen Vinh "Say no to any sanction against Vietnam" at http://www.usvtc.org accessed August 11, 2003.
[113] Official of Vietnam's Embassy to the United States. Interview by author. Washington DC, July 11, 2003.

the hope that it would receive more favorable outcomes in the future from multilateral settlement of trade disputes.[114]

On the basis of the BTA, Vietnam has been able to more than double its exports to the United States. While the agreement has brought mutual benefits, the treaty also directly reflects the unequal power relationship. Vietnam had to undertake a major overhaul of its policies to gain MFN access to US markets. Yet when the United States adopted policies against Vietnam's successful catfish exports, Vietnam had no bargaining leverage. The bilateral agreement lacked the institutional framework for dispute settlement, and Vietnam had few options against unilateral US policies. Vietnam was unable to hold the United States accountable to its commitments, or even insist that the legal text of the BTA should serve as the basis for negotiation over trade disputes. Switching standards, US policy could at the same time declare Vietnamese basa and tra fish to be completely different from catfish and a like product with catfish. Thus a labeling regulation that appears to blatantly represent an unnecessary obstacle to trade was established and a controversial antidumping decision goes unchallenged.

4   Concluding remarks

Food labeling involves domestic regulations with both legitimate concerns about consumer information and opportunities for hidden protectionism. Increasingly countries try to use geographical indicators or quality distinctions to maintain advantages for local producers – reduction of the tariffs, quotas, and subsidies that long protected sensitive primary goods sectors leaves labeling regulations as the last barrier. As difficult trade disputes continue to occur, it will be important for both sides to engage in negotiations based on science rather than arbitrary justifications. The WTO rules are a key factor to influence whether even small countries can insist upon the use of common standards.

The first hurdle for a developing country is to get its more powerful trade partner to engage in a negotiation to find a mutually acceptable solution. There is little that a small country can do when requests to discuss a trade problem are ignored as happened to Vietnam. The United States refused to negotiate with Vietnam after legislating a unilateral change of its labeling policy. Then the United States took an inflexible position during negotiations to suspend the antidumping investigation. In contrast, the WTO adjudication process mandates at least an effort at negotiation during the consultation phase, and guarantees the right of members to a

---

[114] *Business Week*, November 24, 2003.

panel judgment on their complaint. Thus even when the EC refused to offer any concessions during bilateral talks and during the DSU consultation phase, it had to face Peru in court.

The second challenge is to shape the terms of agreement to conform with common rules rather than the will of the more powerful. An important role of the WTO is to establish a clear set of standards to regulate trade. Any member can appeal to these rules when calling for non-discriminatory treatment of its exports. Thus Peru could use the WTO adjudication process to force the EC to engage it in a negotiation based on the standard of WTO policies for labeling. With its legal complaint, Peru could also focus the discussion on the exact article in the agreements that it felt was most beneficial for its argument. Vietnam should have been able to use a legal standard for leverage because the BTA and TBT Agreement include the same text prohibiting regulations that serve as unnecessary obstacles to trade. Without an appeal to the WTO, however, it could not force the United States to take this standard into consideration. Moreover, when the representatives for Vietnamese catfish producers tried to use the same arguments presented by the CFA during the labeling dispute to counter the like product definition in the antidumping dispute, their case was rejected. Outside of an institutional context with established standards and procedures, more powerful countries can pick and choose any standard to justify the policy they choose.

Thirdly, the WTO dispute settlement process can help developing countries by means of legal bandwagoning. Having several countries join together to argue against a particular interpretation of the rules bolsters the legal arguments and legitimacy of the complaint. For a developing country it can be especially useful to have legal points addressed by developed countries as part of the panel hearing process.[115] Where Vietnam stood alone, Peru had Canada and the United States along with other developing countries jointly arguing its case. At the same time, the pressure for eventual compliance grows with the number of countries that could potentially issue sanctions. Even more important than the weight of sanctions, normative pressure from the entire membership supports the obligation for compliance. This shift in the cost analysis is critical for developing countries who fear damaging bilateral relations and lack both legal expertise and retaliatory capacity.

---

[115] This could be a double-edged sword, since third parties could also support the defendant and argue for a negative ruling. The addition of third parties will only help a developing country that is making an uncontroversial legal claim for compliance with treaty obligations. Under these circumstances, however, it is likely that a broader coalition offers support.

Finally, the WTO process brought compliance by changing the alternative to a negotiated settlement. Within the WTO dispute system, the EC had to be concerned about a ruling that would set a precedent with a broader impact. This encouraged early settlement in the scallops case. For the more narrow legal case regarding sardines, winning the ruling gave Peru the leverage to bring a policy change that it had been unable to reach in bilateral talks. On the other hand, even though Vietnam was losing trade benefits that it could legitimately have expected from the BTA, there was no mechanism for it to challenge the US labeling policy. While Vietnam offered concessions towards a compromise on the dumping problem, the DOC refused to compromise. Developing countries lack the market power to issue threats or bribes, but those that are members of the WTO can use its dispute mechanism to challenge such domestic legal proceedings. A negative ruling raises the costs of continued protection so that governments will be more cautious about upholding the protectionist demands of their domestic industry.

The negotiation process matters in terms of how well states use the institutional system. WTO membership is a necessary condition to gain leverage through legal framing, but members must also opt to use the rules by initiating a complaint. Choosing to initiate a complaint together with other members further enhances bargaining leverage while reducing costs. Chapter 8 demonstrates how creative legal tactics in managing a dispute case (Ecuador's complaint against the EU banana import regime) can improve the negotiation outcome. As this chapter has shown, the possibilities for using skillful negotiation tactics to improve outcomes are more limited for states outside of the WTO.

Dispute settlement mechanisms in bilateral free trade agreements also have significant effects on the context for compliance bargaining between trade partners. These dispute mechanisms offer some of the advantages of legal framing found in the WTO dispute settlement. Yet the WTO provides developing countries with the option to enhance their leverage through coalition action, which was important in the case of Peru. As the proliferation of bilateral free trade agreements expands the options for managing trade problems, the choice of negotiation forum will become an important first step in negotiation strategies.

Many have feared that legal costs transfer the power asymmetry of bilateral negotiations into WTO disputes. Certainly developing countries suffer from their lack of comparative advantage in international trade lawyers and are unable to afford to hire a US law firm for every case. Discounted legal services offered by the Advisory Centre on WTO Law, however, are an important step that reduces this problem. Moreover, as developing countries build experience using the DSU, they can begin to improve their skills. Participating as a third party or co-complainant offers a kind of apprenticeship for states to learn how to effectively use the rules to their advantage.[116]

Through examination of specific cases, this chapter highlights how legal framing of the negotiation allows a developing country to gain a better outcome than it could achieve in bilateral negotiations. Two general hypotheses emerge that could be tested on a broader range of cases: developing countries that are members of the WTO will gain better negotiation outcomes than non-members, and developing countries that file a complaint with the support of interested developed country members will gain better outcomes than those that act alone. The broader implication of the study is that the institutional context of a negotiation can reduce the effect of asymmetric power relations. This opens up space for small countries to negotiate for concessions from their most powerful trade partners.

The WTO adds to the tactical toolkit available to a developing country. When facing discrimination against their exports, WTO members can respond with a distributive strategy supported by the rules of the WTO dispute settlement process. Filing a complaint forces the other side to listen to this demand for a unilateral policy change, establishes a neutral standard to settle the dispute, and increases the opportunity to find allies. The institutional context shapes bargaining incentives for both sides so that even a weak country can use a strong legal case to push forward with its distributive strategy while a strong country may offer concessions to avoid a negative precedent or damage to the rules system. Although the legal resources required for adjudication are an obstacle for using legal tactics, the alternative of a bilateral negotiation leaves developing countries in a situation with a far worse outlook for ending the discrimination against their goods by a developed country. With more progress in the area of legal assistance for developing countries, the WTO rules for dispute settlement can help to establish a level playing field.

For issues that are outside of existing WTO commitments, however, the legal framing tactic will not be relevant. New trade issues can only be negotiated through bilateral agreements or in trade rounds to expand on existing rules. In addition, cases with questionable legal interpretation will be more difficult. Developing countries lack the legal capacity to manage the more complicated legal cases and are less likely to find allies to support their case when their interpretation involves stretching

---

[116] Statistical analysis of 74 developing countries from 1995 to 2003 shows that those with more experience as initiators, third parties, or even as defendants were more likely to initiate complaints in the WTO DSU. Davis and Bermeo 2005.

existing legal commitments. Disputed rulings that raise legal controversy among members are less likely to exert the compliance pull from international legitimacy that accompanies most rulings. While unable to solve all trade problems, legal framing offers developing countries an effective tactic against trade barriers that represent a clear violation of existing commitments.

REFERENCES

Bello, Judith Hippler. 1996. "The WTO Dispute Settlement Understanding: Less is More." *American Journal of International Law* 90 (3): 416–18

Blonigen, Bruce and Chad Bown. 2003. "Antidumping and Retaliation Threats." *Journal of International Economics* 60 (2): 249–73

Bown, Chad. 2004. "On the Economic Success of GATT/WTO Dispute Settlement." *The Review of Economics and Statistics* 86 (2): 811–23

Busch, Marc. 2000. "Democracy, Consultation, and the Paneling of Disputes Under GATT." *Journal of Conflict Resolution* 44 (4): 425–46

Busch, Marc and Eric Reinhardt. 2002. "Testing International Trade Law: Empirical Studies of GATT/WTO Dispute Settlement." In *The Political Economy of International Trade Law: Essays in Honor of Robert E. Hudec*, eds. Daniel Kennedy and James Southwick. Cambridge: Cambridge University Press, 457–81

  2003. "Developing Countries and GATT/WTO Dispute Settlement." *Journal of World Trade* 37 (4): 719–35

Davis, Christina. 2003. *Food Fights Over Free Trade: How International Institutions Promote Agricultural Trade Liberalization.* Princeton: Princeton University Press

  2004. "International Institutions and Issue Linkage: Building Support for Agricultural Trade." *The American Political Science Review* 98 (1): 153–69

Davis, Christina and Sarah Blodgett Bermeo. 2005. "Who Files? Developing Country Participation in GATT/WTO Dispute Settlement." Paper presented at the Annual Meeting of the Political Science Association, Washington, DC

Goldstein, Judith and Lisa L. Martin. 2000. "Legalization, Trade Liberalization, and Domestic Politics: A Cautionary Note." *International Organization* 54 (3): 603–32

Guzman, Andrew and Beth Simmons. 2002. "To Settle or Empanel? An Empirical Analysis of Litigation and Settlement at the World Trade Organization." *Journal of Legal Studies* 31 (1): 205–35

Horn, Henrik, Petros Mavroidis, and Hakan Nordstrom. 1999. "Is the Use of the WTO Dispute Settlement System Biased?" Center for Economic Policy Research Discussion Paper 2340

Hudec, Robert. 1993. *Enforcing International Trade Law: The Evolution of the Modern GATT Legal System.* Salem, NH: Butterworth

Hudec, Robert. 2002. "The Adequacy of WTO Dispute Settlement Remedies: A Developing Country Perspective." In *Development, Trade, and the WTO,*

256   *Christina L. Davis*

eds. Bernard Hoekman, Aaditya Mattoo, and Philip English. Washington, DC: The World Bank, 81–91

Jackson, John H. 1997. *The World Trading System: Law and Policy of International Economic Relations*. Second ed. Cambridge Mass: The MIT Press

Johnston, Alastair Iain. 2001. "Treating International Institutions as Social Environments." *International Studies Quarterly* 45 (4): 487–515

Kovenock, Dan and Marie Thursby. 1992. "GATT, Dispute Settlement and Cooperation." *Economics and Politics* 4 (4): 151–70

Odell, John. 2000. *Negotiating the World Economy*. Ithaca, NY: Cornell University Press

Ostry, Sylvia. 2002. "The Uruguay Round North–South Grand Bargain." In *The Political Economy of International Trade Law: Essays in Honor of Robert E. Hudec*, eds. Daniel Kennedy and James Southwick. Cambridge: Cambridge University Press, 285–300

Oxfam. 2002. *Rigged Rules and Double Standards: Trade, Globalisation, and the Fight Against Poverty*. Oxford: Oxfam

Palmeter, N. David. 1996. *Anti-Dumping Under the WTO: A Comprehensive Review*. London: Kluwer Law. Chapter on the United States, 261–79

Ricupero, Rubens. 1998. "Integration of Developing Countries into the Multilateral Trading System." In *The Uruguay Round and Beyond*, eds. Jagdish Bhagwati and Mathias Hirsch. Ann Arbor: The University of Michigan Press, 9–36

Shaffer, Gregory. 2003. *Defending Interests: Public-private Partnerships in WTO Litigation*. Washington, DC: Brookings Institution Press

Shaffer, Gregory and Victor Mosoti. 2002. "EC Sardines: A New Model for Collaboration in Dispute Settlement?" *Bridges* 6 (7): 15–22

Steinberg, Richard. 2002. "In the Shadow of Law or Power? Consensus-based Bargaining and Outcomes in the GATT/WTO." *International Organization* 56 (2): 339–74

8 Compliance bargaining in the WTO: Ecuador and the bananas dispute

James McCall Smith

Introduction

Studies of bargaining in the international economy routinely focus on negotiations regarding the original terms of agreements ex ante rather than on discussions regarding compliance with those commitments ex post. A few scholars have called attention to this often neglected aspect of international negotiations: compliance bargaining.[1] The dynamics of compliance bargaining have particular importance for developing countries, whose post-agreement negotiating power is arguably constrained in many settings. This chapter examines compliance bargaining in the World Trade Organization (WTO) through a case study of Ecuador's tactics in its challenge against the banana import regime of the European Union (EU).

After prevailing in its legal case against the EU banana scheme (as a co-complainant with others), Ecuador pursued an aggressive strategy to encourage compliance with the ruling. In the framework of Odell, Ecuador's stance in this high-profile dispute was a purely distributive strategy.[2] In the universe of international economic negotiations, all compliance bargaining tilts toward the distributive end of the spectrum, as one party claims another has failed to deliver benefits that were previously promised. In the bananas dispute, Ecuador's negotiators creatively sought to maximize their leverage within the specific institutional framework of WTO rules. What is striking about this case is the extent to which those rules – some interpreted and applied for the first time – enabled Ecuador, in effect, to punch above its weight in the multilateral trade system.

As a test of developing country leverage in WTO compliance bargaining, the bananas dispute is a least likely case. At the outset of the dispute, as Ecuador rushed its WTO accession to join the proceedings, the odds

---

[1] See, e.g., Albin 2001, 49; Jönsson and Tallberg 1998 and 2001.   [2] Odell 2000.

of success were hardly high. The EU had already defied two GATT panel rulings against its banana regime in 1993 and 1994. A broad coalition of African, Caribbean, and Pacific (ACP) countries staunchly defended their preferential access to the European market, playing the same developing country card on which Ecuador would in part rely. Although by no means heavyweights in international economic affairs, the ACP banana exporters had two advantages: many enjoyed deep-rooted economic ties to former colonial powers, and their coalition sought to defend the status quo rather than to change it. Finally, despite the obvious advantages of joining a complaint filed by the United States, Ecuador's economic interests diverged in several crucial respects from those of Chiquita International, the firm on whose behalf the United States (and others) initiated the dispute. Facing the prospect of pressure from the United States, rather than from Latin American countries alone, the EU was more likely to comply with an adverse ruling than in the past – but whether it would accommodate Ecuador's specific concerns in choosing how to do so was an open question.

Conventional measures of political power suggested that Ecuador's demands would carry little weight in this cacophony of competing interests. Ecuador is the world's largest banana exporter, but market power in that limited economic realm offered it little or no direct political leverage over the broad issue in dispute: EU trade preferences for former colonial territories. Power in the trade realm typically accrues to states that control market access, not to those that seek it, and Ecuador had little with which to threaten the EU. Despite overwhelming asymmetries (in market size, political clout, and legal resources) between Ecuador and the principal disputants on either side of the Atlantic, Ecuador managed to play an influential role throughout the controversy. Its negotiators did so by charting an independent and assertive course through the maze of WTO dispute settlement procedures, many of which at that time remained untested.

While collaborating with the other complainants, Ecuador's negotiators were careful to maintain their independence at several crucial junctures. When the United States moved quickly to retaliate against the EU, for example, Ecuador refused to follow its lead, insisting that a WTO compliance panel first rule on the legality of the revised European regulations. Although this move drew criticism from Washington, it won support from other member states and has since been adopted as customary practice in subsequent WTO disputes. Similarly, when the EU and United States finally reached a settlement, Ecuador initially refused to ratify their deal, threatening to challenge it before a second compliance panel unless important modifications were made.

Ecuador's negotiators also made assertive use of certain WTO rules to enhance their bargaining leverage. Two instances stand out as worthy of note. First, Ecuador sought and won the authority to retaliate against the EU by suspending benefits in areas outside of merchandise trade in goods – marking the first time that the WTO ever endorsed the right of cross-retaliation. Ecuador's innovative request to cross-retaliate focused on the intellectual property rights of European firms in several sensitive sectors, including industrial design patents, copyrights in the music industry, and (most significantly) geographical indications for alcoholic beverages. By obtaining this authority, Ecuador signaled its commitment to press for full compliance on the part of the EU, enhancing its leverage in subsequent negotiations.

Second, after reaching a settlement in the case, Ecuador continued to adopt an aggressive stance by demanding special institutional guarantees that the EU would honor its commitment to comply fully with the WTO rulings by 2006. During the Doha ministerial meetings, Ecuador made its support of two waivers sought by the EU (for the Cotonou pact and for the transitional banana regime, both of which give preferences to ACP countries) contingent on the creation of a special ad hoc arbitration procedure. This institutional innovation, which is outside of the normal WTO dispute settlement system, guaranteed a timely review of whether the EU's banana regime (for 2006 and beyond) will diminish the market access of Ecuador and other Latin American banana exporters. These countries successfully challenged the EU's tariff proposal through arbitration in 2005.

This combination of tactics enabled Ecuador to wield surprising influence over the ultimate resolution of the bananas dispute, considering the high profile of the case and the diversity of interests at stake. Although some distance from Ecuador's ideal point, the outcome was a compromise that incorporated many of Ecuador's core demands. The EU's twin settlements with the United States and Ecuador included a firm commitment to adopt by 2006 a tariff-only system, which favors Ecuador as the world's lowest-cost banana exporter. During the transitional phase of tariff quotas that began in 2001, Ecuador gained market access advantages over its Latin American competitors. The EU also made specific commitments that favored Ecuador's banana trading companies in the allocation of import licenses. Finally, in exchange for the waivers at Doha, Ecuador (and other Latin banana producers) obtained a special arbitration procedure from the EU that enhanced the speed and finality of third-party review.

In my view, Ecuador's negotiators achieved these results by capitalizing on the bargaining leverage afforded by certain WTO rules. The primary hypothesis for evaluation in this case is that Ecuador's tactics improved its position during compliance bargaining with the EU, generating a more favorable outcome than would otherwise have been available. To test this claim, it is important first to compare Ecuador's results with those of other Latin banana producers whose leaders chose a different path. The reference set includes governments that did not join the WTO case at all (such as Costa Rica and Colombia), as well as those that filed complaints but delegated more negotiating responsibility to the United States during the implementation phase (such as Guatemala and Honduras). In a second test, it may also be helpful to consider a counterfactual scenario: namely, what was the likely outcome if Ecuador had not asserted its independence from the US, threatened cross retaliation, contested the terms of the EU–US settlement, and held the waivers hostage at Doha?

Examining the details of the case with a focus on these twin tests, I conclude that Ecuador's bargaining strategy yielded demonstrable benefits. Had Ecuador not played its hand aggressively in negotiations with the EU, the result of the case would have been less advantageous to its banana producers and trading companies. The bargaining process, in my view, influenced the outcome of this dispute. It would be very difficult to understand the terms of the final settlements – especially the concessions Ecuador successfully exacted – without investigating details of the negotiations and understanding the specific institutional context in which they unfolded.

Generalizing from Ecuador's experience, this study emphasizes the way in which developing country negotiators may be able to utilize certain details of institutional design in the WTO to improve negotiated outcomes in bilateral trade disputes. The institution, in this approach, essentially operates as an intervening variable that affects the selection of bargaining strategies. These strategies, in turn, shape the distribution of benefits in any negotiated settlement. For political scientists, this study underscores the importance of attention to details of institutional design and their impact on bargaining.

I take the institutional setting of the WTO as exogenous in order to focus on compliance bargaining within that framework. Nevertheless, it is interesting to note that the very same details of institutional design utilized by Ecuador to gain leverage in the bananas dispute were originally established at the insistence of more powerful WTO members. The United States, in particular, was the foremost proponent of the right to cross-retaliate, which was an issue of critical importance to its intellectual property and service sectors during the Uruguay Round. Ironically, US negotiators had to overcome the objections of developing countries such as India. The common assumption was that cross retaliation would serve only to enforce the new areas agreements, not to legitimate violations of them. Similarly, the United States has been the staunchest defender of the tradition of consensus decision-making. Despite several provisions in WTO agreements for super-majority votes, the United States has objected to voting in any form whenever the topic has been broached – which the EU did twice in this dispute.[3] These institutional provisions, while obviously beneficial to powerful states, may also present opportunities for developing countries to improve their bargaining position, often in unanticipated ways.

The remainder of the chapter explores the details of Ecuador's role in the bananas dispute and assesses the implications of its strategy for other developing countries engaged in WTO compliance bargaining. The first section offers a brief overview of the complex economic and political terrain on which the bananas dispute took place, emphasizing the divergent interests of the various parties. Subsequent sections examine the results of Ecuador's bargaining tactics at four stages of the compliance bargaining process in turn: the sequencing crisis, the cross-retaliation request, the twin settlements, and the waivers.

1   Origins of the banana wars

The banana wars of the 1990s, which generated no fewer than five separate GATT and WTO rulings against the EU regime, originated in Europe's attempt to forge a common external trade policy with the advent of the single market in 1993. Beforehand, European countries had sharply divergent national regimes for banana imports. At the liberal end of the spectrum were Germany, Denmark, Ireland, and the Benelux countries, most of which applied a 20 percent tariff (Germany had no tariff) and imported bananas almost exclusively from the "dollar banana" zone of Central and South America. At the protectionist end of the spectrum were France, the United Kingdom, Italy, Greece, Spain, and Portugal, all of which used quota systems and tariff discrimination to grant preferential status to bananas from national producers or ACP countries, most of which were former colonial territories.[4]

After considerable debate and several months of delay, the EU Council of Ministers narrowly adopted Regulation 404 establishing the Common

---

[3] During the sequencing crisis (on whether the United States had to request a compliance panel before retaliating), the EU threatened to seek an authoritative interpretation from three-fourths of the member states. Later it raised the possibility of a similar three-fourths vote on the waivers.

[4] Tangermann 2003a, 19–28. Spain and Greece met domestic demand by producing their own bananas in the Canary Islands and Crete, respectively. Portugal met 40 percent of its consumption through production in the Azores and Madeira.

Organisation of the Market for Bananas (COMB), which went into effect on July 1, 1993.[5] The COMB, informally known as the European banana regime, harmonized the various national policies by erecting an extraordinarily complex system of quotas, tariffs, and licenses that restricted the market access of Central and South American bananas in favor of imports from ACP countries. These preferences reflected the fact that production costs in ACP countries were roughly twice those in the dollar banana zone.[6] This regime led to artificially high (and thus lucrative) banana prices in Europe.

The COMB regime, rather predictably, also led to a series of legal challenges. A coalition of Latin American banana producers – Colombia, Costa Rica, Guatemala, Nicaragua, and Venezuela – filed two complaints under GATT, the first against the policies of individual European countries in 1993 and the second against the COMB in 1994. Both GATT panels ruled against the EU, but in both cases the EU blocked adoption of the panel reports. At the same time, the EU separately attempted to appease the Latin American countries. In 1994 the EU signed the Banana Framework Agreement with four of the five complainants. Only Guatemala held out, refusing to settle. Colombia, Costa Rica, Nicaragua, and Venezuela agreed not to push for adoption of the second panel report and not to challenge the COMB until 2003.[7] In exchange, the EU offered increases in country-specific quota allocations, improving their market access. The EU also enabled them to issue export licenses for 70 percent of their quotas, transferring part of the quota rent formerly held by European importers.[8]

This attempt by the EU to settle the first two GATT complaints through the provision of country-specific side payments introduced sharp divisions within the dollar banana zone and eventually gave rise to a third case under the WTO. The Framework Agreement offered benefits only to certain Latin American producers – namely, those that had filed GATT complaints. Others in the region saw their market access in Europe, already jeopardized by the COMB, further deteriorate. By attempting to satisfy some of the larger Latin producers, in particular Colombia and Costa Rica, the EU alienated others.[9] In addition to Guatemala, which had refused to settle, the list of aggrieved countries now included Ecuador, Honduras, Mexico, and Panama.

---

[5] In two Council votes the COMB proposal barely exceeded the qualified majority of 54 votes, with margins of 4 votes in December 1992 and 2 votes in February 1993 (Tangermann 2003a, 35).
[6] Paggi and Spreen 2003, 14.   [7] Dickson 2002, 3.   [8] Tangermann 2003b, 47.
[9] Josling 2003, 175.

Also opposed to the COMB and the Framework Agreement were two influential US-based multinationals, Chiquita International and Dole Foods, which together account for more than half of world banana trade.[10] These two companies had pursued divergent corporate strategies for the single European market. Dole positioned itself to maintain market access in Europe. It diversified its holdings by investing in ACP banana production, and it acquired European ripening facilities in order to qualify for import licenses.[11] Chiquita bet instead that the single market in Europe would be essentially free and that it would be able to expand from its stronghold in Germany.[12] Under the new regime, Chiquita paid a heavy price for this miscalculation. Its share of the European market fell from 30 percent in 1992 to 19 percent by 1995. During the same period, by contrast, Dole's share rose from 12 to 16 percent.[13]

The United States had traditionally been laissez-faire in its approach to the banana trade. Attempts by US banana interests to involve the Bush administration in the first GATT case failed, in part because the Latin American complainants – presciently, in retrospect – did not want their interests to be lost in a US–EU battle.[14] Chiquita intensified its lobbying of the Clinton administration and Congress, however, and US Trade Representative (USTR) Mickey Kantor eventually agreed to initiate a WTO complaint against the EU in September 1995. Honduras and Guatemala, which were important suppliers of Chiquita, also joined the case at that time, as did Mexico (which then had links to Del Monte, the third largest trading company).

Meanwhile, the US had threatened Colombia and Costa Rica, both of which had settled their earlier complaints against Europe, with retaliatory action under Section 301. Although fearful of being caught in the transatlantic crossfire, Colombia and Costa Rica in January 1996 signed understandings with the United States that committed them to support an open market for bananas in Europe – despite the gains they stood to reap under the Framework Agreement. That pact obligated them not to join the case as complainants, but the United States ensured these two major banana exporters were no longer in the EU's camp before terminating its Section 301 actions.[15]

The missing piece in the coalition assembled by the United States was Ecuador. US officials were eager to have Ecuador join the WTO proceedings. Ecuador – as the "Saudi Arabia" of bananas – was in a special position to lend credibility to the US case.[16] The United States

---

[10] Paggi and Spreen 2003, 12.   [11] Stovall and Hathaway 2003, 152.
[12] Taylor 2003, 88.   [13] Ibid., 85.   [14] Stovall and Hathaway 2003, 153.
[15] Ibid., 155–56.   [16] Telephone interview with US official, Geneva, July 10, 2003.

obviously does not produce bananas, and both Honduras and Guatemala (relatively minor players, accounting for 7 percent of world exports) were seen as extensions of Chiquita, which had extensive operations in both countries.[17]

In this context, Ecuador was unique in several respects. First, it is by far the world's largest banana exporter, a distinction it has enjoyed since 1953.[18] Ecuador alone accounts for more than one-third of global banana exports (34 percent), with roughly twice the share of the next largest exporter (Costa Rica) in the late 1990s.[19] Second, in sharp contrast to other countries in the dollar banana zone, multinationals play a very limited role in the Ecuadorian industry. Significantly, Chiquita owns no banana farms in Ecuador, while Dole has only minor holdings.[20] Production lies almost exclusively in private local hands. Multinationals are active as traders of Ecuadorian bananas, but the largest export company in Ecuador, Grupo Noboa, is domestically owned.[21] There are also scores of other local trading companies whose combined market share is substantial. Finally, Ecuador is among the most efficient banana producers in the world, with production costs and average purchase prices even lower than those of its neighbors.[22]

Given Ecuador's status in the global market, bananas play a significant role in its domestic economy. In 1997 bananas become Ecuador's leading export product, and they have long been an important source of hard currency.[23] Bananas account for roughly 30 percent of total exports, making the economy dependent on secure access to banana markets overseas. Ecuador's position in Europe was impaired by Regulation 404 and especially by the Framework Agreement.[24] Given its competitive advantages in production and its firms' investments in the export business, Ecuador also stood to gain substantially from any further liberalization of Europe's banana markets.

In summary, Ecuador was important to the US case, and the WTO dispute was clearly of consequence to Ecuador. The only problem was that Ecuador was not a member of the WTO in 1995 when the case began.

---

[17] Paggi and Spreen 2003, 11–13.   [18] Brenes and Madrigal 2003, 105.

[19] Paggi and Spreen 2003, 11; Brenes and Madrigal 2003, 102.

[20] Taylor 2003, 97.

[21] Grupo Noboa is the fourth-largest banana trading company in the world (after Chiquita, Dole, and Del Monte). It controls more than 10 percent of global trade and more than one-third of Ecuador's exports. It also has the world's largest shipping operation; is the most diversified exporter among the large trading companies; and controls a significant share of the European market (Brenes and Madrigal 2003, 107).

[22] Paggi and Spreen 2003, 14; Brenes and Madrigal 2003, 108.

[23] Brenes and Madrigal 2003, 105.

[24] Stovall and Hathaway 2003, 156; Brenes and Madrigal 2003, 116.

Officials in Ecuador decided that the case was of such paramount concern that they rushed their negotiations to gain entry to the WTO in order to ensure their status as a complainant. Domestic firms in other sectors complained about the speed of the accession process, but the timetable was driven by the bananas dispute.[25] Panama, which also suffered under the Framework Agreement, was in a similar position, but it did not manage to complete the accession process until September 1997, after the initial panel ruling had been issued.[26] Ecuador's accession was tenuous also within the WTO, where it barely collected enough votes to clear the two-thirds threshold in time.[27] Ecuador officially joined the WTO on January 26, 1996. Less than two weeks later, it joined the request for consultations in the bananas dispute.[28]

2   The sequencing crisis

The early stages of the banana dispute unfolded largely as expected. With previous GATT panel rulings on their side, the complainants were confident in the legal merits of the case. To gain maximum leverage, their strategy was to allege a broad array of violations under WTO agreements covering both goods and services.[29] This approach paid off, as both the panel and the Appellate Body found the EU regime to be incompatible with a variety of WTO commitments.[30] The EU's quota allocation and import licensing systems violated the non-discrimination and national treatment provisions of both GATT and GATS. The rulings also held that the existing waiver for the EU–ACP Lomé Convention did not cover these violations.[31] The EU was given fifteen months to comply. In late 1998 it adopted a revised import scheme, but neither Ecuador nor the United States viewed the modified rules as WTO compliant.

How to proceed at this point in the dispute was not clear under the rules of the WTO Dispute Settlement Understanding (DSU). The EU contended that its revised regime should be deemed acceptable until a compliance panel convened under DSU Article 21.5 ruled otherwise. The United States, by contrast, argued that it could move immediately

---

[25] Interview with Ecuadorian official, Geneva, October 1, 2002.
[26] See list of accession dates at <http://www.wto.org/english/thewto_e/acc_e/completeacc_e. htm>.
[27] Interview with WTO official, Geneva, November 7, 2003. To avoid uncertainty during future accessions, the WTO General Council reinforced its preference for consensus decisions (among members present) in a contemporaneous "statement" by the Chairman; see WTO Document WT/L/93 (November 24, 1995).
[28] Josling 2003, 175–76.   [29] Stovall and Hathaway 2003, 156.
[30] For the appellate decision, see WTO Document WT/DS27/AB/R (September 9, 1997).
[31] Josling 2003, 178–85.

to request authority to retaliate at the conclusion of the reasonable time period for implementation. In its view, a panel requested by the EU under DSU Article 22.6 to determine the appropriate level of sanctions did not have to await a ruling by a compliance panel. The text of the DSU did not clearly specify the relationship between the two review processes under Articles 21 and 22, creating what became known as the "sequencing" problem.[32]

Any debate regarding how to interpret these two DSU provisions would not seem to involve terribly high stakes. What appeared to be a minor procedural glitch, however, became a full-blown institutional crisis. Both the United States and the EU depicted the issue as a threat to the viability of the DSU itself. For the United States, if sanctions were not available at the end of the (already lengthy) reasonable time period for compliance, the credibility of the entire system would suffer as countries that ignored or evaded WTO rulings further delayed the day of reckoning. For the EU, if complainants were allowed unilaterally to judge whether replacement measures were lawful – and to request sanctions on the basis of that judgment alone – the WTO's guarantee of multilateral review would mean little.

Brooking no compromise, the two sides brought the work of the Dispute Settlement Body (DSB) to a halt over the usually routine adoption of the agenda, an unprecedented departure from customary practice. The EU threatened to seek an authoritative interpretation of the DSU from WTO members, which could issue such a decision by a three-fourths vote. The United States adamantly refused to allow the WTO to vote on such a sensitive issue. Although it seems odd in retrospect, it is no exaggeration to claim that the future of the WTO dispute settlement system hung in the balance for several days. Eventually, both sides moved forward on their preferred paths simultaneously, but no agreement was reached on how to resolve the sequencing problem.[33]

This crisis placed Ecuador in an extremely delicate situation.[34] Its leaders were lobbied heavily by USTR (itself under pressure from Congress) to join the US move toward immediate retaliation.[35] To the disappointment of hardliners in Washington, Ecuador decided to go it alone. Instead of pursuing retaliation, Ecuador requested that the original panel first

---

[32] For a legal overview of the crisis, see Salas and Jackson 2000.
[33] This account draws on interviews with various US and EU officials in Geneva, Washington, and Brussels during 1999 and 2002.
[34] Telephone interview with Ecuadorian official, Geneva, October 16, 2002.
[35] There were some divisions within the US camp. At least one official from the State Department quietly encouraged Ecuador early on to request an Article 21.5 panel, hoping such a move would prompt the United States to do the same. Telephone interview with US official, Geneva, July 10, 2003.

be reconstituted under Article 21.5 to review the legality of the EU's revised regime.[36] The United States then moved alone to retaliate against the EU and filed a new complaint against the revised banana scheme with Guatemala, Honduras, Mexico, and Panama (which had become a WTO member).[37] As the compliance panel began its work, Ecuador's Ambassador to the EU explained his government's decision – and chided the twin trade powers: "Both the US and the EU need to recognize that other countries are heavily impacted by the prolonged bilateral 'to-ing and fro-ing' that is taking place. While these two giants battle it out, Ecuador, whose industry is really at stake, is being caught in the middle."[38]

Ecuador's establishment of the compliance panel under Article 21.5 proved to be helpful in resolving the sequencing crisis. Rather bizarrely, three separate panels – all with the same members as the original panel – were working at the same time: two under Article 21.5 (as requested by the EU and Ecuador), and one under Article 22.6 (to determine the level of US sanctions). The panelists strategically delayed their Article 22.6 ruling so that all three reports could be issued at the same time in April 1999. Through this maneuver, they were able to rely on the findings of Ecuador's compliance panel that the EU regime remained illegal when authorizing the United States to suspend concessions against Europe. The US–EU sequencing debate was by no means resolved, but Ecuador's decision to have a compliance panel review any replacement measure before requesting sanctions became customary practice in subsequent WTO disputes.

This somewhat risky move to distance itself from the United States offered several advantages to Ecuador. First, it helped the disputants and panelists overcome the sequencing impasse, allowing the case to move forward. Second, in contrast to the other Latin co-complainants, it sig-naled Ecuador's willingness to act independently and to disagree openly with the United States. Finally, as an integrative tactic of sorts in the framework of Odell,[39] the move also won Ecuador appreciation from the EU and support from other delegations that shared its interpretation of the DSU. The EU representative in the DSB, for example, stated that the EU "recognized, in particular, that Ecuador, unlike other Members, had followed all the correct steps under the DSU in order to defend

---

[36] WTO Document WT/DS27/41 (December 18, 1998).
[37] WTO Documents WT/DS27/43 (January 14, 1999) and WT/DS158/1 (January 25, 1999).
[38] "Ecuador Charges US and EU with Exploiting Banana Issue," *South-North Development Monitor* (available on web at <http://www.twnside.org.sg/title/eu-cn.htm>).
[39] Odell 2000.

its rights."[40] This accumulated goodwill with the EU was reportedly helpful to Ecuador as negotiators from all sides later worked to reach a settlement.[41]

3   The cross-retaliation request

While the United States moved quickly to impose sanctions, Ecuador opted to allow time for negotiations with the EU, even after the compliance panel's ruling, in the hopes of reaching a settlement. In a creative maneuver, Ecuador had specifically asked the compliance panel to go beyond its traditional mandate by offering policy guidance. The panel, in response, identified three general approaches that might bring the EU regime into compliance with WTO rules.[42] These recommendations were the basis for talks that continued throughout the summer of 1999. During this period there was movement, as both the United States and Ecuador modified certain demands.[43] By the fall, however, it became clear that the EU was not easily going to be able to forge a settlement that would win approval from the United States, Ecuador, and EU member states.[44]

After this series of intensive consultations yielded little progress, Ecuador was eventually prompted to threaten sanctions itself, despite the obvious obstacles it faced as a small developing country. On November 8, 1999, the EU delivered a routine status report on its efforts to comply with the WTO rulings. The report, however, also noted that the EU Commission would issue a formal proposal on ways to resolve the dispute later that week.[45] Ecuador's negotiators, frustrated and aware that matters could be coming to a head, filed their request for authority to retaliate against the EU the very next day. Given the timing, the request seems to have been an attempt to enhance Ecuador's leverage at a crucial juncture; the text notes that Ecuador "does not rule out the possibility that progress may be made in the coming days in bilateral consultations" on the issue of compensation, which Ecuador clearly preferred to retaliation.[46] Of course, no quick progress was made. Ecuador had instead opened a new phase of the dispute.

---

[40] WTO Document WT/DSB/M/78 (May 12, 2000), 8.
[41] Telephone interview with EU official, Brussels, July 18, 2003.
[42] Josling 2003, 190.
[43] "US, EU Wrestle over Three Proposals for New Banana Trade Rules," *Inside U.S. Trade* 17 (3 September 1999), 15.
[44] "EU Official Reports Failure to Reach Consensus on New Banana Regime," *Inside U.S. Trade* 17 (10 September 1999), 3–6.
[45] WTO Document WT/DS27/51Add.3 (November 8, 1999).
[46] WTO Document WT/DS27/52 (November 9, 1999).

The WTO enforcement system relies on decentralized sanctions, a remedy that is intrinsically more attractive to larger, less trade dependent economies than to small developing countries. In the bananas dispute, several factors made any move toward retaliation a daunting prospect for Ecuador. First, Ecuador's imports from Europe were an infinitesimal share of EU trade. Losing access to the Ecuadorian market was unlikely to do serious harm to any European exporters. Second, the majority of imports from Europe were capital goods and raw materials without which the Ecuadorian economy was almost certain to suffer. Finally, the level of injury caused by the EU banana regime was large as a proportion of imports from Europe. Ecuador estimated that the level of nullification and impairment in the case (which it put at $450 million per year) amounted to more than half of all goods exported by the EU to Ecuador.[47]

Aware of these obstacles, Ecuador adopted an innovative and unprecedented strategy in its request for sanctions. Instead of relying on the goods sector, it proposed to suspend the application of intellectual property rights under the TRIPS Agreement. DSU Article 22 included certain rules enabling complainants to suspend obligations under one WTO treaty in order to induce compliance with another covered agreement. A coalition of developed countries led by the United States had insisted on these cross-retaliation provisions during the Uruguay Round. Their objective was to ensure that the United States, for example, could use its leverage as an importer of goods to compel compliance by developing countries with new rules on services and intellectual property. Ecuador aimed to reverse the arrow, retaliating under TRIPS – an agreement highly valued by the software, entertainment, and pharmaceutical industries – to ensure EU compliance with GATT. Histories of the Uruguay Round negotiations suggest that no delegations anticipated such a move; many developing countries, in fact, were staunch opponents of cross-retaliation.

With this request, Ecuador was charting new legal territory. Not only was it the first attempt by a developing country to retaliate against a developed country in the GATT or WTO, it was also the first use of cross-retaliation by any WTO member.[48] Ecuador's initial request did not offer many details on how it would seek to utilize any authority to retaliate under TRIPS. It simply identified three general types of intellectual property that were in the cross-hairs: music copyrights, geographical

[47] WTO Document WT/DS27/52 (November 9, 1999), 2.
[48] Technically, US retaliation in the bananas dispute also crossed agreements, as the US imposed sanctions under GATT for EU violations of both GATT and GATS.

indications, and industrial designs.[49] The EU immediately demanded arbitration on both the amount and the form of retaliation that Ecuador proposed, raising a host of legal objections.

It was during this arbitration that the details of Ecuador's strategy came to light. The first aspect to note is the sophistication of Ecuador's target selection. On the political side, Ecuador exempted both the Netherlands and Denmark from its request, in recognition of their 1998 votes against the revised banana regime.[50] Ecuador's objective was to focus on EU members (such as France, Spain, and the United Kingdom) that were most hostile to liberalization. In terms of economic impact, Ecuador restricted its targets to categories of intellectual property in which there was little or no technology transfer, protecting its access to valuable technologies.

To defend itself against legal challenges, Ecuador proposed an innovative system of limited and revocable licenses. In effect, the government would grant licenses to domestic firms to violate TRIPS only up to certain specified levels – and for markets only within Ecuador. The EU had objected that Ecuador would have few means of ensuring that its sanctions did not exceed the authorized level. But Ecuador rebutted these assertions using estimates calculated by European industry associations regarding the size of its domestic market. For example, the combined value of its markets for European music and for alcoholic products with European geographical indications was smaller than the level of authorized sanctions.[51] Another crucial aspect of the licensing system is that the licenses would be temporary and could be revoked once the EU came into compliance.

In March 2000, the arbitrators delivered their decision, siding with Ecuador almost across the board.[52] By effectively playing "the developing country card," in the words of one EU negotiator, Ecuador had persuaded the arbitrators that it met the standards set forth under DSU Article 22.3.[53] In particular, Ecuador demonstrated to the panel's satisfaction that it was neither "practicable" nor "effective" for it to retaliate exclusively against European goods and services, and that circumstances were "serious enough" for it to justify suspending concessions under TRIPS.

The arbitrators required that Ecuador begin its retaliation against consumer non-durable goods, but permitted it to apply the balance of its $201.6 million annual authority under TRIPS. They also warned that any suspension of TRIPS, even if carefully crafted, involved a number of

---

[49] WTO Document WT/DS27/52 (November 9, 1999), 3.
[50] Josling 2003, 190.   [51] Interview with Ecuadorian official, Geneva, October 1, 2002.
[52] WTO Document WT/DS27/ARB/ECU (March 24, 2000).
[53] Telephone interview with EU official, Brussels, July 18, 2003.

potential legal complications of which Ecuador should remain aware. Ecuador had always acknowledged that any use of TRIPS would be messy – one official likened it to "using a shotgun to hit a precise target"– but part of the strategy's utility came from this very fact.[54] Ecuador's negotiators, admitting the limited size of their markets, stressed the implications of their TRIPS maneuver as an example for larger developing countries such as India and Brazil.

The response to Ecuador's request and the arbitration ruling was predictably mixed. Other developing countries, such as Honduras and Guatemala, applauded Ecuador on its "great achievement" and expressed gratitude to it for having "removed the obstacles faced by small and weak economies."[55] The United States, another co-complainant, was far more restrained. While some US officials welcomed any development that placed additional pressure on the EU, USTR quickly sent a team of lawyers from Washington to ask questions and express concerns to Ecuador's WTO Ambassador – who refused to meet with them, sending his senior staff aide instead.[56]

EU officials initially viewed Ecuador's proposed retaliation as a "real concern," primarily because of the precedent it would set for future disputes.[57] Even if Ecuador were to act on its authority, the economic impact on the EU would be relatively minor. This fact was of little consolation, however, to certain EU industries that feared what the precedent could mean for their rights under TRIPS in other disputes. A number of EU governments and firms requested meetings with Ecuadorian diplomats across Europe, mainly to ask questions about the intended targets.[58] The only industry to mount a concerted lobbying effort was the European Confederation of Spirits Producers (CEPS). Its representatives informed EU officials that they were prepared to apply aggressive measures if Ecuador violated their geographical indications, including a boycott and a campaign to label it as an international pariah.[59] In its annual report, CEPS touted its efforts: "CEPS secured the European Commission's assurance that it would seek to prevent any WTO retaliation by Ecuador, including its threatened withdrawal of protection for spirits with geographical indications."[60]

Ecuador soon took steps to move forward on its threat, issuing a lengthy target list of consumer non-durable imports from Europe, as

[54] Telephone interview with Ecuadorian official, Geneva, October 16, 2002.
[55] WTO Document WT/DSB/M/78 (May 12, 2000), 9.
[56] Telephone interview with Ecuadorian official, Geneva, October 16, 2002.
[57] Telephone interview with EU official, Brussels, July 18, 2003.
[58] Interview with Ecuadorian official, Geneva, October 1, 2002.
[59] Interview with EU official, Geneva, June 10, 2002.
[60] *CEPS Annual Report 2000* (Brussels: European Confederation of Spirits Producers), 23.

required by the arbitrators, in May 2000.[61] By that time, however, many observers suspected that Ecuador would not actually impose sanctions. Press reports from that period suggested that Ecuadorian officials had given assurances to the EU that retaliation would not occur.[62] It is not clear why Ecuador backed down. One official pointed to the intrinsic risks of violating TRIPS, emphasizing that it could easily discourage the foreign investment that Ecuador (like other developing countries) was eager to attract.[63] Another official suggested that the authority was mainly intended to be of symbolic value, establishing a precedent of concern to the EU.[64]

Other reports, however, suggest that Ecuador did in fact obtain material assistance on a separate issue – namely, its severe financial crisis – in return for forgoing its authority to retaliate. In particular, the EU is said to have quietly "supported Ecuador in the reduction of its external debt in the Club of Paris in exchange for Ecuador's not implementing cross retaliation."[65] Confirming this quid pro quo through official sources is difficult, but the timeline of events makes it plausible. In 1999 Ecuador's real GDP tumbled, its currency collapsed, and it became the first Latin country to default on its Brady bonds. A plan to adopt the US dollar as the national currency led to political crisis and military intervention in January 2000.

Against this dramatic backdrop – during critical negotiations with the IMF, multilateral development banks, the Paris Club, and private creditors – Ecuador decided to pursue cross-retaliation. In March 2000, the same month in which it won authority to retaliate from the WTO, Ecuador secured a $2 billion financial support package from the IMF, World Bank, Inter American Development Bank, and Andean Development Corporation.[66] Negotiations with creditors in the Paris Club were the next step. After three difficult days of talks, the Paris Club agreed in September 2000 – just four months after Ecuador published its list of targets – to reschedule $880 million of Ecuador's external debt.[67] Of the ten Paris Club governments participating in this debt reorganization, five were EU members. The twin agreements ensured that Ecuador was able

---

[61] WTO Document WT/DS27/54 (May 8, 2000).
[62] Saint Lucia's representative referred with relief to these reports in the DSB. See WTO Document WT/DSB/M/78 (May 12, 2000), 10.
[63] Telephone interview with Ecuadorian official, Brussels, July 22, 2003.
[64] Telephone interview with Ecuadorian official, Geneva, October 16, 2002.
[65] Vranes 2002, 214.
[66] "IMF, World Bank, IDB and CAF Prepared to Support Ecuador", IMF News Brief 00–14 (March 9, 2000), International Monetary Fund, Washington, DC.
[67] "The Paris Club Agrees to a Debt Rescheduling for Ecuador," Paris Club Press Release (September 15, 2000).

to meet its financial obligations. Many considerations (such as macroeco-
nomic policy commitments) shaped these talks, but Ecuador might have
gained some informal leverage with international financial institutions by
declining to retaliate in the WTO.

Whatever the rationale for Ecuador's decision to forgo sanctions,
observers in the WTO and participants in the dispute agree that the
pace of negotiations with the EU on bananas accelerated as the prospect
of cross-retaliation approached.[68] The EU attempted, for example, to
arrange compensation for Ecuador – in terms of trade preferences, development aid, or debt reduction – but the Commission encountered obstacles to all three forms of formal compensation (any of which Ecuador
would have preferred to retaliating).[69] It also continued to consult with
Ecuador while trying to forge a settlement with the different stakehold-
ers. And there is evidence that EU leaders offered assistance on Ecuador's
financial crisis if it abstained from retaliation. In sum, Ecuador's innovative cross-retaliation gambit – which it undertook alone – appeared to
enhance its leverage beyond what WTO remedies would normally provide
a small developing country.

4   The twin settlements

Throughout late 1999 and 2000, the EU had conducted extensive consultations with the various parties to the dispute. Since at least November
1999, it seemed clear that the most likely resolution would involve two
stages, with a revised tariff quota system as a transitional device en route
to a tariff-only regime. Within its coalition, EU officials were juggling
competing claims from ACP countries, banana importers, and divided
member states. The chief difficulty confronted by the EU vis-à-vis the
complainants, however, was that the United States and Ecuador sharply
disagreed on what a transitional tariff quota system should look like.
As Ecuador moved forward with its authority to retaliate, the EU's representative in the DSB summed up its dilemma as follows: "The EC
had a choice either to satisfy Ecuador and to remain under sanctions of
US$191.4 million or to satisfy the United States and to remain under
sanctions of US$201.6 million."[70]

---

[68] Telephone interviews with WTO Secretariat official, Geneva, June 12, 2003; with U.S.
official, Geneva, July 10, 2003; and with Ecuadorian official, Geneva, October 16, 2002.
[69] Interview with EU official, Geneva, June 10, 2002; telephone interview with EU official,
Brussels, July 18, 2003.
[70] WTO Document WT/DSB/M/78 (May 12, 2000), 8.

This assertion was not entirely accurate, but there were indeed a number of basic issues on which the United States and Ecuador differed. The first was regarding the desirability of a tariff-only system as the ultimate outcome. In the early stages of the dispute, both the United States and Ecuador favored such a solution, but under pressure from Chiquita – which, facing the prospect of bankruptcy, came to value the guaranteed market shares and rents associated with quota allocations – US officials later signaled their willingness to accept a revised tariff quota system during a transitional period of indeterminate length.[71] Even Ecuador wavered at times on this point, but in the end its negotiators pressed for a firm commitment from the EU to adopt a tariff-only regime by a date certain.

The more fundamental differences between the complainants dealt with the design of any transitional tariff quota system. One issue was the size of the quotas for each of the exporting countries in the dollar banana zone. If allocated on a country-specific basis, these quotas obviously imply a zero-sum game between Ecuador and the Central American complainants. The more complicated issues, however, dealt with the administration of the import licensing system for banana trading companies. One recurring debate was the selection of a historical reference period. This period would be used to determine the licenses allocated to "traditional" importers under any new regime. Chiquita, which lost market share immediately after Regulation 404 went into effect, pushed the United States to insist on a pre-1993 period. Ecuador, by contrast, at first opposed any reference period and later requested a more recent period, 1995–97, because its trading companies had gained licenses by that time.[72] Ecuador also wanted to secure improved access for so-called "newcomers" – which Chiquita clearly was not. In particular, Ecuador pressed for newcomers to have no less than a 20 percent market share, while the United States proposed only 12.5 percent.[73]

With the Bush administration in power and with a growing list of transatlantic trade disputes, both sides sought in early 2001 to resolve the festering banana dispute once and for all. On April 11, 2001, the United States and EU announced an agreement to settle the case. As expected,

[71] "US, EU Wrestle over Three Proposals for New Banana Trade Rules," *Inside U.S. Trade* 17 (September 3, 1999), 15–17.
[72] "US, EU Wrestle over Three Proposals for New Banana Trade Rules," *Inside U.S. Trade* 17 (3 September 1999), 15–16. Also "US, EU Continue Wrangling Over Commission Banana Proposal," *Inside U.S. Trade* 18 (November 17, 2000), 10.
[73] "US, EU Banana Deal will be Implemented in Stages, Beginning in July," *Inside U.S. Trade* 19 (April 13, 2001), 19; and "Banana Deal Effectively Locks in US Share of EU Market," *Inside U.S. Trade* 19 (April 13, 2001), 24.

the EU would adopt a transitional tariff quota system before moving to a tariff-only regime by 2006.[74] Ecuador's response was swift and, on the surface, severe. Its negotiators denounced the agreement in an April 16 press release: "In order to defend the two million Ecuadorians for whom the banana industry is their livelihood, the government of Ecuador will not declare that the 'banana war' is over until a fair agreement is reached which takes into account the interests of Ecuador, the largest banana exporter in the world, and the main supplier to the EU."[75]

Ecuador immediately requested consultations with the EU, threatening to reconvene an Article 21.5 compliance panel to review the US–EU agreement if its concerns were not addressed.[76] From a legal perspective, this threat was all too credible, as even an internal EU study admitted that any licensing system based on a historical reference period "would be vulnerable" to a legal challenge.[77] For the case to be fully resolved and removed from the WTO agenda, Ecuador would have to agree, and this fact gave it leverage during the consultations that followed.

While Ecuadorian officials condemned the agreement in the press, observers noted that the US–EU deal already included substantial benefits for Ecuador.[78] The EU had anticipated Ecuador's response in its talks with the US, playing that card openly to resist certain US demands. According to one US negotiator, the EU frequently exclaimed, "But what about Ecuador? We can't agree to that."[79] Because several of Ecuador's concerns had already been accommodated, its aggressive stance was primarily a negotiating tactic to extract additional concessions from the EU – and this strategy was successful in many respects.

Still, it was not a course without risks. As one official noted, "Ecuador is also keenly aware of the price it may pay for pursuing a dispute settlement panel . . . It is difficult for Ecuador as a small developing country with severe economic problems to resist major pressure from the US and EU over the banana issue."[80] Ecuador enjoyed support from certain EU member states: Sweden, Finland, Austria, and Germany all complained

---

[74] "US, EU Banana Deal will be Implemented in Stages, Beginning in July," *Inside U.S. Trade* 19 (April 13, 2001), 1, 18–21.
[75] "Ecuador Seeks Changes in Banana Deal, Threatens Consultations," *Inside U.S. Trade* 19 (April 20, 2001), 19.
[76] WTO Document WT/DS27/55 (April 20, 2001).
[77] "Internal EU Paper Says Banana Deal Could Run Afoul of the WTO," *Inside U.S. Trade* 19 (April 27, 2001).
[78] "Ecuador Seeks Changes in Banana Deal, Threatens Consultations," *Inside U.S. Trade* 19 (April 20, 2001), 1, 18–19.
[79] Telephone interview with US official, Geneva, July 10, 2003.
[80] "Ecuador Seeks Changes in Banana Deal, Threatens Consultations," *Inside U.S. Trade* 19 (April 20, 2001), 18.

that the settlement did not adequately protect Ecuador's interests.[81] After two weeks of talks, Ecuador and the EU reached a separate agreement that modified aspects of the US–EU deal, adding terms that improved Ecuador's access to import licenses.[82]

What did Ecuador receive in these twin settlements? First, in terms of the original US–EU deal, Ecuador was pleased to see a firm commitment by the EU to adopt a tariff-only system by 2006. Throughout the negotiations, Ecuador had insisted on such a system, with strong support from certain EU members, especially Germany. The US–EU agreement also called for an increase of 100,000 tons in the quota allocated to dollar zone bananas, which was more than the EU had previously offered to transfer from the ACP quota. Also crucial was the removal of the country-specific quota allocations that had been part of the EU's Framework Agreement. This reform favored Ecuador at the expense of Costa Rica and Colombia, which was to be "particularly hurt" by the change.[83] In terms of the historical reference period, Ecuador had to accept 1994–96 rather than 1995–97, but in its view either was better than the pre-1993 period the United States had backed. Moreover, this historical reference period applied only through 2003; during the final two years of the transitional regime, import licenses would be allocated on the basis of usage during 2002 and 2003, which Ecuador applauded. Finally, although it had pressed for a 20 per cent market share for newcomers, Ecuador preferred the 17 percent on which the United States and EU settled to the 12.5 percent formerly proposed by the United States.

Despite these accommodations, Ecuador still had a series of specific concerns regarding implementation of the US–EU deal. In particular, it worried that the EU's management of import licenses in the newcomer (or "non-traditional" operator) category would deny its traders access to the increased quota for dollar zone bananas. Noboa was guaranteed to retain a share of roughly 5 or 6 percent of available licenses, but there were concerns that a politically important Ecuadorian operator, Costa Trading, and others could suffer under the transitional regime.[84] Ecuador pressed for and received a number of new rules that would ensure its operators a fair chance to compete for licenses. Among other provisions,

[81] "EU Members Unlikely to Block Banana Deal as Ecuador Seeks Changes," *Inside U.S. Trade* 19 (April 27, 2001), 5.

[82] WTO Document WT/DS27/60 (July 9, 2001).

[83] "Ecuador Seeks Changes in Banana Deal, Threatens Consultations," *Inside U.S. Trade* 19 (April 20, 2001), 18.

[84] US, EU Banana Deal will be Implemented in Stages, Beginning in July," *Inside U.S. Trade* 19 (April 13, 2001), 19; "Ecuador Seeks Changes in Banana Deal, Threatens Consultations," *Inside U.S. Trade* 19 (April 20, 2001), 1, 18.

the Ecuador–EU pact established minimum thresholds (on years of registration and import volumes) and operational requirements (regarding shipping and security deposits) that would discourage speculators from applying for import licenses that they intended only to resell to operators actually in possession of bananas.[85]

These additional provisions discouraging secondary market speculators and fraud reassured Ecuador substantially. Less widely publicized was another development of value to Ecuador. In additional to increasing the quota for dollar zone bananas by 100,000 tons, the EU reassigned the Dominican Republic in June 2001 from the Latin American quota to the ACP quota.[86] The effect of this move was to increase the available market share for dollar zone bananas by almost another 100,000 tons.[87]

Did the deal Ecuador negotiated work to its advantage once the EU implemented the transitional regime in 2001? The answer, at this point, is clearly yes. Perhaps the best evidence of Ecuador's successful tactics leading up to the twin settlements is its growing share of the EU market in the brief interval since July 2001. In terms of export trends, the volume of Ecuador's banana exports (measured in tons) to the EU fell 6 percent overall between 1997 and 2000, but then began to rise – growing by 2 per cent in 2001, then by a full 18 per cent in 2002, before leveling off in 2003 and 2004.[88] Ecuador's share of the total EU market reached a low point of 14.7 per cent in 1998; after the settlement, it jumped to 17.8 per cent in 2001 and then to a record high of 20.3 per cent in 2002.[89] Similarly, the value of Ecuador's banana exports to the EU, after falling 1 per cent in 2000, rose 12 per cent in 2001 and 22 per cent in 2002, then fell 5 per cent in 2003 before increasing 6 per cent in 2004.[90]

To assess Ecuador's tactics, it is obviously important to compare its results to those of its Latin competitors. After the settlement, Ecuador quickly began to outperform its rivals in the EU banana market. Colombia and Costa Rica, which – having benefited from the country-specific quotas of the 1994 Framework Agreement – did not join the WTO case, saw their market shares stagnate around 16 per cent in 2000–2002 as

[85] WTO Document WT/DS27/58 (July 2, 2001), 6–7.
[86] The Dominican Republic only joined the ACP in 1990 upon ratifying the Lomé IV Convention. See web at <http://www.rvhb.com/faq_15.htm>. Unlike other ACP banana producers, it lacked a former colonial patron in Europe. These factors could explain its anomalous connection to the dollar zone quota and subsequent transfer.
[87] Telephone interview with Ecuadorian official, Brussels, July 22, 2003.
[88] Data from EUROSTAT.
[89] Data from 1990–2002 provided by the European Community Banana Trade Association, Brussels, Belgium.
[90] Data from EUROSTAT and Haver Analytics / Eurostat Data Shop, New York.

Ecuador's climbed above 20 per cent. Between 2001 and 2002, the market shares of co-complainants Guatemala, Honduras, and Mexico all fell, as did that of latecomer Panama.[91] In terms of tons sold in the EU, Ecuador's increase – both overall and in percentage terms – between 2000 and 2004 was larger than that of its Latin rivals.[92]

These results are consistent with market projections. Using a partial equilibrium model, Guyomard and Le Mouël estimate that Latin banana producers are likely to capture the lion's share of increases in EU consumption between 2000 and 2005.[93] Those gains, however, are not equally distributed. Using 1996–98 as a base period, they predict Ecuador's global banana exports to grow 20 per cent by 2005. Their simulation projects that none of the Latin governments that joined the WTO case, nor those that remained on the sidelines, are likely to see their global banana exports increase by nearly as much as Ecuador's – even in percentage terms. Measured in tons, Ecuador's estimated increase is larger than that of all other Latin banana exporters combined.[94]

What is striking is that Ecuador is gaining under a transitional EU system designed to restrict its market access on behalf of ACP countries. From January 2006 onward, the EU is to abolish the tariff-rate quotas of the transitional regime in favor of a tariff-only system. Although much will depend on how high the EU sets its tariffs (as emphasized in the next section), analysts expect Ecuador's banana exporters to perform even better once the EU terminates the transitional regime and complies fully with its WTO obligations in 2006.

Initial reports are positive for Ecuador in terms of Latin banana exports to the EU. Data on the performance and license allocations of Ecuador's banana trading companies, by contrast, are far more difficult to obtain. Nevertheless, applying the counterfactual test, it is reasonable to conclude that had Ecuador not bargained assertively and independently of the United States during settlement negotiations, its trading companies would have seen their access to import licenses diminished in favor of US multinationals. The United States, as noted, sought to limit the access of

---

[91] Measured on the basis of tons sold in the EU, the declining market shares for each country were as follows in 2001 and 2002: Guatemala fell from 0.08 to 0.001 per cent; Honduras from 2.7 to 0.5 per cent; Mexico from 0.0014 to 0.0009 per cent; and Panama from 8.8 to 7.5 per cent. Colombia's share held steady at 16.3 per cent, while Costa Rica's increased slightly from 16 to 16.8 per cent. Data provided by the European Community Banana Trade Association, Brussels, Belgium.
[92] In tons sold, Ecuador's increase was 15 per cent; Costa Rica's, 14 per cent; and Colombia's, 8 per cent. The total for Guatemala decreased 93 per cent; for Honduras, 83 per cent; and for Panama, 18 per cent. Data from EUROSTAT.
[93] Guyomard and Le Mouël 2003.   [94] Ibid., 151.

newcomers from Ecuador and elsewhere and pushed to adopt historical reference periods most favorable to US-based Chiquita. The eventual US–EU settlement split the difference between Ecuador and the United States on these license allocation issues, and the subsequent Ecuador-EU agreement added additional conditions of value to Ecuadorian operators. Had Ecuador chosen the path of its Latin co-complainants, which delegated more fully to the United States, its banana trading companies would have faced larger obstacles in competing for EU licenses.

5   The waivers

Although satisfied generally with the terms of the twin settlements, Ecuador and other Latin American producers remained anxious about how the EU would transition to a tariff-only system in 2006. In particular, they feared that the EU would set the tariffs on dollar zone bananas so high, compared to their ACP competitors, that it would price them out of the market. For the EU to maintain any kind of tariff differential between ACP and Latin bananas would require waivers from WTO rules. The waiver that applied to the Lomé IV pact between the EU and ACP expired in February 2000, like that agreement itself. To fully resolve the banana dispute, given the WTO rulings, the EU needed two waivers: one from GATT Article XIII for its transitional banana regime until the end of 2005, and another from GATT Article I for the new EU–ACP Cotonou agreement, which was to be in effect until the end of 2007.

In the WTO, waivers are traditionally granted only through consensus. The EU knew that this decision rule opened the door to mischief on the part of the complainants in the banana dispute (among others). As a result, its settlements with the United States and Ecuador obligated each of them to "lift its reserve" regarding the Article I waiver and to "actively work toward promoting the acceptance" of the Article XIII waiver.[95] The EU hoped that the road to these waivers would be relatively smooth after the settlements. Ecuador, after all, had been the most active opponent of the waivers when it sought changes in the US–EU pact.[96] There was likely to be opposition from Costa Rica and Colombia, the two parties most harmed by the twin settlements, but the EU hoped to be able to compensate them.

In the months after the settlements, the EU resumed trying to commence the required working party review of its waiver requests in the

---

[95] WTO Document WT/DS27/58 (July 2, 2001), 2, 5.
[96] In an April 18, 2001, meeting of the Goods Council, Ecuador "tried unsuccessfully to block the agenda item" on the waiver. See, "Latin WTO Members Speak out against EU Tariff Banana Waiver," *Inside U.S. Trade* 19 (April 20, 2001), 10.

Council on Trade in Goods. Each time it placed this issue on the agenda, however, a coalition of Latin countries objected on the basis that the EU had not provided adequate documentation regarding the future tariff-only regime. As soon as a working party is formed, the clock begins and WTO members have 90 days to decide on the waiver. By blocking the establishment of a working party, the Latin countries indefinitely delayed the waivers. This coalition – which included Guatemala, Honduras, Nicaragua, and Panama – feared that if they granted the EU carte blanche, it could enact unlimited tariff differentials between Latin and ACP bananas during 2006 and 2007 while remaining immune from challenge under the DSU. The coalition continued to use this procedural ploy to prevent formal consideration of the EU waiver requests throughout the summer of 2001.

As the fall approached, the frustration of many EU officials was building. They resented both Ecuador and the United States for not doing more to encourage progress on the waivers. To break the impasse, the EU suggested its interest in invoking a formal voting clause in the WTO Agreement that allows for approval of waivers by a three-fourths majority when no consensus can be reached. This move got the attention of the United States, which did not want to confront another institutional crisis. The United States and EU then began to apply intense pressure on the Central American delegations, "including offers of new trade benefits and threats that potential ones may not be realized."[97] The campaign paid off, as Guatemala, Nicaragua, and Panama dropped their objections. Honduras, the last holdout, did not want to be perceived as undermining the tradition of consensus decision-making by itself. On October 5, 2001, the Council on Trade in Goods finally formed a working party to review the EU requests.[98]

With the clock having begun on October 5, the expectation was that the WTO should be able to decide on the waivers before January 1, 2002, when the EU had to begin implementing its revised tariff quota for ACP bananas. That timetable, however, was regarded as inadequate by the EU. Its leaders preferred to resolve the waivers before the November 2001 Doha ministerial meetings, at which WTO members would attempt to launch another round. The reason was that ACP countries, anxious about the legal status of their Cotonou preferences in the WTO, had begun to insist that the waivers be approved before they would support any launch. In light of the many issues under discussion leading up to

[97] "WTO Moves to Consider EU Banana Waivers, Roadblock Dropped," *Inside U.S. Trade* 19 (October 12, 2001), 16.
[98] "WTO Moves to Consider EU Banana Waivers, Roadblock Dropped," *Inside U.S. Trade* 19 (October 12, 2001), 15–16.

Doha, the EU had difficulty persuading other members that the waivers required urgent consideration. As the ministerial approached, the waivers were not on the agenda – much to the relief of the Latin countries, which did not want to confront the intense political pressures likely to be applied at Doha.[99]

At Doha, however, the representative from Kenya, as chair of the ACP group, surprised the assembled delegations by placing the waivers on the agenda without having undertaken the traditional preliminary consultations in the Council on Trade in Goods.[100] With this move, the ACP countries capitalized on a procedural opening to gain leverage rather like Ecuador had done. The Latin American countries suspected that the EU arranged this maneuver, but both it and the United States professed surprise. The result was several days of intense consultations between the EU, the Latin American countries, and ACP delegations, with the United States serving as mediator. The Latin American countries – which included Colombia, Costa Rica, Ecuador, Honduras, and Panama – began the discussions together, but their coalition soon fractured.

Several Latin demands were rejected out of hand by the EU and ACP delegations. One casualty was a proposal to limit the Article I waiver to the end of 2005, at which point it could be renewed through 2007 if the tariff-only regime proved acceptable.[101] Costa Rica dropped its demand that approval of the waiver be contingent on the acceptance of new tariff negotiations by the ACP countries. The coalition abandoned its insistence on the right to request suspension of the waiver at any time after it came into effect. And they also gave up a demand for assurances that expanded market access after EU enlargement would be available to all suppliers on a competitive basis. After several meetings, Colombia, Costa Rica, Honduras, and then Panama all agreed to drop their objections and approve the waiver early on November 13, 2001 – one day before the final Doha plenary session.[102]

With only hours remaining before the conclusion of the ministerial, Ecuador stood alone as the solitary holdout. It wanted the EU to offer some guarantee that its market access would not be diminished during 2006 and 2007, after the transition to a tariff-only regime. In particular, it sought a numerical target for the level of tariff that would be applied.

[99] Interview with US official, Geneva, June 11, 2002.
[100] Telephone interview with EU official, Brussels, June 17, 2002.
[101] "WTO Moves to Consider EU Banana Waivers, Roadblock Dropped," *Inside U.S. Trade* 19 (October 12, 2001), 16.
[102] "EU Waivers Approved as Latin Americans Drop Banana Demands," *Inside U.S. Trade* 19 (15 November 2001), 10–11.

The EU refused to offer any such assurance, arguing that it could not guarantee market outcomes under a tariff system and was not prepared to limit its rights prematurely in the Article XXVIII negotiations that would later set the new tariff levels. The result was an impasse that lasted late into the evening on November 13. Ecuador had signaled that its banana concerns were serious enough to justify its trade minister taking the blame for spoiling the launch. Ecuador claimed that such a story would play well at home, despite the obvious international costs.

The credibility of this threat was never put to the test. Late on the evening of November 13, soon after the departure of a key Ecuadorian official for the airport, Ecuador agreed to accept a compromise crafted by the United States, Colombia, and others.[103] Instead of numerical targets on market share or tariff levels, the compromise gave Ecuador and other Latin countries a special procedural guarantee. Attached to the Article I waiver, as an annex, is a procedure for arbitral review of the EU's proposed tariff-only regime prior to its implementation.[104] Ecuador won the status of "principal supplier" in the GATT Article XXVIII negotiations that will determine the new tariff levels on bananas, but other Latin countries received the right to be notified of the results of the talks. The EU agreed that its revised tariffs would not "diminish the total market access" of the Latin banana producers. If the arbitrator finds otherwise, Ecuador (or others) could suspend the effect of the waiver, returning parts of the Cotonou agreement to legal limbo. Ecuador, moreover, could arguably reactivate its case against the banana regime and potentially move again to request authority to retaliate against the EU at once.

While not the bedrock guarantee Ecuador was seeking on the future tariff level, this procedural compromise offered the Ecuadorian delegation several advantages. It included a guarantee on timelines, obligating the EU to complete its Article 28 negotiations in a timely fashion – well before its deadline at the end of 2005. Ecuador also received a speedier and more focused form of multilateral review than would have been available under the DSU. Finally, the EU agreed not to diminish the total market access of the Latin banana producers, which eased Ecuador's fears regarding the potential for punitive tariff differentials between Latin and ACP bananas. US officials report that the EU was reluctant to endorse even this procedural compromise, but Ecuador viewed the absence of any constraints on future tariff levels as a deal breaker.[105] Ecuador's extreme threat to hold the entire ministerial hostage did not produce its desired

[103] Telephone interview with Ecuadorian official, Brussels, July 22, 2003.
[104] WTO Document WT/MIN(01)/15 (November 14, 2001).
[105] Interview with US official, Geneva, June 11, 2002.

result, but the coalition of Latin producers – capitalizing on leverage provided by Ecuador's aggressive posture – did extract important institutional commitments from the EU.

Late in 2004, the EU announced its intention to apply a uniform tariff of 230 Euros per ton.[106] Ecuador promptly challenged the EU proposal as excessively high and requested WTO arbitration under the waiver agreement.[107] The Director-General appointed a former Canadian ambassador and two Appellate Body members to serve as arbitrators.[108] The panel determined that the EU proposal would not maintain total market access for the Latin exporters.[109] EU officials fear that the Latin coalition – or ACP countries, which are anxious as well–will again link this dispute to the Hong Kong ministerial in an attempt to increase pressure on Brussels.[110] Such a result would hardly be surprising.

6   Conclusion

The independent and often creative path that Ecuador charted through the torturously complex bananas dispute was not without risks. As a small developing country highly dependent on access to markets in Europe and the US (not to mention investment, financial, and development assistance from those same powers), Ecuador was not expected to wield significant negotiating leverage in the transatlantic banana war. Nevertheless, its leaders made a costly decision to rush Ecuador's accession to the WTO in order to join the complaint. It pressed the case aggressively at each stage and devised an unprecedented approach to compliance bargaining after winning at the panel and appellate levels. Even after reaching a transitional settlement, its leaders continued to agitate for Ecuador's interests, threatening to torpedo the launch of the Doha round.

As the experiences of its regional competitors suggest, there were other policy paths available to Ecuador. Like Panama, Ecuador could have opted not to hurry its WTO accession, relying on others to press for reform of the EU banana regime. Instead it paid the price of a swift entry, having borne the higher cost of being outside during earlier GATT complaints against the EU banana scheme. Like Colombia and Costa Rica after their GATT case, Ecuador could have accepted the EU's offer

---

[106] "Split over EU Tariff Threatens to Restart Banana Wars," *Financial Times* (October 29, 2004), 9.

[107] WTO Document WT/L/607 Add. 3 (April 1, 2005).

[108] WTO Document WT/L/607/Add.12 (May 2, 2005).

[109] WTO Document WT/L/616 (August 1, 2005), 24.

[110] "WTO to Arbitrate over EU Single Tariff for Bananas," *Agra Europe* 2150 (April 1, 2005), EP/1.

of increased country-specific quotas despite their obvious inconsistency with the WTO rulings. Instead it realized that the WTO system offered it an opportunity to press for full compliance. Like Guatemala, Honduras, and Mexico, Ecuador could have relied almost entirely on the United States to negotiate on its behalf during the implementation phase of the dispute. Instead it charted an independent course, aware that its interests diverged from those of the United States.

Despite a lengthy delay from start to finish, Ecuador's sophisticated strategy eventually bore fruit (so to speak). In one test of the primary hypothesis, Ecuador's settlement with the EU conferred significant benefits when compared to regional competitors in the banana industry. For example, Costa Rica and Colombia – the chief beneficiaries of the 1994 Banana Framework Agreement – saw their competitive position diminished after the EU agreed to abolish its country-specific quotas during the transitional period. During the first year and a half of the transitional regime, from July 2001 to December 2002, Ecuador's share of the EU banana market rose sharply while the shares of Costa Rica and Colombia stagnated – and those of its Latin co-complainants fell. As the lowest-cost producer of bananas, Ecuador stands to gain even better market access after the EU's transition to a tariff-only system in 2006 – a commitment on which Ecuador insisted there be a date certain.

A second test is counterfactual analysis of the likely outcome had Ecuador not threatened cross retaliation, challenged the US–EU settlement, and held the waivers hostage. Especially in the latter stages of the dispute, co-complainants Guatemala and Honduras (along with Mexico and Panama) relied more heavily than Ecuador on the United States to represent their views, thanks to their more extensive ties to US trading companies. Ecuador disagreed with the United States on a number of basic issues – in particular the system for allocating EU import licenses, which was crucial to Ecuador's own trading companies. Tracing the divergent preferences of the United States and Ecuador reveals that the twin settlements accommodated many of Ecuador's demands. It thus seems safe to conclude that if Ecuador had not actively pushed its agenda, a settlement endorsed by the United States on its behalf would have been much less to its liking.

In another counterfactual, there is also evidence to suggest that Ecuador's cross-retaliation threat bolstered its position during debt rescheduling talks with the Paris Club. The terms and timing of this debt reorganization might have been less favorable for Ecuador in the absence of the WTO authority to retaliate against sensitive targets (such as geographical indications for European alcoholic beverages) under TRIPS. Whatever the extent of this issue linkage, no linkage at all would have been possible on the financial front without the authority to cross-retaliate in the WTO.

Finally, the specific guarantee at Doha that the tariff-only system the EU eventually implements will not diminish the market access of Latin producers in 2006, along with a novel procedural mechanism to ensure this commitment is honored, may also prove to be of value to Ecuador. The outcome of ongoing tariff negotiations with the EU remains unclear. Although Ecuador would have preferred to fix a limit on the EU tariff level, its negotiators believed that the institutional compromise brokered by the United States and the Latin coalition to end the standoff at Doha would provide some leverage at the bargaining table.

In addition to being intrinsically interesting for these reasons, the bananas dispute offers perhaps the only opportunity (to date) to investigate a difficult case of compliance bargaining in the WTO by a developing country. In almost every other dispute filed by developing countries against developed WTO members, the defendants have complied with rulings of violation before the reasonable time period for implementation has expired. Examples include the complaint by Brazil and Venezuela against US gasoline standards; Costa Rica's case against US restrictions on imported underwear; the complaint by India, Malaysia, Pakistan, and Thailand against the US shrimp ban; Brazil's initial case against Canadian aircraft subsidies; India's complaint against EU antidumping duties on bed linen; and Pakistan's case against US cotton safeguards. In all of these disputes, the defendant complied more fully and faster than the EU in the bananas case (arguably because the stakes were smaller and the issues less complicated).

Because those early cases were relatively easy in no way suggests that difficult disputes do not lie ahead. In fact, Brazil has already begun to pursue a number of politically sensitive challenges to agricultural policies in the United States and Europe. The question is whether the Ecuador case offers lessons for other developing country complainants such as Brazil, and I believe the answer is yes. Ecuador's strategies are a model for developing countries seeking to maximize their bargaining leverage by utilizing certain procedural maneuvers within the institutional context of the WTO.

In terms of the specifics of its strategy, Ecuador's pathbreaking move to request cross-retaliation should now be a weapon in the arsenal of every developing country complainant. As with any form of sanctions, there are considerable obstacles to using cross-retaliation.[111] Nevertheless, WTO arbitrators have endorsed the move in principle, and scholars

[111] Vranes 2003.

such as Subramanian and Watal have begun to trumpet its attractive attributes.[112] Although Ecuador opted not to implement its authority to cross-retaliate, observers suggest that the mere possibility of TRIPs retaliation focused additional EU attention on Ecuador's demands. For larger developing countries that are more attractive to (or less dependent on) foreign investment, the threat of cross-retaliation against intellectual property could serve as an even more effective tool in compliance bargaining with the United States, EU, and other advanced industrial powers.

Ecuador's moves during the sequencing crisis and cross-retaliation request speak to a more general truth regarding the DSU. Despite its detail, it is very much an evolving instrument, open to surprising interpretations and potentially advantageous procedural moves. With regard to the negotiations in Doha, the tradition of approving waivers in the WTO by consensus gave Ecuador and other Latin banana producers the chance to attempt to extract certain concessions at Doha. It was an uphill climb in that case, but there are likely to be occasions on which developing countries will be able to gain leverage by wielding their veto carefully – especially when they do so as a coalition.

Ecuador, in sum, capitalized repeatedly on certain institutional rules to enhance its bargaining leverage. Institutions may cast a longer shadow over compliance bargaining than over other forms of international economic negotiation. This seems certain whenever there are procedural rules in place for dispute settlement, as is the case in the WTO. Still, multilateral economic negotiations have a structure all their own,[113] making it useful for developing countries to pay close attention to institutional details in that setting as well. That advice also applies to scholars of international relations. This study emphasizes the value of paying additional heed both to details of institutional design and to bargaining processes, which – as they did in this case – often have an independent effect on distributional outcomes.

REFERENCES

Albin, Cecilia. 2001. *Justice and Fairness in International Negotiation.* Cambridge: Cambridge University Press

Brenes, E. R., and K. Madrigal. 2003. Banana Trade in Latin America. In *Banana Wars: The Anatomy of a Trade Dispute*, eds. T. Josling and T. Taylor. Cambridge, Mass: CABI Publishing, 97–122

---

[112] Subramanian and Watal 2000.   [113] Odell 2003; Winham 1986.

CEPS. 2000. *Annual Report 2000.* Brussels: European Confederation of Spirits Producers. Available on web at http://www.europeanspirits.org

Dickson, Anna K. 2002. "The EU Banana Regime: History and Interests." Available on web at http://www.bananalink.org

Guyomard, Hervé, and Chantal Le Mouël. 2003. "The New Banana Import Regime in the European Union: A Quantitative Assessment." *The Estey Centre Journal of International Law and Trade Policy* 4 (2): 143–61

Jackson, John H., and Patricio Grane. 2001. "The Saga Continues: An Update on the Banana Dispute and its Procedural Offspring." *Journal of International Economic Law* 4 (3): 581–95

Jönsson, Christer, and Jonas Tallberg. 1998. "Compliance and Post-Agreement Bargaining," *European Journal of International Relations* 4 (4): 371–408

2001. "Compliance Bargaining in the European Union." Paper prepared for presentation at ECSA's International Conference, Madison, Wisconsin May 31–June 2

Josling, T. 2003. "Bananas and the WTO: Testing the New Dispute Settlement Process." In *Banana Wars: The Anatomy of a Trade Dispute*, eds. T. Josling and T. Taylor. Cambridge, Mass: CABI Publishing, 169–95

Odell, John 2000. *Negotiating the World Economy.* Ithaca, NY: Cornell University Press

2003. "Making and Breaking Impasses in International Regimes: The WTO, Seattle, and Doha." Working paper presented at the Center for International Studies, The University of Southern California, January 22

Paggi, M. and T. Spreen. 2003. "Overview of the World Banana Market." In *Banana Wars: The Anatomy of a Trade Dispute*, eds. T. Josling and T. Taylor. Cambridge, Mass: CABI Publishing, 7–16

Salas, Mauricio, and John H. Jackson. 2000. "Procedural Overview of the WTO EC – Banana Dispute." *Journal of International Economic Law* 3 (1): 145–66

Stovall, J. G., and D. E. Hathaway. 2003. "US Interests in the Banana Trade Controversy." In *Banana Wars: The Anatomy of a Trade Dispute*, eds. T. Josling and T. Taylor. Cambridge, Mass: CABI Publishing

Subramanian, Arvind, and Jayashree Watal. 2000. "Can TRIPS Serve as an Enforcement Device for Developing Countries in the WTO?" *Journal of International Economic Law*, 403–16

Tangermann, S. 2003a. "European Interests in the Banana Market." In *Banana Wars: The Anatomy of a Trade Dispute*, eds. T. Josling and T. Taylor. Cambridge, Mass: CABI Publishing, 17–44

2003b. "The European Common Banana Policy." In *Banana Wars: The Anatomy of a Trade Dispute*, eds. T. Josling and T. Taylor. Cambridge, Mass: CABI Publishing, 45–66

Taylor, T. 2003. "Evolution of the Banana Multinationals." In *Banana Wars: The Anatomy of a Trade Dispute*, eds. T. Josling and T. Taylor. Cambridge, Mass: CABI Publishing, 67–96

Vranes, Erich. 2002. "Policy Lessons from Transatlantic Trade Disputes." In *External Economic Relations and Foreign Policy in the European Union*, eds. S. Griller and B. Weidel. Vienna: Springer, 205–36

2003. "Cross Retaliation under GATS and TRIPS – An Optimal Enforcement Device for Developing Countries?" In *The Banana Dispute: An Economic and Legal Analysis*, eds. F. Breuss, S. Griller, and E. Vranes. Vienna: Springer, 113–30

Winham, Gilbert.1986. *International Trade and the Tokyo Round Negotiation.* Princeton: Princeton University Press

Index